DATE DUE

THE GREEK BUCOLIC POETS

28

THE GREEK
BUCOLIC POETS

WITH AN ENGLISH TRANSLATION BY
J. M. EDMONDS

LATE FELLOW OF JESUS COLLEGE
LECTURER IN THE UNIVERSITY OF CAMBRIDGE

CAMBRIDGE, MASSACHUSETTS
HARVARD UNIVERSITY PRESS
LONDON
WILLIAM HEINEMANN LTD
MCMLXXVII

American SBN 674 99031 5
British SBN 434 99028 0

First printed 1912
Reprinted 1916, 1919, 1923
Reprinted and revised 1928
Reprinted 1938, 1950, 1960, 1970, 1977

Printed in Great Britain

CONTENTS

Λύρα δή σοι καὶ κιθάρα λείπεται ὡς κατὰ πόλιν χρήσιμα καὶ αὖ κατ' ἀγροὺς τοῖς νομεῦσι σῦριγξ ἄν τις εἴη.

PLATO, *Republic* 399 d.

PREFACE

TO THE FIRST EDITION

THE translator wishes to record his indebtedness to many predecessors, from the author of the *Sixe Idillia* to the late Andrew Lang. His thanks are also due, among other friends, to Mr. A. S. F. Gow for allowing him access to the results of his investigations into the "Bucolic Masquerade" and the Pattern-Poems.[1]

8 *October*, 1912.

---

[1] These are also in the *Greek Anthology*, XV, 21 ff., and so in Vol. 5 of the Loeb Anthology, pp. 124 ff., translated by Paton. —Ed. 1969.

PREFACE

TO THE SIXTH REPRINT

THIS time I have made certain changes and additions in the light of the Papyri and of the best recent work, and included five older emendations, of Hiller's at Theocr. 17. 54, of Schaefer's at Mosch. 3. 74 and 118, of Ahrens' at Mosch. 3. 118, and of Hermann's at *Meg.* 32, and five newer, two of Legrand's at Theocr. 23. 50 and Bion 7. 11, and three of my own at Theocr. 15. 124, 26. 28, and 27. 68. As a step towards what fresh discoveries may some day make practicable I have given the Doric accentuation where it is attested by the Papyri, *e.g.* κορύδοι, ὦμες, μακαρίτις. I am indebted for kind comment and correction to Mr. A. S. F. Gow as before, and to Professor A. Y. Campbell.

J. M. E.

CAMBRIDGE,
15 *November*, 1937.

viii

INTRODUCTION

I.—THE LIFE OF THEOCRITUS

THE external evidence for the life of Theocritus is scanty enough. Beyond a brief statement in Suidas, a casual phrase in Choeroboscus, the epigram Ἄλλος ὁ Χῖος, and a comment upon a passage of Ovid, we have only a few short and not always consistent notes in the commentaries which are contained in the manuscripts. His poems tell us plainly that he was a native of Syracuse, and was familiar also with the districts of Croton and Thurii in Italy, with the island of Cos, with Miletus, and with Alexandria, and that he wrote certain of his works about the twelfth year of Ptolemy Philadelphus. The inscriptions he composed for the statues of Gods and poets connect him, or at least his fame, also with Teos, Paros, Ephesus, and Camirus. The rest—and that means much of the following account—is conjecture.

His parents were Praxagoras and Philinna, both possibly of Coan birth or extraction. His early manhood was spent in the Aegean. He seems to have studied medicine,[1] probably at Samos, under the

---

[1] In the Argument to XI read προσδιαλέγεται ὁ Θ. ἰατρῷ Νικίᾳ Μιλησίῳ τὸ γένος, ᾧ (mss ὃς, ὁ) συμφοιτητὴς γέγονεν Ἐρασιστράτου ἰατρὸς ἂν καὶ αὐτὸς (mss ἰατροῦ ὄντος καὶ αὐτοῦ): otherwise both συν- and καὶ αὐτ. are unintelligible.

famous physician Erasistratus, along with the Milesian
Nicias to whom he dedicates the *Cyclops* and the
Hylas. Theocritus is also said to have been a pupil
of the Samian poet Asclepiades, whose epigrams we
know in the Anthology. He certainly spent some
years at Cos, sitting at the feet of the great poet and
critic Philitas, who numbered among his pupils
Zenodotus the grammarian, Hermesianax the elegist,
and the young man who was afterwards Ptolemy II.
This happy period of our author's life is almost cer-
tainly recalled in a poem written at a later time, the
Harvest-home. Philitas probably died about the year
283. Ten years later we find Theocritus at Syracuse,
seeking the favour of the young officer who in 274
had been elected general-in-chief after the troubles
of Pyrrhus' *régime* and was soon to be known as
Hiero II. The poem we know as *Charites* or *The
Graces* probably appeared as epistle-dedicatory to a
collection of poems, *Charites* being really the title of
the whole book.[1] Such fancy titles were the fashion
of the day. Alexander of Aetolia, for instance, pub-
lished a collection called *The Muses*; the "night-
ingales" of Callimachus' famous little poem on Hera-
cleitus are best explained as the name of his old
friend's collected poems; and Aratus published a
collection actually called by this name, for Helladius[2]

[1] The scholion on ἡμετέρας χάριτας (l. 6) is τὰ οἰκεῖα
ποιήματα. The phrase σποράδες ποκὰ in Artemidorus' intro-
ductory poem does not, of course, necessarily imply that
hitherto each poem of the three authors had existed separ-
ately. There were no magazines. [2] ap. Phot. *Bibl.* p. 531 *b*
14, cf. 532 *a* 36.

writes " As Aratus says in the first of his Charites,"
ἐν Χαρίτων πρώτῃ. Whether Theocritus' little book
contained any of the extant poems we cannot say.
It very possibly contained the *Cyclops* and the
Beloved, and from the title it may be judged to have
comprised no more than three pieces. One bio-
graphical point should be noted here; Theocritus
was newly come to Syracuse. We gather from the
Charites that Hiero was by no means the first great
man to whom Theocritus had gone for patronage,
and it is to be remarked that the poet ascribes the
indifference with which he had hitherto been received,
not to the disturbed state of the country, but to the
commercial spirit of the age. There were no doubt
other possible patrons than Hiero in Sicily, but peace
and tranquillity had not been known there for many
years. The same argument may be used to show
that his sojourn in Magna Graecia was not during
the decade preceding the publication of the *Charites.*
The poem apparently failed like its predecessors;
for Theocritus, like his own Aeschinas, was fain to
go overseas and seek his fortune at Alexandria.[1]

The voyage to Egypt lay by way of the southern
Aegean, and we are credibly informed that he now
spent some time at Cos. He doubtless had many
old friends to see. It was probably on this voyage
that he wrote the *Distaff,* to accompany the gift he
was taking from Syracuse to the wife of his old friend

---

[1] Beloch and others put the *Ptolemy* before the *Charites;*
but when the latter was written Hiero cannot have been
king. See the introduction to the poem.

Nicias, who was now settled in practice at Miletus. The *Cyclops* is generally regarded as a consolation addressed to the lovesick Nicias. If this is true, it would follow on this placing of the *Distaff* that the *Cyclops* was written before the *Charites*; for it implies that Nicias, to whom it was doubtless sent as a letter, was then unmarried. The probable age of the two friends in 273 points, as we shall see, the same way. If on the other hand we may regard the *Cyclops* as an outpouring of soul on the part of the lovesick Theocritus, the author likening himself, and not Nicias, to Polyphemus, the two lines—all that has been preserved—of Nicias' reply [1] may be interpreted with more point: " Love has, it seems, made you a poet," a compliment upon the first serious piece of work of his friend's that he had seen. This interpretation puts the *Cyclops* long before the *Charites*, independently of the dating of the *Distaff*. In any case, the *Cyclops* is certainly an early poem. The same visit to Nicias may have been the occasion of the eighth epigram, an inscription for the base of the new statue of Asclepius with which the doctor had adorned his consulting-room. We may well imagine that Nicias employed his friend in order to put a little money in his pocket; for his own epigrams in the Anthology show clearly that he could have written an excellent inscription himself.

The *Love of Cynisca*, with its hint of autobiography

---

[1] ἦν ἄρ' ἀληθὲς τοῦτο, Θεόκριτε· οἱ γὰρ Ἔρωτες | πολλοὺς ποιητὰς ἐδίδαξαν τοὺς πρὶν ἀμούσους.

and its friendly flattery of Philadelphus, was in all probability written about this time. There is no doubt as to the approximate dates of the *Ptolemy* and the *Women at the Adonis Festival*. They must both have been written at Alexandria between the king's marriage with his sister Arsinoë—this took place sometime between 278 and 273—and her death in 270. The *Ptolemy* cannot be much later than 273; for it is clear that the Syrian war was in its early days, and this began in 274.

At this point it becomes necessary to discuss a question of great importance not only to the biographer of Theocritus but to the historian of the Pastoral. Does the *Harvest-home* deal with real persons? The scene of the poem is Cos. We have the characters Simichidas and Lycidas and the dumb characters Eucritus and Amyntas; the two songs mention in connexion with one or other of these persons Ageanax, Tityrus, Aratus, Aristis, Philinus, and two unnamed shepherds of Acharnae and Lycopè; in another part of the poem—though these are not necessarily to be reckoned as friends of the others—we have Philitas, and Sicelidas of Samos. Of these, Philitas certainly, and Aratus possibly, are the well-known poets; Philinus may or may not be the Coan Philinus who won at Olympia in 264 and 260 and who is probably the Philinus of the *Spell*; Aristis is a clip-form of some compound like Aristodamus; Amyntas is also called Amyntichus. The Tityrus, to whom, in the guise of a goatherd,

INTRODUCTION

Theocritus dedicates the *Serenade*, is almost certainly a real person, and as certainly, Tityrus was not his real name; Tityrus here may or may not be the same person. Sicelidas, on external grounds, is certainly to be identified with the poet Asclepiades; it is to be noted that he is called Sicelidas elsewhere than in Theocritus; but he and Philitas are in a sense outside this discussion. Lastly, Amyntas bears a royal name. We know Ptolemy Philadelphus to have been taught by Philitas; and though his father was reputed the son of Lagus, the Macedonians were proud to believe him to be actually the son of Philip of Macedon, whose father was Amyntas. It is generally thought that Philitas went to Philadelphus; but in view both of the climate of Egypt and of the great probability that from 301 Cos was a vassal either of Ptolemy I or of his son-in-law Lysimachus, it is at least as likely that Philadelphus went to Philitas. Cos, moreover, was Philadelphus' birthplace.[1]

If these were the only facts before us, sufficient evidence would be still to seek; for there is unfortunately some doubt as to the identity of Aratus. But there are other considerations which, taken with these, bring us near to certainty. If Lycidas is not a real person, why does the poet insist upon his characteristic laugh, and emphasise the

---

[1] It is worth noting here that Vergil in his *Bucolics* uses the royal Macedonian name Iollas. Did Theocritus in a lost poem use this for some great Macedonian of the family of Antipater?

excellence of his pastoral get-up ? If Aristis is not a
real person, why is he so carefully described, and
what business has he in the poem ? It is Aratus'
love, not Aristis' knowledge of it, that is important
to the narrative. Lastly, there is the tradition of
the scholia that the narrator is either Theocritus or
one of his friends, of which alternatives the former
is far the more probable. The conclusion we must
come to is that we are dealing throughout with real
persons, some of whom have their ordinary names
and others not. This does not mean, of course, that
the " other-names " were invented for the occasion
by the poet. Rather should they be considered pet-
names by which these persons were known to their
friends. There can be no certain identification.

A further question arises. Whence did Theocritus
derive the notion of staging himself and his friends
as herdsmen ? The answer is not far to seek. First,
the Greek mind associated poetry directly with
music ; and secondly, Greek herdsmen were then, as
they are still, players and singers. The poets of his
day, some of whom dealt like him with country life,
would naturally appear, to a country-loving poet like
Theocritus, the literary counterparts, so to speak, of
the herdsmen, and their poetry in some sense the
art-form of the herdsman's folk-music. It is not
perhaps without ulterior motive that Lycidas the
poet-goatherd is made to claim fellowship with
Comatas the goatherd-poet. The accident that
combined this staging with the use of pet-names in

this poem, is responsible, through Vergil's imitations, for the modern notion of the Pastoral.

Let us now return to the life of Theocritus. If, as is generally believed, the *Harvest-home* is autobiographical, it was written after the author had won some measure of fame—he makes himself say that he is "no match *yet awhile* for the excellent Sicelidas"—, and the passage about the "strutting cocks of the Muses' yard" is a reference to Apollonius of Rhodes and his famous controversy with Callimachus, Theocritus declaring his allegiance to the latter, who maintained that the long epic poem was out of date. This controversy in all probability began upon the publication of the first edition of Apollonius' *Argonautica*. The date of this is unfortunately disputed, but it can hardly have been earlier than 260. A further shred of biography may perhaps be derived from a consideration of the story of Comatas in relation to the cruel death of Sotades.[1] This brave outspoken poet denounced Ptolemy's incestuous marriage, and was thrown into prison. After languishing there for a long time he made good his escape, but falling eventually into the hands of an admiral of the Egyptian fleet, was shut up in a leaden vessel and drowned in the sea. This strange method of execution calls for some explanation. One is tempted to think that Sotades was a friend of Theocritus—he was a writer of love-poems of the type of XII, XXIX, and XXX—, and that after his friend

[1] Plut. *de Puer. Educ.* 15, Athen. 14. 621.

had been some years in prison Theocritus wrote the *Harvest-home*, hinting that Sotades had suffered long enough, and sheltering himself under a reminder of his own early acquaintance with the king and a declaration of his allegiance to the great court-poet Callimachus. On the unfortunate man's escape, we may imagine, the story of the frustration of the my-thical king's cruel purpose became directly applicable to the situation; the phrase κακαῖσιν ἀτασθαλίαισιν ἄνακτος was now genuine censure and the particle θήν real sarcasm; and when the admiral sent word of the recapture, Ptolemy with a grim irony ordered that the modern Comatas should be shut up in a modern chest and put beyond reach of the assistance of the bees. Here again we can arrive at no date. All we know is that Sotades' offence must have been committed about 275 and that he lay a long time in prison.

We do not know for certain where Theocritus spent the rest of his life. Perhaps after the protest of the *Harvest-home* and its tragic sequel he found it prudent to retire from Alexandria. But whether he now left Egypt or not, it is more than probable that he spent some time during his later years in Cos. There was close intercourse during this period be-tween Cos and Alexandria, and if he did not make the island his home, he may well have paid long summer visits there. Besides the *Harvest-home*, there are two certainly Coan poems, the *Thyrsis* and the *Spell*, and these would seem to belong rather to this than to an earlier period. Apart altogether from the question of actual impersonation, it is impossible to resist the conclusion that when speaking of the Sicilian Thyrsis and the song he sang at Cos, Theocritus had himself at the back of his mind, and that when he wrote of Thyrsis' victory over the Libyan, he was thinking of some contest of his own—perhaps one of the Dionysiac contests mentioned in the *Ptolemy*—with Callimachus of Cyrenè. And it can hardly be a mere coincidence that in the *Spell* Theocritus makes the athlete boast of having "outrun the fair Philinus," and that a Coan named Philinus won at Olympia in 264 and 260; it is only reasonable to suppose that Theocritus wrote these words when Philinus' name was on every Coan lip.

Except that in XXX the poet speaks of the first appearance of grey hairs upon his head, and that in the *Beloved* the comparison of the maid to the thrice-wed wife, which could not fail to offend the thrice-wed Arsinoë, must have been written before the author's sojourn at Alexandria, there is nothing to indicate to what period of his life the remaining poems belong.

The list of Theocritus' works given by Suidas tells us that we possess by no means all of the works once ascribed to him. His *Bucolic Poems*, ἔπη or δράματα βουκολικὰ were in the time of Suidas, or rather of the writers upon whom he drew, his chief title to fame. Of the *Epigrams* or *Inscriptions* we have some, if not all, known as his in antiquity. The *Hymns* are now

xviii

represented by the *Ptolemy*, the *Dioscuri*, the *Berenice* fragment, and perhaps the *Charites*. The *Lyric Poems* must have included the *Distaff* and XXIX and XXX, and perhaps also the *Beloved* and the *Epithalamy*. The books known as *Elegies*, *Iambics*, *Funeral Laments*, and *The Heroines*, and the single poem called *The Daughters of Proetus*—perhaps known to Vergil,—all these are lost without a trace. It is strange that Suidas' list apparently omits all mention of the non-pastoral mimes, the *Love of Cynisca*, the *Spell*, and the *Women at the Adonis Festival*, and of the little epics *Hylas* and *The Little Heracles*. The *Spell* may have been included among the Lyric Poems, its claim to be so classed lying in the peculiar way in which, though it is a personal narrative, the refrain is used throughout as if it were a song. We may perhaps guess that the four other poems belonged to the remaining book of Suidas' list, the *Hopes*,[1] and that this was a collection published by Theocritus soon after his arrival in Egypt, with the *Love of Cynisca* standing first as a sort of dedication to his friend Ptolemy and echoing the title's veiled request for his patronage.

The name εἰδύλλια, idyls, as applied to the poems of Theocritus, is certainly as old as the commentaries which accompany the text, and some of these probably go back to the first century before Christ. It was known to Pliny the Younger as a collective

---

[1] A book of the same title is ascribed by Suidas to Callimachus.

title for a volume of short poems; there is a collection bearing this name among the works of Ausonius. But it was apparently unknown as the title of Theocritus' poems to Suidas and his predecessors. The meaning of it is "little poems." We are told that Pindar's Epinician Odes were known as εἴδη, and Suidas uses the same word in describing the works of Sotades. There is no warrant for the interpretation "little pictures."

If we may accept the identification of the " pretty little Amyntas " with Philadelphus, we can get a very close approximation to the date of Theocritus' birth. Philadelphus was born in 309. At the time described in the *Harvest-home* he is obviously about fifteen. In the same poem Theocritus has already attained something of a reputation, but is still a young man. We shall not be far wrong if we put his age at twenty-two or three. He was born then about the year 316, and when he wrote the *Charites* he was about forty-three. This would suit admirably the autobiographical hint in the *Love of Cynisca* that the poet's hair at the time of writing was just beginning to go grey. If the Berenice of the fragment preserved by Athenaeus is the wife, not of Soter, but of Euergetes, it would follow that Theocritus was at the Alexandrian court in his seventieth year. It is at any rate certain that he did not die young; for Statius calls him *Siculus senex*.[1]

[1] *Silv.* 5. 3. 151.

INTRODUCTION

A scholiast on Ovid's *Ibis* l. 549

Utve Syracosio praestricta fauce poetae,
Sic animae laqueo sit via clausa tuae,

tells us that this is "the Syracusan poet Theocritus, who was arrested by king Hiero for making an attack upon his son, the king's object being merely to make him think that he was going to be put to death. But when Hiero asked him if he would avoid abusing his son in future, he began to abuse him all the more, and not only the son but the father too. Whereat the king in indignation ordered him to be put to death in real earnest, and according to some authorities he was strangled and according to others beheaded." There is nothing improbable in this story. When Theocritus was sixty-five Hiero's son Gelo would be nineteen; we know of no other Syracusan poet who met such a fate; and Antigonus' treatment of Theocritus of Chios and Ptolemy's of Sotades show how the most enlightened rulers of the day could deal with adverse criticism. But whether we believe it or no, the story is evidence for a tradition that Theocritus' last days were spent in Sicily; and we may well imagine that he died at Syracuse, that birthplace, as he calls it, of good men and true, where his fellow-citizens long afterwards pointed out to the collector of inscriptions the statue of his great forerunner Epicharmus, and the words which he once wrote for its base, little thinking perhaps that the time would come when his eulogy would apply as truly to himself: " They that have their habitation in the most mighty city of Syracuse have set him up here, as became fellow-townsmen, in bronze in the stead of the flesh, and thus have remembered to pay him his wages for the great heap of words he hath builded; for many are the things he hath told their children profitable unto life. He hath their hearty thanks."

II.—The Life of Moschus

The evidence for the life of Moschus is contained in a notice in Suidas and a note appended to the *Runaway Love* in the Anthology. These tell us that he was of Syracuse, a grammarian and a pupil of Aristarchus, and that he was accounted the second Bucolic poet after Theocritus. Aristarchus taught at Alexandria from 180 to about 144. The year 150 will then be about the middle of Moschus' life. He is almost certainly to be identified with the Moschus who is mentioned by Athenaeus as the author of a work on the Rhodian dialect, in which he explained that λεπαστή was an earthenware vessel like those called πτωματίδες but wider in the mouth. None of Moschus' extant works are really Bucolic; for the *Lament for Bion* is certainly by another hand.

III.—The Life of Bion

All we know of Bion is gathered from references in Suidas and Diogenes Laertius, from the above-mentioned note in the Anthology, and from the poem upon his death written by a pupil who was a native of Magna Graecia. The third of the Bucolic poets, as he was apparently reckoned in antiquity, was born at a little place called Phlossa near Smyrna. His pupil calls his poetry Dorian and connects him with Syracuse and the Muses of Sicily. But this may be no more biographical than his phrase " Bion the neatherd." According to his pupil he was the leading Bucolic poet of his day, and it is unfortunate that most of the poems that have come down to us under his name,[1] though all quoted as extracts from his *Bucolica*, are really not pastorals at all. It is noteworthy that Diogenes calls him μελικὸς ποιητής, a lyric poet. The description lyric poems would apply —in Alexandrian times— to the *Adonis* and perhaps to some of the smaller poems too. Either Diogenes knew the collection by the title of μέλη βουκολικά, or there were two collections of which he knew only one.

If we may take his pupil literally, Bion was murdered by means of poison. There is really nothing to settle his date. Suidas' order, Theocritus, Moschus, Bion, is probably to be regarded as chronological, and a comparison of the styles of the two last poets points to Bion having been the later. In the present state of our knowledge it would be unwise to draw a contrary conclusion from the omission of Moschus' name from the autobiographical passage of the *Lament*.

[1] The *Adonis* has been ascribed to him on the authority of the *Lament for Bion*.

INTRODUCTION

IV.—THE TEXT[1]

The text of this edition is based upon Ahrens and
Ziegler. It owes much also to von Wilamowitz-
Moellendorff. To the last scholar's excellent edition,
as also to his various books and articles, particularly
the brilliant *Textgeschichte der griechischen Bukoliker*,
I am deeply indebted throughout the volume. In
many passages, as is well known, the text of the
Bucolic poets is by no means settled. In most of
these I have adopted the emendations of other
scholars, giving my acknowledgments, where the
change is important, at the foot of the page. In
some cases—those marked E in the notes—I have
preferred my own. Most editors of the classics
will be human enough, I hope, to sympathise with
my lack of modesty in this respect. There has not
always been room for more than the merest indica-
tion of my reasons. These will however be found,
by the kindness of the editors, in the *Classical Review*.[2]
There is much to be said for Professor von Wilamo-
witz-Moellendorff's re-arrangement of the order of
the poems. The usual position of the *Spell* is par-
ticularly unfortunate; for it leads the student to
reckon, it as a pastoral, which it is not. But the
post-Renaissance order has been too long established,
I think, to be upset now without great inconvenience;
and so I have ventured to retain it.

[1] See pp. xxvii–xxviii.
[2] In a few important cases the full references to the *C.R.* are
(1916) given in the notes.

INTRODUCTION

V.—The Translation

In translating the Bucolic Poets my aim has been
briefly this : to translate not so much the words as
their meaning, to observe not merely the obvious
English idioms of syntax but the more evasive but
equally important ones of stress, word-order, and
balance, and to create an atmosphere of association
in some sense akin to the atmosphere of the original.
The present fashion, set by Mr. Myers in his Pindar,
of translating classical verse into archaic prose, has
much in its favour, and in rendering the songs of
Theocritus' shepherds into verse I have not dis-
carded it without due consideration. In Theocritus'
day there was a convention which made it possible
for him, without violating literary propriety, to re-
present the folk-song of a shepherd in the metre of
the Epic. Some generations before, this would have
been out of the question. A song in hexameters
would have been a contradiction in terms. A some-
what similar convention nowadays makes prose the
suitable literary vehicle of dialogue or narrative, but
there is no firmly-established convention of using
prose to represent song. A literary folk-song, if one
may use the term, would now be impossible in blank
verse, let alone prose.

So I have chosen to render the songs of Theocritus'
shepherds in rhyme, and used with only two excep-
tions the common ballad-metre written long, with
seven, or where there is a medial pause, six, stresses

to the line, employing occasional archaisms of word or rhythm not alien, I hope, to a metre which has for us associations of simple living and unsophisticated modes of thought.

In the prose parts of my translation of the pastorals I have adopted an archaic style partly because the shepherd in modern literature does not talk the only modern dialect I know, that of the upper middle-class, and partly in an endeavour to create in them an atmosphere similar to that of the songs. I have extended archaism to two of the three non-pastoral mimes for kindred reasons, to the Love-Poems because they are so Elizabethan in spirit, to the Epic poems because the Epic is necessarily, under modern conditions, archaic, and to the rest because it is the fashion of the day.[1] The *Women at the Adonis Festival* is on a separate footing. It is so entirely modern in spirit, and the chief characters so closely resemble the average educated Englishwoman, that the only thing to do is to disregard the few anachronisms of name and custom and render it into Colloquial Suburban.

[1] Verse-translations of the *Distaff* will be found in the *Cambridge Review* for Dec. 8, 1910, and of XXIX and XXX in the *Classical Review* for March and May, 1911.

BIBLIOGRAPHY

Editiones Principes:—

Theocritus was first printed with the *Works and Days* of
Hesiod at Milan about the year 1480, but the edition con-
tains only I—XVIII. The Aldine edition of 1495 contains
Theocritus I—XXVIII and lines 1–24 of XXIX, Bion I,
Moschus I—III, *Megara, The Dead Adonis,* and the *Pipe.*
The Juntine edition of 1515 added the *Inscriptions,* and the
Wings and *Axe* of Simias. The *Altar* of Dosiadas first
appeared in the edition of Callierges in 1516. The rest of
Bion and Moschus as well as the *Egg* of Simias were added in
the editions of Mekerchus (1565), Stephanus (1566), or
Ursinus (1568); but the poems and fragments of Bion and
Moschus quoted by Stobaeus in his *Florilegium* had already
been printed in the early editions of that work, the first of
which was published by Victor Trincavellus in 1536. The
latter half of Theocritus XXIX was first edited by Casaubon
on page 75 of his Commentary to Diogenes Laertius pub-
lished at Morges in 1583. The *Second Altar* was first com-
mented on by Scaliger in his Letters (*Opera Posthuma,* Paris,
1610, p. 469), and first edited by Salmasius in his *Inscrip-
tionum Herodis Attici Explicatio* (Paris, 1619). Theocritus
XXX, which, till the discovery of the Antinoë Papyrus
published by Hunt and Johnson in 1930, occurred only in
the Ambrosian MS. known as B 75, was long overlooked, but
was discovered by Ziegler in 1864, and first published by
Bergk in 1865.

When this volume was first issued the latest critical text of
the Bucolic Poets was that of von Wilamowitz-Moellendorff
(Oxford, 1905–1906), and the best English commentary
(*Theocritus* and *Megara* only) was Cholmeley's. For detailed
study there are now available:

    A. S. F. Gow, *Bucolici Graeci* (Oxford Classical Texts,
1952).

BIBLIOGRAPHY

C. Gallavotti, *Theocritus quique feruntur Bucolici Graeci* (Rome, 1946).

A. S. F. Gow, *Greek Bucolic Poets* (with translation and brief notes) (Cambridge, 1953).

A. S. F. Gow, *Theocritus* I, introduction, text, translation: II, commentary (Cambridge, 1950, 2nd edn., 1952).

P. Legrand, *Bucoliques Grecs*, Text and French translation and notes. (Vol. I, 1925; 3rd edn., 1946, Vol. II, 1927, Paris, Budé.)

T. Breitenstein, *Recherches sur le poème Mégara* (Copenhagen, 1966).

Older books helpful to the student are:

Ahrens: *Bucolicorum Reliquiae* (Leipzig, 1855), an edition with Latin critical notes and copious introduction dealing with the MSS, early printed editions and versions, etc.

Fritzsche: *Theocriti Idyllia* (Leipzig, 1870), an edition with Latin notes critical and exegetical.

Ziegler: *Theocriti Carmina* (Tübingen, 1879) and *Bionis et Moschi Carmina* (Tübingen, 1868), texts with Latin critical notes.

von Wilamowitz-Moellendorff: *Textgeschichte der griechischen Bukoliker* (Berlin, 1906), a history of the text, accompanied by a series of articles dealing with certain poems and passages; and *Bion von Smyrna* (Berlin, 1900), an edition of the *Lament for Adonis* with notes introductory, critical and exegetical, accompanied by a verse translation in German.

Legrand: *Étude sur Théocrite* (Paris, 1898).

Lang: *Theocritus, Bion, and Moschus* (London, 1880, etc.), an English prose translation with an introduction on *Theocritus and his Age*.

Haeberlin: *Carmina Figurata Graeca* (Hanover, 1887), a text of the Pattern-Poems with Latin notes introductory, critical and exegetical.

Wendel: *Scholia in Theocritum Vetera* (Lipsiae, 1913).

THE BUCOLIC POETS

ΒΟΥΚΟΛΙΚΑ

Βουκολικαὶ Μοῖσαι σποράδες ποκά, νῦν δ᾽ ἅμα πᾶσαι
    ἐντὶ μιᾶς μάνδρας, ἐντὶ μιᾶς ἀγέλας.

Ἄλλος ὁ Χῖος· ἐγὼ δὲ Θεόκριτος, ὃς τάδ᾽ ἔγραψα
    εἷς ἀπὸ τῶν πολλῶν εἰμὶ Συρακοσίων,
υἱὸς Πραξαγόραο περικλειτῆς τε Φιλίνης·
    Μοῦσαν δ᾽ ὀθνείην οὔτιν᾽ ἐφελκυσάμην.

THE BUCOLIC POETS

INTRODUCTORY POEMS

THE Muses of the country, scattered abroad ere this, are now of one fold and of one flock.

THE Chian is another man; the Theocritus who wrote this book is one of the many that are of Syracuse, the son of Praxagoras and the famed Philina, and his Muse is the Muse of his native land.

The first of the above poems would appear to have been written for the title-page of the first collected edition of the Bucolic poets, published by the grammarian Artemidorus early in the first century before Christ; the second is thought to have stood upon the title-page of a separate edition of Theocritus, published by Artemidorus' son Theon. "The Chian" is believed by some to be Homer, but is more probably the orator and epigrammatist Theocritus of Chios.

I

THE POEMS OF THEOCRITUS

I.—THYRSIS

A SHEPHERD *and a goatherd meet in the pastures* **one** *noontide, and compliment each other upon their piping. The shepherd, Thyrsis by name, is persuaded by the other—for a cup which he describes but does not at first show—to sing him* The Affliction of Daphnis, *a ballad which tells how the ideal shepherd, friend not only of Nymph and Muse, but of all the wild creatures, having vowed to his first love that she should be his last, pined and died for the love of another. The ballad is divided into three parts marked by changes in the refrain. The first part, after a complaint to the Nymphs of their neglect, tells how the herds and the herdsmen gathered about the dying man, and Hermes his father, and Priapus the country-god of fertility whom he had flouted, came and spoke and got no answer. In the second part, the slighted Love-Goddess comes, and gently upbraids him, whereat he breaks silence with a threat of vengeance after death. The lines of his speech which follow tell in veiled ironic terms what the vengeance of this friend of wild things will be; for Anchises was* *afterwards blinded by bees, Adonis slain by a boar, and Cypris herself wounded by Diomed. The speech is continued with a farewell to the wild creatures, and to the wells and rivers of Syracuse. In the third part he bequeaths his pipe to Pan, ends his dying speech with an address to all Nature, and is overwhelmed at last in the river of Death. The scene of the mime is Cos, but Thyrsis comes from Sicily, and Sicily is the scene of his song.*

NOTE.—For able discussions of the Cup see A. S. F. Gow, *Journal of Hellenic Studies* 1913. 207, and A. Y. Campbell, *Annual of Archaeology and Anthropology* 1931. 19.

ΘΕΟΚΡΙΤΟΥ

I.—ΘΥΡΣΙΣ

ΘΥΡΣΙΣ

Ἁδύ τι τὸ ψιθύρισμα καὶ ἁ πίτυς αἰπόλε τήνα
ἁ ποτὶ ταῖς παγαῖσι μελίσδεται, ἁδὺ δὲ καὶ τὺ
συρίσδες· μετὰ Πᾶνα τὸ δεύτερον ἆθλον ἀποισῇ.
αἴκα τῆνος ἕλῃ κεραὸν τράγον, αἶγα τὺ λαψῇ·
αἴκα δ᾽ αἶγα λάβῃ τῆνος γέρας, ἐς τὲ καταρρεῖ
ἁ χίμαρος· χιμάρῳ δὲ καλὸν κρέας, ἔστε κ᾽
ἀμέλξῃς.

ΑΙΠΟΛΟΣ

ἅδιον ὦ ποιμὴν τὸ τεὸν μέλος ἢ τὸ καταχὲς
τῆν᾽ ἀπὸ τᾶς πέτρας καταλείβεται ὑψόθεν ὕδωρ.
αἴκα ταὶ Μοῖσαι τὰν οἴιδα δῶρον ἄγωνται,
ἄρνα τὺ σακίταν λαψῇ γέρας· αἰ δέ κ᾽ ἀρέσκῃ   10
τήνας ἄρνα λαβεῖν, τὺ δὲ τὰν ὄιν ὕστερον ἀξῇ.

ΘΥΡΣΙΣ

λῇς ποτὶ τᾶν Νυμφᾶν, λῇς αἰπόλε τεῖδε καθίξας,
ὡς τὸ κάταντες τοῦτο γεώλοφον αἵ τε μυρῖκαι,
συρίσδεν; τὰς δ᾽ αἶγας ἐγὼν ἐν τῷδε νομευσῶ.

THE POEMS OF THEOCRITUS

I.—THYRSIS

THYRSIS

SOMETHING sweet is the whisper of the pine that makes her music by yonder springs, and sweet no less, master Goatherd, the melody of your pipe. Pan only shall take place and prize afore you; and if they give him a horny he-goat, then a she shall be yours; and if a she be for him, why, you shall have her kid; and kid's meat's good eating till your kids be milch-goats.

GOATHERD

As sweetly, good Shepherd, falls **your** music as the resounding water that gushes down from the top o' yonder rock. If the Muses get the ewe-lamb to their meed, you shall carry off the cosset; and if so be they choose the cosset, the ewe-lamb shall come to you.

THYRSIS

'Fore the Nymphs I pray you, master Goatherd, come now and sit ye down here by this shelving bank and these brush tamarisks and play **me a** tune. I'll keep your goats the while.

" cosset " : a pet lamb.

ΑΙΠΟΛΟΣ

οὐ θέμις ὦ ποιμὴν τὸ μεσαμβρινὸν οὐ θέμις
    ἄμμιν
συρίσδεν. τὸν Πᾶνα δεδοίκαμες· ἦ γὰρ ἀπ' ἄγρας
τανίκα κεκμακὼς ἀμπαύεται· ἔστι δὲ πικρός,
καί οἱ ἀεὶ δριμεῖα χολὰ ποτὶ ῥινὶ κάθηται.
ἀλλὰ τὺ γὰρ δὴ Θύρσι τὰ Δάφνιδος ἄλγε' ἄειδες
καὶ τᾶς βουκολικᾶς ἐπὶ τὸ πλέον ἵκεο Μοίσας,   2
δεῦρ' ὑπὸ τὰν πτελέαν ἐσδώμεθα τῶ τε Πριήπω
καὶ τᾶν κραναιᾶν κατεναντίον, ᾇπερ ὁ θῶκος
τῆνος ὁ ποιμενικὸς καὶ ταὶ δρύες. αἱ δέ κ' ἀείσῃς,
ὡς ὅκα τὸν Λιβύαθε ποτὶ Χρόμιν ᾆσας ἐρίσδων,
αἶγά τέ τοι δωσῶ διδυματόκον ἐς τρὶς ἀμέλξαι,
ἃ δύ' ἔχοισ' ἐρίφως ποταμέλγεται ἐς δύο πέλλας,
καὶ βαθὺ κισσύβιον κεκλυσμένον ἀδέι κηρῷ,
ἀμφῶες, νεοτευχές, ἔτι γλυφάνοιο ποτόσδον.

τῶ περὶ μὲν χείλη μαρύεται ὑψόθε κισσός,[1]
κισσὸς ἑλιχρύσῳ κεκονιμένος· ἁ δὲ κατ' αὐτὸν   3
καρπῷ ἕλιξ εἰλεῖται ἀγαλλομένα κροκόεντι.[2]
ἔντοσθεν δὲ γυνά τι θεῶν δαίδαλμα τέτυκται,
ἀσκητὰ πέπλῳ τε καὶ ἄμπυκι. πὰρ δέ οἱ ἄνδρες
καλὸν ἐθειράζοντες ἀμοιβαδὶς ἄλλοθεν ἄλλος
νεικείουσ' ἐπέεσσι. τὰ δ' οὐ φρενὸς ἅπτεται αὐτᾶς·
ἀλλ' ὁκὰ μὲν τῆνον ποτιδέρκεται ἄνδρα γελᾶσα,
ἄλλοκα δ' αὖ ποτὶ τὸν ῥιπτεῖ νόον. οἱ δ' ὑπ'
    ἔρωτος
δηθὰ κυλοιδιόωντες ἐτώσια μοχθίζοντι.

---

[1] mss also τῶ ποτὶ   ὑψόθε Junt: mss ὑψόθι   [2] ἁ δὲ is
ἑλίχρυσος and ἕλιξ an adjective E (*Cl. Rev.* 1912. 241): others
ἁ δὲ ἕλιξ "the ivy-tendril"

GOATHERD

No, no, man; there's no piping for me at high
noon. I go in too great dread of Pan for that. I
wot high noon's his time for taking rest after the
swink o' the chase; and he's one o' the tetchy sort;
his nostril's ever sour wrath's abiding-place. But for
singing, you, Thyrsis, used to sing *The Affliction of
Daphnis* as well as any man; you are no 'prentice in
the art of country-music. So let's come and sit
yonder beneath the elm, this way, over against
Priapus and the fountain-goddesses, where that
shepherd's seat is and those oak-trees. And if you
but sing as you sang that day in the match with
Chromis of Libya, I'll not only grant you three
milkings of a twinner goat that for all her two young
yields two pailfuls, but I'll give you a fine great
mazer to boot, well scoured with sweet beeswax, and
of two lugs, bran-span-new and the smack of the
graver upon it yet.

The lip of it is hanged about with curling ivy,
ivy freaked with a cassidony which goes twisting
and twining among the leaves in the pride of her
saffron fruitage. And within this bordure there's
a woman, fashioned as a God might fashion her,
lapped in a robe and a snood about her head.
And either side the woman a swain with fair and
flowing locks, and they bandy words the one with
the other. Yet her heart is not touched by aught
they say; for now 'tis a laughing glance to this,
and anon a handful of regard to that, and for all
their eyes have been so long hollow for love of

"Priapus and the fountain-goddesses": effigies. "Mazer":
a carved wooden cup. "freaked": *lit.* "dusted." "Cas-
sidony": the Everlasting or Golden-Tufts; for another
interpretation see p. 527.

τοῖς δὲ μέτα γριπεύς τε γέρων πέτρα τε τέτυκται
λεπράς, ἐφ' ᾇ σπεύδων μέγα δίκτυον ἐς βόλον
   ἕλκει
ὁ πρέσβυς κάμνοντι τὸ καρτερὸν ἀνδρὶ ἐοικώς.
φαίης κα γυίων νιν ὅσον σθένος ἐλλοπιεύειν·
ὧδέ οἱ ᾠδήκαντι κατ' αὐχένα πάντοθεν ἶνες
καὶ πολιῷ περ ἐόντι, τὸ δὲ σθένος ἄξιον ἄβας.

τυτθὸν δ' ὅσσον ἄπωθεν ἁλιτρύτοιο γέροντος
πυρναίαις σταφυλαῖσι καλὸν βέβριθεν ἀλωά,
τὰν ὀλίγος τις κῶρος ἐφ' αἱμασιαῖσι φυλάσσει
ἥμενος· ἀμφὶ δέ νιν δύ' ἀλώπεκες, ἁ μὲν ἀν' ὄρχως
φοιτῇ σινομένα τὰν τρώξιμον, ἁ δ' ἐπὶ πήρᾳ
πάντα δόλον τεύχοισα τὸ παιδίον οὐ πρὶν ἀνησεῖν
φατὶ πρὶν ἢ 'κρατίσδον[1] ἐπὶ ξηροῖσι καθίξῃ.
αὐτὰρ ὅγ' ἀνθερίκοισι καλὰν πλέκει ἀκριδοθήραν
σχοίνῳ ἐφαρμόσδων· μέλεται δέ οἱ οὔτε τι
   πήρας
οὔτε φυτῶν τοσσῆνον, ὅσον περὶ πλέγματι γαθεῖ.
παντᾷ δ' ἀμφὶ δέπας περιπέπταται ὑγρὸς ἄκανθος,
αἰολίχον θάημα[2]· τέρας κέ τυ θυμὸν ἀτύξαι.

τῶ μὲν ἐγὼ πορθμῆϊ Καλυδνίῳ[3] αἶγά τ' ἔδωκα
ὦνον καὶ τυρόεντα μέγαν λευκοῖο γάλακτος·

---

[1] ἢ (ἀ)κρατίσδον E, cf. Suidas ἀκρατίζω: mss ἀκράτιστον
(scholia also ἀκρατισμόν), which some editors explain
"till he have wrecked (or safely docked) the breakfast" [2] αἰολίχον schol., cf. αἰόλος, πυρρός, πυρρίχος (4. 20): schol.
also with Hesychius αἰολικόν: mss αἰπολικόν   θάημα
Wilamowitz-Moellendorff, cf. Anth. P. 9. 101, Auson. Epist.
14. 33, Hesych.: mss τι θάημα   [3] πορθμῆϊ Καλυδνίῳ schol.:
schol. also with mss πορθμεῖ Καλυδωνίῳ

her, they spend their labour in vain.   Besides these
there's an old fisher wrought on't and a rugged
rock, and there stands gaffer gathering up his
great net for a cast with a right good will like
one that toils might and main.   You would say that
man went about his fishing with all the strength o's
limbs, so stands every sinew in his neck, for all his
grey hairs, puffed and swollen; for his strength is
the strength of youth.

And but a little removed from master Weather-
beat there's a vineyard well laden with clusters
red to the ripening, and a little lad seated watch-
ing upon the hedge.   And on either side of
him two foxes; this ranges to and fro along the
rows and pilfers all such grapes as be ready for
eating, while that setteth all his cunning at the lad's
wallet, and vows he will not let him be till he have
set him breaking his fast with but poor victuals to
his drink.   And all the time the urchin's got star-
flower-stalks a-platting to a reed for to make him a
pretty gin for locusts, and cares never so much, not
he, for his wallet or his vines as he takes pleasure in
his platting.   And for an end, mark you, spread all
about the cup goes the lissom bear's-foot, a sight
worth the seeing with its writhen leaves; 'tis a
marvellous work, 'twill amaze your heart.

Now for that cup a ferryman of Calymnus had a
goat and a gallant great cheese-loaf of me, and never

"Breaking his fast": the chief feature of a Greek
breakfast, as the word ἀκρατίζω shows, was unmixed wine;
this, being in a bottle, the fox, even if he wished it, could not
expect to get at.   "To his drink": cf. Plato, *Rep.* 372 B,
ἐπιπίνοντες τοῦ οἴνου, "drinking the wine to the food."
Calymnus is an island near Cos.

οὐδέ τί πω ποτὶ χεῖλος ἐμὸν θίγεν, ἀλλ' ἔτι κεῖται
ἄχραντον. τῷ κά τυ μάλα πρόφρων ἀρεσαίμαν, 6
αἴκα μοι τὺ φίλος τὸν ἐφίμερον ὕμνον ἀείσῃς.
κοὔ τί τυ κερτομέω. πόταγ' ὠγαθέ· τὰν γὰρ ἀοιδὰν
οὔ τί πᾳ εἰς 'Αΐδαν γε τὸν ἐκλελάθοντα φυλαξεῖς;

ΘΥΡΣΙΣ

Ἄρχετε βουκολικᾶς Μοῖσαι φίλαι ἄρχετ' ἀοιδᾶς.
Θύρσις ὅδ' ὠξ Αἴτνας, καὶ Θύρσιδος ἀδέα φωνά.
πᾷ ποκ' ἄρ' ἦσθ', ὅκα Δάφνις ἐτάκετο, πᾷ ποκα
    Νύμφαι;
ἢ κατὰ Πηνειῶ καλὰ τέμπεα, ἢ κατὰ Πίνδω;
οὐ γὰρ δὴ ποταμοῖο μέγαν ῥόον εἴχετ' 'Ανάπω,
οὐδ' Αἴτνας σκοπιάν, οὐδ' Ἄκιδος ἱερὸν ὕδωρ.

    ἄρχετε βουκολικᾶς Μοῖσαι φίλαι ἄρχετ' ἀοιδᾶς. 7
τῆνον μὰν θῶες, τῆνον λύκοι ὠρύσαντο,
τῆνον χὠκ δρυμοῖο λέων ἔκλαυσε θανόντα.

    ἄρχετε βουκολικᾶς Μοῖσαι φίλαι ἄρχετ' ἀοιδᾶς.
πολλαί οἱ πὰρ ποσσὶ βόες, πολλοὶ δέ τε ταῦροι,
πολλαὶ δὲ δαμάλαι καὶ πόρτιες ὠδύραντο.

    ἄρχετε βουκολικᾶς Μοῖσαι φίλαι ἄρχετ' ἀοιδᾶς.
ἦνθ' Ἑρμᾶς πράτιστος ἀπ' ὤρεος, εἶπε δέ· 'Δάφνι,
τίς τυ κατατρύχει; τίνος ὠγαθὲ τόσσον ἔρασαι;'[1]
    ἄρχετε βουκολικᾶς Μοῖσαι φίλαι ἄρχετ' ἀοιδᾶς.

---

[1] perh. ἔρασαι, cf. 2. 149 n.

yet hath it touched my lip; it still lies unhandselled by. Yet right welcome to it art thou, if like a good fellow thou'lt sing me that pleasing and delightful song. Nay, not so; I am in right earnest. To't, good friend; sure thou wilt not be hoarding that song against thou be'st come where all's forgot?

THYRSIS (sings)

Country-song, sing country-song, sweet Muses.
'Tis Thyrsis sings, of Etna, and a rare sweet voice
  hath he.
Where were ye, Nymphs, when Daphnis pined? ye
  Nymphs, O where were ye?
Was it Peneius' pretty vale, or Pindus' glens? 'twas
  never
Anápus' flood nor Etna's pike nor Acis' holy river.
Country-song, sing country-song, sweet Muses.
When Daphnis died the foxes wailed and the
  wolves they wailed full sore,
The lion from the greenwood wept when Daphnis
  was no more.
Country-song, sing country-song, sweet Muses.
O many the lusty steers at his feet, and many the
  heifers slim,
Many the calves and many the kine that made their
  moan for him.
Country-song, sing country-song, sweet Muses.
Came Hermes first, from the hills away, and said "O
  Daphnis, tell,
" Who is't that fretteth thee, my son? whom lovest
  thou so well?"
Country-song, sing country-song, sweet Muses.

"Peneius, Pindus": a river and a mountain in Thessaly.
"Anapus, Acis": rivers of Sicily.

15

ἦνθον τοὶ βοῦται, τοὶ ποιμένες, ᾡπόλοι ἦνθον·
πάντες ἀνηρώτευν, τί πάθοι κακόν. ἦνθ' ὁ Πρίηπος
κῆφα· 'Δάφνι τάλαν, τί νυ τάκεαι; ἁ δὲ τὲ
    κώρα [1]
πάσας ἀνὰ κράνας, πάντ' ἄλσεα ποσσὶ φορεῖται—
    ἄρχετε βουκολικᾶς Μοῖσαι φίλαι ἄρχετ'
    ἀοιδᾶς—
ζάτεισ'· ἁ δύσερώς τις ἄγαν καὶ ἀμήχανος ἐσσί.
βούτας μὲν ἐλέγευ, νῦν δ' αἰπόλῳ ἀνδρὶ ἐοίκας·
ᾡπόλος ὅκκ' ἐσορῇ τὰς μηκάδας οἷα βατεῦνται,
τάκεται ὀφθαλμώς, ὅτι οὐ τράγος αὐτὸς ἔγεντο,—
    ἄρχετε βουκολικᾶς Μοῖσαι φίλαι ἄρχετ'
    ἀοιδᾶς—
καὶ τὺ δ' ἐπεί κ' ἐσορῇς τὰς παρθένος οἷα γελᾶντι,
τάκεαι ὀφθαλμώς, ὅτι οὐ μετὰ ταῖσι χορεύεις.'
τὼς δ' οὐδὲν ποτελέξαθ' ὁ βουκόλος, ἀλλὰ τὸν
    αὐτῶ
ἄννε πικρὸν ἔρωτα, καὶ ἐς τέλος ἄννε μοίρας.

    ἄρχετε βουκολικᾶς Μοῖσαι πάλιν ἄρχετ' ἀοιδᾶς.
ἦνθέ γε μὰν ἀδεῖα καὶ ἁ Κύπρις γελάοισα,[2]
λάθρη μὲν γελάοισα, βαρὺν δ' ἀνὰ θυμὸν ἔχοισα,
κεῖπε· 'τύ θην τὸν Ἔρωτα κατεύχεο Δάφνι
    λυγιξεῖν·

---

[1] τὲ Wil. from Laur. 32. 16 and Paris. 3832: other mss γε,
τοι, τι   [2] ἀδεῖα = ἡδέα Sch. Gen. (Reiske)

The neatherds came, the shepherds came, and the
  goatherds him beside,
All fain to hear what ail'd him ; Priápus came and
  cried
" Why peak and pine, unhappy wight, when thou
  mightest bed a bride ?
" For there's nor wood nor water but hath seen her
  footsteps flee—
  Country-song, sing country-song, sweet Muses—
" In search o' thee.   O a fool-in-love and a feeble is
  here, perdye !
" Neatherd, forsooth ? 'tis goatherd now, or 'faith, 'tis
  like to be ;
" When goatherd in the rutting-time the skipping
  kids doth scan,
" His eye grows soft, his eye grows sad, because he's
  born a man ;—
  Country-song, sing country-song, sweet Muses—
" So you, when ye see the lasses laughing in gay ríot,
" Your eye grows soft, your eye grows sad, because
  you share it not."
But never a word said the poor neathérd, for a
  bitter love bare he ;
And he bare it well, as I shall tell, to the end that
  was to be.

  Country-song, more country-song, ye Muses.
But and the Cyprian came him to, and smiled on
  him full sweetly—
For though she fain would foster wrath, she could not
  choose but smile—
And cried " Ah, braggart Daphnis, that wouldst
  throw Love so featly !

ἦρ' οὐκ αὐτὸς Ἔρωτος ὑπ' ἀργαλέω ἐλυγίχθης;'
ἄρχετε βουκολικᾶς Μοῖσαι πάλιν ἄρχετ' ἀοιδᾶς.
τὰν δ' ἄρα χὠ Δάφνις ποταμείβετο· ' Κύπρι
βαρεῖα,
Κύπρι νεμεσσατά, Κύπρι θνατοῖσιν ἀπεχθής,
ἤδη γὰρ φράσδῃ πάνθ' ἄλιον ἄμμι δεδυκεῖν·
Δάφνις κἠν Ἀΐδα κακὸν ἔσσεται ἄλγος Ἔρωτι—
ἄρχετε βουκολικᾶς Μοῖσαι πάλιν ἄρχετ'
ἀοιδᾶς—
οὐ[1] λέγεται τὰν Κύπριν ὁ βουκόλος; ἕρπε ποτ'
Ἴδαν,
ἕρπε ποτ' Ἀγχίσαν. τηνεῖ δρύες ἠδὲ[2] κύπειρος,
αἱ δὲ[3] καλὸν βομβεῦντι ποτὶ σμάνεσσι μέλισσαι.
ἄρχετε βουκολικᾶς Μοῖσαι πάλιν ἄρχετ' ἀοιδᾶς.
ὡραῖος χὤδωνις, ἐπεὶ καὶ μῆλα νομεύει
καὶ πτώκας βάλλει καὶ θηρία πάντα διώκει.

ἄρχετε βουκολικᾶς Μοῖσαι πάλιν ἄρχετ' ἀοιδᾶς.
αὖτις ὅπως στασῇ Διομήδεος ἄσσον ἰοῖσα,
καὶ λέγε· τὸν βούταν νικῶ Δάφνιν, ἀλλὰ μάχευ
μοι.

ἄρχετε βουκολικᾶς Μοῖσαι πάλιν ἄρχετ' ἀοιδᾶς.
ὦ λύκοι, ὦ θῶες, ὦ ἀν' ὤρεα φωλάδες ἄρκτοι,
χαίρεθ'· ὁ βουκόλος ὔμμιν ἐγὼ Δάφνις οὐκέτ' ἀν'
ὕλαν,

---

[1] οὐ Graefe: mss and schol. οὖ against the dialect   [2] ἠδὲ
Wil from Plutarch: mss ὥδε   [3] αἱ δὲ Wil from Plutarch:
mss ὥδε

"Thou'rt thrown, methinks, thyself of Love's so
   grievous guile."
   Country-song, more country-song, ye Muses.
   Then out he spake; "O Cypris cruel, Cypris
   vengeful yet,
" Cypris hated of all flesh! think'st all my sun be
   set?
" I tell thee even 'mong the dead Daphnis shall
   work thee ill :—
   Country-song, more country-song, ye Muses—
" Men talk of Cypris and the hind; begone to Ida
   hill,
" Begone to hind Anchises; sure bedstraw there
   doth thrive
" And fine oak-trees and pretty bees all humming
   at the hive.
   Country-song, more country-song, ye Muses.
" Adonis too is ripe to woo, for a' tends his sheep o'
   the lea
" And shoots the hare and a-hunting goes of all the
   beasts there be.
   Country-song, more country-song, ye Muses.
" And then I'ld have thee take thy stand by
   Diomed, and say
" ' I slew the neatherd Daphnis; fight me thou
   to-day.'
   Country-song, more country-song, ye Muses.
   " But 'tis wolf farewell and fox farewell and bear
   o' the mountain den,
" Your neatherd fere, your Daphnis dear, ye'll
   never see agen,

οὐκέτ᾽ ἀνὰ δρυμώς, οὐκ ἄλσεα. χαῖρ᾽ Ἀρέθοισα
καὶ ποταμοί, τοὶ χεῖτε καλὸν κατὰ Θυμβρίδος
ὕδωρ.

ἄρχετε βουκολικᾶς Μοῖσαι πάλιν ἄρχετ᾽ ἀοιδᾶς.
Δάφνις ἐγὼν ὅδε τῆνος ὁ τὰς βόας ὧδε νομεύων,
Δάφνις ὁ τὼς ταύρως καὶ πόρτιας ὧδε ποτίσδων.

ἄρχετε βουκολικᾶς Μοῖσαι πάλιν ἄρχετ᾽ ἀοιδᾶς.

ὦ Πὰν Πάν, εἴτ᾽ ἐσσὶ κατ᾽ ὤρεα μακρὰ Λυκαίω,
εἴτε τύγ᾽ ἀμφιπολεῖς μέγα Μαίναλον, ἔνθ᾽ ἐπὶ
νᾶσον
τὰν Σικελάν, Ἑλίκας δὲ λίπε ῥίον αἰπύ τε σᾶμα
τῆνο Λυκαονίδαο, τὸ καὶ μακάρεσσιν ἀγητόν.

λήγετε βουκολικᾶς Μοῖσαι ἴτε λήγετ᾽ ἀοιδᾶς.
ἔνθ᾽ ὦναξ καὶ τάνδε φέρευ πακτοῖο [1] μελίπνουν
ἐκ κηρῶ σύριγγα καλὰν περὶ χεῖλος ἑλικτάν·
ἦ γὰρ ἐγὼν ὑπ᾽ ἔρωτος ἐς Ἅιδος ἕλκομαι ἤδη.

λήγετε βουκολικᾶς Μοῖσαι ἴτε λήγετ᾽ ἀοιδᾶς.
νῦν ἴα μὲν φορέοιτε βάτοι, φορέοιτε δ᾽ ἄκανθαι,
ἁ δὲ καλὰ νάρκισσος ἐπ᾽ ἀρκεύθοισι κομάσαι·
πάντα δ᾽ ἔναλλα [2] γένοιντο, καὶ ἁ πίτυς ὄχνας
ἐνείκαι,
Δάφνις ἐπεὶ θνάσκει, καὶ τὰς κύνας ὤλαφος
ἕλκοι,

[1] So Reiske from Schol.: mss φέρ᾽ εὐπάκτοιο   [2] mss also
with *Oxyrhynchus Papyrus* 2064 (c. A.D. 180) read ἄναλλα

" By glen no more, by glade no more. And 'tis
    O farewell to thee,
" Sweet Arethuse, and all pretty watèrs down
    Thymbris vale that flee ;
 Country-song, more country-song, ye Muses ;
" For this, Ò this is that Daphnís, your kine to field
    did bring,
" This Daphnis he, led stirk and steer **to** you
    a-watering.
 Country-song, more country-song, ye Muses.

" And Pan, O Pan, whether at this hour by Lycee's
    mountain-pile
" Or Maenal steep thy watch thou keep, come away
    to the Sicil isle,
" Come away from the knoll of Helicè and the howe
    lift high i' the lea,
" The howe of Lycáon's child, the howe that Gods in
    heav'n envye ;
 Country-song, leave country-song, ye Muses ;
" Come, Master, and take this pretty pipe, this pipe
    of honey breath,
" Of wax well knit round lips to fit ; for Love hales
    mé to my death.
 Country-song, leave country-song, ye Muses.
" Bear violets now ye briers, ye thistles violets
    too ;
" Daffodilly may hang on the juniper, and all things
    go askew ;
" Pines may grow figs now Daphnis dies, **and** hind
    tear hound if she will,

" Arethusa ": the fountain of Syracuse. " Helicè, Lycaon's
child ": the tombs of Helicè and her son Arcas were famous
sights of Arcadia.

κἠξ ὀρέων τοὶ σκῶπες ἀηδόσι δηρίσαιντο'.[1]

λήγετε βουκολικᾶς Μοῖσαι ἴτε λήγετ' ἀοιδᾶς.

χὠ μὲν τόσσ' εἰπών ἀπεπαύσατο· τὸν δ' Ἀφροδίτα
ἤθελ' ἀνορθῶσαι· τά γε μὰν λίνα πάντα λελοίπει
ἐκ Μοιρᾶν, χὠ Δάφνις ἔβα ῥόον. ἔκλυσε δίνα[2]   1
τὸν Μοίσαις φίλον ἄνδρα, τὸν οὐ Νύμφαισιν
ἀπεχθῆ.

λήγετε βουκολικᾶς Μοῖσαι ἴτε λήγετ' ἀοιδᾶς.

καὶ τὺ δίδου τὰν αἶγα τό τε σκύφος, ὥς κεν[3]
ἀμέλξας

σπείσω ταῖς Μοίσαις. ὦ χαίρετε πολλάκι Μοῖσαι,
χαίρετ'· ἐγὼ δ' ὔμμιν καὶ ἐς ὕστερον ἅδιον ᾀσῶ.

ΑΙΠΟΛΟΣ

πλῆρές τοι μέλιτος τὸ καλὸν στόμα Θύρσι γένοιτο,
πλῆρες δὲ σχαδόνων, καὶ ἀπ' Αἰγίλω ἰσχάδα
τρώγοις

ἀδεῖαν, τέττιγος ἐπεὶ τύγα φέρτερον ᾄδεις.
ἠνίδε τοι τὸ δέπας· θᾶσαι φίλος, ὡς καλὸν ὄσδει·
Ὡρᾶν πεπλύσθαι νιν ἐπὶ κράναισι δοκησεῖς.   1
ὧδ' ἴθι Κισσαίθα, τὺ δ' ἄμελγέ νιν. αἱ δὲ χίμαιραι,
οὐ μὴ σκιρτασεῖτε[4], μὴ ὁ τράγος ὔμμιν ἀναστῇ.

---

[1] δηρίσαιντο Scaliger from Verg. *Ecl.* 8. 55: mss γαρύσαιντο
[2] perh. ἔκλιε δίνα E = the encircling Acheron shut him in:
cf. Cramer *A. O.* 4. 195. 8 κλείω ὁ β ἀόριστος ἔκλιον διὰ τοῦ ῑ ὡς
ἔπιθον   [3] κεν : mss also νιν   [4] Porson : mss σκιρτασῆτε

"And the sweet nightingále be outsung i' the dale
  by the scritch-owl from the hill."
    Country-song, leave country-song, ye Muses
  Such words spake he, and he stayed him still;
    and O, the Love-Ladye,
She would fain have raised him where he lay, but
  that could never be.
For the thread was spun and the days were done
  and Daphnis gone to the River,
And the Nymphs' good friend and the Muses' fere
  was whelmed i' the whirl for ever.
    Country-song, leave country-song, ye Muses.

There; give me the goat and the tankard, man;
and the Muses shall have a libation of her milk.
Fare you well, ye Muses, and again fare you well,
and I'll e'en sing you a sweeter song another day.

GOATHERD

Be your fair mouth filled with honey and the
honeycomb, good Thyrsis; be your eating of the
sweet figs of Aegilus; for sure your singing's as
delightful as the cricket's chirping in spring.
Here's the cup (*taking it from his wallet*). Pray mark
how good it smells; you'll be thinking it hath been
washed at the well o' the Seasons. Hither, Brown-
ing; and milk her, you. A truce to your skip-
ping, ye kids yonder, or the buckgoat will be after
you.

"Gone to the River": Acheron, the river of Death; *or*
"over the River" (ἔβα = crossed, so schol.) "Whelmed
i' the whirl": *or* "pent by the flood."

23

II.—THE SPELL

THIS *monologue, which preserves the dialogue-form by a dumb character, consists of two parts; in the first a Coan girl named Simaetha [1] lays a fire-spell upon her neglectful lover, the young athlete Delphis, and in the second, when her maid goes off to smear the ashes upon his lintel, she tells the Moon how his love was won and lost. The scene lies not far from the sea, at a place where three roads meet without the city, the roads being bordered with tombs. The Moon shines in the background, and in the foreground is a wayside shrine and statue of Hecate with a little altar before it. Upon this altar, in the first part of the rite, the poor girl burns successively barley-meal, bay-leaves, a waxen puppet, and some bran; next, the coming of the Goddess having been heralded by the distant barking of dogs and welcomed with the beating of brass, amid the holy silence that betokens her presence Simaetha pours the libation and puts up her chief prayer; lastly she burns the herb hippomanes and a piece of the fringe of her lover's cloak. The incantation which begins and ends*

[1] She is not a professional sorceress, see l. 91.

24

the four-line stanza devoted to the burning of each of these things, as well as the two central stanzas belonging to the holy silence and the libation, is addressed to the magic four-spoked wheel which still bears the name of the bird that was originally bound to such wheels, and which is kept turning by Simaetha throughout the rite.[1] When Thestylis withdraws with the collected ashes in the libation-bowl, her mistress begins her soliloquy. This consists of two halves, the first of which is divided, by a refrain addressed to the listening Moon, into stanzas, all, except the last, of five lines; then instead of the refrain comes the climax of the story, put briefly in two lines, and the second half begins, with its tale of desertion. In the latter half the absence of the refrain with its lyric and romantic associations is intended to heighten the contrast between then and now, between the fulness of joy and the emptiness of despair. Towards the end both of the first and of the second parts of the poem there is a suggestion that Simaetha only half believes in the efficacy of her spell; for she threatens that if it fails to bring back Delphis' love to her, poison shall prevent his bestowing it elsewhere.

---

[1] See an able article by A. S. F. Gow, *Journal of Hellenic Studies* 1934.

II.—ΦΑΡΜΑΚΕΥΤΡΙΑΙ

Πᾷ μοι ταὶ δάφναι; φέρε Θεστυλί. πᾷ δὲ τὰ
    φίλτρα;
στέψον τὰν κελέβαν φοινικέῳ οἰὸς ἀώτῳ,
ὡς τὸν ἐμὸν βαρὺν εὖντα φίλον καταθύσομαι
    ἄνδρα,
ὅς μοι δωδεκαταῖος ἀφ' ὧ τάλας[1] οὐδὲ ποθίκει,
οὐδ' ἔγνω, πότερον τεθνάκαμες ἢ ζοοὶ εἰμές,
οὐδὲ θύρας ἄραξεν ἀνάρσιος. ἦρά οἱ ἀλλᾷ
οἴχετ'[2] ἔχων ὅ τ' Ἔρως ταχινὰς φρένας ἅ τ'
    Ἀφροδίτα;
βασεῦμαι ποτὶ τὰν Τιμαγήτοιο παλαίστραν
αὔριον, ὥς νιν ἴδω καὶ μέμψομαι οἷά με ποιεῖ.
νῦν δέ νιν ἐκ θυέων καταδήσομαι.[3] ἀλλὰ Σελάνα
φαῖνε καλόν· τὶν γὰρ ποταείσομαι, ἅσυχε[4]
    δαῖμον,
τᾷ χθονίᾳ θ' Ἑκάτᾳ, τὰν καὶ σκύλακες τρομέοντι
ἐρχομέναν νεκύων ἀνὰ τήρία καὶ μέλαν αἷμα.
χαῖρ' Ἑκάτα δασπλῆτι, καὶ ἐς τέλος ἄμμιν ὀπάδει
φάρμακα ταῦτ' ἔρδοισα χερείονα μήτε τι Κίρκας
μήτε τι Μηδείας μήτε ξανθᾶς Περιμήδας.

ἴυγξ. ἕλκε τὺ τῆνον ἐμὸν ποτὶ δῶμα τὸν ἄνδρα.
ἄλφιτά τοι πρᾶτον πυρὶ τάκεται· ἀλλ' ἐπίπασσε
Θεστυλί. δειλαία, πεῖ τὰς φρένας ἐκπεπότασαι;

---

[1] Papyrus Antinoensis (c. 500 A.D.) with some mss *τάλαν*
[2] *οἴχετ'* E: mss *ῷχετ'*   [3] so Toup and *P. Ant.* here and at
3 and 159: mss *καταθύσομαι*   [4] *ἅσυχε* Kiessling: mss *ἅσυχα*,
from l. 100?

II.—THE SPELL

Where are my bay-leaves? Come, Thestylis; where are my love-charms? Come crown me the bowl with the crimson flower o' wool; I would fain have the fire-spell to my cruel dear that for twelve days hath not so much as come anigh me, the wretch, nor knows not whether I be alive or dead, nay nor even hath knocked upon my door, implacable man. I warrant ye Love and the Lady be gone away with his feat fancy. In the morning I'll to Timagetus' school and see him, and ask what he means to use me so; but, for to-night, I'll put the spell o' fire upon him.

So shine me fair, sweet Moon; for to thee, still Goddess, is my song, to thee and that Hecat infernal who makes e'en the whelps to shiver on her goings to and fro where these tombs be and the red blood lies. All hail to thee, dread and awful Hecat! I prithee so bear me company that this medicine of my making prove potent as any of Circe's or Medea's or Perimed's of the golden hair.

Wryneck, wryneck, draw him hither.

First barley-meal to the burning. Come, Thestylis; throw it on. Alack, poor fool! whither are thy wits gone wandering? Lord! am I become a thing

ἠρά γέθην[1]μυσαρὰ καὶ τὶν ἐπίχαρμα τέτυγμαι;
πάσσ' ἅμα καὶ λέγε· 'ταῦτα τὰ Δέλφιδος ὄστια
πάσσω.'

ἶυγξ, ἕλκε τὺ τῆνον ἐμὸν ποτὶ δῶμα τὸν ἄνδρα.
Δέλφις ἔμ' ἀνίασεν· ἐγὼ δ' ἐπὶ Δέλφιδι δάφναν
αἴθω· χὡς αὕτα λακεῖ μέγα κἀκπυρίσασα
ἐξαπίνας[2] ἄφθη κοὐδὲ σποδὸν εἴδομες αὐτᾶς,
οὕτω τοι καὶ Δέλφις ἐνὶ φλογὶ σάρκ' ἀμαθύνοι.

ἶυγξ, ἕλκε τὺ τῆνον ἐμὸν ποτὶ δῶμα τὸν ἄνδρα.
ὡς τοῦτον τὸν κωρον[3] ἐγὼ σὺν δαίμονι τάκω,
ὣς τάκοιθ' ὑπ' ἔρωτος ὁ Μύνδιος αὐτίκα Δέλφις.
χὡς δινεῖθ' ὅδε ρόμβος ὁ χάλκεος ἐξ 'Αφροδίτας,
ὣς τῆνος δινοῖτο ποθ' ἀμετέραισι θύραισιν.[4]

ἶυγξ, ἕλκε τὺ τῆνον ἐμὸν ποτὶ δῶμα τὸν ἄνδρα.
νῦν θυσῶ τὰ πίτυρα. τὺ δ' Ἄρτεμι καὶ τὸν ἐν
"Αιδα
κινήσαις ἀδάμαντα καὶ εἴ τί περ ἀσφαλὲς ἄλλο.
Θεστυλί, ταὶ κύνες ἄμμιν ἀνὰ πτόλιν ὠρύονται.
ἁ θεὸς ἐν τριόδοισι· τὸ χαλκέον ὡς τάχος ἄχει.

ἶυγξ, ἕλκε τὺ τῆνον ἐμὸν ποτὶ δῶμα τὸν ἄνδρα.
ἠνίδε σιγῇ μὲν πόντος, σιγῶντι δ' ἀῆται·
ἁ δ' ἐμὰ οὐ σιγῇ στέρνων ἔντοσθεν ἀνία,
ἀλλ' ἐπὶ τήνῳ πᾶσα καταίθομαι, ὅς με τάλαιναν
ἀντὶ γυναικὸς ἔθηκε κακὰν καὶ ἀπάρθενον εἶμεν.

ἶυγξ, ἕλκε τὺ τῆνον ἐμὸν ποτὶ δῶμα τὸν ἄνδρα.
ἐς τρὶς ἀποσπένδω κὴς τρὶς τάδε, πότνια, φωνῶ·
εἴτε γυνὰ τήνῳ παρακέκλιται εἴτε καὶ ἀνήρ,

---

[1] So *P. Ant.*: mss τοι   [2] κἀκπυρίσασα ἐξαπίνας *Et Mag.*
and Hdn. (cf. Garin *Stud. Ital. Filol. cl.* 1907): mss καππυ-
ρίσασα (or καπυρ.) κἠξαπίνας, *P. Ant.* κακκ.υρισασα   [3] κωρον
E, cf. Verg. *Ecl.* 8, Hor. *Epod.* 17, Ov. *Her.* 6. 91 ; Soph. *fr.*
481a κόρον ἀϊστώσας πυρί ; 15. 120: mss κηρόν, from a gloss
[4] ll. 27–31 follow 41 in *P. Ant.* and one ms

a filthy drab like thee may crow over? On, on
with the meal, and say "These be Delphis' bones
I throw."

Wryneck, wryneck, draw him hither.

As Delphis hath brought me pain, so I burn the
bay against Delphis. And as it crackles and then
lo! is burnt suddenly to nought and we see not so
much as the ash of it, e'en so be Delphis' body
whelmed in another flame.

Wryneck, wryneck, draw him hither.

As this puppet melts for me before Hecat,
so melt with love, e'en so speedily, Delphis of
Myndus. And as this wheel of brass turns by grace
of Aphrodite, so turn he and turn again before my
threshold.

Wryneck, wryneck, draw him hither.

Now to the flames with the bran. O Artemis, as
thou movest the adamant that is at the door of Death,
so mayst thou move all else that is unmovable.
Hark, Thestylis, where the dogs howl in the town.
Sure the Goddess is at these cross-roads. Quick,
beat the pan.

Wryneck, wryneck, draw him hither.

Lo there! now wave is still and wind is still,
though never still the pain that is in my breast; for
I am all afire for him, afire alas! for him that hath
made me no wife and left me to my shame no
maid.

Wryneck, wryneck, draw him hither.

Thrice this libation I pour, thrice, Lady, this
prayer I say: be woman at this hour or man his

"Myndus": a town of Caria, opposite Cos. "Turn and
turn again before my threshold": waiting to be let in; cf.
7. 122.

τόσσον ἔχοι λάθας, ὅσσον ποκὰ Θησέα φαντὶ
ἐν Δίᾳ λασθῆμεν ἐϋπλοκάμω Ἀριάδνας.
 ἶυγξ, ἕλκε τὺ τῆνον ἐμὸν ποτὶ δῶμα τὸν ἄνδρα.
ἱππομανὲς φυτόν ἐστι παρ᾽ Ἀρκάσι, τῷ δ᾽ ἐπὶ
  πᾶσαι
καὶ πῶλοι μαίνονται ἀν᾽ ὤρεα καὶ θοαὶ ἵπποι.
ὣς καὶ Δέλφιν ἴδοιμι, καὶ ἐς τόδε δῶμα περᾶσαι
μαινομένῳ ἴκελος λιπαρᾶς ἔκτοσθε παλαίστρας.
 ἶυγξ, ἕλκε τὺ τῆνον ἐμὸν ποτὶ δῶμα τὸν ἄνδρα.
τοῦτ᾽ ἀπὸ τᾶς χλαίνας τὸ κράσπεδον ὤλεσε
  Δέλφις,
ὠγὼ νῦν τίλλοισα κατ᾽ ἀγρίῳ ἐν πυρὶ βάλλω.
αἰαῖ Ἔρως ἀνιαρέ, τί μευ μέλαν ἐκ χροὸς αἷμα
ἐμφὺς ὡς λιμνᾶτις ἅπαν ἐκ βδέλλα πέπωκας;
 ἶυγξ, ἕλκε τὺ τῆνον ἐμὸν ποτὶ δῶμα τὸν ἄνδρα.
σαύραν τοι τρίψασα κακὸν ποτὸν αὔριον οἰσῶ.
Θεστυλί, νῦν δὲ λαβοῖσα τὺ τὰ θρόνα ταῦθ᾽
  ὑπόμαξον
τᾶς τήνω φλιᾶς καθ᾽ ὑπέρτερον ἇς ἔτι καὶ νύξ,[1]
καὶ λέγ᾽ ἐπιφθύζοισα· ‘τὰ Δέλφιδος ὄστια μάσσω.’[2]
 ἶυγξ, ἕλκε τὺ τῆνον ἐμὸν ποτὶ δῶμα τὸν ἄνδρα.

νῦν δὴ μώνα ἐοῖσα πόθεν τὸν ἔρωτα δακρύσω;
τηνῶθ᾽ ἀρξεῦμαι,[3] τίς μοι κακὸν ἄγαγε τοῦτο.
 ἦνθ᾽ ἁ τῶ Ὑβούλοιο καναφόρος ἄμμιν Ἀναξὼ
ἄλσος ἐς Ἀρτέμιδος, τᾷ δὴ πύκα[4] πολλὰ μὲν ἄλλα
θηρία πομπεύεσκε περισταδόν, ἐν δὲ λέαινα.
 φράζεό μευ τὸν ἔρωθ᾽ ὅθεν ἵκετο, πότνα Σελάνα.

---

 [1] νύξ Buech. : mss, *P. Ant.* νῦν [2] μάσσω Ahlwardt : mss
πάσσω, from l. 21 [3] τηνῶθ᾽ ἀρξεῦμαι Wil : mss ἐκ τήνω δ᾽
ἄρξω οἱ ἐκ τίνος ἄρξωμαι (and ἄρξομαι) [4] πύκα Th. Fritzsche:
mss ποκα
 61 ἐκ θυμῶ δέδεμαι, ὃ δέ μευ λόγον οὐδένα ποιεῖ, not in the
best mss nor in *P. Ant.*

30

love-mate, O be that mate forgotten even as old Theseus once forgat the fair-tressed damsel in Dia.

Wryneck, wryneck, draw him hither.

Horse-madness is a herb grows in Arcady, and makes every filly, every flying mare run a-raving in the hills. In like case Delphis may I see, aye, coming to my door from the oil and the wrestling-place like one that is raving mad.

Wryneck, wryneck, draw him hither.

This fringe hath Delphis lost from his cloak, and this now pluck I in pieces and fling away into the ravening flame. Woe's me, remorseless Love ! why hast clung to me thus, thou muddy leech, and drained my flesh of the red blood every drop?

Wryneck, wryneck, draw him hither.

I'll bray thee an eft to-morrow, and an ill drink thou shalt find it. But for to-night take thou these ashes, Thestylis, while 'tis yet dark, and smear them privily upon his lintel above, and spit for what thou doest and say " Delphis' bones I smear."

Wryneck, wryneck, draw him hither.

Now I am alone. Where shall I begin the lament of my love? Here be 't begun; I'll tell who 'twas brought me to this pass.

One day came Anaxo daughter of Eubulus our way, came a-basket-bearing in procession to the temple of Artemis, with a ring of many beasts about her, a lioness one.

List, good Moon, where I learnt my loving

" Dia ": Naxos, where Theseus abandoned Ariadne. " Spit for what thou doest " : to avert ill-luck.

καί μ' ἁ Θευμαρίδα Θρᾶσσα τροφός, ἁ μακαρῖτις,
ἀγχίθυρος[1] ναίοισα, κατεύξατο καὶ λιτάνευσε
τὰν πομπὰν θάσασθαι· ἐγὼ δέ οἱ ἁ μεγάλοιτος
ὠμάρτευν βύσσοιο καλὸν σύροισα χιτῶνα
κἀμφιστειλαμένα τὰν ξυστίδα τὰν Κλεαρίστας.
    φράζεό μευ τὸν ἔρωθ' ὅθεν ἵκετο, πότνα Σελάνα.
ἤδη δ' εὖσα μέσαν κατ' ἀμαξιτόν, ἇ τὰ Λύκωνος,
εἶδον Δέλφιν ὁμοῦ τε καὶ Εὐδάμιππον ἰόντας·
τοῖς δ' ἦς ξανθοτέρα μὲν ἑλιχρύσοιο γενειάς,
στήθεα δὲ στίλβοντα πολὺ πλέον ἢ τὺ Σελάνα,
ὡς ἀπὸ γυμνασίοιο καλὸν πόνον ἄρτι λιπόντων.
    φράζεό μευ τὸν ἔρωθ' ὅθεν ἵκετο, πότνα Σελάνα.
χὤς ἴδον, ὥς ἐμάνην, ὥς μευ περὶ[2]θυμὸς ἰάφθη
δειλαίας· τὸ δὲ κάλλος ἐτάκετο, κοὐδέ τι πομπᾶς
τήνας ἐφρασάμαν· οὐδ' ὡς πάλιν οἴκαδ' ἀπῆνθον
ἔγνων· ἀλλά μέ τις καπυρὰ νόσος ἐξαλάπαξε·[3]
κεῖμαν δ' ἐν κλιντῆρι δέκ' ἄματα καὶ δέκα
    νύκτας.
    φράζεό μευ τὸν ἔρωθ' ὅθεν ἵκετο, πότνα Σελάνα.
καί μευ χρὼς μὲν ὁμοῖος ἐγίνετο πολλάκι θάψῳ,
ἔρρευν δ' ἐκ κεφαλᾶς πᾶσαι τρίχες, αὐτὰ δὲ
    λοιπὰ
ὀστί' ἔτ' ἦς καὶ δέρμα. καὶ ἐς τίνος οὐκ ἐπέρασα,
ἢ ποίας ἔλιπον γραίας δόμον, ἅτις ἐπᾷδει;
ἀλλ' ἦς οὐδὲν ἐλαφρόν· ὁ δὲ χρόνος ἄνυτο φεύγων.
    φράζεό μευ τὸν ἔρωθ' ὅθεν ἵκετο, πότνα Σελάνα.
χοὔτω τᾷ δώλᾳ τὸν ἀλαθέα μῦθον ἔλεξα·
εἰ' ἄγε Θεστυλί μοι χαλεπᾶς νόσω εὑρέ τι μᾶχος.
πᾶσαν ἔχει με τάλαιναν ὁ Μύνδιος· ἀλλὰ μολοῖσα

---

[1] ἀγχίθυρος E: mss ἀγχ.   [2] Taylor and P. Ant. πυρὶ
[3] Schol. also with P. Ant. ἐξεσάλαξε

Now Theumaridas' Thracian nurse that dwelt next door, gone ere this to her rest, had begged and prayed me to go out and see the pageant, and so— ill was my luck—I followed her, in a long gown of fine silk, with Clearista's cloak over it.

List, good Moon, where I learnt my loving.

I was halfway o' the road, beside Lycon's, when lo! I espied walking together Delphis and Eudamippus, the hair o' their chins as golden as cassidony, and the breasts of them, for they were on their way from their pretty labour at the school, shone full as fair as thou, great Moon.

List, good Moon, where I learnt my loving.

And O the pity of it! in a moment I looked and was lost, lost and smit i' the heart ; the colour went from my cheek ; of that brave pageant I bethought me no more. How I got me home I know not ; but this I know, a parching fever laid me waste and I was ten days and ten nights abed.

List, good Moon, where I learnt my loving.

And I would go as wan and pale as any dyer's-boxwood ; the hairs o' my head began to fall ; I was nought but skin and bone. There's not a charmer in the town to whom I resorted not, nor witch's hovel whither I went not for a spell. But 'twas no easy thing to cure a malady like that, and time sped on apace.

List, good Moon, where I learnt my loving.

At last I told my woman all the truth. " Go to, good Thestylis," cried I, " go find me some remedy for a sore distemper. The Myndian, alack ! he possesseth me altogether. Go thou, pray, and watch

---

"Clearista": perh. her sister.   "Cassidony": the Ever-lasting or Golden-Tufts.   "smit i' the heart": or perh. 'and my heart pierced with fire' (metaph. from fire-darts used in war).

τήρησον ποτὶ τὰν Τιμαγήτοιο παλαίστραν·
τηνεῖ γὰρ φοιτῇ, τηνεῖ δέ οἱ ἁδὺ καθῆσθαι.

φράζεό μευ τὸν ἔρωθ' ὅθεν ἵκετο, πότνα Σελάνα·
κἠπεί κά νιν ἐόντα μάθῃς μόνον, ἄσυχα νεῦσον·
κεἶφ' ὅτι Σιμαίθα τυ καλεῖ, καὶ ὑφαγέο τᾷδε.'[1]
ὣς ἐφάμαν· ἁ δ' ἦνθε καὶ ἄγαγε τὸν λιπαρόχρων
εἰς ἐμὰ δώματα Δέλφιν· ἐγὼ δέ νιν ὡς ἐνόησα
ἄρτι θύρας ὑπὲρ οὐδὸν ἀμειβόμενον ποδὶ κούφῳ,—

φράζεό μευ τὸν ἔρωθ' ὅθεν ἵκετο, πότνα Σελάνα·
πᾶσα μὲν ἐψύχθην χιόνος πλέον, ἐκ δὲ μετώπω
ἱδρώς μευ κοχύδεσκεν ἴσον νοτίαισιν ἐέρσαις,
οὐδέ τι φωνῆσαι δυνάμαν, οὐδ' ὅσσον ἐν ὕπνῳ
κνυζῶνται φωνεῦντα φίλαν ποτὶ ματέρα τέκνα·
ἀλλ' ἐπάγην δαγῦδι καλὸν χρόα πάντοθεν ἴσα.

φράζεό μευ τὸν ἔρωθ' ὅθεν ἵκετο, πότνα Σελάνα.
καί μ' ἐσιδὼν ὤστοργος ἐπὶ χθονὸς ὄμματα πάξας
ἕζετ' ἐπὶ κλιντῆρι καὶ ἑζόμενος φάτο μῦθον·
'ἦρά με Σιμαίθα τόσον ἔφθασας, ὅσσον ἐγώ θην
πράν ποκα τὸν χαρίεντα τράχων ἔφθασσα Φιλῖνον,
ἐς τὸ τεὸν καλέσασα τόδε στέγος ἢ 'μὲ παρεῖμεν.

φράζεό μευ τὸν ἔρωθ' ὅθεν ἵκετο, πότνα Σελάνα.
ἦνθον γάρ κεν ἐγών, ναὶ τὸν γλυκὺν ἦνθον Ἔρωτα
ἢ τρίτος ἠὲ τέταρτος ἐὼν φίλος αὐτίκα νυκτός,
μᾶλα μὲν ἐν κόλποισι Διωνύσοιο φυλάσσων,
κρατὶ δ' ἔχων λεύκαν, Ἡρακλέος ἱερὸν ἔρνος,
πάντοθι πορφυρέαισι περὶ ζώστραισιν ἑλικτάν.

φράζεό μευ τὸν ἔρωθ' ὅθεν ἵκετο, πότνα Σελάνα.

[1] P. Ant. αφαγέο (with most mss) and τεῖδε with the τῶδε
of some mss over it

for him by Timagetus' wrestling-place : 'tis thither
he resorts, 'tis there he loves well to sit.

List, good Moon, where I learnt my loving.

" And when so be thou be'st sure he's alone,
give him a gentle nod o' the head and say Simaetha
would see him, and bring him hither." So bidden
she went her ways and brought him that was so
sleek and gay to my dwelling. And no sooner
was I ware of the light fall o's foot across my
threshold,—

List, good Moon, where I learnt my loving—

than I went cold as ice my body over, and the sweat
dripped like dewdrops from my brow ; aye, and for
speaking I could not so much as the whimper of a
child that calls on's mother in his sleep ; for my
fair flesh was gone all stiff and stark like a puppet's.

List, good Moon, where I learnt my loving.

When he beheld me, heartless man ! he fixed his
gaze on the ground, sat him upon the bed, and
sitting thus spake : " Why, Simaetha, when thou
bad'st me hither to this thy roof, marry, thou didst
no further outrun my own coming than I once
outran the pretty young Philinus.

List, good Moon, where I learnt my loving.

" For I had come of myself, by sweet Love I had,
of myself the very first hour of night, with comrades
twain or more, some of Dionysus' own apples in my
pocket, and about my brow the holy aspen sprig of
Heracles with gay purple ribbons wound in and out.

List, good Moon, where I learnt my loving.

"Heartless man" : to behave so and then desert me.
"Philinus" : of Cos, here spoken of as a youth ; he won at
Olympia in 264 and 260.

καί κ' εἰ μέν μ'[1]ἐδέχεσθε, τὰ δ' ἧς φίλα· καὶ γὰρ
    ἐλαφρὸς
καὶ καλὸς πάντεσσι μετ' ἠϊθέοισι καλεῦμαι,
εὐαδέ[2] τ' εἰ μῶνον τὸ καλὸν στόμα τεῦς ἐφίλησα·
εἰ δ' ἀλλᾷ μ' ὠθεῖτε καὶ ἁ θύρα εἴχετο μοχλῷ,
πάντως κα πελέκεις καὶ λαμπάδες ἦνθον ἐφ' ὑμέας.
    φράζεό μευ τὸν ἔρωθ' ὅθεν ἵκετο, πότνα Σελάνα.
νῦν δὲ χάριν μὲν ἔφαν τᾷ Κύπριδι πρᾶτον ὀφείλειν,
καὶ μετὰ τὰν Κύπριν τύ με δευτέρα ἐκ πυρὸς εἵλευ
ὦ γύναι ἐσκαλέσασα τεὸν ποτὶ τοῦτο μέλαθρον
αὔτως ἡμίφλεκτον· Ἔρως δ' ἄρα καὶ Λιπαραίω
πολλάκις Ἀφαίστοιο σέλας φλογερώτερον αἴθει
    φράζεό μευ τὸν ἔρωθ' ὅθεν ἵκετο, πότνα Σελάνα·
σὺν δὲ κακαῖς μανίαις καὶ παρθένον ἐκ θαλάμοιο
καὶ νύμφαν ἐσόβησ'[3] ἔτι δέμνια θερμὰ λιποῖσαν
ἀνέρος.' ὡς ὃ μὲν εἶπεν· ἐγὼ δέ οἱ ἁ ταχυπειθὴς
χειρὸς ἐφαψαμένα μαλακῶν ἔκλιν' ἐπὶ λέκτρων·
καὶ ταχὺ χρὼς ἐπὶ χρωτὶ πεπαίνετο, καὶ τὰ
    πρόσωπα
θερμότερ' ἧς ἢ πρόσθε, καὶ ἐψιθυρίσδομες ἁδύ.
ὡς καί[4] τοι μὴ μακρὰ φίλα θρυλέοιμι Σελάνα,
ἐπράχθη τὰ μέγιστα, καὶ ἐς πόθον ἤνθομες ἄμφω.
    κοὔτε τι τῆνος ἐμὶν ἐπεμέμψατο μέσφα τό γ'
    ἐχθές,
οὔτ' ἐγὼ αὖ τήνῳ. ἀλλ' ἦνθέ μοι ἅ τε Φιλίστας
μάτηρ τᾶς ἀμᾶς αὐλητρίδος ἅ τε Μελιξοῦς
σάμερον, ἁνίκα πέρ τε ποτ' ὠρανὸν ἔτραχον ἵπποι
Ἀῶ τὰν ῥοδόπαχυν ἀπ' Ὠκεανοῖο φέροισαι,

---

[1] So Meineke and *P. Ant*: mss καί μ' . . . . κ'   [2] εὐαδέ
L. Schmidt: mss εὖδον   [3] ἐσόβησ' Jacobs from schol. cf.
13. 48: mss ἐφόβησ'   [4] καί Wil. from Vat. 915 and Laur.
32. 16: other mss κά, *P. Ant.* κεν

"And had ye received me so, it had been joy;
for I have a name as well for beauty of shape as
speed of foot with all the bachelry o' the town,
and I had been content so I had only kissed thy
pretty lips.   But and if ye had sent me packing with
bolt and bar, then I warrant ye axes and torches had
come against you.

List, good Moon, where I learnt my loving.

"But, seeing thou hadst sent for me, I vowed my
thanks to the Cyprian first—but after the Cyprian
'tis thou, in calling me to this roof, sweet maid, didst
snatch the brand from a burning that was all but
done; for i' faith, Cupid's flare oft will outblaze the
God o' Lipara himself,—

List, good Moon, where I learnt my loving—

"And with the dire frenzy of him bride is
driven from groom ere his marriage-bed be cold,
much more a maid from the bower of her virginity."
So he ended, and I, that was so easy to win,
took him by the hand and made him to lie along
the bed.   Soon cheek upon cheek grew ripe, our
faces waxed hotter, and lo! sweet whispers went
and came.   My prating shall not keep thee too
long, good Moon: enough that all was done, enough
that both desires were sped.

And till 'twas but yesterday, he found never
a fault in me nor I in him.   But lo! to-day, when
She o' the Rose-red Arms began her swift chariot-
ing from sea to sky, comes me the mother of
Melixo and of our once flute-girl Philista, and

"I have a name": the self-complimentary details of
Delphis' speech are due to the reporter.   "God of
Lipara": the Liparaean Islands contain volcanoes.   "Our
flute-girl": the girl who used to play to him and me; the

κεῖπέ μοι ἄλλα τε πολλὰ καὶ ὡς ἄρα Δέλφις ἔραται.[1]
κεῖτε νιν αὖτε γυναικὸς ἔχει πόθος εἴτε καὶ ἀνδρός,
οὐκ ἔφατ' ἀτρεκὲς ἴδμεν, ἀτὰρ τόσον· 'αἰὲν Ἔρωτος
ἀκράτω ἐπεχεῖτο καὶ ἐς τέλος ᾤχετο φεύγων,
καὶ φάτο οἱ στεφάνοισι τὰ δώματα τῆνα πυκαξεῖν.'[2]
ταῦτά μοι ἁ ξείνα μυθήσατο, ἔστι δ' ἀλαθής.
ἦ γάρ μοι καὶ τρὶς καὶ τετράκις ἄλλοκ' ἐφοίτη,
καὶ παρ' ἐμὶν ἐτίθει τὰν Δωρίδα πολλάκις ὄλπαν·
νῦν δὲ δυωδεκαταῖος[3] ἀφ' ὧτέ νιν οὐδὲ ποτεῖδον.
ἦρ' οὐκ ἄλλο τι τερπνὸν ἔχει, ἁμῶν δὲ λέλασται;
    νῦν μὰν τοῖς φίλτροις καταθύσομαι· αἱ δ' ἔτι
        κά με[4]
λυπῇ, τὰν Ἀΐδαο πύλαν, ναὶ Μοίρας, ἀραξεῖ·
τοῖά οἱ ἐν κίστᾳ κακὰ φάρμακα φαμὶ φυλάσσειν
Ἀσσυρίω, δέσποινα, παρὰ ξείνοιο μαθοῖσα.
ἀλλὰ τὺ μὲν χαίροισα ποτ' ὠκεανὸν τρέπε πώλως,
πότνι'· ἐγὼ δ' οἰσῶ τὸν ἐμὸν πόθον ὥσπερ ὑπέσταν.[5]
χαῖρε Σελαναία λιπαρόχροε,[6] χαίρετε τὤλλοι[7]
ἀστέρες εὐκάλοιο κατ' ἄντυγα Νυκτὸς ὀπαδοί.

---

[1] P. Ant. ερᾶται   [2] πυκαξεῖν E: mss πυκάσδεν   [3] δυωδ.
Wil: mss τε (ἔτι, τι) δωδ.   [4] κά με Ahr, P. Ant. καμε: mss
κήμέ   [5] Cf. Cl. Rev. 1911, pp. 68–69   [6] P. Ant. λιπαρο-
θρονε   [7] τὤλλοι E: mss δ' (or κ') ἄλλοι, P. Ant. χαιρεθ' αλλοι

38

among divers other talk would have me believe Delphis was in love. And she knew not for sure, so she said, whether this new love were of maid or of man, only " he was ever drinking " quoth she " to the name of Love, and went off in haste at the last saying his love-garlands were for such-and-such a house." So ran my gossip's story, and sure 'tis true ; for ah! though time was, i' faith, when he would come thrice and four times a day, and often left his Dorian flask with me to fetch again, now 'tis twelve days since I so much as set eyes upon him. I am forgot, for sure ; his joy doth lie otherways.

To-night these my fire-philtres shall lay a spell upon him ; but if so be they make not an end of my trouble, then, so help me Fate, he shall be found knocking at the gate of Death ; for I tell thee, good Mistress, I have in my press medicines evil enough, that one out of Assyria told me of. So fare thee well, great Lady ; to Ocean with thy team. And I, I will bear my love as best I may. Farewell sweet Lady o' the Shining Face, and all ye starry followers in the train of drowsy Night, farewell, farewell.

same is still employed by Delphis, and it is through her mother that Simaetha learns that he loves another, a second daughter of the same woman being one of Simaetha's serving-maids. "Assyria": the land of magic herbs. For "Shining Face" there was an ancient variant 'Shining Throne.'

III.—THE SERENADE

THE *poet appears to personate a young goatherd, who after five lines dedicatory to a friend whom he calls Tityrus, serenades his mistress Amaryllis. The poem is a monologue, but, like II, preserves the dialogue-form of the mime by means of a dumb character. The appeal to Amaryllis may be regarded as consisting of three parts each ending with the offer of a gift—apples, garland, goat—and a fourth part containing a love-song of four stanzas. The reciter would doubtless make a slight pause to mark the rejection of each gift and the failure of the song before the renewal of the cry of despair*

III.—ΚΩΜΟΣ

Κωμάσδω ποτὶ τὰν Ἀμαρυλλίδα, ταὶ δέ μοι αἶγες
βόσκονται κατ᾽ ὄρος, καὶ ὁ Τίτυρος αὐτὰς ἐλαύνει.
Τίτυρ᾽ ἐμὶν τὸ καλὸν πεφιλημένε, βόσκε τὰς αἶγας,
καὶ ποτὶ τὰν κράναν ἄγε Τίτυρε, καὶ τὸν ἐνόρχαν,
τὸν Λιβυκὸν κνάκωνα, φυλάσσεο μή τυ κορύψῃ.

ὦ χαρίεσσ᾽ Ἀμαρυλλί, τί μ᾽ οὐκέτι τοῦτο κατ᾽
    ἄντρον
παρκύπτοισα καλεῖς; τὸν ἐρωτύλον ἦρά με μισεῖς;
ἦρά γέ τοι σιμὸς καταφαίνομαι ἐγγύθεν ἦμεν,
νύμφα, καὶ προγένειος; ἀπάγξασθαί με ποησεῖς.
ἠνίδε τοι δέκα μᾶλα φέρω· τηνῶθε καθεῖλον,
ὦ μ᾽ ἐκέλευ καθελεῖν τύ· καὶ αὔριον ἄλλα τοι οἰσῶ.

θᾶσαι μάν· θυμαλγὲς ἐμὶν ἄχος. αἴθε γενοίμαν
ἁ βομβεῦσα μέλισσα καὶ ἐς τεὸν ἄντρον ἱκοίμαν
τὸν κισσὸν διαδὺς καὶ τὰν πτέριν, ᾇ τὺ πυκάσδεις.
νῦν ἔγνων τὸν Ἔρωτα· βαρὺς θεός· ἦρα λεαίνας
μαζὸν ἐθήλαξε[1], δριμῷ τέ νιν ἔτραφε μάτηρ·
ὥς[2] με κατασμύχων καὶ ἐς ὄστιον ἄχρις ἰάπτει.
ὦ τὸ καλὸν ποθορεῦσα, τὸ πᾶν λίθος· ὦ κυάνοφρυ
νύμφα, πρόσπτυξαί με τὸν αἰπόλον, ὥς τυ φιλήσω.
ἔστι καὶ ἐν κενεοῖσι φιλήμασιν ἁδέα τέρψις.
τὸν στέφανον τιλαί με κατ᾽ αὐτίκα λεπτὰ ποησεῖς,
τόν τοι ἐγὼν Ἀμαρυλλὶ φίλα κίσσοιο φυλάσσω
ἀμπλέξας καλύκεσσι καὶ εὐόδμοισι σελίνοις.

---

[1] ἐθήλαξε Stobaeus : mss -αζε   [2] ὥς E cf. 25. 53 : mss ὅς

III.—THE SERENADE

I GO a-courting of Amaryllis, and my goats they go browsing on along the hill with Tityrus to drive them on. My well-beloved Tityrus, pray feed me my goats; pray lead them to watering, good Tityrus, and beware or the buckgoat, the yellow Libyan yonder, will be butting you.

Beautiful Amaryllis, why peep you no more from your cave and call me in? Hate you your sweetheart? Can it be a near view hath shown him snubnosed, Nymph, and over-bearded? I dare swear you'll be the death of me. See, here have I brought you half a score of apples plucked yonder where you bade me pluck them, and to-morrow I'll bring you as many again. . .

Look, ah! look upon me; my heart is torn with pain. I wish I were yon humming bee to thread my way through the ivy and the fern you do prink your cave withal and enter in! O now know I well what Love is. 'Tis a cruel god. I warrant you a she-lion's dugs it was he sucked and in a forest was reared, so doth he slow-burn me, aye, pierce me to the very bone. O Nymph of the pretty glance, but all stone; O Nymph of the dark dark eyebrow, come clasp thy goatherd that is so fain to be kissing thee. E'en in an empty kiss there's a sweet delight. You'll make me tear in pieces the ivy-wreath I have for you, dear Amaryllis; of rosebuds twined it is, and of fragrant parsley leaves. . .

ὤμοι ἐγών, τί πάθω, τί ὁ δύσσοος; οὐχ ὑπα-
  κούεις.
τὰν βαίταν ἀποδὺς εἰς κύματα τηνῶ ἀλεῦμαι,
ὧπερ τὼς θύννως σκοπιάζεται Ὄλπις ὁ γριπεύς·
καἴκα μὴ 'ποθάνω, τό γε μὰν τεὸν ἁδὺ τέτυκται.
ἔγνων πρᾶν, ὅκ' ἐμεῦ μεμναμένω, εἰ φιλέεις με,
οὐδὲ τὸ τηλέφιλον ποτεμάξατο τὸ πλατάγημα,
ἀλλ' αὔτως ἁπαλῶ ποτὶ πάχεος[1] ἐξεμαράνθη·
εἶπε καὶ Ἀγροιὼ τἀλαθέα κοσκινόμαντις,
ἁ πρᾶν ποιολογεῦσα παραιβάτις, ὥνεκ' ἐγὼ μὲν
τὶν ὅλος ἔγκειμαι, τὺ δέ μευ λόγον οὐδένα ποιῇ.
ἦ μάν τοι λευκὰν διδυματόκον αἶγα φυλάσσω,
τάν με καὶ ἁ Μέρμνωνος ἐριθακὶς ἁ μελανόχρως
αἰτεῖ, καὶ δωσῶ οἱ, ἐπεὶ τύ μοι ἐνδιαθρύπτῃ.

ἅλλεται ὀφθαλμός μευ ὁ δεξιός· ἦρά γ' ἰδησῶ
αὐτάν; ᾀσεῦμαι ποτὶ τὰν πίτυν ὧδ' ἀποκλινθείς·
καί κέ μ' ἴσως ποτίδοι, ἐπεὶ οὐκ ἀδαμαντίνα ἐστίν·

Ἱππομένης ὅκα δὴ τὰν παρθένον ἤθελε γᾶμαι,
μᾶλ' ἐν χερσὶν ἑλὼν δρόμον ἄνυεν· ἁ δ' Ἀταλάντα
ὡς ἴδεν, ὡς ἐμάνη, ὡς ἐς βαθὺν ἅλατ' ἔρωτα.

---

[1] ἁπαλῶ ποτὶ πάχεος, cf. 12. 24

Alas and well-a-day! what's to become of me?
Ay me! you will not answer. I'll doff my plaid and
go to Olpis' watching-place for tunnies and leap
from it into the waves; and if I die not, 'twill be
through no fault of yours. I found it out t'other
day; my thoughts were of you and whether or no
you loved me, and when I played slap to see, the
love-in-absence that should have stuck on, shrivelled
up forthwith against the soft of my arm. Agroeo
too, the sieve-witch that was out the other day
a-simpling beside the harvesters, she spoke me true
when she said you made me of none account, though
I was all wrapt up in you. Marry, a white twinner-
goat have I to give you, which that nut-brown
little handmaiden of Mermnon's is fain to get of me
—and get her she shall, seeing you choose to play
me the dainty therein. . .

Lo there! a twitch o' my right eye. Shall I be
seeing her? I'll go lean me against yon pine-tree
and sing awhile. It may be she'll look upon me
then, being she's no woman of adamant.

(*sings*) When Schoenus' bride-race was begun,
   Apples fell from one that run;
   She looks, she's lost, and lost doth leap
   Into love so dark and deep.

"Through no fault of yours": the Greek is "at any rate
as far as you are concerned it has (*i.e.* will have) been done
as you wished." "Love-in-absence: a flower. The Greek
is "stuck not on at the slapping-game." "A twitch o'
my right eye": a good omen. "Schoenus' bride-race":
Hippomenes won Atalanta the fleet-footed daughter of
Schoenus by throwing an apple in the race for her hand: the

45

τὰν ἀγέλαν χὠ μάντις ἀπ᾿ Ὄθρυος ἆγε Μελάμπους
ἐς Πύλον· ἃ δὲ Βίαντος ἐν ἀγκοίναισιν ἐκλίνθη
μάτηρ ἁ χαρίεσσα περίφρονος Ἀλφεσιβοίας.
τὰν δὲ καλὰν Κυθέρειαν ἐν ὤρεσι μῆλα νομεύων
οὐχ οὕτως Ὤδωνις ἐπὶ πλέον ἄγαγε λύσσας,
ὥστ᾿ οὐδὲ φθίμενόν νιν ἄτερ μαζοῖο τίθητι;
ζαλωτὸς μὲν ἐμὶν ὁ τὸν ἄτροπον ὕπνον ἰαύων
Ἐνδυμίων, ζαλῶ δὲ φίλα γύναι Ἰασίωνα,
ὃς τοσσῆν᾿ ἐκύρησεν, ὅσ᾿ οὐ πευσεῖσθε βέβαλοι.

ἀλγέω τὰν κεφαλάν, τὶν δ᾿ οὐ μέλει. οὐκέτ᾿
ἀείδω,
κεισεῦμαι δὲ πεσών, καὶ τοὶ λύκοι ὧδέ μ᾿ ἔδονται.
ὡς μέλι τοι γλυκὺ τοῦτο κατὰ βρόχθοιο γένοιτο.

When the seer in's brother's name
With those kine to Pylus came,
Bias to the joy-bed hies
Whence sprang Alphesibee the wise.

When Adonis o'er the sheep
In the hills his watch did keep,
The Love-Dame proved so wild a wooer,
E'en in death she clips him to her.

O would I were Endymion
That sleeps the unchanging slumber on,
Or, Lady, knew thy Jasion's glee
Which prófane eyes may never see! . . .

My head aches sore, but 'tis nought to you. I'll
make an end, and throw me down, aye, and stir not
if the wolves devour me—the which I pray be as
sweet honey in the throat to you.

seer Melampus by bringing to the king of Pylus the oxen of
Iphiclus won the king's daughter Pero for his brother Bias:
although he was slain long ago, Aphrodite Cytherea loves
her Adonis so dearly that she still clasps him—at the Adonis
festival—to her breast: Endymion was loved by the Moon,
and Jasion—as in the Eleusinian mysteries—by Demeter.

IV.—THE HERDSMEN

A CONVERSATION *between a goatherd named Battus and his fellow goatherd Corydon, who is acting oxherd in place of a certain Aegon who has been persuaded by one Milon son of Lampriadas to go and compete in a boxing-match at Olympia. Corydon's temporary rise in rank gives occasion for some friendly banter—which the sententious fellow does not always understand—varied with bitter references to Milon's having supplanted Battus in the favours of Amaryllis. The reference to Glaucè fixes the imaginary date as contemporary with Theocritus. This is not the great Milon, but a fictitious strong man of the same town called, suitably enough, by his name.[1] The poem, like all the other genuine shepherd-mimes, contains a song. Zacynthus is still called the flower of the Levant. The scene is near Crotona in Southern Italy.*

---

[1] The identification of Milon with the great athlete is incorrect. The great Milon flourished B.C. 510; the scholiast knows of no such feats in connexion with him ; and the feats ascribed to him by authors ap. Athen. 10. 412 e, f, are by no means identical with these.

IV.—NOMEIΣ

ΒΑΤΤΟΣ
Εἰπέ μοι ὦ Κορύδων, τίνος αἱ βόες; ἦρα Φιλώνδα;

ΚΟΡΥΔΩΝ
οὔκ, ἀλλ' Αἴγωνος· βόσκειν δέ μοι αὐτὰς ἔδωκεν.

ΒΑΤΤΟΣ
ἦ πά ψε κρύβδαν τὰ ποθέσπερα πάσας ἀμέλγεις;

ΚΟΡΥΔΩΝ
ἀλλ' ὁ γέρων ὑφίητι τὰ μοσχία κἠμὲ φυλάσσει.

ΒΑΤΤΟΣ
αὐτὸς δ' ἐς τίν' ἄφαντος ὁ βουκόλος ᾤχετο χώραν;

ΚΟΡΥΔΩΝ
οὐκ ἄκουσας; ἄγων νιν ἐπ' Ἀλφεὸν ᾤχετο Μίλων.

ΒΑΤΤΟΣ
καὶ πόκα τῆνος ἔλαιον ἐπ' ὀφθαλμοῖσιν ὀπώπει;

ΚΟΡΥΔΩΝ
φαντί νιν Ἡρακλῆι βίην καὶ κάρτος ἐρίσδειν.

ΒΑΤΤΟΣ
κἤμ' ἔφαθ' ἁ μάτηρ Πολυδεύκεος ἦμεν ἀμείνω.

IV.—THE HERDSMEN

BATTUS (*in a bantering tone*)
What, Corydon man ; whose may your cows be ?
Philondas's ?

CORYDON
Nay, Aegon's ; he hath given me the feeding of
them in his stead.

BATTUS
And I suppose, come evening, you give them all
a milking hugger-mugger ?

CORYDON
Not so ; the old master sees me to that ; he puts
the calves to suck, himself.

BATTUS
But whither so far was their own proper herds-
man gone ?

CORYDON
Did you never hear ? Milon carried him off with
him to the Alpheus.

BATTUS
Lord ! When had the likes of him ever so much
as set eyes upon a flask of oil ?

CORYDON (*sententiously*)
Men say he rivals Heracles in might.

BATTUS (*scoffing*)
And mammy says I'm another Polydeuces.

"Hugger-mugger": on the sly.   "Oil": used by athletes
upon their bodies.

THE BUCOLIC POETS

ΚΟΡΥΔΩΝ
κὦχετ᾽ ἔχων σκαπαναν τε καὶ εἴκατι τουτόθε μῆλα.

ΒΑΤΤΟΣ
πείσαι κα[1] Μίλων καὶ τὼς λύκος αὐτίκα λυσσῆν.

ΚΟΡΥΔΩΝ
ταὶ δαμάλαι δ᾽ αὐτὸν μυκώμεναι αἵδε ποθεῦντι.

ΒΑΤΤΟΣ
δειλαίαί γ᾽ αὗται, τὸν βουκόλον ὡς κακὸν εὗρον.

ΚΟΡΥΔΩΝ
ἦ μὰν δειλαῖαι γε, καὶ οὐκέτι λῶντι νέμεσθαι.

ΒΑΤΤΟΣ
τήνας μὲν δή τοι τᾶς πόρτιος αὐτὰ λέλειπται
τὦστία.   μὴ πρῶκας σιτίζεται ὥσπερ ὁ τέττιξ;

ΚΟΡΥΔΩΝ
οὐ Δᾶν, ἀλλ᾽ ὁκὰ μέν νιν ἐπ᾽ Αἰσάροιο νομεύω
καὶ μαλακῶ χόρτοιο καλὰν κώμυθα δίδωμι,
ἄλλοκα δὲ σκαίρει τὸ βαθύσκιον ἀμφὶ Λάτυμνον.

ΒΑΤΤΟΣ
λεπτὸς μὰν χὦ ταῦρος ὁ πυρρίχος. αἴθε
  λάχοιεν

---

[1] κα Ahrens : mss κε, τοι, τ

52

CORYDON

Well, he took a score of sheep and a spade with him, when he went.

BATTUS (*with a momentary bitterness*)

Ah, that Milon! he'ld persuade a wolf to run mad for the asking.

CORYDON

And his heifers miss him sore; hark to their lowing.

BATTUS (*resuming his banter*)

Aye; 'twas an ill day for the kine; how sorry a herdsman it brought them!

CORYDON (*misunderstanding*)

Marry, an ill day it was, and they are off their feed now.

BATTUS

Look you now, yonder beast, she's nought but skin and bone. Pray, doth she feed on dewdrops like the cricket?

CORYDON

Zeus! no. Why, sometimes I graze her along the Aesarus and give her a brave bottle of the tenderest green grass, and oftentimes her playground's in the deep shade of Latymnus.

BATTUS

Aye, and the red-poll bull, he's lean as can be. (*bitterly again*) I only would to God, when there's a

---

"A score of sheep": athletes when training fed largely upon meat, and kept themselves in condition by shovelling sand. "Persuade a wolf": i.e. "he beguiled Aegon to compete at Olympia though he is but a poor hand at boxing (cf. l. 7) just as he beguiled Amaryllis away from me though she never really loved him."

τοὶ τῶ Λαμπριάδα, τοὶ δαμόται ὅκκα θύωντι
τᾷ Ἥρᾳ, τοιόνδε· κακοχράσμων γὰρ ὁ δᾶμος.

ΚΟΡΥΔΩΝ

καὶ μὰν ἐς στομάλιμνον ἐλαύνεται ἔς τε τὰ
  Φύσκων[1],
καὶ ποτὶ τὸν Νήαιθον, ὅπα καλὰ πάντα φύοντι.
αἰγίπυρος καὶ κνύζα καὶ εὐώδης μελίτεια.

ΒΑΤΤΟΣ

φεῦ φεῦ βασεῦνται καὶ ταὶ βόες ὦ τάλαν Αἴγων
εἰς Ἀίδαν, ὅκα καὶ τὺ κακᾶς ἠράσσαο νίκας,
χἁ σύριγξ εὐρῶτι παλύνεται, ἅν ποκ' ἐπάξα.

ΚΟΡΥΔΩΝ

οὐ τήνα γ', οὐ Νύμφας, ἐπεὶ ποτὶ Πῖσαν ἀφέρπων
δῶρον ἐμίν νιν ἔλειπεν· ἐγὼ δέ τις εἰμὶ μελικτάς,   3[0]
κεὖ μὲν τὰ Γλαύκας ἀγκρούομαι, εὖ δὲ τὰ Πύρρω·

  Αἰνέω τάν τε Κρότωνα καλὰν πόλιν ἅτε Ζά-
    κυνθον[2]
καὶ τὸ ποταῷον τὸ Λακίνιον, ἆπερ ὁ πύκτας
Μίλων[3] ὀγδώκοντα μόνος κατεδαίσατο μάζας.
τηνεῖ καὶ τὸν ταῦρον ἀπ' ὤρεος ἆγε πιάξας
τᾶς ὁπλᾶς κῆδωκ' Ἀμαρυλλίδι, ταὶ δὲ γυναῖκες
μακρὸν ἀνάυσαν, χὠ βουκόλος ἐξεγέλασσεν.

---

[1] Φύσκων so Palat. 330, cf. *Philologus*, 1908, p. 466 : other
mss Φύσκω   [2] καλὰν πόλιν ἅτε Ζάκυνθον E, cf. a Laconian
inscription *I. A.* 79 ταυτᾶ ἅτε = οὕτως ὡς, and a modern folk-
saying, ἡ Ζάκυνθος, ἡ Ζάκυνθος, τὸ ἄνθος τῆς Ἀνατολῆς : mss
καλὰ πόλις ἅτε (or ἅ τε) Ζάκυνθος   [3] Μίλων Naber, cf. l. 7 :
mss and schol. Αἴγων

sacrifice to Hera in their ward, the sons of
Lampriadas might get such another as he : they are a
foul mixen sort, they o' that ward.

CORYDON

All the same that bull's driven to the sea-lake and
the Physcian border, and to that garden of good
things, goat-flower, mullet, sweet odorous balsam,
to wit Neaethus.

BATTUS (*sympathising as with another of Milon's victims*)

Heigho, poor Aegon ! thy very kine must needs
meet their death because thou art gone a-whoring
after vainglory, and the herdsman's pipe thou once
didst make thyself is all one mildew.

CORYDON

Nay, by the Nymphs, not it. He bequeathed it to
me when he set out for Pisa. I too am something of
a musician. Mark you, I'm a dabster at Glaucè's
snatches and those ditties Pyrrhus makes : (*sings*)

O Croton is a bonny town as Zacynth by the sea,
And a bonny sight on her eastward height is the
    fane of Laciny,
Where boxer Milon one fine morn made fourscore
    loaves his meal,
        And down the hill another day,
        While lasses holla'd by the way,
        To Amaryllis, laughing gay
        Led the bull by the heel.

"Might get such another ": the greater part of a sacrificed
animal was eaten by the sacrificers. "Mullet ": usually
called ' fleabane.'

THE BUCOLIC POETS

ὦ χαρίεσσ' 'Αμαρυλλί, μόνας σέθεν οὐδὲ θανοίσας
λασεύμεσθ'· ὅσον αἶγες ἐμὶν φίλαι, ὅσσον ἀπέσβης.
αἰαῖ τῶ σκληρῶ μάλα δαίμονος, ὅς με λελόγχει.   4

θαρσεῖν χρὴ φίλε Βάττε· τάχ' αὔριον ἔσσετ'
        ἄμεινον.
ἐλπίδες ἐν ζωοῖσιν, ἀνέλπιστοι δὲ θανόντες.
χὠ Ζεὺς ἄλλοκα μὲν πέλει αἴθριος, ἄλλοκα δ' ὕει.

θαρσέω. βάλλε κάτωθε, τὰ μοσχία·[1] τᾶς γὰρ
        ἐλαίας
τὸν θαλλὸν τρώγοντι τὰ δύσσοα.

                        σίτθ' ὁ Λέπαργος,
σιτθ' ἁ Κυμαίθα ποτὶ τὸν λόφον. οὐκ ἐσακούεις;
ἡξῶ ναὶ τὸν Πᾶνα κακὸν τέλος αὐτίκα δωσῶν,
εἰ μὴ ἄπει τουτῶθεν. ἴδ' αὖ πάλιν ἅδε ποθέρπει.
εἴθ' ἦς μοι ῥοικόν τι[2] λαγωβόλον, ὥς τυ πάταξα.

θᾶσαί μ' ὦ Κορύδων ποττῶ Διός· ἁ γὰρ ἄκανθα   50
ἁρμοῖ μ' ὧδ' ἐπάταξ' ὑπὸ τὸ σφυρόν. ὡς δὲ
        βαθεῖαι
τἀτρακτυλλίδες ἐντί. κακῶς ἁ πόρτις ὄλοιτο·
εἰς ταύταν ἐτύπην χασμεύμενος. ἦρά γε λεύσσεις;

ναὶ ναί, τοῖς ὀνύχεσσιν ἔχω τέ νιν· ἄδε καὶ αὐτά.

---

[1] βάλλε κάτωθε, τὰ μ. E, cf. βάλλ' ἐς κόρακας : others βάλλε
κάτωθε τὰ μ.   [2] ῥοικόν τι Hermann : mss ῥ. τὸ or τυ

BATTUS (*not proof against the tactless reference;*
apostrophising)

O beautiful Amaryllis, though you be dead, I am
true, and I'll never forget you. My pretty goats are
dear to me, but dear no less a maiden that is no
more. O well-a-day that my luck turned so ill!

CORYDON

Soft you, good Battus; be comforted. Good luck
comes with another morn; while there's life there's
hope; rain one day, shine the next.

BATTUS

Let be. 'tis well. (*changing the subject*) Up with
you, ye calves; up the hill! They are at the green
of those olives, the varlets.

CORYDON

Hey up, Snowdrop! hey up, Goodbody! to the
hill wi' ye! Art thou deaf? 'Fore Pan I'll
presently come thee an evil end if thou stay there.
Look ye there; back she comes again. Would
there were but a hurl-bat in my hand! I had had
at thee.

BATTUS

Zeus save thee, Corydon; see here! It had at
me as thou saidst the word, this thorn, here under
my ankle. And how deep the distaff-thistles go!
A plague o' thy heifer! It all came o' my gaping
after her. (*Corydon comes to help him*) Dost see
him, lad?

CORYDON

Aye, aye, and have got him 'twixt my nails; and
lo! here he is.

ΒΑΤΤΟΣ

ὁσσίχον ἐστὶ τὸ τύμμα καὶ ἁλίκον ἄνδρα δαμάζει.

ΚΟΡΥΔΩΝ

εἰς ὄρος ὄκχ᾽ ἕρπῃς, μὴ νήλιπος ἔρχεο Βάττε·
ἐν γὰρ ὄρει ῥάμνοι τε καὶ ἀσπάλαθοι κομέονται.

ΒΑΤΤΟΣ

εἴπ᾽ ἄγε μ᾽ ὦ Κορύδων, τὸ γερόντιον ἦρ᾽ ἔτι μύλλει
τήναν τὰν κυάνοφρυν ἐρωτίδα, τᾶς ποκ᾽ ἐκνίσθη;

ΚΟΡΥΔΩΝ

ἀκμάν γ᾽ ὦ δειλαῖε· πρόαν γέ μεν αὐτὸς ἐπενθὼν
καὶ ποτὶ τᾷ μάνδρᾳ κατελάμβανον ἇμος ἐνήργει.

ΒΑΤΤΟΣ

εὖ γ᾽ ὤνθρωπε φιλοῖφα· τό τοι γένος ἢ Σατυρίσκοις
ἐγγύθεν ἢ Πάνεσσι κακοκνάμοισιν ἐρίσδεις.

BATTUS (*in mock-heroic strain*)
O what a little tiny wound to overmaster so mighty a man!

CORYDON (*pointing the moral*)
Thou should'st put on thy shoes when thou goest into the hills, Battus; 'tis rare ground for thorns and gorse, the hills.

BATTUS
Pray tell me, Corydon, comes gaffer yet the gallant with that dark-browed piece o' love he was smitten of?

CORYDON
Aye, that does he, ill's his luck. I happened of them but two days agone, and near by the byre, too, and faith, gallant was the word.

BATTUS (*apostrophising*)
Well done, goodman Light-o'-love. 'Tis plain thou comest not far below the old Satyrs and ill-shanked Pans o' the country-side for lineage.

"Old Satyrs": effigies of Pan and the Satyrs were a feature of the country-side.

V.—THE GOATHERD AND THE SHEPHERD

THE *scene of this shepherd-mime is laid in the wooded pastures near the mouth of the river Crathis in the district of Sybaris and Thurii in Southern Italy. The foreground is the shore of a lagoon near which stand effigies of the Nymphs who preside over it, and there is close by a rustic statue of Pan of the seaside. The characters are a goatherd named Comatas and a young shepherd named Lacon who are watching their flocks. Having seated themselves some little distance apart, they proceed to converse in no very friendly spirit, and the talk gradually leads to a contest of song with a woodcutter named Morson for the judge and a lamb and a goat for the stakes. The contest is a spirited, not to say a bitter, one, and consists of a series of alternate couplets, the elder man first singing his couplet and the younger then trying to better him at the same theme. The themes Comatas chooses are various, but the dominant note, as often in Theocritus, is love. In some of the lines there is more meaning than appears on the surface. After fourteen pairs of couplets, Morson breaks in before Lacon has replied and awards his lamb to Comatas.*[1]

[1] See Gow, *Classical Quarterly* 1935. 65.

V.—ΑΙΠΟΛΙΚΟΝ ΚΑΙ ΠΟΙΜΕΝΙΚΟΝ

ΚΟΜΑΤΑΣ

Αἶγες ἐμαί, τῆνον τὸν ποιμένα τὸν Συβαρίταν
φεύγετε τὸν Λάκωνα· τό μευ νάκος ἐχθὲς ἔκλεψεν.

ΛΑΚΩΝ

οὐκ ἀπὸ τᾶς κράνας σίττ' ἀμνίδες; οὐκ ἐσορῆτε
τόν μευ τὰν σύριγγα πρόαν κλέψαντα Κομάταν;

ΚΟΜΑΤΑΣ

τὰν ποίαν σύριγγα; τὺ γάρ ποκα δῶλε Σιβύρτα
ἐκτάσα σύριγγα; τί δ' οὐκέτι σὺν Κορύδωνι
ἀρκεῖ τοι καλάμας αὐλὸν ποππύσδεν ἔχοντι;

ΛΑΚΩΝ

τάν μοι ἔδωκε Λύκων ὠλεύθερε. τὶν δὲ τὸ ποῖον
Λάκων ἀγκλέψας πόκ' ἔβαν νάκος; εἰπὲ Κομάτα.
οὐδὲ γὰρ Εὐμάρᾳ τῷ δεσπότᾳ ἦς τι ἐνεύδειν.

ΚΟΜΑΤΑΣ

τὸ Κροκύλος μοι ἔδωκε, τὸ ποικίλον, ἁνίκ' ἔθυσε
ταῖς Νύμφαις τὰν αἶγα· τὺ δ' ὦ κακὲ καὶ τόκ'
    ἐτάκευ
βασκαίνων, καὶ νῦν με τὰ λοίσθια γυμνὸν ἔθηκας.

62

V.—THE GOATHERD AND THE SHEPHERD

COMATAS

Beware, good my goats, of yonder shepherd from Sybaris, beware of Lacon; he stole my skin-coat yesterday.

LACON

Hey up! my pretty lambkins; away from the spring. See you not Comatas that stole my pipe two days agone?

COMATAS

Pipe? Sibyrtas' bondman possessed of a pipe? he that was content to sit with Corydon and toot upon a parcel o' straws?

LACON

Yes, master freeman, the pipe Lycon gave me. And as for your skin-coat, what skin-coat and when has ever Lacon carried off o' yours? Tell me that, Comatas; why, your lord Eumaras, let alone his bondman, never had one even to sleep in.

COMATAS

'Tis that Crocylus gave me, the dapple skin, after that he sacrificed that she-goat to the Nymphs. And as your foul envious eyes watered for it then, so your foul envious hands have bid me go henceforth naked now.

THE BUCOLIC POETS

ΛΑΚΩΝ

οὐ μαύτὸν τὸν Πᾶνα τὸν ἄκτιον, οὐ τέ γε Λάκων
τὰν βαίταν ἀπέδυσ' ὁ Καλαίθιδος,[1] ἢ κατὰ τήνας
τᾶς πέτρας ὤνθρωπε μανεὶς εἰς Κράθιν ἀλοίμαν.

ΚΟΜΑΤΑΣ

οὐ μὰν οὐ ταύτας τὰς λιμνάδας ὠγαθὲ Νύμφας,
αἴτε μοι ἵλαοί τε καὶ εὐμενέες τελέθοιεν,
οὔ τευ τὰν σύριγγα λαθὼν ἔκλεψα Κομάτας.

ΛΑΚΩΝ

αἲ τοι πιστεύσαιμι, τὰ Δάφνιδος ἄλγε' ἀροίμαν.
ἀλλ' ὢν αἴκα λῇς ἔριφον θέμεν, ἔστι μὲν οὐδὲν
ἱερόν, ἀλλ' ἄγε τοι διαείσομαι, ἔστε κ' ἀπείπῃς.

ΚΟΜΑΤΑΣ

ὗς ποτ' Ἀθαναίαν ἔριν ἤρισεν. ἠνίδε κεῖται
ὦριφος· ἀλλ' ἄγε καὶ τὺ τὸν εὔβοτον ἀμνὸν ἔρισδε.[2]

ΛΑΚΩΝ

καὶ πῶς ὦ κιναδεῦ τάδ' ἐρίσσεται[3] ἐξ ἴσω ἄμμιν;
τίς τρίχας ἀντ' ἐρίων ἐποκίξατο; τίς δὲ παρεύσας
αἰγὸς πρατοτόκοιο κακὰν κύνα δήλετ' ἀμέλγειν;

ΚΟΜΑΤΑΣ

ὅστις νικασεῖν τὸν πλατίον ὡς τὺ πεποίθει,[4]
σφὰξ βομβέων τέττιγος ἐναντίον. ἀλλὰ γὰρ
    οὔ τι
ὦριφος ἰσοπαλής τοι,[5] ἴδ' ὁ τράγος οὗτος· ἔρισδε.

---

[1] Κυλαίθιδος Bechtel from Herodas 6. 50   [2] ἔρισδε with
accus. of stake: mss also ἔρειδε   [3] τάδ' ἐρίσσεται (passive)
E: mss τάδ' (τάγ', τάδε γ') ἔσσεται   [4] πεποίθει Heinsius:
mss πεποίθεις   [5] τοι Ahrens: mss τυ

64

LACON

Nay, nay, by Pan o' the Shore; Lacon son of Calaethis never filched coat of thine, fellow, may I run raving mad else and leap into the Crathis from yonder rock.

COMATAS

No, no, by these Nymphs o' the lake, man; so surely as I wish 'em kind and propitious, Comatas never laid sneaking hand on pipe o' thine.

LACON

Heaven send me the affliction of Daphnis if e'er I believe that tale. But enough of this; if thou'lt wage me a kid—'tis not worth the candle, but nevertheless come on; I'll have a contention o' song with thee till thou cry hold.

COMATAS

'Tis the old story—teach thy grandam. There; my wage is laid. And thou, for thine, lay me thy fine fat lamb against it.

LACON

Thou fox! prithee how shall such laying fadge? As well might one shear himself hair when a' might have wool, as well choose to milk a foul bitch before a young milch-goat.

COMATAS

He that's as sure as thou that he'll vanquish his neighbour is like the wasp buzzing against the cricket's song. But 'tis all one; my kid it seems is no fair stake. So look, I lay thee this full-grown he-goat; and now begin.

" Teach thy grandam" : the Greek is "the sow contended against Athena."   "Fadge" : be suitable.

ΛΑΚΩΝ

μὴ σπεῦδ᾽· οὐ γάρ τοι πυρὶ θάλπεαι. ἅδιον ᾀσῇ
τεῖδ᾽ ὑπὸ τὰν κότινον καὶ τἄλσεα ταῦτα καθίξας.
ψυχρὸν ὕδωρ τηνεῖ καταλείβεται· ὧδε πεφύκει
ποία χὰ στιβὰς ἅδε, καὶ ἀκρίδες ὧδε λαλεῦντι.

ΚΟΜΑΤΑΣ

ἀλλ᾽ οὔ τι σπεύδω· μέγα δ᾽ ἄχθομαι, εἰ τύ με τολμῇς
ὄμμασι τοῖσδ᾽[1] ὀρθοῖσι ποτιβλέπεν, ὅν ποκ᾽ ἐόντα
παῖδ᾽ ἔτ᾽ ἐγὼν ἐδίδασκον. ἴδ᾽ ἁ χάρις εἰς τί
   ποθέρπει.
θρέψαι τοι λυκιδεῖς, θρέψαι κυνάς, ὥς τυ φάγωντι.

ΛΑΚΩΝ

καὶ πόκ᾽ ἐγὼν παρὰ τεῦς τι μαθὼν καλὸν ἢ καὶ
   ἀκούσας
μέμναμ᾽; ὦ φθονερὸν τὺ καὶ ἀπρεπὲς ἀνδρίον
   αὔτως.

ΚΟΜΑΤΑΣ

ἁνίκ᾽ ἐπύγιζόν τυ, τὺ δ᾽ ἄλγεες· αἱ δὲ χίμαιραι
αἵδε κατεβληχῶντο, καὶ ὁ τράγος αὐτὰς ἐτρύπη.

ΛΑΚΩΝ

μὴ βάθιον τήνω πυγίσματος ὕβε ταφείης.
ἀλλὰ γὰρ ἔρφ᾽, ὧδ᾽ ἕρπε, καὶ ὕστατα βουκο-
   λιαξῇ.

ΚΟΜΑΤΑΣ

οὐχ ἑρψῶ τηνεῖ· τουτεῖ δρύες, ὧδε κύπειρος,
ὧδε καλὸν βομβεῦντι ποτὶ σμάνεσσι μέλισσαι·
ἔνθ᾽ ὕδατος ψυχρῶ κρᾶναι δύο· ταὶ δ᾽ ἐπὶ δένδρει
ὄρνιχες λαλαγεῦντι· καὶ ἁ σκιὰ οὐδὲν ὁμοία
τᾷ παρὰ τίν· βάλλει δὲ καὶ ἁ πίτυς ὑψόθε κώνοις.

------

[1] ὄμμασι τοῖσδ᾽ Hermann : mss ἴ. τοῖς

LACON

Soft, soft; no fire's burning thee. You'll sing better sitting under the wild olive and this coppice. There's cool water falling yonder, and here's grass and a greenbed, and the locusts at their prattling.

COMATAS

I'm in no haste, not I, but in sorrow rather that you dare look me in the face, I that had the teaching of you when you were but a child. Lord! look where kindness goes. Nurse a wolf-cub,—nay rather nurse a puppy-dog—to be eaten for't.

LACON

And when, pray, do I mind me to have learnt or heard aught of good from thee? Fie upon thee for a mere envious and churlish piece of a man!

COMATAS

When I was poking you and you were sore; and these she-kids were bleating and the billy-goat bored into them.

LACON

I hope you won't be buried, hunchback, deeper than that polang!

But a truce, man; hither, come thou hither, and thou shalt sing thy country-song for the last time.

COMATAS

Thither will I never come. Here I have oaks and cyperus, and bees humming bravely at the hives, here's two springs of cool water to thy one, and birds, not locusts, a-babbling upon the tree, and, for shade, thine's not half so good; and what's more the pine overhead is casting her nuts.

ΛΑΚΩΝ

ἦ μὰν ἀρνακίδας τε καὶ εἴρια τεῖδε πατησεῖς,
αἴκ' ἔνθῃς, ὕπνω μαλακώτερα· ταὶ δὲ τραγεῖαι
ταὶ παρὰ τὶν ὄσδοντι κακώτερον ἢ τύ περ ὄσδεις.
στασῶ δὲ κρατῆρα μεγαν λευκοῖο γάλακτος
ταῖς Νύμφαις, στασῶ δὲ καὶ ἁδέος ἄλλον ἐλαίω.

ΚΟΜΑΤΑΣ

αἰ δέ κε καὶ τὺ μόλῃς, ἀπαλὰν πτέριν ὧδε πατησεῖς
καὶ γλάχων' ἀνθεῦσαν· ὑπεσσεῖται δὲ χιμαιρᾶν
δέρματα τᾶν παρὰ τὶν μαλακώτερα τετράκις
     ἀρνῶν.
στασῶ δ' ὀκτὼ μὲν γαυλὼς τῷ Πανὶ γάλακτος,
ὀκτὼ δὲ σκαφίδας μέλιτος πλέα κηρί' ἐχοίσας.

ΛΑΚΩΝ

αὐτόθε μοι ποτέρισδε καὶ αὐτόθε βουκολιάσδευ·
τὰν σαυτῶ πατέων ἔχε τὰς δρύας. ἀλλὰ τίς ἄμμε,
τίς κρινεῖ; αἴθ' ἔνθοι ποχ' ὁ βουκόλος ὧδ' ὁ
     Λυκώπας.

ΚΟΜΑΤΑΣ

οὐδὲν ἐγὼ τηνω ποτιδεύομαι· ἀλλὰ τὸν ἄνδρα,
αἰ λῇς, τὸν δρυτόμον βωστρήσομες, ὃς τὰς ἐρείκας
τήνας τὰς παρὰ τὶν ξυλοχίζεται· ἔστι δὲ Μόρσων.

ΛΑΚΩΝ

βωστρεωμες.

ΚΟΜΑΤΑΣ

     τὺ κάλει νιν.

ΛΑΚΩΝ

          ἰὼ ξένε μικκὸν ἄκουσον
τεῖδ' ἐνθών· ἄμμες γὰρ ἐρίσδομες, ὅστις ἀρείων,
βουκολιαστάς ἐστι. τὺ δ' ὠγαθὲ μήτ' ἐμὲ Μόρσων
ἐν χάριτι κρίνῃς, μήτ' ὦν τύγα τοῦτον ὀνάσῃς.

LACON

An you'll come here, I'll lay you shall tread
lambskins and sheep's wool as soft as sleep. Those
buckgoat-pelts of thine smell e'en ranker than thou.
And I'll set up a great bowl of whitest milk to
the Nymphs, and eke I'll set up another of
sweetest oil.

COMATAS

If come you do, you shall tread here taper fern
and organy all a-blowing, and for your lying down
there's she-goat-skins four times as soft as those
lambskins of thine. And I'll set up to Pan eight
pails of milk and eke eight pots of full honey-
combs.

LACON

Go to; be where you will for me for the match o'
country-song. Go your own gate; you're welcome
to your oaks. But who's to be our judge, say who?
Would God neatherd Lycopas might come this way
along.

COMATAS

I suffer no want of him. We'll holla rather, an't
please ye, on yon woodcutter that is after fuel in
the heather near where you be. Morson it is.

LACON

We will.

COMATAS

Call him, you.

LACON

Ho, friend! hither and lend us your ears awhile.
We two have a match toward, to see who's the
better man at a country-song. (MORSON *approaches*)
Be you fair, good Morson; neither judge me out of
favour nor yet be too kind to him.

69

ΚΟΜΑΤΑΣ

ναὶ ποτὶ τᾶν Νυμφᾶν Μόρσων φίλε μήτε Κομάτᾳ
τὸ πλέον εὐθύνῃς, μήτ᾽ ὢν τύγα τῷδε χαρίξῃ.
ἅδε τοι ἁ ποίμνα τῶ Θουρίω ἐστὶ Σιβύρτα.

ΛΑΚΩΝ

μή τύ τις ἠρώτη ποττῶ Διός, αἴτε Σιβύρτα
αἴτ᾽ ἐμόν ἐστι κάκιστε τὸ ποίμνιον; ὡς λάλος ἐσσί.

ΚΟΜΑΤΑΣ

βέντισθ᾽ οὗτος, ἐγὼ μὲν ἀλαθέα πάντ᾽ ἀγορεύω
κοὐδὲν καυχῶμαι· τὺ δ᾽ ἄγαν φιλοκέρτομος ἐσσί.

ΛΑΚΩΝ

εἶα λέγ᾽, εἴ τι λέγεις, καὶ τὸν ξένον ἐς πόλιν
αὖθις
ζῶντ᾽ ἄφες· ὦ Παιάν, ἦ στωμύλος ἦσθα Κομᾶτα.

ΚΟΜΑΤΑΣ

Ταὶ Μοῖσαί με φιλεῦντι πολὺ πλέον ἦ τὸν ἀοιδὸν
Δάφνιν· ἐγὼ δ᾽ αὐταῖς χιμάρως δύο πρᾶν ποκ᾽
ἔθυσα.

ΛΑΚΩΝ

καὶ γὰρ ἔμ᾽ Ὡπόλλων φιλέει μέγα, καὶ καλὸν
αὐτῷ
κριὸν ἐγὼ βόσκω. τὰ δὲ Κάρνεα καὶ δὴ ἐφέρπει.

---

73 Εὐμάρα δὲ τὰς αἴγας ὁρῇς φίλε τῶ Συβαρίτα. Wil
rightly omits.

COMATAS

'Fore the Nymphs, sweet Morson, pray you neither rule unto Comatas more than his due nor yet give your favour to Lacon.   This flock o' sheep, look you, is Sibyrtas' of Thurii.

LACON

Zeus! and who asked thee, foul knave, whether the flock was mine or Sibyrtas'?   Lord, what a babbler is here !

COMATAS

Most excellent blockhead, all I say, I, is true, though for my part, I'm no braggart ; but Lord ! what a railer is here !

LACON

Come, come ; say thy say and be done, and let's suffer friend Morson to come off with his life. Apollo save us, Comatas ! thou hast the gift o' the gab.

(*The Singing Match*)

COMATAS

The Muses bear me greater love than Daphnis ere
    did see ;
And well they may, for t'other day they had two
    goats of me.

LACON

But Apollo loves me all as well, and an offering too
    have I,
A fine fat ram a-batt'ning ; for Apollo's feast draws
    nigh.

" Foul knave " : Comatas' apparently innocent remark implies the taunt of slavery ; cf. ll. 5 and 8.   " Daphnis " : the Greek has " the poet Daphnis."

ΚΟΜΑΤΑΣ

πλὰν δύο τὰς λοιπὰς διδυματόκος αἶγας ἀμέλγω,
καί μ᾽ ἁ παῖς ποθορεῦσα ʽτάλανʼ λέγει ʽαὐτὸς
  ἀμέλγεις;ʼ

ΛΑΚΩΝ

φεῦ φεῦ· Λάκων τοι ταλάρως σχεδὸν εἴκατι πληροῖ
τυρῶ καὶ τὸν ἄναβον ἐν ἄνθεσι παῖδα μολύνει.

ΚΟΜΑΤΑΣ

βάλλει καὶ μάλοισι τὸν αἰπόλον ἁ Κλεαρίστα
τὰς αἶγας παρελᾶντα καὶ ἁδύ τι ποππυλιάσδει.

ΛΑΚΩΝ

κἠμὲ γὰρ ὁ Κρατίδας τὸν ποιμένα λεῖος ὑπαντῶν 9
ἐκμαίνει·[1] λιπαρὰ δὲ παρ᾽ αὐχένα σείετ᾽ ἔθειρα.

ΚΟΜΑΤΑΣ

ἀλλ᾽ οὐ σύμβλητ᾽ ἐστὶ κυνόσβατος οὐδ᾽ ἀνεμώνα
πρὸς ῥόδα, τῶν ἄνδηρα παρ᾽ αἱμασιαῖσι πεφύκει.

ΛΑΚΩΝ

οὐδὲ γὰρ οὐδ᾽ ἀκύλοις ὀρομαλίδες· αἱ μὲν ἔχοντι
λεπτὸν[2] ἀπὸ πρίνοιο λεπύριον, αἱ δὲ μελιχραί.

---

[1] *lit.* Cratidas maddens *me* when it is in gentle temper that
he runs to meet me (Gow) [2] λεπτόν: of taste

COMATAS

Nigh all my goats have twins at teat; there's only
two with one;
And the damsel sees and the damsel says 'Poor lad,
dost milk alone?'

LACON

O tale of woe! here's Lacon, though, fills cheese-
racks well-nigh twenty
And fouls his dear not a youth but a boy mid flowers
that blow so plenty.

COMATAS

But when her goatherd boy goes by you should see
my Cleärist
Fling apples, and her pretty lips call pouting to be
kissed.

LACON

But madness 'tis for the shepherd to meet the
shepherd's love,
So brown and bright are the tresses light that toss
that shoulder above.

COMATAS

Ah! but there's no comparing windflower with rose
at all,
Nor wild dog-róse with her that blows beside the
trim orchard's wall.

LACON

There's no better likeness, neither, 'twixt fruit of
pear and holm;
The acorn savours flat and stale, the pear's like
honeycomb.

" Pear ": in the Greek, a sweet kind of wild apple.

THE BUCOLIC POETS

ΚΟΜΑΤΑΣ

κἠγὼ μὲν δωσῶ τᾷ παρθένῳ αὐτίκα φάσσαν
ἐκ τᾶς ἀρκεύθω καθελών· τηνεῖ γὰρ ἐφίσδει.

ΛΑΚΩΝ

ἀλλ᾽ ἐγὼ ἐς χλαῖναν μαλακὸν πόκον, ὁππόκα πέξω
τὰν οἶν τὰν πέλλαν, Κρατίδᾳ δωρήσομαι αὐτός.

ΚΟΜΑΤΑΣ

σίττ᾽ ἀπὸ τᾶς κοτίνω ταὶ μηκάδες· ὧδε νέμεσθε,
ὡς τὸ κάταντες τοῦτο γεώλοφον αἵ τε μυρῖκαι.

ΛΑΚΩΝ

οὐκ ἀπὸ τᾶς δρυὸς οὗτος ὁ Κώναρος ἅ τε Κιναίθα;
τουτεῖ βοσκησεῖσθε ποτ᾽ ἀντολάς,[1] ὡς ὁ Φάλαρος.

ΚΟΜΑΤΑΣ

ἔστι δέ μοι γαυλὸς κυπαρίσσινος, ἔστι δὲ κρατήρ,
ἔργον Πραξιτέλευς· τᾷ παιδὶ δὲ ταῦτα φυλάσσω.

ΛΑΚΩΝ

χἀμῖν ἐστι κύων φιλοποίμνιος, ὃς λύκος ἄγχει,
ὃν τῷ παιδὶ δίδωμι τὰ θηρία πάντα διώκειν.

---

[1] ποτ᾽ ἀντολάς "uphill" E, cf. 4. 44 and ἀνατέλλω Ap. Rhod.
2.1247 : others "towards the east"

COMATAS

In yonder juniper-thicket a cushat sits on her
nest ;
I'll go this day and fetch her away for the maiden I
love best.

LACON

So soon as e'er my sheep I shear, a rare fine gift I'll
take ;
I'll give yon black ewe's pretty coat my darling's
cloak to make.

COMATAS

Hey, bleaters ! away from the olive ; where would
be grazing then ?
Your pasture's where the tamarisk grows and the
slope hill drops to the glen.

LACON

Where are ye browsing, Crumple ? and, Browning,
where are ye ?
Graze up the hill as Piebald will, and let the oak-
leaves be.

COMATAS

I've laid up a piggin of cypress-wood and a bowl for
mixing wine,
The work of great Praxiteles, both for that lass of
mine.

LACON

And I, I have a flock-dog, a wolver of good fame,
Shall go a gift to my dearest and hunt him all
manner of game.

"Praxiteles" : probably the great sculptor ; intended as
an ignorant man's boast (Gow).

ΚΟΜΑΤΑΣ

ἀκρίδες, αἳ τὸν φραγμὸν ὑπερπαδῆτε τὸν ἀμόν,
μή μευ λωβάσησθε τὰς ἀμπέλος· ἐντὶ γὰρ ἄβαι.[1]

ΛΑΚΩΝ

τοὶ τέττιγες ὁρῆτε, τὸν αἰπόλον ὡς ἐρεθίζω·
οὕτως κὔμμες θην ἐρεθίζετε τὼς καλαμευτάς.

ΚΟΜΑΤΑΣ

μισέω τὰς δασυκέρκος ἀλώπεκας, αἳ τὰ Μίκωνος
αἰεὶ φοιτῶσαι τὰ ποθέσπερα ῥαγίζοντι.

ΛΑΚΩΝ

καὶ γὰρ ἐγὼ μισέω τὼς κανθάρος, οἳ τὰ Φιλώνδα
σῦκα κατατρώγοντες ὑπανέμιοι φορέονται.

ΚΟΜΑΤΑΣ

ἦ οὐ μέμνασ᾽, ὅκ᾽ ἐγώ τυ κατήλασα, καὶ τὺ σεσαρὼς
εὖ ποτεκιγκλίζευ καὶ τᾶς δρυὸς εἴχεο τήνας;

ΛΑΚΩΝ

τοῦτο μὲν οὐ μέμναμ᾽· ὅκα μάν τοι[2] τεῖδέ τυ δήσας
Εὐμάρας ἐκάθαρε, καλῶς μάλα τοῦτό γ᾽ ἴσαμι.

ΚΟΜΑΤΑΣ

ἤδη τις Μόρσων πικραίνεται· ἢ οὐχὶ παρᾴσθευ;
σκίλλας ἰὼν γραίας ἀπὸ σάματος αὐτίκα τίλλειν.

[1] ἄβαι : mss αὐαι, ἆβαι, ἄβαι, schol. αὐαι, ἄζαι, αὐταί : probably special name of a choice sort of vine, cf. Hesych. ἤβη· ἄμπελος : some take it as "youths," i.e. young vines
[2] μάν τοι Wil : mss μάν ποκα or μάν

COMATAS

Avaunt, avaunt, ye locusts o'er master's fence that
    spring;
These be none of your common vines; have done
    your ravaging.

LACON

See, crickets, see how vexed he be! see master
    Goatherd boiling!
'Tis even so you vex, I trow, the reapers at their
    toiling.

COMATAS

I hate the brush-tail foxes, that soon as day declines
Come creeping to their vintaging mid goodman
    Micon's vines.

LACON

So too I hate the beetles come riding on the breeze,
Guttle Philondas' choicest figs, and off as quick as
    you please.

COMATAS

Don't you remember when I poked you, and you
grinning jerked your tail finely at me, and clung to
that oak-tree?

LACON

That indeed I don't remember; however, when
Eumaras fastened you up here and cleaned you out—
that anyway I know all about.

COMATAS

Somebody's waxing wild, Morson; see you not what
    is plain?
Go pluck him squills from an oldwife's grave to cool
    his heated brain.

"At their toiling": more likely 'at their (noontide)
rest' (Gow).

ΛΑΚΩΝ

κἠγὼ μὰν κνίζω Μόρσων τινά· καὶ τὺ δὲ λεύσσεις.
ἐνθὼν τὰν κυκλάμινον ὄρυσσέ νυν ἐς τὸν Ἄλεντα.

ΚΟΜΑΤΑΣ

Ἱμέρα ἀνθ' ὕδατος ῥείτω γάλα, καὶ τὺ δὲ Κρᾶθι
οἴνῳ πορφύροις, τὰ δέ τοι σία καρπὸν ἐνείκαι.

ΛΑΚΩΝ

ῥείτω χἀ Συβαρῖτις ἐμὶν μέλι, καὶ τὸ πότορθρον
ἁ παῖς ἀνθ' ὕδατος τᾷ καλπίδι κηρία βάψαι.

ΚΟΜΑΤΑΣ

ταὶ μὲν ἐμαὶ κύτισόν τε καὶ αἴγιλον αἶγες ἔδοντι,
καὶ σχῖνον πατέοντι καὶ ἐν κομάροισι κέονται.

ΛΑΚΩΝ

ταῖσι δ' ἐμαῖς ὀίεσσι πάρεστι μὲν ἁ μελίτεια
φέρβεσθαι, πολλὸς δὲ καὶ ὡς ῥόδα κίσθος ἐπανθεῖ.

ΚΟΜΑΤΑΣ

οὐκ ἔραμ' Ἀλκίππας, ὅτι με πρᾶν οὐκ ἐφίλησε
τῶν ὤτων καθελοῖσ', ὅκα οἱ τὰν φάσσαν ἔδωκα.

LACON

Nay, I be nettling somebody; do you not see it,
    then?
Be off to Haleis[1] bank, Morson, and dig him some
    cyclamen.

COMATAS

Let Himera's stream run white with cream, and
    Crathis, as for thine,
Mid apple-bearing beds of reed may it run red with
    wine.

LACON

Let Sybaris' well spring honey for me, and ere the
    sun is up
May the wench that goes for water draw honeycombs
    for my cup.

COMATAS

My goats eat goat-grass, mine, and browze upon the
    clover,
Tread mastich green and lie between the arbutes
    waving over.

LACON

It may be so, but I'ld have ye know these pretty
    sheep of mine
Browze rock-roses in plenty and sweet as eglantine.

COMATAS

When I brought the cushat 'tother night 'tis true
    Alcippa kissed me,
But alack! she forgot to kiss by the pot, and since,
    poor wench, she's missed me.

"Kiss by the pot": to kiss taking hold of both ears.

THE BUCOLIC POETS

ΛΑΚΩΝ

ἀλλ’ ἐγὼ Εὐμήδευς ἔραμαι μέγα· καὶ γὰρ ὅκ’
  αὐτῷ
τὰν σύριγγ’ ὤρεξα, καλόν τί με κάρτ’ ἐφίλησεν.

ΚΟΜΑΤΑΣ

οὐ θεμιτὸν Λάκων ποτ’ ἀηδόνα κίσσας ἐρίσδειν,
οὐδ’ ἔποπας κύκνοισι· τὺ δ’ ὦ τάλαν ἐσσὶ
  φιλεχθής.

ΜΟΡΣΩΝ

παύσασθαι κέλομαι τὸν ποιμένα. τὶν δὲ Κομᾶτα
δωρεῖται Μόρσων τὰν ἀμνίδα· καὶ τὺ δὲ θύσας
ταῖς Νύμφαις Μόρσωνι καλὸν κρέας αὐτίκα
  πέμψον.

ΚΟΜΑΤΑΣ

πεμψῶ ναὶ τὸν Πᾶνα. φριμάσσεο πᾶσα τραγίσκων
νῦν ἀγέλα· κἠγὼν γὰρ ἰδ’ ὡς μέγα τοῦτο καχάσδω[1]
καττῶ Λάκωνος τῶ ποιμένος, ὅττι ποκ’ ἤδη
ἀνυσάμαν τὰν ἀμνόν· ἐς ὠρανὸν ὕμμιν ἁλεῦμαι.
αἶγες ἐμαὶ θαρσεῖτε κερουχίδες[2]· αὔριον ὔμμε
πάσας ἐγὼ λουσῶ Συβαρίτιδος ἔνδοθι λίμνας.[3]
οὗτος ὁ λευκίτας ὁ κορυπτίλος, εἴ τιν’ ὀχευσεῖς
τᾶν αἰγῶν, φλασσῶ τυ, πρὶν ἤ ἐμὲ καλλιερῆσαι
ταῖς Νύμφαις τὰν ἀμνόν. ὃ δ’ αὖ πάλιν. ἀλλὰ
  γενοίμαν,
αἰ μή τυ φλάσσαιμι, Μελάνθιος ἀντὶ Κομᾶτα.

---

[1] καχάσδω E, cf. 2. 153, 23. 46 : mss καχαξῶ   [2] mss and
O. P. 1618 (c. 450 A.D.) κερουχίδες, schol. also κερουλίδες (so
prob. P. Ant.), κερουλκίδες   [3] P. Ant. with some mss κράνας

LACON

When fair Eumédes took the pipe that was his
  lover's token
He kissed him sweet as sweet could be; his lover's
  love's unbroken.

COMATAS

'Tis nature's law that no jackdaw with nightingale
  shall bicker,
Nor owl with swan, but poor Lacón was born a
  quarrel-picker.

MORSON

I bid the shepherd cease. You, Comatas, may
take the lamb; and when you offer her to the
Nymphs be sure you presently send poor Morson a
well-laden platter.

COMATAS

That will I, 'fore Pan. Come, snort ye, my merry
buck-goats all. Look you how great a laugh I have
of shepherd Lacon for that I have at last achieved
the lamb. Troth, I'll caper you to the welkin.
Horned she-goats mine, frisk it and be merry; to-
morrow I'll wash you one and all in Sybaris lake.
What, Whitecoat, thou butt-head! if thou leave not
poking the she's, before ever I sacrifice the lamb to
the Nymphs I'll break every bone in thy body. Lo
there! he's at it again. If I break thee not, be my
last end the end of Melanthius.

"owl": the Greek has "hoopoe."   "Melanthius":
the goatherd mutilated by Odysseus and Telemachus in the
twenty-second book of the *Odyssey*.

VI.—A COUNTRY SINGING-MATCH

THEOCRITUS *dedicates the poem to the Aratus of whom he speaks in the* Harvest-Home. *The scene is a spring in the pastures, and the time a summer noon. The theme is a friendly contest between a certain Damoetas and 'the neatherd Daphnis.' This is probably the Daphnis of the* Thyrsis. *If so, the two singers are meant to be contemporary with the persons of whom they sing, as are the singers of IV, V, and X. Each sings one song. Daphnis, apostrophising Polyphemus, asks why he is blind to the love of the sea-nymph Galatea. Damoetas, personating him, declares that his apathy is all put on, to make her love secure.*

VI.—ΒΟΥΚΟΛΙΑΣΤΑΙ

Δαμοίτας χὠ Δάφνις ὁ βουκόλος εἰς ἕνα χῶρον
τὰν ἀγέλαν πόκ', Ἄρατε, συνάγαγον· ἧς δ' ὁ μὲν
αὐτῶν
πυρρός, ὁ δ' ἡμιγένειος· ἐπὶ κράναν δέ τιν' ἄμφω
ἐσδόμενοι θέρεος μέσῳ ἄματι τοιάδ' ἄειδον.
πρᾶτος δ' ἄρξατο Δάφνις, ἐπεὶ καὶ πρᾶτος ἔρισδε·

Βάλλει τοι Πολύφαμε τὸ ποίμνιον ἁ Γαλάτεια
μάλοισιν, δυσέρωτα τὸν αἰπόλον ἄνδρα καλεῦσα·
καὶ τύ νιν οὐ ποθόρησθα τάλαν τάλαν[1], ἀλλὰ
κάθησαι
ἀδέα συρίσδων. πάλιν ἅδ' ἴδε τὰν κύνα βάλλει,
ἅ τοι τᾶν ὀΐων ἔπεται σκοπός· ἁ δὲ βαΰσδει
εἰς ἅλα δερκομένα, τὰ δέ νιν καλὰ κύματα
φαίνει[2]
ἅσυχα καχλάζοντος ἐπ' αἰγιαλοῖο θέοισαν.
φράζεο μὴ τᾶς παιδὸς ἐπὶ κνάμαισιν ὀρούσῃ
ἐξ ἁλὸς ἐρχομένας, κατὰ δὲ χρόα καλὸν ἀμύξῃ.
ἁ δὲ καὶ αὐτόθε τοι διαθρύπτεται· ὡς ἀπ' ἀκάνθας
ταὶ καπυραὶ χαῖται, τὸ καλὸν θέρος ἀνίκα
φρύγει,
καὶ φεύγει φιλέοντα καὶ οὐ φιλέοντα διώκει,

---

[1] τάλαν E accus. neut. cf. Men. *Ep.* 217 : others voc. masc.
[2] φαίνει : schol. also ῥαίνει

VI.—A COUNTRY SINGING-MATCH

Damoetas and neatherd Daphnis, Aratus, half-bearded the one, the other's chin ruddy with the down, had driven each his herd together to a single spot at noon of a summer's day, and sitting them down side by side at a water-spring began to sing. Daphnis sang first, for from him came the challenge :

See, Cyclops ! Galatéa's at thy flock with apples,
    see !
The apples fly, and she doth cry 'A fool's-in-love
    are ye ' ;
But with never a look to the maid, poor heart, thou
    sit'st and pipest so fine.
Lo yonder again she flings them amain at that
    good flock-dog o' thine !
See how he looks to seaward and bays her from the
    land !
See how he's glassed where he runs so fast i' the
    pretty wee waves o' the strand '
Beware or he'll leap as she comes from the deep,
    leap on her legs so bonny,
And towse her sweet pretty flesh—But lo where
    e'en now she wantons upon ye !
O the high thistle-down and the dry thistle-down i'
    the heat o' the pretty summer O !—
She'll fly ye and deny ye if ye'll a-wooing go,

"Apples": a love-gift, cf. 2. 120, 3. 10.   "glassed":
there is an ancient variant "splashed."

καὶ τὸν ἀπὸ γραμμᾶς κινεῖ λίθον· ἦ γὰρ ἔρωτι
πολλάκις ὦ Πολύφαμε τὰ μὴ καλὰ καλὰ
πέφανται.

τῷ δ' ἐπὶ Δαμοίτας ἀνεβάλλετο καὶ τάδ' ἄειδεν·

Εἶδον ναὶ τὸν Πᾶνα, τὸ ποίμνιον ἁνίκ' ἔβαλλε,
κοὔ μ' ἔλαθ', οὐ τὸν ἐμὸν τὸν ἕνα γλυκύν, ᾧ
  ποθορῷμι
ἐς τέλος, αὐτὰρ ὁ μάντις ὁ Τήλεμος ἔχθρ' ἀγορεύων
ἐχθρὰ φέροι ποτὶ οἶκον, ὅπως τεκέεσσι φυλάσσοι.
ἀλλὰ καὶ αὐτὸς ἐγὼ κνίζων πάλιν οὐ ποθόρημι,
ἀλλ' ἄλλαν τινὰ φαμὶ γυναῖκ' ἔχεν· ἁ δ' ἀΐοισα
ζαλοῖ μ' ὦ Παιὰν καὶ τάκεται, ἐκ δὲ θαλάσσας
οἰστρεῖ παπταίνοισα ποτ' ἄντρα τε καὶ ποτὶ
  ποίμνας.
σίξα[1] δ' ὑλακτεῖν νιν καὶ τᾷ κυνί· καὶ γὰρ ὅκ' ἤρων
αὐτᾶς, ἐκνυζῆτο ποτ' ἰσχία ῥύγχος ἔχοισα.
ταῦτα δ' ἴσως ἐσορῶσα ποεῦντά με πολλάκι,
  πεμψεῖ
ἄγγελον. αὐτὰρ ἐγὼ κλαξῶ θύρας, ἔστε κ' ὀμόσσῃ
αὐτά μοι στορεσεῖν καλὰ δέμνια τᾶσδ' ἐπὶ νάσω.

---

[1] σίξα Ruhnken : mss σίγα, σῖγα, σιγᾶ, σιγα

But cease to woo and she'll pursue, aye, then the
    king's the move;
For oft the foul, good Polypheme, is fair i' the eyes
    of love.

    Then Damoetas in answer lifted up his voice,
singing:

    I saw, I saw her fling them, Lord Pan my witness
    be;
I was not blind, I vow, by this my one sweet—this
Wherewith Heav'n send I see to the end, and
    Télemus when he
Foretells me woe, then be it so, but woe for him
    and his!—;
'Tis tit for tat, to tease her on I look not on the jade
And say there's other wives to wed, and lo! she's
    jealous made,
Jealous for me, Lord save us ' and 'gins to pine for
    me
And glowers from the deep on the cave and the
    sheep like a want-wit lass o' the sea.
And the dog that bayed, I hissed him on; for when
    'twas I to woo
He'ld lay his snout to her lap, her lap, and whine
    her friendly to.
Maybe she'll send me messages if long I go this
    gate;
But I'll bar the door till she swear o' this shore to
    be my wedded mate.

    " The king ": moved as a last resource in some game like
draughts or backgammon.   " Telemus ": prophesied the
blinding of Polyphemus by Odysseus.

καὶ γάρ θην οὐδ' εἶδος ἔχω κακόν, ὥς με λέγοντι.
ἦ γὰρ πρᾶν ἐς πόντον ἐσέβλεπον, ἦς δὲ γαλάνα,
καὶ καλὰ μὲν τὰ γένεια, καλὰ δέ μευ ἁ μία κώρα,
ὡς παρ' ἐμὶν κέκριται, κατεφαίνετο, τῶν δέ τ'
    ὀδόντων
λευκοτέρα αὐγὰ[1] Παρίας ὑπέχαινε[2] λίθοιο.
ὡς μὴ βασκανθῶ δέ, τρὶς εἰς ἐμὸν ἔπτυσα κόλπον·
ταῦτα γὰρ ἁ γραία με Κοτυτταρὶς ἐξεδίδαξε.   4

τόσσ' εἰπὼν τὸν Δάφνιν ὁ Δαμοίτας ἐφίλησε,   4
χὣ μὲν τῷ σύριγγ' ὁ δὲ τῷ καλὸν αὐλὸν ἔδωκεν.
αὔλει Δαμοίτας, σύρισδε δὲ Δάφνις ὁ βούτας·
ὠρχεῦντ' ἐν μαλακᾷ ταὶ πόρτιες αὐτίκα ποίᾳ.
νίκη μὰν οὐδάλλος, ἀνήσσατοι δ' ἐγένοντο.

[1] λευκοτέρα αὐγά Meineke, cf. e.g. 2.152, 10. 30, 11. 12 : mss λευκοτέραν αὐγάν   [2] ὑπέχαινε E : mss ὑπέφαινε from κατεφαίνετο above
41 & πρᾶν ἀμάντεσσι παρ' Ἱπποκίωνι ποταύλει. Not in the best ms, after 42 in another.

Ill-favoured ? nay, for all they say ; I have looked i'
    the glassy sea,
And, for aught I could spy, both beard and eye
    were pretty as well could be,
And the teeth all a-row like marble below,—and
    that none should o'erlook me of it,
As Goody Cotyttaris taught me, thrice in my breast
    I spit.

So far Damoetas, and kissed Daphnis, and that to
this gave a pipe and this to that a pretty flute.
Then lo ! the piper was neatherd Daphnis and the
flute-player Damoetas, and the dancers were the
heifers who forthwith began to bound mid the
tender grass. And as for the victory, that fell to
neither one, being they both stood unvanquished in
the match.

    " And the teeth all a-row " : the Greek has " of my teeth
below, the sheen gaped whiter than marble."   " O'erlook
me " : to see one's reflexion made one liable to the effects of
the evil eye ; spitting averted this.

VII.—THE HARVEST-HOME

THE *poet tells in the first person how three friends went out from Cos to join in a harvest-home at a farm in the country. On the way they overtake a Cretan goatherd named Lycidas, and the conversation leads to a friendly singing-match between him and the narrator Simichidas. Lycidas' song, which was apparently composed the previous November, is primarily a song of good wishes for the safe passage of his beloved Ageanax to Mitylenè, but the greater part of it is concerned with the merrymaking which will celebrate his safe arrival, and includes an address to the mythical goatherd-poet Comatas, whose story is to be sung by Tityrus on the festive occasion. Simichidas replies with a prayer to Pan and the Loves to bring the fair Philinus to his lover Aratus, a prayer which passes, however, into an appeal to Aratus to cease such youthful follies. Lycidas now bestows the crook which he had laughingly offered as a stake, and leaves the three friends at the entrance to the farm. The rest of the poem is a description of the feast. The scholia preserve a tradition that Simichidas is Theocritus himself, and indeed there is great probability that we are dealing throughout the poem with real persons. A discussion of this question will be found in the Introduction.*

VII.—ΘΑΛΥΣΙΑ

Ἧς χρόνος ἁνίκ' ἐγών τε καὶ Εὔκριτος εἰς τὸν
   Ἅλεντα
εἵρπομες ἐκ πόλιος, σὺν καὶ τρίτος ἄμμιν Ἀμύντας.
τᾷ Δηοῖ γὰρ ἔτευχε θαλύσια καὶ Φρασίδαμος
κ' Ἀντιγένης, δύο τέκνα Λυκώπεος, εἴ τί περ ἐσθλόν
χαῶν τῶν ἐπάνωθεν [1] ἀπὸ Κλυτίας τε καὶ αὐτῶ
Χάλκωνος, Βούριναν ὃς ἐκ ποδὸς ἄνυε κράναν
εὖ [2] ἐνερεισάμενος πέτρᾳ γόνυ, ταὶ δὲ παρ' αὐτὰν
αἴγειροι πτελέαι τε ἐΰσκιον ἄλσος ὕφαινον [3]
χλωροῖσιν πετάλοισι κατηρεφέες κομόωσαι.
κοὔπω τὰν μεσάταν ὁδὸν ἄνυμες, οὐδὲ τὸ σᾶμα
ἁμῖν τὸ Βρασίλα κατεφαίνετο, καί τιν' ὁδίταν
ἐσθλὸν σὺν Μοίσαισι Κυδωνικὸν εὕρομες ἄνδρα,
οὔνομα μὲν Λυκίδαν, ἦς δ' αἰπόλος, οὐδέ κέ τίς νιν
ἠγνοίησεν ἰδών, ἐπεὶ αἰπόλῳ ἔξοχ' ἐῴκει.
ἐκ μὲν γὰρ λασίοιο δασύτριχος εἶχε τράγοιο
κνακὸν δέρμ' ὤμοισι νέας ταμίσοιο ποτόσδον,
ἀμφὶ δέ οἱ στήθεσσι γέρων ἐσφίγγετο πέπλος
ζωστῆρι πλακερῷ [4], ῥοικὰν δ' ἔχεν ἀγριελαίω
δεξιτερᾷ κορύναν. καί μ' ἀτρέμας εἶπε σεσαρὼς
ὄμματι μειδιόωντι, γέλως δέ οἱ εἴχετο χείλευς·
'Σιμιχίδα, πᾷ δὴ τὸ μεσαμέριον πόδας ἕλκεις,

---

[1] ἐπάνωθεν Reiske, cf. *Ep.* 22. 3: mss ἔτ' ἄνωθεν   [2] εὖ
Herm., *O. P.* 2064 (*c.* A.D. 180): mss εὖ γ'   [3] ὕφαινον
Heinsius from Verg. *Ecl.* 9. 42: mss ἔφαινον   [4] Schol. also
πλοκερῷ

VII.—THE HARVEST-HOME

Once upon a time went Eucritus and I, and for a third, Amyntas, from the town to the Haleis. 'Twas to a harvest-feast holden that day unto Deo by Phrasidamus and Antigenes the two sons of Lycopeus, sons to wit of a fine piece of the good old stuff that came of Clytia, of Clytia and of that very Chalcon whose sturdy knee planted once against the rock both made Burina fount to gush forth at his feet and caused elm and aspen to weave above it a waving canopy of green leaves and about it a precinct of shade. Ere we were halfway thither, ere we saw the tomb of Brasilas, by grace of the Muses we overtook a fine fellow of Cydonia, by name Lycidas and by profession a goatherd, which indeed any that saw him must have known him for, seeing liker could not be. For upon his shoulders there hung, rank of new rennet, a shag-haired buck-goat's tawny fleece, across his breast a broad belt did gird an ancient shirt, and in's hand he held a crook of wild olive. Gently, broadly, and with a twinkling eye he smiled upon me, and with laughter possessing his lip, " What, Simichidas," says he; " whither away this sultry

"Deo": Demeter.   "Clytia and Chalcon": legendary queen and king of Cos.   "Burina": the fountain still bears this name.

ἀνίκα δὴ καὶ σαῦρος ἐν αἱμασιαῖσι καθεύδει,
οὐδ᾿ ἐπιτυμβίδιαι κορυδαλλίδες ἠλαίνοντι;
ἦ μετὰ δαῖτα κλητὸς ἐπείγεαι; ἦ τινος ἀστῶν
λανὸν ἔπι θρῴσκεις; ὥς τευ ποσὶ νισσομένοιο
πᾶσα λίθος πταίοισα ποτ᾿ ἀρβυλίδεσσιν ἀείδει.᾿
  τὸν δ᾿ ἐγὼ ἀμείφθην· ᾿Λυκίδα φίλε, φαντί τυ
      πάντες
ἦμεν συρικτὰν μέγ᾿ ὑπείροχον ἔν τε νομεῦσιν
ἔν τ᾿ ἀματήρεσσι.   τὸ δὴ μάλα θυμὸν ἰαίνει
ἀμέτερον· καίτοι κατ᾿ ἐμὸν νόον ἰσοφαρίζειν
ἔλπομαι. ἁ δ᾿ ὁδὸς ἅδε θαλυσιάδ᾿[1]· ἦ γὰρ ἑταῖροι
ἀνέρες εὐπέπλῳ Δαμάτερι δαῖτα τελεῦντι
ὄλβω ἀπαρχόμενοι· μάλα γάρ σφισι πίονι μέτρῳ
ἁ δαίμων εὔκριθον ἀνεπλήρωσεν ἀλωάν.
ἀλλ᾿ ἄγε δή, ξυνὰ γὰρ ὁδός ξυνὰ δὲ καὶ ἀώς,
βουκολιασδώμεσθα· τάχ᾿ ὥτερος ἄλλον ὀνασεῖ.
καὶ γὰρ ἐγὼ Μοισᾶν καπυρὸν στόμα, κἠμὲ λέγοντι
πάντες ἀοιδὸν ἄριστον· ἐγὼ δέ τις οὐ ταχυπειθής,
οὐ Δᾶν· οὐ γάρ πω κατ᾿ ἐμὸν νόον οὔτε τὸν ἐσθλὸν
Σικελίδαν νίκημι τὸν ἐκ Σάμω οὔτε Φιλίταν[2]
ἀείδων, βάτραχος δὲ ποτ᾿ ἀκρίδας ὥς τις ἐρίσδω.᾿
  ὣς ἐφάμαν ἐπίταδες· ὁ δ᾿ αἰπόλος ἁδὺ γελάσσας
᾿τάν τοι᾿ ἔφα ᾿κορύναν δωρύττομαι, οὕνεκεν ἐσσὶ
πᾶν ἐπ᾿ ἀλαθείᾳ πεπλασμένον ἐκ Διὸς ἔρνος.
ὥς μοι καὶ τέκτων μέγ᾿ ἀπέχθεται, ὅστις ἐρευνῇ
ἴσον ὄρευς κορυφᾷ τελέσαι δόμον Ὡρομέδοντος[3],

---

[1] θαλύσιάδ(ε) E: mss θαλυσιάς   [2] Φιλίταν Crönert : mss
Φιλήταν   [3] Schol. also εὐρυμέδοντος

94

noontide, when e'en the lizard will be sleeping i' th' hedge and the crested larks go not afield? Is 't even a dinner you be bidden to or a fellow-townsman's vintage-rout that makes you scurry so? for 'faith, every stone i' the road strikes singing against your hastening brogues."

" 'Tis said, dear Lycidas," answered I, " you beat all comers, herdsman or harvester, at the pipe. So 'tis said, and right glad am I it should be said ; howbeit to my thinking I'm as good a man as you. This our journey is to a harvest-home ; some friends of ours make holyday to the fair-robed Demeter with first-fruits of their increase, because the Goddess hath filled their threshing-floor in measure so full and fat. So come, I pray you, since the way and the day be yours as well as ours, and let you and me make country-music. And each from the other may well take some profit, seeing I, like you, am a clear-voiced mouthpiece of the Muses, and, like you, am accounted best of musicians everywhere,—albeit I am not so quick, Zeus knows, to believe what I'm told, being to my thinking no match in music yet awhile for the excellent Sicelidas of Samos nor again for Philitas, but I am even as a frog that is fain to outvie the pretty crickets."

So said I of set purpose, and master Goatherd with a merry laugh " I offer you this crook," says he, " as to a sprig of great Zeus that is made to the pattern of truth. Even as I hate your mason who will be striving to rear his house high as the peak of Mount Oromedon, so hate I likewise your

---

"The pipe": here it implies music generally.   "Sprig of great Zeus": Truth was daughter of Zeus.   Oromedon is probably the highest mountain in Cos.

καὶ Μοισᾶν ὄρνιχες, ὅσοι ποτὶ Χῖον ἀηδώ[1]
ἀντία κοκκύζοντες ἐτώσια μοχθίζοντι.
ἀλλ' ἄγε βουκολικᾶς ταχέως ἀρξώμεθ' ἀοιδᾶς,
Σιμιχίδα· κἠγὼ μέν, ὅρη φίλος, εἴ τοι ἀρέσκει   5
τοῦθ' ὅτι πρᾶν ἐν ὄρει τὸ μελύδριον ἐξεπόνασα·

'Εσσεται 'Αγεάνακτι καλὸς πλόος εἰς Μιτυ-
λήναν,
χὤκκεν[2] ἐφ' ἑσπερίοις 'Ερίφοις νότος ὑγρὰ διώκῃ
κύματα, χ' Ὠρίων ὅκ'[3] ἐπ' ὠκεανῷ πόδας ἴσχῃ,
αἴ κεν τὸν Λυκίδαν ὀπτεύμενον ἐξ 'Αφροδίτας
ῥύσηται· θερμὸς γὰρ ἔρως αὐτῷ με καταίθει.
χαλκυόνες στορεσεῦντι τὰ κύματα τάν τε θάλασ-
σαν
τόν τε νότον τόν τ' εὖρον, ὃς ἔσχατα φυκία
κινεῖ,
ἀλκυόνες, γλαυκαῖς Νηρηΐσι ταὶ τὰ μάλιστα
ὀρνίχων ἐφίληθεν, ὅσαις[4] τέ περ ἐξ ἁλὸς ἄγρα.   e
'Αγεάνακτι πλόον διζημένῳ εἰς Μιτυλήναν
ὥρια πάντα γένοιτο, καὶ εὔπλοος ὅρμον ἵκοιτο.
κἠγὼ τῆνο κατ' ἆμαρ ἀνήτινον ἢ ῥοδόεντα
ἢ καὶ λευκοΐων στέφανον περὶ κρατὶ φυλάσσων
τὸν πτελεατικὸν οἶνον ἀπὸ κρατῆρος ἀφυξῶ
πὰρ πυρὶ κεκλιμένος, κύαμον δέ τις ἐν πυρὶ
φρυξεῖ.

[1] ἀηδώ E, cf. 1. 136, 5. 136, Bacch. 3. 98, and Bergk *Poet. Lyr.* [4] III p. 140 : mss ἀοιδόν   [2] χὤκκεν E : mss χῶταν
[3] ὅκ' E : mss ὅτ'   [4] Greverus (Gow) ὅσοις

strutting cocks o' the Muses' yard whose crowing
makes so pitiful contention against the Chian
nightingale. But enough; let's begin our country-
songs, Simichidas. First will I—pray look if you
approve the ditty I made in the hills 'tother
day : (*sings*)

What though the Kids above the flight of wave
    before the wind
Hang westward, and Orion's foot is e'en upon the sea?
Fair voyage to Mitylenè town Agéanax shall find,
Once from the furnace of his love his Lycidas be free.
The halcyons—and of all the birds whose living's of
    the seas
The sweet green Daughters of the Deep love none
    so well as these—
O they shall still the Southwind and the tangle-toss-
    ing East,
And lay for him wide Ocean and his waves along to
    rest.
Ageanax late though he be for Mitylene bound
Heav'n bring him blest wi' the season's best to haven
    safe and sound ;
And that day I'll make merry, and bind about my brow
The anise sweet or snowflake neat or rosebuds all a-
    row,
And there by the hearth I'll lay me down beside the
    cheerful cup,
And hot roast beans shall make my bite and elmy
    wine my sup ;

  "The Chian nightingale": Homer. "The Kids": the
time of the year indicated is at the end of November.
"The halcyons": said to command a calm for their nesting
about the winter-solstice. "Elmy wine": wine flavoured
with elm-catkins, or else "wine of Ptelea."

χὰ στιβὰς ἐσσεῖται πεπυκασμένα ἔστ' ἐπὶ πᾶχυν
κνύζᾳ τ' ἀσφοδέλῳ τε πολυγνάμπτῳ τε σελίνῳ,
καὶ πίομαι μαλακῶς μεμναμένος Ἀγεάνακτος
αὐταῖσιν κυλίκεσσι[1] καὶ ἐς τρύγα χεῖλος ἐρείδων.

αὐλησεῦντι δέ μοι δύο ποιμένες, εἷς μὲν
            Ἀχαρνεύς,
εἷς δὲ Λυκωπείτας· ὁ δὲ Τίτυρος ἐγγύθεν ᾀσεῖ,
ὥς ποκα τᾶς Ξενέας ἠράσσατο Δάφνις ὁ βούτας,
χὥς ὄρος ἀμφεπονεῖτο, καὶ ὡς δρύες αὐτὸν ἐθρή-
            νευν,
Ἱμέρα αἵτε φύοντο[2] παρ' ὄχθαισιν ποταμοῖο,
εὖτε χιὼν ὥς τις κατετάκετο μακρὸν ὑφ' Αἷμον
ἢ Ἄθω ἢ Ῥοδόπαν ἢ Καύκασον ἐσχατόωντα.

ᾀσεῖ δ' ὥς ποκ' ἔδεκτο τὸν αἰπόλον εὐρέα
            λάρναξ
ζωὸν ἐόντα κακαῖσιν ἀτασθαλίαισιν ἄνακτος,
ὥς τέ νιν αἱ σιμαὶ λειμωνόθε φέρβον ἰοῖσαι
κέδρον ἐς ἀδεῖαν μαλακοῖς ἄνθεσσι μέλισσαι,
οὕνεκά οἱ γλυκὺ Μοῖσα κατὰ στόματος χέε νέκταρ.
ὦ μακαριστὲ Κομᾶτα, τύ θην τάδε τερπνὰ πεπόν-
            θεις,
καὶ τὺ κατεκλάσθης ἐς λάρνακα, καὶ τὺ
            μελισσᾶν

---

[1] cf. Ar. *Ran.* 560; Burns's "right guid-willie waught"
[2] So *O. P.* 2064: *O. P.* 1618 εφυοντο, mss φύοντι

And soft I'll lie, for elbow-high my bed strown thick
and well
Shall be of crinkled parsley, mullet, and asphodel ;
And so t' Ageanax I'll drink, drink wi' my dear in
mind,
Drink wine and wine-cup at a draught and leave no
lees behind.
   My pipers shall be two shepherds, a man of
Acharnae he,
And he a man of Lycópè ; singer shall Tityrus be,
And sing beside me of Xénea and neatherd Daphnis'
love,
How the hills were troubled around him and the
oaks sang dirges above,
Sang where they stood by Himeras flood, when he
a-wasting lay
Like snow on Haemus or Athos or Caucasus far far
away.
   And I'll have him sing how once a king, of wilful
malice bent,
In the great coffer all alive the goatherd-poet
pent,
And the snub bees came from the meadow to the
coffer of sweet cedar-tree,
And fed him there o' the flowerets fair, because his
lip was free
O' the Muses' wine ; Comátas ! 'twas joy, all joy to
thee ;
Though thou wast hid 'neath cedarn lid, the bees thy
meat did bring,

"Mullet": usually called 'fleabane.'   "His lip was
free of the Muses' wine": the Greek has "nectar," and the
meaning is that he was a poet.

κηρία φερβόμενος ἔτος ὥριον ἐξεπόνησας.
αἴθ' ἐπ' ἐμεῦ ζωοῖς ἐναρίθμιος ὤφελες ἦμεν,
ὥς τοι ἐγὼν ἐνόμευον ἀν' ὤρεα τὰς καλὰς αἶγας
φωνᾶς εἰσαΐων, τὺ δ' ὑπὸ δρυσὶν ἢ ὑπὸ πεύκαις
ἁδὺ μελισδόμενος κατεκέκλισο θεῖε Κομᾶτα.'

χὠ μὲν τόσσ' εἰπὼν ἀπεπαύσατο· τὸν δὲ μέτ' αὖτις[1]
κἠγὼν τοῖ' ἐφάμαν· 'Λυκίδα φίλε, πολλὰ μὲν ἄλλα
Νύμφαι κἠμὲ δίδαξαν ἀν' ὤρεα βουκολέοντα
ἐσθλά, τά που καὶ Ζηνὸς ἐπὶ θρόνον ἄγαγε φάμα·
ἀλλὰ τό γ' ἐκ πάντων μέγ' ὑπείροχον, ᾧ τυ γεραίρειν
ἀρξεῦμ'· ἀλλ' ὑπάκουσον, ἐπεὶ φίλος ἔπλεο Μοί-
σαις·

'Σιμιχίδᾳ μὲν Ἔρωτες ἐπέπταρον· ἦ γὰρ ὁ δειλὸς
τόσσον ἐρᾷ Μυρτοῦς, ὅσον εἴαρος αἶγες ἐρᾶντι.
Ὥρατος δ' ὁ τὰ πάντα φιλαίτατος ἀνέρι τήνῳ
παιδὸς ὑπὸ σπλάγχνοισιν ἔχει πόθον· οἶδεν Ἄρισ-
τις,
ἐσθλὸς ἀνήρ, μέγ' ἄριστος, ὃν οὐδέ κεν αὐτὸς
ἀείδειν
Φοῖβος σὺν φόρμιγγι παρὰ τριπόδεσσι μεγαίροι,
ὡς ἐκ παιδὸς Ἄρατος ὑπ' ὀστέον αἴθετ' ἔρωτι.
τόν μοι Πάν, Ὁμόλας ἐρατὸν πέδον ὅστε λέλογχας,
ἄκλητον κείνοιο φίλας ἐς χεῖρας ἐρείσαις,

---

[1] αὖτις Ahr : mss αὖθις

Till thou didst thole, right happy soul, thy twelve
  months' prisoning.
And O of the quick thou wert this day ! How
  gladly then with mine
I had kept thy pretty goats i' the hills, the while
  'neath oak or pine
Thou 'dst lain along and sung me a song, Comatas
  the divine !"

So much sang Lycidas and ended ; and thereupon
" Dear Lycidas " said I, " afield with my herds on the
hills I also have learnt of the Nymphs, and there's
many a good song of mine which Rumour may well
have carried up to the throne of Zeus. But this of
all is far the choicest, this which I will sing now for
your delight. Pray give ear, as one should whom
the Muses love : (*sings*)

The Loves have sneezed, for sure they have, on poor
  Simichidas :
For he loves maid Myrto as goats the spring : but
  where he loves a lass
His dear'st Aratus sighs for a lad. Aristis, dear
  good man—
And best in fame as best in name, the Lord o' the
  Lyre on high
Beside his holy tripod would let him make melody—
Aristis knows Aratus' woes. O bring the lad, sweet
  Pan,
Sweet Lord of lovely Homolè, bring him unbid to 's
  fere,

  " Have sneezed ": a sneeze meant good luck, and a man
deeply in love was said to have been sneezed upon by the
Loves.   " Lord of the Lyre ": the Greek has " Apollo."

εἴτ' ἔστ' ἆρα Φιλῖνος ὁ μαλθακὸς εἴτε τις ἄλλος.

κεἰ μὲν ταῦτ' ἔρδοις ὦ Πὰν φίλε, μή τι τυ
  παῖδες

Ἀρκαδικοὶ σκίλλαισιν ὑπὸ πλευράς τε καὶ ὤμως

τανίκα μαστίσδοιεν, ὅτε κρέα τυτθὰ παρείη·

εἰ δ' ἄλλως νεύσαις, κατὰ μὲν χρόα πάντ'
  ὀνύχεσσι

δακνόμενος κνάσαιο καὶ ἐν κνίδαισι καθεύδοις,   110

εἴης δ' Ἠδωνῶν μὲν ἐν ὤρεσι χείματι μέσσῳ

Ἕβρον πὰρ ποταμὸν[1] τετραμμένος ἐγγύθεν Ἄρκτω,

ἐν δὲ θέρει πυμάτοισι παρ' Αἰθιόπεσσι νομεύοις

πέτρᾳ ὕπο Βλεμύων, ὅθεν οὐκέτι Νεῖλος ὁρατός.

 ὔμμες δ' Ὑετίδος καὶ Βυβλίδος ἁδὺ λιπόντες

νᾶμα καὶ Οἰκεῦντα, ξανθᾶς ἕδος αἰπὺ Διώνας,

ὦ μάλοισιν Ἔρωτες ἐρευθομένοισιν ὁμοῖοι,

βάλλετέ μοι τόξοισι τὸν ἱμερόεντα Φιλῖνον,

βάλλετ', ἐπεὶ τὸν ξεῖνον ὁ δύσμορος οὐκ ἐλεεῖ
  μευ.

καὶ δὴ μὰν[2] ἀπίοιο πεπαίτερος, αἱ δὲ γυναῖκες   120

'αἰαῖ' φαντὶ 'Φιλῖνε, τό τοι καλὸν ἄνθος ἀπορρεῖ.'

μηκέτι τοι φρουρέωμες ἐπὶ προθύροισιν Ἄρατε,

μηδὲ πόδας τρίβωμες· ὁ δ' ὄρθριος ἄλλον ἀλέκτωρ

---

[1] O. P. 1618 Εβρω παρ ποταμω correcting accusative
[2] δὴ μὰν: mss also δὴ μάλ'

Whether Philínus, sooth to say, or other be his dear.
This do, sweet Pan, and never, when slices be too few,
May the leeks o' the lads of Arcady beat thee black
    and blue;
But O if othergates thou go, may nettles make thy
    bed
And set thee scratching tooth and nail, scratching
    from heel to head,
And be thy winter-lodging nigh the Bear up Hebrus
    way
I' the hills of Thrace; when summer's in, mid
    furthest Africa
Mayst feed thy flock by the Blemyan rock beyond
    Nile's earliest spring.
  Ɔ come ye away, ye little Loves like apples red-
    blushing,
From Byblis' fount and Oecus' mount that is fair-
    haired Dion's joy,
Come shoot the fair Philinus, shoot me the silly boy
That flouts my friend! Yet after all, the pear's o'er-
    ripe to taste,
And the damsels sigh and the damsels say 'Thy
    bloom, child, fails thee fast';
So let's watch no more his gate before, Aratus, o'
    this gear,
But ease our aching feet, my friend, and let old
    chanticleer

"Leeks": the sea-leek had purificatory uses; the poet refers here to what was apparently the current explanation of a flogging rite—the choristers flogged the statue of Pan at the feast because they had once received short commons. "Dion": Diōne is Aphrodite or her mother; the Loves are summoned from the district of Miletus. "O' this gear": in this way. "Aching feet": from standing about at the door, one of the conventional signs of being in love.

κοκκύζων νάρκαισιν ἀνιαραῖσι διδοίη,
εἰς δ' ἀπὸ τᾶσδε φέριστε μολὼν ἄγχοιτο παλαί-
    στρας.[1]
ἄμμιν δ' ἀσυχία τε μέλοι γραία τε παρείη,
ἅτις ἐπιφθύζοισα τὰ μὴ καλὰ νόσφιν ἐρύκοι.'

    τόσσ' ἐφάμαν· ὁ δέ μοι τὸ λαγωβόλον, ἁδὺ
    γελάσσας
ὡς πάρος, ἐκ Μοισᾶν ξεινήιον ὤπασεν ἦμεν.
χὠ μὲν ἀποκλίνας ἐπ' ἀριστερὰ τὰν ἐπὶ Πύξας
εἷρφ' ὁδόν, αὐτὰρ ἐγώ τε καὶ Εὔκριτος ἐς Φρα-
    σιδάμω
στραφθέντες χὠ καλὸς Ἀμύντιχος ἔν τε βαθείαις
ἀδείας σχοίνοιο χαμευνίσιν ἐκλίνθημες
ἔν τε νεοτμάτοισι γεγαθότες οἰναρέαισι.

    πολλαὶ δ' ἄμμιν ὕπερθε κατὰ κρατὸς δονέοντο
αἴγειροι πτελέαι τε· τὸ δ' ἐγγύθεν ἱερὸν ὕδωρ
Νυμφᾶν ἐξ ἄντροιο κατειβόμενον κελάρυζε.
τοὶ δὲ ποτὶ σκιαραῖς ὀροδαμνίσιν αἰθαλίωνες
τέττιγες λαλαγεῦντες ἔχον πόνον· ἁ δ' ὀλολυγὼν
τηλόθεν ἐν πυκιναῖσι βάτων τρύζεσκεν ἀκάνθαις·
ἄειδον κόρυδοι καὶ ἀκανθίδες, ἔστενε τρυγών,
πωτῶντο ξουθαὶ περὶ πίδακας ἀμφὶ μέλισσαι.
πάντ' ὦσδεν θέρεος μάλα πίονος, ὦσδε δ' ὀπώρας.
ὄχναι μὲν πὰρ ποσσί, περὶ πλευραῖσι δὲ μᾶλα
δαψιλέως ἁμῖν ἐκυλίνδετο· τοὶ δ' ἐκέχυντο
ὄρπακες βραβίλοισι καταβρίθοντες ἔραζε.
τετράενες δὲ πίθων ἀπελύετο κρατὸς ἄλειφαρ·
Νύμφαι Κασταλίδες Παρνάσσιον αἶπος ἔχοισαι,

---

[1] Cf. Plat. *Gorg.* 493 D ἄλλην σοι εἰκόνα λέγω ἐκ τοῦ αὐτοῦ
γυμνασίου τῇ νῦν, and Ar. *Vesp.* 526

Cry 'shiver' to some other when he the dawn shall
    sing ;
One scholar o' that school's enough to have met his
    death i' the ring.
'Tis peace of mind, lad, we must find, and have a
    beldame nigh
To sit for us and spit for us and bid all ill go by."

So far my song ; and Lycidas, with a merry laugh
as before, bestowed the crook upon me to be the
Muses' pledge of friendship, and so bent his way to
the left-hand and went down the Pyxa road ; and
Eucritus and I and pretty little Amyntas turned in
at Phrasidamus's and in deep greenbeds of fragrant
reeds and fresh-cut vine-strippings laid us rejoicing
down.

Many an aspen, many an elm bowed and rustled
overhead, and hard by, the hallowed water welled
purling forth of a cave of the Nymphs, while the
brown cricket chirped busily amid the shady leafage,
and the tree-frog murmured aloof in the dense
thornbrake. Lark and goldfinch sang and turtle
moaned, and about the spring the bees hummed and
hovered to and fro. All nature smelt of the opulent
summer-time, smelt of the season of fruit. Pears
lay at our feet, apples on either side, rolling abun-
dantly, and the young branches lay splayed upon the
ground because of the weight of their damsons.

Meanwhile we broke the four-year-old seal from
off the lips of the jars, and O ye Castalian Nymphs
that dwell on Parnassus' height, did ever the aged

    "One scholar o' that school": one dallier with such
follies. "Castalian Nymphs": all nymphs were
Castalian.

ἠρά γέ πα τοιόνδε Φόλω κατὰ λάϊνον ἄντρον
κρατὴρ' Ἡρακλῆι γέρων ἐστάσατο Χείρων;
ἠρά γέ πα τῆνον τὸν ποιμένα τὸν ποτ' Ἀνάπῳ,
τὸν κρατερὸν Πολύφαμον, ὃς ὤρεσι νᾶας[1] ἔβαλλε,
τοῖον νέκταρ ἔπεισε κατ' αὔλια ποσσὶ χορεῦσαι,
οἷον δὴ τόκα πῶμα διεκρανάσατε Νύμφαι
βωμῷ πὰρ Δάματρος ἀλωίδος; ἃς ἐπὶ σωρῷ
αὖτις ἐγὼ πάξαιμι μέγα πτύον, ἃ δὲ γελάσσαι
δράγματα καὶ μάκωνας ἐν ἀμφοτέραισιν ἔχοισα.

[1] νᾶας Heinsius : mss λᾶας

Cheiron in Pholus' rocky cave set before Heracles such a bowlful as that? And the mighty Polypheme who kept sheep beside the Anapus and had at ships with mountains, was it for such nectar he footed it around his steading—such a draught as ye Nymphs gave us that day of your spring by the altar of Demeter o' the Threshing-floor? of her, to wit, upon whose cornheap I pray I may yet again plant the great purging-fan while she stands smiling by with wheatsheaves and poppies in either hand.

"Of your spring": the wine was drunk mixed with water. "Demeter": a harvest-effigy.

VIII.—THE SECOND COUNTRY SINGING-MATCH

THE *characters of this shepherd-mime are the mythical personages Daphnis the neatherd and Menalcas the shepherd, and an unnamed goatherd who plays umpire in their contest of song. After four lines by way of stage-direction, the conversation opens with mutual banter between the two young countrymen, and leads to a singing-match with pipes for the stakes. Each sings four alternate elegiac quatrains and an envoy of eight hexameters. In the first three pairs of quatrains Menalcas sets the theme and Daphnis takes it up. The first pair is addressed to the landscape, and contains mutual compliments; the remainder deal with love. The last pair of quatrains and the two envoys do not correspond in theme. The resemblance of most of the competing stanzas has caused both loss and transposition in the manuscripts. From metrical and linguistic considerations the poem is clearly not the work of Theocritus.*

VIII.—ΒΟΥΚΟΛΙΑΣΤΑΙ

Δάφνιδι τῷ χαρίεντι συνάντετο βουκολέοντι
μᾶλα νέμων, ὡς φαντί, κατ᾽ ὤρεα μακρὰ Μενάλκας.
ἄμφω τώγ᾽ ἤστην πυρροτρίχω, ἄμφω ἀνήβω,
ἄμφω συρίσδεν δεδαημένω, ἄμφω ἀείδεν.
πρᾶτος δ᾽ ὦν ποτὶ Δάφνιν ἰδὼν ἀγόρευε Μενάλκας·
ʿ μυκητᾶν ἐπίουρε βοῶν Δάφνι, λῇς μοι ἀεῖσαι;
φαμί τυ νικασεῖν ὅσσον θέλω, αὐτὸς ἀείδων.᾽
τὸν δ᾽ ἄρα χὠ Δάφνις τοιῷδ᾽ ἀπαμείβετο μύθῳ·
ʿ ποιμὴν εἰροπόκων οἴων συρικτὰ Μενάλκα,
οὔποτε νικασεῖς μ᾽, οὐδ᾽ εἴ τι πάθοις τύγ᾽ ἀείδων.᾽

ΜΕΝΑΛΚΑΣ
χρήσδεις ὦν ἐσιδεῖν; χρήσδεις καταθεῖναι ἄεθλον;

ΔΑΦΝΙΣ
χρήσδω τοῦτ᾽ ἐσιδεῖν, χρήσδω καταθεῖναι ἄεθλον.

ΜΕΝΑΛΚΑΣ
καὶ τίνα θησεύμεσθ᾽, ὅτις ἀμὶν ἄρκιος εἴη;

ΔΑΦΝΙΣ
μόσχον ἐγὼ θησῶ· τὺ δὲ θὲς ἰσομάτορα τῆνον.[1]

---

[1] τῆνον E : mss ἀμνόν (with unlikely hiatus) from gloss

VIII.—THE SECOND COUNTRY SINGING-MATCH

Once on a day the fair Daphnis, out upon the long hills with his cattle, met Menalcas keeping his sheep. Both had ruddy heads, both were striplings grown, both were players of music, and both knew how to sing. Looking now towards Daphnis, Menalcas first 'What, Daphnis,' cries he, 'thou watchman o' bellowing kine, art thou willing to sing me somewhat? I'll warrant, come my turn, I shall have as much the better of thee as I choose.' And this was Daphnis' answer : 'Thou shepherd o' woolly sheep, thou mere piper Menalcas, never shall the likes of thee have the better of me in a song, strive he never so hard.'

MENALCAS
Then will 't please you look hither? Will't please you lay a wage?

DAPHNIS
Aye, that it will ; I'll both look you and lay you, too.

MENALCAS
And what shall our wage be? what shall be sufficient for us?

DAPHNIS
Mine shall be a calf, only let yours be that mother-tall fellow yonder.

ΜΕΝΑΛΚΑΣ

οὐ θησῶ ποκα τῆνον[1], ἐπεὶ χαλεπὸς ὁ πατήρ μευ
χἀ μάτηρ, τὰ δὲ μᾶλα ποθέσπερα πάντ᾽ ἀριθ-
μεῦντι.

ΔΑΦΝΙΣ

ἀλλὰ τί μὰν θησεῖς; τί δὲ τὸ πλέον ἑξεῖ ὁ νικῶν;

ΜΕΝΑΛΚΑΣ

σύριγγ᾽ ἃν ἐπόησα καλὰν ἐγὼ ἐννεάφωνον,
λευκὸν κηρὸν ἔχοισαν ἴσον κάτω ἴσον ἄνωθεν·
ταύταν κα θείην, τὰ δὲ τῶ πατρὸς οὐ καταθησῶ.

ΔΑΦΝΙΣ

ἦ μάν τοι κἠγὼ σύριγγ᾽ ἔχω ἐννεάφωνον,
λευκὸν κηρὸν ἔχοισαν ἴσον κάτω ἴσον ἄνωθεν.
πρώαν νιν συνέπαξ· ἔτι καὶ τὸν δάκτυλον ἀλγέω
τοῦτον, ἐπεὶ κάλαμός με διασχισθεὶς νιν ἔτμαξεν.[2]

ΜΕΝΑΛΚΑΣ

ἀλλὰ τίς ἄμμε κρινεῖ; τίς ἐπάκοος ἔσσεται ἁμέων;

ΔΑΦΝΙΣ

τῆνόν πως ἐνταῦθα τὸν αἰπόλον, ἢν καλέσωμες,
ᾧ ποτὶ ταῖς ἐρίφοις ὁ κύων ὁ φαλαρὸς ὑλακτεῖ.

χοἰ μὲν παῖδες ἄϋσαν, ὁ δ᾽ αἰπόλος ἦνθ᾽ ἐπα-
κοῦσαι,
οἱ[3] μὲν παῖδες ἄειδον, ὁ δ᾽ αἰπόλος ἤθελε κρίνειν.
πρᾶτος δ᾽ ὦν ἄειδε λαχὼν ἰυκτὰ Μενάλκας,
εἶτα δ᾽ ἀμοιβαίαν ὑπελάμβανε Δάφνις ἀοιδὰν
βουκολικάν· οὕτω δὲ Μενάλκας ἄρξατο πρᾶτος·

---

[1] ποκα τῆνον E : mss ποκα ἀμνὸν, cf. 14   [2] νιν ἔτμαξεν
Meineke : mss διέτμαξε   [3] οἱ E : mss χοἰ

MENALCAS

He shall be no wage of mine. Father and mother are both sour as can be, and tell the flock to a head every night.

DAPHNIS

Well, but what is't to be? and what's the winner to get for's pains?

MENALCAS

Here's a gallant nine-stop pipe I have made, with good white beeswax the same top and bottom; this I'm willing to lay, but I'll not stake what is my father's.

DAPHNIS

Marry, I have a nine-stop pipe likewise, and it like yours hath good white beeswax the same top and bottom. I made it t'other day, and my finger here sore yet where a split reed cut it for me. (*each stakes a pipe*)

MENALCAS

But who's to be our judge? who's to do the hearing for us?

DAPHNIS

Peradventure that goatherd yonder, if we call him; him wi' that spotted flock-dog a-barking near by the kids.

So the lads holla'd, and the goatherd came to hear them, the lads sang and the goatherd was fain to be their judge. Lots were cast, and 'twas Menalcas Loud-o'-voice to begin the country-song and Daphnis to take him up by course. Menalcas thus began:

"By course": stanza by stanza

Ἄγκεα καὶ ποταμοί, θεῖον γένος, αἴ τι Μενάλκας
πήποχ' ὁ συρικτὰς προσφιλὲς ᾆσε μέλος,
βόσκοιτ' ἐκ ψυχᾶς τὰς ἀμνάδας· ἢν δέ ποκ' ἔνθη
Δάφνις ἔχων δαμάλας, μηδὲν ἔλασσον ἔχοι.

ΔΑΦΝΙΣ

κράναι καὶ βοτάναι, γλυκερὸν φυτόν, αἴπερ ὁμοῖον
μουσίσδει Δάφνις ταῖσιν ἀηδονίσι,
τοῦτο τὸ βουκόλιον πιαίνετε· κἤν τι Μενάλκας
τεῖδ' ἀγάγῃ, χαίρων ἄφθονα πάντα νέμοι.

ΜΕΝΑΛΚΑΣ

ἔνθ' ὄϊς, ἔνθ' αἶγες διδυματόκοι, ἔνθα μέλισσαι[1]
σμάνεα πληροῦσιν, καὶ δρύες ὑψίτεραι,
ἔνθ' ὁ καλὸς Μίλων βαίνει ποσίν· αἱ δ' ἂν ἀφέρπῃ,
χὠ ποιμὴν ξηρὸς τηνόθι χαἰ βοτάναι.

ΔΑΦΝΙΣ

παντᾷ ἔαρ, παντᾷ δὲ νομοί, παντᾷ δὲ γάλακτος
οὔθατα πιδῶσιν,[2] καὶ τὰ νέα τρέφεται,
ἔνθα καλὰ Ναῒς[3] ἐπινίσσεται· αἱ δ' ἂν ἀφέρπῃ,
χὠ τὰς βῶς βόσκων χαἰ βόες αὐότεραι.

ΜΕΝΑΛΚΑΣ

ὦ τράγε, τᾶν λευκᾶν αἰγῶν ἄνερ, ὦ βάθος[4] ὕλας
μυρίον (αἱ σιμαὶ[5] δεῦτ' ἐφ' ὕδωρ ἔριφοι)·

[1] 41–47 transposed by Anon. *Ephem. Goth.* 1803. 22
[2] πιδῶσιν Ahrens : mss πηδῶσιν, schol. also πλήθουσιν   [3] Ναῒς
Mein : mss παῖς   [4] ὦ βάθος schol. : mss ὦ β.   [5] αἱ σιμαὶ
Wil : mss ὦ σ.

Ye woods and waters, wondrous race,
Lith and listen of your grace;
If e'er my song was your delight
Feed my lambs with all your might;
And if Daphnis wend this way,
Make his calves as fat as they.

DAPHNIS

Ye darling wells and meadows dear,
Sweets o' the earth, come lend an ear;
If like the nightingales I sing,
Give my cows good pasturing;
And if Menalcas e'er you see,
Fill his flock and make him glee.

MENALCAS

Where sweet Milon trips the leas
There's fuller hives and loftier trees;
Where'er those pretty footings fall
Goats and sheep come twinners all;
If otherwhere those feet be gone,
Pasture's lean and shepherd lone.

DAPHNIS

Where sweet Naïs comes a-straying
There the green meads go a-maying;
Where'er her pathway lies along,
There's springing teats and growing young;
If otherwhere her gate be gone,
Cows are dry and herd fordone.

MENALCAS

Buck-goat, husband of the she's,
Hie to th' wood's infinities—
Nay, snubbies, hither to the spring;
This errand's not for your running;—

"Snubbies": kids.

ἐν τήνῳ γὰρ τῆνος· ἴθ' 'ὦ καλὲ[1]' καὶ λέγε, 'Μίλων,
ὁ Πρωτεὺς φώκας καὶ θεὸς ὢν[2] ἔνεμε.'

ΔΑΦΝΙΣ

*　*　*　*　*　*　*　*　*

ΜΕΝΑΛΚΑΣ

μή μοι γᾶν Πέλοπος, μή μοι Κροίσεια[3] τάλαντα
εἴη ἔχειν, μηδὲ πρόσθε θέειν ἀνέμων·
ἀλλ' ὑπὸ τᾷ πέτρᾳ τᾷδ' ᾄσομαι ἀγκὰς ἔχων τυ,
σύννομε[4] κάλ'[5], ἐσορῶν τὰν Σικελάν ἐς ἅλα.

ΔΑΦΝΙΣ

δένδρεσι μὲν χειμὼν φοβερὸν κακόν, ὕδασι δ'
　　αὐχμός,
ὄρνισιν δ' ὕσπλαγξ, ἀγροτέροις δὲ λίνα,
ἀνδρὶ δὲ παρθενικᾶς ἀπαλᾶς πόθος. ὦ πάτερ ὦ Ζεῦ,
οὐ μόνος ἠράσθην· καὶ τὺ γυναικοφίλας.

ταῦτα μὲν ὦν, δι' ἀμοιβαίων οἱ παῖδες ἄεισαν·
τὰν πυματὰν δ' ᾠδὰν οὕτως ἐξᾶρχε Μενάλκας·

Φείδευ τᾶν ἐρίφων, φείδευ λύκε τᾶν τοκάδων μευ,
μηδ' ἀδίκει μ', ὅτι μικκὸς ἐὼν πολλαῖσιν ὁμαρτέω.
ὦ Λάμπουρε κύον, οὕτω βαθὺς ὕπνος ἔχει τυ;
οὐ χρὴ κοιμᾶσθαι βαθέως σὺν παιδὶ νέμοντα.
ταὶ δ' ὄϊες, μηδ' ὕμμες ὀκνεῖθ' ἀπαλᾶς κορέσασθαι
ποίας· οὔ τι καμεῖσθ', ὅκκα πάλιν ἅδε φύηται.

---

[1] καλέ schol. : mss and schol. κολέ　　　[2] ὢν Mein : mss ὡς
[3] Κροίσεια Jortin : mss χρύσεια　　　[4] σύννομε Graefe : mss
σύννομα　　　[5] κάλ' Mein : mss μὰλ'

Go, buck, and " Fairest Milon " say,
" A God kept seals once on a day."

[Daphnis' reply is lost]

MENALCAS

I would not Pelops' tilth untold
Nor all Croesus' coffered gold,
Nor yet t' outfoot the storm-wind's breath,
So I may sit this rock beneath,
Pretty pasture-mate, wi' thee,
And gaze on the Sicilian sea.

DAPHNIS

Wood doth fear the tempest's ire,
Water summer's drouthy fire,
Beasts the net and birds the snare.
Man the love of maiden fair ;
Not I alone lie under ban ;
Zeus himself 's a woman's man.

So far went the lads' songs by course.   Now 'twas
the envoy, and Menalcas thus began :

Spare, good Wolf, the goats you see,
Spare them dam and kid for me ;
If flock is great and flockman small,
Is't reason you should wrong us all ?
Come, White-tail, why so sound asleep ?
Good dogs wake when boys tend sheep.
Fear not, ewes, your fill to eat ;
For when the new blade sprouteth sweet,
Then ye shall no losers be ;

" A God kept seals " : Proteus ; the message means ' Do
not despise your lover because he keeps sheep.'   " Lie
under ban " : the Greek has ' have fallen in love.'

σίττα νέμεσθε νέμεσθε, τὰ δ' οὔθατα πλήσατε
    πᾶσαι,
ὡς τὸ μὲν ὦρνες ἔχωντι, τὸ δ' ἐς ταλάρως ἀποθῶμαι. 7

    δεύτερος αὖ Δάφνις λιγυρῶς ἀνεβάλλετ' ἀείδεν·

    Κἤμ' ἐκ σπήλυγγος[1] σύνοφρυς κόρα ἐχθὲς ἰδοῖσα
τὰς δαμάλας παρελᾶντα καλὸν καλὸν ἦμεν
    ἔφασκεν·
οὐ μὰν οὐδὲ λέγων ἐκρίθην ἄπο τὸν πικρὸν αὐτᾶς,[2]
ἀλλὰ κάτω βλέψας τὰν ἀμετέραν ὁδὸν εἰρπον.
ἀδεῖ' ἁ φωνὰ τᾶς πόρτιος, ἁδὺ τὸ πνεῦμα·   7
ἁδὺ δὲ τῶ θέρεος παρ' ὕδωρ ῥέον αἰθριοκοιτεῖν.   7
τᾷ δρυῒ ταὶ βαλάνοι κόσμος, τᾷ μαλίδι μᾶλα,
τᾷ βοῒ δ' ἁ μόσχος, τῷ βουκόλῳ αἱ βόες αὐταί.   8

    ὣς οἱ παῖδες ἄεισαν, ὁ δ' αἰπόλος ὧδ' ἀγόρευεν·
'ἁδύ τι τὸ στόμα τοι καὶ ἐφίμερος ὦ Δάφνι φωνά.
κρέσσον μελπομένω τευ ἀκουέμεν ἢ μέλι λείχειν.
λάζεο τᾶς σύριγγος·[3] ἐνίκασας γὰρ ἀείδων.
αἰ δέ τι λῇς με καὶ αὐτὸν ἅμ' αἰπολέοντα διδάξαι,
τήναν τὰν μιτύλαν[4] δωσῶ τὰ δίδακτρά τοι αἶγα,
ἄτις ὑπὲρ κεφαλᾶς αἰεὶ τὸν ἀμολγέα πληροῖ.'

    [1] σπήλυγγος E, cf. 16. 53 : mss τῶ ἄντρω   [2] λέγων and
αὐτᾶς E, taking ἀπεκρίθην as 'parted from,' supplying λόγον :
mss λόγων or λόγον and αὐτᾷ   [3] τᾶς σύριγγος Scaliger :
mss τὰς σύριγγας   [4] μιτύλαν 'youngest and smallest' E :
others as Lat. mutilus 'that has lost her horns': mss μιτάλαν,
μιτύλαν

    77 ἁδὺ δὲ χὠ μόσχος γαρύεται, ἁδὺ δὲ χἀ βῶς. From 9. 7 ;
Valckenaer rightly omits, though it is found in O. P. 2064

To 't, and feed you every she,
Feed till every udder teem
Store for lambs and store for cream.

Then Daphnis, for his envoy, lifted up his tuneful
voice, singing—

Yestermorn a long-browed maid,
Spying from a rocky shade
Neat and neatherd passing by,
Cries " What a pretty boy am I ! "
Did pretty boy the jape repay ?
Nay, bent his head and went his way.
Sweet to hear and sweet to smell,
God wot I love a heifer well,
And sweet alsó 'neath summer sky
To sit where brooks go babbling by ;
But 'tis berry and bush, 'tis fruit and tree,
'Tis calf and cow, wi' my kine and me.

So sang those two lads, and this is what the goat-
herd said of their songs : " You, good Daphnis, have
a sweet and delightful voice. Your singing is to the
ear as honey to the lip. Here's the pipe; take it;
your song has fairly won it you. And if you are
willing to teach me how to sing as you sing while I
share pasture with you, you shall have the little
she-goat yonder to your school-money, and I warrant
you she'll fill your pail up to the brim and further."

" Long-browed ": the Greek is 'with meeting eye-brows.'
" 'Tis berry and bush ": the Greek is 'acorn adorns oak,
apple apple-tree, calf cow, and cows cowherd.'

ὡς μὲν ὁ παῖς ἐχάρη καὶ ἀνάλατο καὶ πλατάγησε
νικάσας, οὕτως ἐπὶ ματέρι νεβρὸς ἄλοιτο.
ὡς δὲ κατεσμύχθη καὶ ἀνετράπετο φρένα λύπᾳ
ὥτερος, οὕτω καὶ νύμφα δμαθεῖσ᾽[1] ἀκάχοιτο.
κἠκ τούτω πρᾶτος παρὰ ποιμέσι Δάφνις ἔγεντο,
καὶ Νύμφαν ἄκρηβος ἐὼν ἔτι Ναΐδα γᾶμεν.

---

[1] δμαθεῖσ᾽ Ahrens : mss γαμεθεῖσ᾽, γαμηθεῖσ᾽

At that the lad was transported, and capered and clapped hands for joy of his victory; so capers a fawn at the sight of his dam. At that, too, the other's fire was utterly extinct, and his heart turned upside-down for grief; so mourns a maiden that is forced against her will.

From that day forth Daphnis had the pre-eminence of the shepherds, insomuch that he was scarce come to man's estate ere he had to wife that Naïs of whom he sang.

"Naïs": apparently the nymph to whom Daphnis afterwards swore the oath which, when he fell in love with Xenea, he died rather than break.

IX.—THE THIRD COUNTRY SINGING-MATCH

THIS *poem would seem to be merely a poor imitation of the last. The characters are two neatherds, Daphnis and Menalcas, and the writer himself. We are to imagine the cattle to have just been driven out to pasture. There is no challenge and no stake. At the request of the writer that they shall compete in song before him, each of the herdsmen sings seven lines, Daphnis setting the theme; and then the writer, leaving it to be implied that he judged them equal, tells us how he gave them each a gift and what it was. The writer now appeals to the Muses to tell him the song he himself sang on the occasion, and he sings a six-line song in their praise.*

IX.—ΒΟΥΚΟΛΙΑΣΤΑΙ

Βουκολιάζεο Δάφνι, τὺ δ᾽ ᾠδᾶς ἄρχεο πρᾶτος,
ᾠδᾶς ἄρχεο πρᾶτος, ἐφεψάσθω δὲ Μενάλκας,
μόσχως βουσὶν ἀφέντες ἔπι[1], στείραισι δὲ ταύρως.
χοὶ μὲν ἁμᾷ βόσκοιντο καὶ ἐν φύλλοισι πλανῶντο
μηδὲν ἀτιμαγελεῦντες· ἐμὶν δὲ τὺ βουκολιάζευ
ἐκ τόθεν,[2] ἄλλωθεν δὲ ποτικρίνοιτο Μενάλκας.

ΔΑΦΝΙΣ

Ἁδὺ μὲν ἁ μόσχος γαρύεται, ἁδὺ δὲ χἀ βῶς,
ἁδὺ δὲ χἀ σύριγξ χὠ βουκόλος, ἁδὺ δὲ κἠγών.
ἔστι δέ μοι παρ᾽ ὕδωρ ψυχρὸν στιβάς, ἐν δὲ
νένασται
λευκᾶν ἐκ δαμαλᾶν καλὰ δέρματα, τάς μοι ἁπάσας
λὶψ κόμαρον τρωγοίσας ἀπὸ σκοπιᾶς ἐτίναξε.
τῶ δὲ θέρευς φρύγοντος ἐγὼ τόσσον μελεδαίνω,
ὅσσον ἐρῶν γα[3] πατρὸς μύθων καὶ ματρὸς ἀκούει.

οὕτως Δάφνις ἄεισεν ἐμίν, οὕτως δὲ Μενάλκας·

Αἴτνα μᾶτερ ἐμά, κἠγὼ καλὸν ἄντρον ἐνοικέω
κοίλαις ἐν πέτραισιν· ἔχω δέ τοι, ὅσσ᾽ ἐν ὀνείρῳ
φαίνονται, πολλὰς μὲν ὄϊς, πολλὰς δὲ χιμαίρας,
ὧν μοι πρὸς κεφαλᾷ καὶ πρὸς ποσὶ κώεα κεῖται.

---

[1] ἀφέντες ἔπι E: mss ὑφέντες ὑπό (Vat. 915 ἐπί) from 4. 4?
[2] ἐκ τόθεν Cholmeley from Ap. Rhod. 2. 531 (of time): mss and Schol. ἔμποθεν and ἐν ποθ᾽ ἐν   [3] mss τό, -τα, -τι

IX.—THE THIRD COUNTRY SINGING-MATCH

SING a country-song, Daphnis. Be you the **first** and Menalcas follow when you have let out the calves to run with the cows and the bulls with the barren heifers. As for the cattle, may they feed together and wander together among the leaves and never stray alone, but do you come and sing me your song on this side and Menalcas stand for judgment against you on that.

DAPHNIS (*sings*)

O sweet the cry o' the calf, and sweet the cry o' the
      cow,
And sweet the tune o' the neatherd's pipe, and I
      sing sweet enow ;
      And a greenbed's mine by the cool brook-side
      Piled thick and thick with many a hide
      From the pretty heifers wi' skin so white
      Which the storm found browzing on the height
        And hurled them all below :
      And as much reck I o' the scorching heat
      As a love-struck lad of his father's threat.

So sang me Daphnis, and then Menalcas thus :—

Etna, mother o' mine ! my shelter it is a grot,
A pretty rift in a hollow clift, and for skins to **my**
      bed, God wot,
      Head and foot 'tis goats and sheep
      As many as be in a vision o' sleep,

ἐν πυρὶ δὲ δρυΐνῳ χόρια ζεῖ, ἐν πυρὶ δ' αὖαι
φαγοὶ χειμαίνοντος· ἔχω δέ τοι οὐδ' ὅσον ὥραν
χείματος ἢ νωδὸς καρύων ἀμύλοιο παρόντος.

τοῖς μὲν ἐπεπλατάγησα καὶ αὐτίκα δῶρον ἔδωκα,
Δάφνιδι μὲν κορύναν, τάν μοι πατρὸς ἔτραφεν
    ἀγρός,
αὐτοφυῆ, τὰν δ' οὐδ' ἂν ἴσως μιμάσατο[1] τέκτων,
τήνῳ δὲ στρόμβῳ καλὸν ὄστρακον, ὧ κρέας αὐτὸς
σιτήθην πέτραισιν ἐν Ἰκαρίαισι δοκεύσας
πέντε ταμὼν πέντ' οὖσιν· ὁ δ' ἐγκαναχήσατο
    κόχλῳ.
    βουκολικαὶ Μοῖσαι μάλα χαίρετε, φαίνετε δ'
    ᾠδάν,[2]
τὰν τόκ' ἐγὼ τήνοισι παρὼν ἄεισα νομεῦσι·
μηκέτ' ἐπὶ γλώσσας ἄκρας ὀλοφυγγόνα φύσῃ·[3]

Τέττιξ μὲν τέττιγι φίλος, μύρμακι δὲ μύρμαξ,
ἴρηκες δ' ἴρηξιν, ἐμὶν δ' ἁ Μοῖσα καὶ ᾠδά.
τᾶς μοι πᾶς εἴη πλεῖος δόμος. οὔτε γὰρ ὕπνος
οὔτ' ἔαρ ἐξαπίνας[4] γλυκερώτερον, οὔτε μελίσ-
    σαις
ἄνθεα· τόσσον ἐμὶν Μοῖσαι φίλαι· οὓς γὰρ[5]
    ὁρεῦντι[6]
γαθεῦσαι,[7] τούσδ' οὔ τι ποτῷ δαλήσατο Κίρκα.

---

[1] μιμάσατο Adert : mss μωμάσατο   [2] mss also ᾠδὰς τάς
[3] φύσῃ Wil : mss φύσῃς   [4] Perhaps ἐξάπινον adj., cf. Hipp.
de Aff. 517. 19 (adv.) and ἐξάπινα adv. LXX, N.T., and
Byzant.   [5] mss also οὓς μὲν   [6] Schol. also ὁρῆτε, ὁρῶσαι
[7] γαθεῦσαι Brunck : mss and Schol. γαθεῦσι(ν)

And an oaken fire i' the winter days
With chestnuts roasting at the blaze
  And puddings in the pot:
And as little care I for the wintry sky
As the toothless for nuts when porridge is by.

 Then clapped I the lads both, and then and there
gave them each a gift, Daphnis a club which grew
upon my father's farm and e'en the same as it grew—
albeit an artificer could not make one to match it—,
and Menalcas a passing fine conch, of which the fish
when I took it among the Icarian rocks furnished
five portions for five mouths,—and he blew a blast
upon the shell.
 All hail, good Muses o' the countryside! and the
song I did sing that day before those herdsmen, let
it no longer raise pushes on the tip o' my tongue,
but show it me you:

(the song)
O cricket is to cricket dear, and ant for ant doth
   long,
The hawk's the darling of his fere, and o' me the
   Muse and her song:
  Of songs be my house the home alway,
  For neither sleep, nor a sudden spring-day,
  Nor flowers to the bees, are as sweet as they;
   I love the Muse and her song:
  For any the Muses be glad to see,
  Is proof agen Circè's witcherye.

 "Pushes": pimples on the tongue, the scholiast tells us,
were a sign that one refuses to give up what another has
entrusted to him.

X.—THE REAPERS

THE *characters of this pastoral mime are two reapers,*
Milon, the man of experience, and Bucaeus, called also
Bucus, the lovesick youth. The conversation takes place
in the course of their reaping, and leads to a love-song
from the lover and a reaping-song from his kindly
mentor. When Milon calls his song the song of the
divine Lityerses he is using a generic term. There was
at least one traditional reaping-song which told how
Lityerses, son of Midas, of Celaenae in Phrygia, after
entertaining strangers hospitably, made them reap with
him till evening, when he cut off their heads and hid their
bodies in the sheaves. This apparently gave the name to
all reaping-songs. Milon's song, after a prayer to
Demeter, addresses itself in succession to binders,
threshers, and reapers, and lastly to the steward. Both
songs are supposed to be impromptu, and sung as the
men reap on.

X.—ΕΡΓΑΤΙΝΑΙ Η ΘΕΡΙΣΤΑΙ

ΜΙΛΩΝ

Ἐργατίνα Βουκαῖε, τί νῦν ᾤζυρὲ πεπόνθεις;
οὔτε τὸν ὄγμον ἄγειν ὀρθὸν δύνᾳ, ὡς τὸ πρὶν ᾇγες,
οὔθ᾽ ἅμα λᾳοτομεῖς τῷ πλατίον, ἀλλ᾽ ἀπολείπῃ
ὥσπερ ὄϊς ποίμνας, ᾆς τὸν πόδα κάκτος ἔτυψε.
ποῖός τις δείλαν τὺ καὶ ἐκ μέσω ἅματος ἐσσῇ,
ὃς νῦν ἀρχόμενος τᾶς αὔλακος οὐκ ἀποτρώγεις;

ΒΟΥΚΑΙΟΣ

Μίλων ὀψαμᾶτα, πέτρας ἀπόκομμ᾽ ἀτεράμνω,
οὐδαμά τοι συνέβα ποθέσαι τινὰ τῶν ἀπεόντων;

ΜΙΛΩΝ

οὐδαμά. τίς δὲ πόθος τῶν ἔκτοθεν ἐργάτᾳ ἀνδρί;

ΒΟΥΚΑΙΟΣ

οὐδαμά νυν συνέβα τοι ἀγρυπνῆσαι δι᾽ ἔρωτα;

ΜΙΛΩΝ

μηδέ γε συμβαίη· χαλεπὸν χορίω κύνα γεῦσαι.

ΒΟΥΚΑΙΟΣ

ἀλλ᾽ ἐγὼ ὦ Μίλων ἔραμαι σχεδὸν ἐνδεκαταῖος·

X.—THE REAPERS

MILON

Husbandman Bucaeus, what ails ye now, good drudge? you neither can cut your swath straight as once you did, nor keep time in your reaping with your neighbour. You're left behind by the flock like a ewe with a thorn in her foot. How will it be wi' you when noon is past and day o' the wane, if thus early you make not a clean bite o' your furrow?

BUCAEUS

Good master early-and-late-wi'-sickle, good Sir chip-o'-the-flint, good Milon, hath it never befallen thee to wish for one that is away?

MILON

Never, i' faith; what has a clown like me to do with wishing where there's no getting?

BUCAEUS

Then hath it never befallen thee to lie awake o' nights for love?

MILON

Nay, and God forbid it should. 'Tis ill letting the dog taste pudding.

BUCAEUS

But I've been in love, Milon, the better part of ten days;—

THE BUCOLIC POETS

ΜΙΛΩΝ
ἐκ πίθω ἀντλεῖς δῆλον, ἐγὼ δ᾽ ἔχω οὐδ᾽ ἄλις ὄξος.

ΒΟΥΚΑΙΟΣ
τοιγὰρ τὰ πρὸ θυρᾶν μοι ἀπὸ σπόρω ἄσκαλα
πάντα.

ΜΙΛΩΝ
τίς δέ τυ τᾶν παίδων λυμαίνεται;

ΒΟΥΚΑΙΟΣ
ἁ Πολυβώτα,
ἃ πρᾶν ἀμάντεσσι παρ᾽ Ἱπποκίωνι ποταύλει.

ΜΙΛΩΝ
εὗρε θεὸς τὸν ἀλιτρόν· ἔχεις πάλαι ὧν ἐπεθύμεις.
μάντις τοι τὰν νύκτα χροΐξεῖθ᾽ ἁ καλαμαία.

ΒΟΥΚΑΙΟΣ
μωμᾶσθαί μ᾽ ἄρχῃ τύ· τυφλὸς δ᾽ οὐκ αὐτὸς ὁ
Πλοῦτος,
ἀλλὰ καὶ ὠφρόντιστος Ἔρως. μὴ δὴ μέγα μυθεῦ.

ΜΙΛΩΝ
οὐ μέγα μυθεῦμαι· τὺ μόνον κατάβαλλε τὸ λᾶον,
καί τι κόρας φιλικὸν μέλος ἀμβάλευ. ἅδιον οὕτως
ἐργαξῇ· καὶ μὰν πρότερόν ποκα μουσικὸς ἦσθα.

ΒΟΥΚΑΙΟΣ
Μῶσαι Πιερίδες, συναείσατε τὰν ῥαδινάν μοι
παῖδ᾽· ὧν γάρ χ᾽ ἄψησθε θεαί, καλὰ πάντα ποεῖτε.

132

MILON

Then 'tis manifest thou draw'st thy wine from the hogshead the while I am short of vinegar-water.

BUCAEUS

—And so it is that the land at my very door since was seed-time hath not felt hoe.

MILON

And which o' the lasses is thy undoing?

BUCAEUS

'Tis Polybotas' daughter, she that was at Hippocion's t'other day a-piping to the reapers.

MILON

Lord! thy sin hath found thee out. Thou'dst wished and wished, and now, 'faith, thou'st won. There'll be a locust to clasp thee all night long.

BUCAEUS

Thou bid'st fair to play me fault-finder. But there's blind men in heaven besides Him o' the Money-bags, fool Cupid for one. So prithee talk not so big.

MILON

I talk not big, not I; pray be content, go thou on wi' thy laying o' the field, and strike up a song o' love to thy leman. 'Twill sweeten thy toil. Marry, I know thou wast a singer once.

BUCAEUS (*sings*)

Pierian Muses, join with me a slender lass to sing;
For all ye Ladies take in hand ye make a pretty thing.

"Since was seed-time": a proverbial exaggeration; for he has been in love only ten days, and this is harvest-time.

Βομβύκα χαρίεσσα, Σύραν καλέοντί τυ πάντες,
ἰσχνὰν ἁλιόκαυστον, ἐγὼ δὲ μόνος μελίχλωρον,
καὶ τὸ ἴον μέλαν ἐστὶ καὶ ἁ γραπτὰ ὑάκινθος,
ἀλλ' ἔμπας ἐν τοῖς στεφάνοις τὰ πρᾶτα λέγονται.
ἁ αἲξ τὰν κύτισον, ὁ λύκος τὰν αἶγα διώκει,
ἁ γέρανος τὤροτρον, ἐγὼ δ' ἐπὶ τὶν μεμάνημαι.
αἴθε μοι ἦς, ὅσσα Κροῖσόν ποκα φαντὶ πεπᾶσθαι,
χρύσεοι ἀμφότεροί κ' ἀνεκείμεθα τᾷ 'Αφροδίτᾳ,
τὼς αὐλὼς μὲν ἔχοισα καὶ ἢ ῥόδον ἢ τύγα
    μᾶλον,
σχῆμα δ' ἐγὼ καὶ καινὰς ἐπ' ἀμφοτέροισιν
    ἀμύκλας.
Βομβύκα χαρίεσσ', οἱ μὲν πόδες ἀστράγαλοί τευ
ἁ φωνὰ δὲ τρύχνος· τὸν μὰν τρόπον οὐκ ἔχω
    εἰπεῖν.

ΜΙΛΩΝ

ἦ καλὰς ἄμμε[1] ποῶν ἐλελάθει Βοῦκος ἀοιδάς.
ὡς εὖ τὰν ἰδέαν τᾶς ἁρμονίας ἐμέτρησεν.
ὤμοι τῶ πώγονος, ὃν ἀλιθίως ἀνέφυσα.
θᾶσαι δὴ καὶ ταῦτα τὰ τῶ θείω Λιτυέρσα.

Δάματερ πολύκαρπε πολύσταχυ, τοῦτο τὸ
    λᾷον

<hr>

ἄμμε : mss also ἄμμι

Bombýca fair, to other folk you may a Gipsy be ;
Sunburnt and lean they call you ; you're honey-
     brown to me.
Of flowers the violet's dark, and dark the lettered
     flag-flower tall,
But when there's nosegays making they choose them
     first of all.
Dame Goat pursues the clover, Gray Wolf doth goat
     pursue,
Sir Stork pursues the plough ; and I—O ! I am wild
     for you.
Would all old Croesus had were mine ! O then
     we'ld figured be
In good red gold for offerings rare before the Love-
     Ladye,
You with your pipes, a rose in hand or apple, I bedight
Above with mantle fine, below, new buskins left and
     right.
Bombyca fair, your pretty feet are knucklebones,
     and O !
Your voice is poppy, but your ways—they pass my
     power to show.

MILON

Marry, 'twas no 'prentice hand after all. Mark
how cunningly he shaped his tune! Alackaday,
what a dolt was I to get me a beard ! But come
hear this of the divine Lityerses :   *(sings)*
Demeter, Queen of fruit and ear, bless O bless our
     field ;

"Gipsy": the Greek is 'Syrian.'   "Knucklebones":
Bombýca pipes, dances, and sings by profession (cf. ll. 16
and 34) ; she flings her feet about as a player tosses the
knucklebones, lightly and easily, and her singing soothes the
listener like a narcotic.   "What a dolt was I": 'what a
thing it is to be young !'

εὔεργόν τ' εἴη καὶ κάρπιμον ὅττι μάλιστα.

σφίγγετ' ἀμαλλοδέται τὰ δράγματα, μὴ παριών
τις

εἴπῃ· ' σύκινοι ὦνδρες·[1] ἀπώλετο χοῦτος ὁ μισθός.'
ἐς βορέαν ἄνεμον τᾶς κόρθυος ἀ τομὰ ὔμμιν
καὶ ζέφυρον[2] βλεπέτω· πιαίνεται ὁ στάχυς οὕτως.
σῖτον ἀλοιῶντας φεύγειν τὸ μεσαμβρινὸν ὕπνον·
ἐκ καλάμας ἄχυρον τελέθει τημόσδε μάλιστα.
ἄρχεσθαι δ' ἀμῶντας ἐγειρομένω κορυδαλλῶ,
καὶ λήγειν εὔδοντος, ἐλινῦσαι δὲ τὸ καῦμα.
εὐκτὸς ὁ τῶ βατράχω, παῖδες, βίος· οὐ μελεδαίνει
τὸν τὸ πιεῖν ἐγχεῦντα· πάρεστι γὰρ ἄφθονον
αὐτῷ.[3]
καλλίον'[4] ὦ 'πιμελητὰ φιλάργυρε τὸν φακὸν
ἕψειν·
μὴ 'πιτάμῃς τὰν χεῖρα καταπρίων τὸ κύμινον.

ταῦτα χρὴ μοχθεῦντας ἐν ἁλίῳ ἄνδρας ἀείδειν,
τὸν δὲ τεὸν Βουκαῖε πρέπει λιμηρὸν ἔρωτα
μυθίσδεν τᾷ ματρὶ κατ' εὐνὰν ὀρθρευοίσᾳ.

---

[1] εἴπῃ Brunck : mss εἴποι   ἄνδρες E : mss ἄνδρες   [2] καὶ
E ; ἐς βορέαν καὶ ζέφυρον means " North-west," cf. Schol. Pind.
P. 10. ἅ ἐστι πρὸς ἀνατολὴν καὶ μεσημβρίαν = South-east : mss
ἢ ζέφυρον   [3] cf. Pherecr. ap. Athen. 10. 430 and Zenob.
2. 78   [4] καλλίον' E, cf. 11. 44 : mss κάλλιον

Grant our increase greatest be that toil therein may
    yield.
Grip tight your sheaves, good Binders all, or passers-
    by will say
' These be men of elder-wood; more wages thrown
    away.'
'Twixt Northwind and Westwind let straws endlong
    be laid;
The breeze runs up the hollow and the ear is plumper
    made.
For Threshers, lads, the noontide nap's a nap beside
    the law,
For noontide's the best tide for making chaff of
    straw;
But Reapers they are up wi' the lark, and with the
    lark to bed;
To rest the heat o' the day, stands Reapers in good
    stead.
And 'tis O to be a frog, my lads, and live aloof from
    care!
He needs no drawer to his drink; 'tis plenty every-
    where.
Fie, fie, Sir Steward! better beans, an't please ye,
    another day;
Thou'lt cut thy finger, niggard, a-splitting caraway.

    That's the sort o' song for such as work i' the sun;
but that starveling love-ditty o' thine, Bucaeus,
would make brave telling to thy mammy abed of a
morning.

" Elder-wood ": the Greek has " figwood," which was
useless; cf. Shaks. *Merry Wives* 2.3.30 ' My heart of elder.'
" 'Tis O to be a frog ": the steward is stingy with the drink
as with the lentils.

XI.—THE CYCLOPS

THEOCRITUS *offers a* consolatio amoris *to his friend
the poet-physician Nicias of Miletus,*[1] *with whom he
studied under the physician Erasistratus. After a brief
introduction by way of stage-direction, he tells him the
song the Cyclops sang to his love the sea-nymph.
Metrical and grammatical considerations make it prob-
able that the poem was an early one; it may well be
anterior to* The Distaff. *There is 'tragic irony' in the
Cyclops' reference to his eye when speaking of singeing
his beard, and also in his mention of the possible advent
of a stranger from overseas.*

[1] For another interpretation see the Introduction.

XI.—ΚΥΚΛΩΨ

Οὐδὲν ποττὸν ἔρωτα πεφύκει φάρμακον ἄλλο,
Νικία, οὔτ' ἔγχριστον, ἐμὶν δοκεῖ, οὔτ' ἐπίπαστον,
ἢ ταὶ Πιερίδες· κοῦφον δέ τι τοῦτο καὶ ἁδὺ
γίνετ' ἐπ' ἀνθρώποις, εὑρεῖν δ' οὐ ῥᾴδιόν ἐστι.
γινώσκειν δ' οἶμαί τυ καλῶς ἰατρὸν ἐόντα
καὶ ταῖς ἐννέα δὴ πεφιλημένον ἔξοχα Μοίσαις.
οὕτω γοῦν ῥάιστα διᾶγ' ὁ Κύκλωψ ὁ παρ' ἁμῖν,
ὡρχαῖος Πολύφαμος, ὅκ' ἤρατο τᾶς Γαλατείας,
ἄρτι γενειάσδων περὶ τὸ στόμα τὼς κροτάφως τε.
ἤρατο δ' οὐ μάλοις οὐδὲ ῥόδῳ οὐδὲ κικίννοις,
ἀλλ' ὀρθαῖς μανίαις, ἁγεῖτο δὲ πάντα πάρεργα.
πολλάκι ταὶ ὄιες ποτὶ τωὔλιον αὐταὶ ἀπῆνθον
χλωρᾶς ἐκ βοτάνας· ὁ δὲ τὰν Γαλάτειαν ἀείδων
αὐτὸς ἐπ' ἀϊόνος κατετάκετο φυκιοέσσας
ἐξ ἀοῦς, ἔχθιστον ἔχων ὑποκάρδιον ἕλκος,
Κύπριδος ἐκ μεγάλας τό οἱ ἥπατι πᾶξε βέλεμνον.
ἀλλὰ τὸ φάρμακον εὗρε, καθεζόμενος δ' ἐπὶ
    πέτρας
ὑψηλᾶς ἐς πόντον ὁρῶν ἄειδε τοιαῦτα·

'Ω λευκὰ Γαλάτεια, τί τὸν φιλέοντ' ἀποβάλλῃ,
λευκοτέρα πακτᾶς ποτιδεῖν, ἀπαλωτέρα ἀρνός,
μόσχω γαυροτέρα, φιαρωτέρα[1] ὄμφακος ὠμᾶς;

---

[1] Mss φιαρωτέρα: Schol. also σφιγγανεωτέρα (i.e. σφριγανω-
τέρα)

XI.—THE CYCLOPS

It seems there's no medicine for love, Nicias, neither salve nor plaster, but only the Pierian Maids. And a gentle medicine it is and sweet for to use upon the world, but very hard to find, as indeed one like you must know, being both physician and well-belov'd likewise of the Nine. 'Twas this, at least, gave best comfort to my countryman the Cyclops, old Polyphemus, when he was first showing beard upon cheek and chin and Galatea was his love. His love was no matter of apples, neither, nor of rose-buds nor locks of hair, but a flat frenzy which recked nought of all else. Time and again his sheep would leave the fresh green pasturage and come back unbidden to fold, while their master must peak and pine alone upon the wrack-strown shore a-singing all the day long of Galatea, sick at heart of the spite-ful wound the shaft of the great Cyprian had dealt him. Nevertheless he found the medicine for it, and sitting him down upon an upstanding rock looked seawards and sang :

O Galatea fair and white, white as curds in whey,
Dapper as lamb a-frisking, wanton as calf at play,
And plump o' shape as ruddying grape, O why deny
   thy lover?

φοιτῆς δαῦθ᾽ [1] οὕτως, ὅκκα γλυκὺς ὕπνος ἔχῃ με,
οἴχῃ δ᾽ εὐθὺς ἰοῖσ᾽, ὅκκα γλυκὺς ὕπνος ἀνῇ με,
φεύγεις δ᾽ ὥσπερ ὄϊς πολιὸν λύκον ἀθρήσασα.
ἠράσθην μὲν ἔγωγα τεοῦς κόρα, ἁνίκα πρᾶτον
ἦνθες ἐμᾷ σὺν ματρὶ θέλοισ᾽ ὑακίνθινα φύλλα
ἐξ ὄρεος δρέψασθαι, ἐγὼ δ᾽ ὁδὸν ἁγεμόνευον.
παύσασθαι δ᾽ ἐσιδών τυ καὶ ὕστερον οὐδ᾽ ἔτι
    πα νῦν
ἐκ τήνω δύναμαι· τὶν δ᾽ οὐ μέλει, οὐ μὰ Δί᾽
    οὐδέν.
    γινώσκω χαρίεσσα κόρα, τίνος ὤνεκα φεύγεις·
ὤνεκά μοι λασία μὲν ὀφρὺς ἐπὶ παντὶ μετώπῳ
ἐξ ὠτὸς τέταται ποτὶ θὤτερον ὡς μία μακρά,
εἷς δ᾽ ὀφθαλμὸς ὕπεστι,[2] πλατεῖα δὲ ῥὶς ἐπὶ
    χείλει.
ἀλλ᾽ οὗτος τοιοῦτος ἐὼν βοτὰ χίλια βόσκω,
κἠκ τούτων τὸ κράτιστον ἀμελγόμενος γάλα
    πίνω·
τυρὸς δ᾽ οὐ λείπει μ᾽ οὔτ᾽ ἐν θέρει οὔτ᾽ ἐν ὀπώρᾳ,
οὐ χειμῶνος ἄκρω· ταρσοὶ δ᾽ ὑπεραχθέες αἰεί.
συρίσδεν δ᾽ ὡς οὔτις ἐπίσταμαι ὧδε Κυκλώπων,
τίν τε φίλον γλυκύμαλον ἁμᾷ κἠμαυτὸν ἀείδω [3]
πολλάκι νυκτὸς ἀωρί. τρέφω δέ τοι ἔνδεκα
    νεβρώς
πάσας μαννοφόρως [4] καὶ σκύμνως τέσσαρας
    ἄρκτων.

3

4

---

[1] δαῦθ᾽ (or δεῦθ᾽?) = δὴ αὖτε (δηῦτε) : mss δ᾽αῦθ᾽   [2] ὕπεστι Winsem: mss ἔπεστι   [3] τε and ἀείδω E; he could not play and sing at the same time : mss τό and ἀείδων   [4] μαννοφόρως Schol. v. 1: mss ἀμνοφόρως

O soon enow thou'rt here, I trow, when sweet sleep
    comes me over,
But up and gone when sleeping's done—O never
    flees so fast
Ewe that doth spy gray wolf anigh, as thou when
    slumber's past.
My love of thee began, sweeting, when thou—I
    mind it well—
Wast come a-pulling luces wi' my mother on the fell;
I showed ye where to look for them, and from that
    hour to this
I've loved ye true; but Lord! to you my love as
    nothing is.
  O well I wot pretty maid, pretty maid, for why
    thou shun'st me so,
One long shag eyebrow ear to ear my forehead o'er
    doth go,
And but one eye beneath doth lie, and the nose
    stands wide on the lip;
Yet be as I may, still this I say, I feed full a
    thousand sheep,
And the milk to my hand's the best i' the land, and
    my cheese 'tis plenty alsó;
Come summer mild, come winter wild, my cheese-
    racks ever o'erflow.
And, for piping, none o' my kin hereby can pipe
    like my piping,
And of thee and me, dear sweet-apple, in one song
    oft I sing,
Often at dead of night. And O, there's gifts in store
    for thee,
Eleven fawns, all white-collárs, and cosset bear's cubs
    four for thee.

ἀλλ' ἀφίκευσο ποθ' ἁμέ, καὶ ἑξεῖς οὐδὲν ἔλασσον,
τὰν γλαυκὰν δὲ θάλασσαν ἔα ποτὶ χέρσον ὀρεχ-
    θεῖν.
ἁδίον'[1] ἐν τὤντρῳ παρ' ἐμὶν τὰν νύκτα διαξεῖς·
ἐντὶ δάφναι τηνεῖ, ἐντὶ ῥαδιναὶ κυπάρισσοι,
ἔστι μέλας κισσός, ἔστ' ἄμπελος ἁ γλυκύκαρ-
    πος,
ἔστι ψυχρὸν ὕδωρ, τό μοι ἁ πολυδένδρεος Αἴτνα
λευκᾶς ἐκ χιόνος ποτὸν ἀμβρόσιον προΐητι.
τίς κα τῶνδε θάλασσαν ἔχειν καὶ κύμαθ'[2] ἕλοιτο;
   αἰ δέ τοι αὐτὸς ἐγὼν δοκέω λασιώτερος ἦμεν, 5
ἐντὶ δρυὸς ξύλα μοι καὶ ὑπὸ σποδῷ ἀκάματον
    πῦρ·
καιομενος δ' ὑπὸ τεῦς καὶ τὰν ψυχὰν ἀνεχοίμαν
καὶ τὸν ἕν' ὀφθαλμόν, τῷ μοι γλυκερώτερον
    οὐδέν.
ὤμοι, ὅτ' οὐκ ἔτεκέν μ' ἁ μάτηρ βράγχι' ἔχοντα,
ὡς κατέδυν ποτὶ τὶν καὶ τὰν χέρα τεῦς ἐφί-
    λησα,
αἰ μὴ τὸ στόμα λῇς, ἔφερον δέ τοι ἢ κρίνα
    λευκά
ἢ μάκων' ἁπαλὰν ἐρυθρὰ πλαταγώνι' ἔχοισαν. 5
νῦν μὰν ὦ κόριον, νῦν αὖ τό γα νεῖν μασεῦμαι,[3] 6
εἴ κα τίς σὺν ναὶ πλέων ξένος ὧδ' ἀφίκηται,
ὡς εἰδῶ, τί πόχ' ἁδὺ κατοικεῖν τὸν βυθὸν ὕμμιν.

---

[1] ἁδίον' E. cf. 10. 54: mss ἅδιον   [2] καὶ κύμαθ' Ahrens
from Schol.: mss ἢ κύμ.   [3] αὖ τό γα νεῖν μασεῦμαι (i.e.
μαθήσομαι, which occurs in the Scholiast's paraphrase) Ahr:
mss αὐτό γα νεῖν μεμαθεῦμαι (γε μαθεῦμαι)

    58 ἀλλὰ τὰ μὲν θέρεος, τὰ δὲ γίνεται ἐν χειμῶνι,
    ὥστ' οὐκ ἄν τοι ταῦτα φέρειν ἅμα πάντ' ἐδυνάθην.
The reasons for rejecting these lines against the mss are too
long to be given here. See *Class. Rev.* 1912, p. 246.

O leave it be, the blue blue sea, to gasp an 't will
    o' the shore,
And come ye away to me, to me ; I'll lay ye'll find
    no ill store.
A sweeter night thou'lt pass i' the cave with me
    than away i' the brine ;
There's laurel and taper cypress, swart ivy and sweet-
    fruit vine,
And for thy drinking the cool watér woody Etna
    pours so free
For my delight from his snow so white, and a
    heav'nly draught it be.
Now who would choose the sea and his waves, and a
    home like this forgo ?
  But if so be the master o' t too shag to thy deem-
    ing show,
There's wood in store, and on the floor a fire that
    smoulders still,
And if thou would'st be burning, mayst burn my
    soul an thou will,
Yea, and the dear'st of all my goods, my one dear
    eye. O me !
That I was not born with fins to be diving down to
    thee,
To kiss, if not thy lips, at least thy hand, and give
    thee posies
Of poppies trim with scarlet rim or snow-white
    winter-roses !
And if a stranger a-shipboard come, e'en now, my
    little sweeting,
E'en now to swim I'll learn of him, and then shall I
    be weeting
Wherefore it be ye folk o' the sea are so lief to be
    living below.

ἐξένθοις, Γαλάτεια, καὶ ἐξενθοῖσα λάθοιο
ὥσπερ ἐγὼν νῦν ὧδε καθήμενος οἴκαδ' ἀπενθεῖν,
ποιμαίνειν δ' ἐθέλοις σὺν ἐμὶν ἅμα καὶ γάλ' ἀμέλγειν
καὶ τυρὸν πᾶξαι τάμισον δριμεῖαν ἐνεῖσα.
ἁ μάτηρ ἀδικεῖ με μόνα, καὶ μέμφομαι αὐτᾷ·
οὐδὲν πήποχ' ὅλως ποτὶ τὶν φίλον εἶπεν ὑπέρ
    μευ,
καὶ ταῦτ' ἆμαρ ἐπ' ἆμαρ ὁρεῦσά με λεπτύνοντα.[1]
φασῶ[2] τὰν κεφαλὰν καὶ τὼς πόδας ἀμφοτέρως
    μευ
σφύζειν, ὡς ἀνιαθῇ, ἐπεὶ κἠγὼν ἀνιῶμαι.

  ὦ Κύκλωψ Κύκλωψ, πᾷ τὰς φρένας ἐκπεπό-
    τασαι;
αἰκ[3] ἐνθὼν ταλάρως τε πλέκοις καὶ θαλλὸν
    ἀμάσας
ταῖς ἄρνεσσι φέροις, τάχα κα πολὺ μᾶλλον ἔχοις
    νῶν.
τὰν παρεοῖσαν ἄμελγε· τί τὸν φεύγοντα διώκεις;
εὑρησεῖς Γαλάτειαν ἴσως καὶ καλλίον' ἄλλαν.
πολλαὶ συμπαίσδεν με κόραι τὰν νύκτα κέλονται,
κιχλίζοντι δὲ πᾶσαι, ἐπεί κ' αὐταῖς ὑπακούσω.
δῆλον ὅτ' ἐν τᾷ γᾷ κἠγών τις φαίνομαι ἦμεν.

  οὕτω τοι Πολύφαμος ἐποίμαινεν τὸν ἔρωτα
μουσίσδων, ῥᾷον δε διᾶγ' ἢ εἰ χρυσὸν ἔδωκεν.

---

[1] λεπτύνοντα Meineke : mss λεπτὸν ἐόντα   [2] Mss φασῶ or
φλασῶ, Schol. φασῶ   [3] αἰκ (i.e. αἰ, cf. οὐ οὐκ) Wil, cf
Epicharmus and Oracle in Hdt. i. 174 : mss αἴκ'

Come forth and away, my pretty fay, and when
    thou comest, O
Forget, as he that sitteth here, thy ways again to go;
Feed flock wi' me, draw milk wi' me, and if 't my
    darling please,
Pour rennet tart the curds to part and set the good
    white cheese.
'Tis all my mother's doing ; she sore to blame hath
    bin ;
Never good word hath spoke you o' me, though she
    sees me waxing so thin.
I'll tell her of throbbing feet, I'll tell her of aching
    eyne ;
I am fain that misery be hers sith misery be mine.

O Cyclops, Cyclops, where be your wits gone flying ?
Up, fetch you loppings for your lambs, or go a withy-
    plying ;
The wearier's oft the wiser man, and that there's no
    denying.
Milk the staying, leave the straying, chase not them
    that shy ;
Mayhap you'll find e'en sweeter Galateas by and by.
There's many a jill says ' Come an you will and play
    all night wi' me,'
And the laugh I hear when I give ear is soft and
    sweet as can be ;
E'en I, 'tis plain, be somebody, ashore, if not i' the sea.

Thus did Polyphemus tend his love-sickness with
music, and got more comfort thereout than he
could have had for any gold.

"Throbbing feet": headache **and** footache—the latter
from waiting on the beloved's threshold—were conventional
signs of being in love.

XII.—THE BELOVED

THE *Greeks sometimes exalted friendship to a passion,
and such a friendship doubtless inspired this fine poem.
Theocritus acknowledges his indebtedness to the Ionian
lyrists and elegists by using their dialect. The passage
rendered here in verse contains what at first sight looks
like a mere display of learning, but has simply this
intention : ' Our love will be famous among so remote a
posterity that the very words for it will be matter for
learned comment.'*

XII.—ΑΙΤΗΣ

Ἤλυθες ὦ φίλε κοῦρε· τρίτῃ σὺν νυκτὶ καὶ ἠοῖ
ἤλυθες[1]· οἱ δὲ ποθεῦντες ἐν ἤματι γηράσκουσιν.
ὅσσον ἔαρ χειμῶνος, ὅσον μῆλον βραβίλοιο
ἥδιον, ὅσσον ὄϊς σφετέρης λασιωτέρη ἀρνός,
ὅσσον παρθενικὴ προφέρει τριγάμοιο γυναικός,
ὅσσον ἐλαφροτέρη μόσχου νεβρός, ὅσσον ἀηδών
συμπάντων λιγύφωνος ἀοιδοτάτη πετεηνῶν,
τόσσον ἔμ' εὔφρηνας σὺ φανείς, σκιερὴν δ' ὑπὸ
    φηγὸν
ἠελίου φρύγοντος ὁδοιπόρος ἔδραμον ὥς τις.
εἴθ' ὁμαλοὶ πνεύσειαν ἐπ' ἀμφοτέροιϊν[2] Ἔρωτες
νῶϊν, ἐπεσσομένοις δὲ γενοίμεθα πᾶσιν ἀοιδή·

'δίω[3] δή τινε τώδε μετὰ προτέροισι[4] γενέσθην
φῶθ', ὁ μὲν εἴσπνηλος, φαίη χ' Ὠμυκλαϊάζων,
τὸν δ' ἕτερον[5] πάλιν, ὡς κεν ὁ Θεσσαλὸς εἴποι,
    ἀΐτην.
ἀλλήλους δ' ἐφίλησαν ἴσῳ ζυγῷ. ἦρα τότ' ἦσαν
χρύσειοι πάλιν ἄνδρες, ὅτ' ἀντεφίλησ' ὁ φιλη-
    θείς.'

[1] For punctuation cf. Sappho 89 (Julian *Epist.* 59 p. 379 Hercher)　[2] ἀμφοτέροιϊν E: mss -οισιν　[3] δίω Ahrens: mss and schol. δοίω　[4] so Taylor from schol., and *P. Ant.*: mss μετ' ἀμφοτέροισι　[5] τὸν ἕτερον attracted for ὁ ἕτερος

XII.—THE BELOVED

THOU'RT come, dear heart; thou'rt come after two days and nights, albeit one will turn a lover gray. As spring is sweeter than winter, and pippin than damson-plum; as mother-ewe is shaggier than her lambkin, and maiden more to be desired than a thrice-wed wife; as the fawn is nimbler-footed than the calf, and the nightingale clearest-tongued of all the wingèd songsters; so am I gladded above all at the sight of thee, and run to thee as a wayfarer runneth to the shady oak when the sun is burning hot. And 'tis O that equal Loves might inspire thee and me, and we become this song and saying unto all them that follow after :—

> *Here were two men of might*
> *The antique years among,*
> *The one* Inspirant *hight*
> *I' th' Amyclaean tongue,*
> *The t'other* Fere *would be*
> *In speech of Thessalye ;*
> *Each lov'd each, even-peise :*
> *O other golden days,*
> *Whenas love-I love-you*
> *All men did hold for true !*

εἰ γὰρ τοῦτο, πάτερ Κρονίδη, πέλοι, εἰ γάρ, ἀγήρῳ
ἀθάνατοι, γενεῆς δὲ διηκοσίῃσιν ἔπειτα
ἀγγείλειεν ἐμοί τις ἀνέξοδον εἰς Ἀχέροντα·
'ἡ σὴ νῦν φιλότης καὶ τοῦ χαρίεντος ἀΐτεω   20
πᾶσι διὰ στόματος, μετὰ δ' ἠϊθέοισι μάλιστα.'
ἀλλ' ἤτοι τούτων μὲν ὑπέρτεροι Οὐρανίωνες·
ἔσσονθ'[1] ὡς ἐθέλουσιν· ἐγὼ δέ σε τὸν καλὸν αἰνέων
ψεύδεα ῥινὸς ὕπερθεν ἀραιῆς οὐκ ἀναφύσω.
ἢν γὰρ καί τι δάκῃς τὸ μὲν ἀβλαβὲς εὐθὺς
          ἔθηκας,
διπλάσιον δ' ὤνησας, ἔχων δ' ἐπίμετρον ἀπῆλθον.

Νισαῖοι Μεγαρῆες ἀριστεύοντες ἐρετμοῖς,
ὄλβιοι οἰκείοιτε, τὸν Ἀττικὸν ὡς περίαλλα
ξεῖνον ἐτιμήσασθε Διοκλέα τὸν φιλόπαιδα.
αἰεί οἱ περὶ τύμβον ἀολλέες εἴαρι πρώτῳ   30
κοῦροι ἐριδμαίνουσι φιλήματος ἄκρα φέρεσθαι.
ὃς δέ κε προσμάξῃ γλυκερώτατα[2] χείλεσι χείλη,
βριθόμενος στεφάνοισιν ἑὴν ἐς μητέρ' ἀπῆλθεν.
ὄλβιος, ὅστις παισὶ φιλήματα κεῖνα διαιτᾷ·
ἦ που τὸν χαροπὸν Γανυμήδεα πόλλ' ἐπιβῶται
Λυδίῃ ἴσον ἔχειν πέτρῃ στόμα, χρυσὸν ὁποίη
πεύθονται μὴ φαῦλος ἐτήτυμον ἀργυραμοιβοί.

<hr/>

[1] ἔσσονθ' E, cf. ἐσσαμένων Thuc., ἔσσατο Pind. *Fr. Oxyrh.*
3. 408, ἔσσαντο Euphorion 99 : mss ἔσσονθ'   [2] γλυκερώτατα
E, cf. 15. 139 : mss -τερα

O would to thee, Father Zeus, and to you, unaging Host of Heaven, that when a hundred hundred years shall be passed away, one bring me word upon the prisoning bank of Acheron our love is yet upon every lip, upon the young men's most of all! Be that or no the People of Heaven shall stablish as they will; for theirs is the dominion; now, when I sing thy praises, there shall no push-o'-leasing rise upon the tip of this tongue; for if e'er thou giv'st me torment, thou healest the wound out of hand, and I am better off than before, seeing I come away with over-measure.

Heaven rest you glad, Nisaean masters o' the oar, for that you have done such exceeding honour unto an Attic stranger—to wit Diocles (who so loved his boys); about whose grave, so surely as Spring cometh round, your children vie in a kissing-match, and whosoever presseth lip sweetliest upon lip, cometh away to's mother loaden with garlands. Happy the justicer holdeth that court of kissing! God wot he prays beamy Ganymed, and prays indeed, to make his lips like the touchstones which show the money-changer whether the gold be gold or dross.

"Push-o'-leasing": in the Greek the tell-tale pimples, themselves called 'lies,' rise, not upon the tongue, but upon the tip of the nose. "Diocles": an Athenian who, while living in exile at Megara, died in battle to save the youth he loved.

XIII.—HYLAS

THEOCRITUS *tells his friend Nicias in epic shape the tale of the Apotheosis of Hylas, the beloved of Heracles. If, as is probable, the words 'as* we *seem to think' are a delicate way of saying 'as* you *seem to think,' the poem may well be an answer to a friendly rebuke of the author of XII, XXIX, and XXX.*

XIII.—ΥΛΑΣ

Οὐχ ἁμῖν τὸν Ἔρωτα μόνοις ἔτεχ᾽, ὡς ἐδο-
    κεῦμες[1],
Νικία, ᾧτινι τοῦτο θεῶν ποκα τέκνον ἔγεντο·
οὐχ ἁμῖν τὰ καλὰ πράτοις καλὰ φαίνεται ἦμεν,
οἳ θνατοὶ πελόμεσθα τὸ δ᾽ αὔριον οὐκ ἐσορῶμες·
ἀλλὰ καὶ Ἀμφιτρύωνος ὁ χαλκεοκάρδιος υἱός,
ὃς τὸν λῖν ὑπέμεινε τὸν ἄγριον, ἤρατο παιδός,
τοῦ χαρίεντος Ὕλα, τοῦ τὰν πλοκαμῖδα φορεῦντος,
καί νιν πάντ᾽ ἐδίδαξε πατὴρ ὡσεὶ φίλον υἱέα,
ὅσσα μαθὼν ἀγαθὸς καὶ ἀοίδιμος αὐτὸς ἔγεντο·
χωρὶς δ᾽ οὐδέποκ᾽ ἦς, οὐδ᾽ εἰ μέσον ἆμαρ ἄροιτο[2],
οὐδ᾽ ἄρ᾽ ὅχ᾽ ἁ λεύκιππος ἀνατρέχοι[3] ἐς Διὸς Ἀώς,
οὐδ᾽ ὁπόκ᾽ ὀρτάλιχοι μινυροὶ ποτὶ κοῖτον ὁροιεν[4]
σεισαμένας πτερὰ ματρὸς ἐπ᾽ αἰθαλόεντι πετεύρῳ,
ὡς αὐτῷ κατὰ θυμὸν ὁ παῖς πεπονᾱμένος εἴη,
αὐτῷ[5] δ᾽ εὖ ἕλκων ἐς ἀλαθινὸν ἄνδρ᾽ ἀποβαίη.

ἀλλ᾽ ὅτε τὸ χρύσειον ἔπλει μετὰ κῶας Ἰάσων
Αἰσονίδας, οἱ δ᾽ αὐτῷ ἀριστῆες συνέποντο
πασᾶν ἐκ πολίων προλελεγμένοι, ὧν ὄφελός τι,

---

[1] ὡς ἐδοκεῦμες, like ἦν ἄρα, 'as it seems we think,' cf. ὡς
δοκεῖ 11. 2, ἄρα i. 66 and 18. 1, νυ Bion 2. 1 and ergo or igitur
Propert. 4. 6, i. 8, 3. 5, Ovid *Trist.* 3. 2, 3. 9, *Am.* 2. 7;
and for the first person cf. Pindar *P.* 3. 107   [2] ἄροιτο E,
cf. 1. 12: mss ὅροιτο   [3] Ahrens-Schaefer: mss οὐδ᾽ ὅκχ᾽
and -χει   [4] ὁροιεν E, cf. Hes. *Scut.* 437: mss ὀρφεν
[5] αὐτῷ = αὐτόθεν, so schol.

XIII.—HYLAS

FROM what God soever sprung, Nicias, Love was not, as we seem to think, born for us alone ; nor first unto us of mortal flesh that cannot see the morrow, look things of beauty beautiful. For Amphitryon's brazen-heart son that braved the roaring lion, he too once loved a lad, to wit the beauteous Hylas of the curly locks, and, even as father his son, had taught him all the lore that made himself a good man and brought him fame ; and would never leave him, neither if Day had risen to the noon, nor when Dawn's white steeds first galloped up into the home of Zeus, nor yet when the twittering chickens went scurrying at the flapping of their mother's wings to their bed upon the smoky hen-roost. This did he that he might have the lad fashioned to his mind, and that pulling a straight furrow from the outset the same might come to be a true man.

Now when Jason son of Aeson was to go to fetch the Golden Fleece with his following of champions that were chosen of the best out of all the cities in

ἵκετο χὢ ταλαεργὸς ἀνὴρ ἐς ἀφνειὸν Ἰωλκόν,
Ἀλκμήνας υἱὸς Μιδεάτιδος ἡρωίνας,
σὺν δ᾽ αὐτῷ κατέβαινεν Ὕλας εὔεδρον ἐς Ἀργώ,
ἅτις κυανεᾶν οὐχ ἅψατο Συνδρομάδων ναῦς,
ἀλλὰ διεξάιξε, βαθὺν δ᾽ εἰσέδραμε Φᾶσιν
αἰετὸς ὣς μέγα λαῖτμα· ἀφ᾽ οὗ τόθι¹ χοιράδες ἔσταν.

  ἆμος δ᾽ ἀντέλλοντι Πελειάδες, ἐσχατιαὶ δὲ
ἄρνα νέον βόσκοντι, τετραμμένου εἴαρος ἤδη,
τᾶμος ναυτιλίας μιμνάσκετο θεῖος ἄωτος
ἡρώων, κοίλαν δὲ καθιδρυθέντες ἐς Ἀργὼ
Ἑλλάσποντον ἵκοντο νότῳ τρίτον ἆμαρ ἀέντι,
εἴσω δ᾽ ὅρμον ἔθεντο Προποντίδος, ἔνθα Κιανῶν
αὔλακας εὐρύνοντι βόες τρίβοντες ἄροτρα.
ἐκβάντες δ᾽ ἐπὶ θῖνα κατὰ ζυγὰ δαῖτα πένοντο
δειελινάν, πολλοὶ δὲ μίαν στορέσαντο χαμεύναν·
λειμὼν γάρ σφιν ἔκειτο, μέγα στιβάδεσσιν ὄνειαρ,
ἔνθεν βούτομον ὀξὺ βαθύν τ᾽ ἐτάμοντο κύπειρον.

  κὤχεθ᾽ Ὕλας ὁ ξανθὸς ὕδωρ ἐπιδόρπιον οἴσων
αὐτῷ θ᾽ Ἡρακλῆι καὶ ἀστεμφεῖ Τελαμῶνι,
οἳ μίαν ἄμφω ἑταῖροι ἀεὶ δαίνυντο τράπεζαν,
χάλκεον ἄγγος ἔχων. τάχα δὲ κράναν ἐνόησεν
ἡμένῳ ἐν χώρῳ· περὶ δὲ θρύα πολλὰ πεφύκει,
κυάνεόν τε χελιδόνιον χλωρόν τ᾽ ἀδίαντον
καὶ θάλλοντα σέλινα καὶ εἰλιτενὴς ἄγρωστις.
ὕδατι δ᾽ ἐν μέσσῳ Νύμφαι χορὸν ἀρτίζοντο,
Νύμφαι ἀκοίμητοι, δειναὶ θεαὶ ἀγροιώταις,

¹ τόθι "there," E: mss τότε; Knox ἀπ᾽ οὖν τότε

158

the land, then came there with them to the rich Iolcus
the great man of toil who was son of the high-born
Alcmena of Midea, and went down with Hylas at his
side to that good ship Argo, even to her that
speeding ungrazed clean through the blue Clappers,
ran into Phasis bay as an eagle into a great gulf,
whereafter those Clappers have stood still, reefs ever-
more.

And at the rising of the Pleiads, what time of
the waning spring the young lambs find pasture
in the uplands, then it was that that divine
flower of hero-folk was minded of its voyaging, and
taking seat in the Argo's hull came after two
days' blowing of the Southwind to the Hellespont,
and made haven within Propontis at the spot where
furrow is broadened and share brightened by the
oxen of the Cianians. Being gone forth upon the
strand, as for their supper they were making it
ready thwart by thwart; but one couch was strown
them for all, for they found to their hand a meadow
that furnished good store of litter, and thence did
cut them taper rushes and tall bedstraw.

Meanwhile the golden-haired Hylas was gone to
bring water against supper for his own Heracles and
for the valiant Telamon—for they two did ever eat
together at a common board—gone with a brazen ewer.
Ere long he espied a spring; in a hollow it lay,
whereabout there grew many herbs, as well blue
swallow-wort and fresh green maidenhair as blooming
parsley and tangling deergrass. Now in the midst
of the water there was a dance of the Nymphs afoot,
of those Nymphs who, like the water, take no rest,
those Nymphs who are the dread Goddesses of the

Εὐνίκα καὶ Μαλὶς ἔαρ θ' ὁρόωσα Νύχεια.
ἤτοι ὁ κοῦρος ἐπεῖχε ποτῷ πολυχανδέα κρωσσὸν
βάψαι ἐπειγόμενος· ταὶ δ' ἐν χερὶ πᾶσαι ἔφυσαν
πασάων γὰρ ἔρως ἁπαλὰς φρένας ἐξεσόβησεν[1]
Ἀργείῳ ἐπὶ παιδί. κατήριπε δ' ἐς μέλαν ὕδωρ
ἀθρόος, ὡς ὅτε πυρσὸς ἀπ' οὐρανοῦ ἤριπεν ἀστὴρ   5
ἀθρόος ἐν πόντῳ, ναύταις δέ τις εἶπεν ἑταίροις
'κουφότερ' ὦ παῖδες ποιεῖσθ' ὅπλα· πλευστικὸς
          οὖρος[2].'
Νύμφαι μὲν σφετέροις ἐπὶ γούνασι κοῦρον ἔχοισαι
δακρυόεντ' ἀγανοῖσι παρεψύχοντ' ἐπέεσσιν.

Ἀμφιτρυωνιάδας δὲ ταρασσόμενος περὶ παιδὶ
ᾤχετο, Μαιωτιστὶ λαβὼν εὐκαμπέα τόξα
καὶ ῥόπαλον, τό οἱ αἰὲν ἐχάνδανε δεξιτερὰ χείρ.
τρὶς μὲν Ὕλαν ἄυσεν, ὅσον βαθὺς ἤρυγε λαιμός·
τρὶς δ' ἄρ' ὁ παῖς ὑπάκουσεν, ἀραιὰ δ' ἵκετο φωνὰ
ἐξ ὕδατος, παρεὼν δὲ μάλα σχεδὸν εἴδετο πόρρω.   6
νεβροῦ φθεγξαμένας τις ἐν οὔρεσιν ὠμοφάγος λῖς   6
ἐξ εὐνᾶς ἔσπευσεν ἑτοιμοτάταν ἐπὶ δαῖτα·
Ἡρακλέης τοιοῦτος ἐν ἀτρίπτοισιν ἀκάνθαις
παῖδα ποθῶν δεδόνητο, πολὺν δ' ἐπελάμβανε χῶρον.
σχέτλιοι οἱ φιλέοντες, ἀλώμενος ὅσσ' ἐμόγησεν
οὔρεα καὶ δρυμούς, τὰ δ' Ἰάσονος ὕστερα πάντ' ἦς.
ναῦς γέμεν[3] ἄρμεν' ἔχοισα μετάρσια τῶν παρεόντων,

---

[1] ἐξεσόβησεν Jacobs, cf. 2. 137 : mss ἐξεφόβησεν or ἀμφε-
κάλυψεν   [2] πλευστικός : mss also πνευστικός   οὖρος E :
mss οὖρος   [3] γέμεν Hermann : mss μέν
          61 ὡς δ' ὁπότ' ἠυγένειος ἀπόπροθι λῖς ἐσακούσας
Omitted by the best ms, the schol. and Pap. ; for asyndetic
introduction of simile, cf. 14. 39.

country-folk, Eunica to wit and Malis and Nycheia
with the springtime eyes. And these, when the lad
put forth the capacious pitcher in haste to dip it in,
lo! with one accord they all clung fast to his arm,
because love of the young Argive had fluttered all
their tender breasts. And down he sank into the
black water headlong, as when a falling star will
sink headlong in the main and a mariner cry to
his shipmates 'Hoist away, my lads; the breeze
freshens.' Then took the Nymphs the weeping lad
upon their knees and offered him comfort of gentle
speech.

Meantime the son of Amphitryon was grown
troubled for the child, and gone forth with that
bow of his that was bent Scythian-wise and the
cudgel that was ever in the grasp of his right hand.
Thrice cried he on Hylas as loud as his deep throttle
could belch sound; thrice likewise did the child
make answer, albeit his voice came thin from the
water and he that was hard by seemed very far away.
When a fawn cries in the hills, some ravening lion
will speed from his lair to get him a meal so ready;
and even so went Heracles wildly to and fro amid the
pathless brake, and covered much country because
of his longing for the child. As lovers know no
flinching, so endless was the toil of his wandering by
wood and wold, and all Jason's business was but a
by-end. And all the while the ship stood tackle
aloft, and so far as might be, laden, and the heroes

"Tackle aloft": with the sail hoisted but not yet turned
to the wind, cf. Alcaeus 156. 9.

οὐρὸν [1] δ' ἡμίθεοι μεσονύκτιον ἐξεκάθαιρον
Ἡρακλῆα μένοντες. ὁ δ' ᾇ πόδες ἆγον ἐχώρει
μαινόμενος· χαλεπὸς γὰρ ἔσω θεὸς ἧπαρ ἄμυσσεν.

οὕτω μὲν κάλλιστος Ὕλας μακάρων ἀριθμεῖται·
Ἡρακλέην δ' ἥρωες ἐκερτόμεον λιποναύταν,
οὕνεκεν ἡρώησε τριακοντάζυγον Ἀργώ·
πεζᾷ δ' εἰς Κόλχους τε καὶ ἄξενον ἵκετο Φᾶσιν.

[1] οὐρόν E, cf. Il. 2. 153 : mss ἰστία a correction of οὐρον

passed the night a-clearing of the channel, waiting upon Heracles. But he alas! was running whithersoever his feet might carry him, in a frenzy, the God did rend so cruelly the heart within him.

Thus came fairest Hylas to be numbered of the Blest, and the heroes to gird at Heracles for a deserter because he wandered and left the good ship of the thirty thwarts. Nevertheless he made the inhospitable land of the Colchians afoot.

"The channel": the hollow in the sand down which the ship would be launched.

XIV.—THE LOVE OF CYNISCA

THE LOVE OF CYNISCA *is a dialogue of common life. The scene is neither Egypt nor Sicily, perhaps Cos. The characters, middle-aged men, one of whom has been crossed in love, meet in the road, and in the ensuing conversation the lover tells the story of his quarrel with Cynisca, and ends with expressing his intention of going for a soldier abroad. His friend suggests that he should enlist in the army of Ptolemy, and gives that monarch a flattering testimonial, which betrays the hand of the rising poet who seeks for recognition at court.*

XIV.—ΚΥΝΙΣΚΑΣ ΕΡΩΣ

ΑΙΣΧΙΝΑΣ
Χαίρειν πολλὰ τὸν ἄνδρα Θυώνιχον.

ΘΥΩΝΙΧΟΣ
ἄλλα τοιαῦτα
Αἰσχίνᾳ.

ΑΙΣΧΙΝΑΣ
ὡς χρόνιος.

ΘΥΩΝΙΧΟΣ
χρόνιος· τί δέ τοι τὸ μέλημα;

ΑΙΣΧΙΝΑΣ
πράσσομες οὐχ ὡς λῷστα Θυώνιχε.

ΘΥΩΝΙΧΟΣ
ταῦτ᾽ ἄρα λεπτός,
χὠ μύσταξ πολὺς οὗτος, ἀϋσταλέοι δὲ κίκιννοι.
τοιοῦτος πρώαν τις ἀφίκετο Πυθαγορικτάς,
ὠχρὸς κἀνυπόδητος· Ἀθηναῖος δ᾽ ἔφατ᾽ ἦμεν.

ΑΙΣΧΙΝΑΣ
ἤρατο μὰν καὶ τῆνος;

ΘΥΩΝΙΧΟΣ
ἐμὶν δοκεῖ, ὀπτῶ ἀλεύρω.

ΑΙΣΧΙΝΑΣ
παίσδεις ὠγάθ᾽ ἔχων· ἐμὲ δ᾽ ἁ χαρίεσσα Κυνίσκα
ὑβρίσδει· λασῶ δὲ μανείς ποκα, θρὶξ ἀνὰ
μέσσον.

XIV.—THE LOVE OF CYNISCA

AESCHINAS

A very good day to master Thyonichus.

THYONICHUS

To Aeschinas the same.

AESCHINAS

Well met!

THYONICHUS

Well met it is; but what ails ye?

AESCHINAS

Luck's way's not my way, Thyonichus.

THYONICHUS

Ah! that's for why thou'rt so lean and the hair o'
thy lip so lank, and thy love-locks all-to-bemoiled.
Thou'rt like one of your Pythagoreaners that came
t'other day, pale-faced and never a shoe to's foot;
hailed from Athens, he said.

AESCHINAS

And was he, too, in love?

THYONICHUS

Aye, marry, was he—with a dish o' porridge.

AESCHINAS

Thou'lt be ever at thy quips, good lad. With me
'tis the pretty Cynisca, and she's playing the jade.
And I doubt 'tis but a hair's-breadth betwixt me and
a madman.

THE BUCOLIC POETS

ΘΥΩΝΙΧΟΣ

τοιοῦτος μὲν ἀεὶ τὺ φίλ' Αἰσχίνα, ἀσυχᾷ[1] ὀξύς,
πάντα θέλων κατὰ καιρόν· ὅμως δ' εἶπον, τί τὸ
    καινόν;

ΑΙΣΧΙΝΑΣ

Ὡργεῖος κἠγὼν καὶ ὁ Θεσσαλὸς ἱπποδιώκτας
Ἄγις[2] καὶ Κλεύνικος ἐπίνομες ὁ στρατιώτας
ἐν χώρῳ παρ' ἐμίν. δύο μὲν κατέκοψα νεοσσὼς
θηλάζοντά τε χοῖρον, ἀνῷξα δὲ Βίβλινον αὐτοῖς
εὐώδη, τετόρων ἐτέων, σχεδὸν ὡς ἀπὸ λανῶ·
βολβοτίνα,[3] κοχλίας ἐξαρέθη. ἧς πότος ἀδύς.

ἤδη δὲ προϊόντος, ἔδοξ' ἐπιχεῖσθαι ἄκρατον
ὥτινος ἤθελ' ἕκαστος· ἔδει μόνον ὥτινος εἰπεῖν.
ἄμμες μὲν φωνεῦντες ἐπίνομες, ὡς ἐδέδοκτο·
ἃ δ' οὐδὲν παρεόντος ἐμεῦ. τίν' ἔχειν με δοκεῖς
    νῶν;
'οὐ φθεγξῇ; λύκον εἶδες; ἔπαιξέ τις. 'ὡς σοφός'
    εἶπε,
κἠφλέγετ'[4]· εὐμαρέως κεν ἀπ' αὐτᾶς καὶ λύχνον
    ἅψας.

ἔστι Λύκος, Λύκος ἐστί, Λάβα τῶ γείτονος υἱός,
εὐμάκης, ἁπαλός, πολλοῖς δοκέων καλὸς ἦμεν·
τούτω τὸν κλύμενον κατετάκετο τῆνον ἔρωτα.
χἀμὶν τοῦτο δι' ὠτὸς ἔγεντό ποχ' ἀσυχᾷ οὕτως·
οὐ μὰν ἐξήταξα μάταν εἰς ἄνδρα γενείων.

ἤδη δ' ὦν πόσιος τοὶ τέσσαρες ἐν βάθει ἦμες,
χὠ Λαρισαῖος 'τὸν ἐμὸν λύκον' ἆδεν ἀπ' ἀρχᾶς,

---

[1] ἀσυχᾷ and 27 ποχ' ἀσυχᾷ οὕτως· cf. Men. *Her.* 20.   [2] Wil,
P. *Ant.*: mss *Ἄπις   [3] βολβοτίνα E: cf. Athen. 318e where
βολβοτίνη is changed by editors to βολβιτίνη: mss βολβός τις
from βολβόν τινα: Wordsworth βολβός, κτείς (cf. Ath. 63 f.,
356 f.)   [4] κηφλέγετ' P. *Ant*: mss κῆφατ'

'Faith, that's ever my Aeschinas; something hastier than might be; will have all his own way. But come, what is it?

There was the Argive and I and Agis the jockey out o' Thessaly, and Cleunicus the man-at-arms a-drinking at my farm. I'd killed a pair of pullets, look you, and a sucking-pig, and broached 'em a hogshead of Bibline fine and fragrant—four years in the cask, mark you, and yet, where new's best, as good as new—and on the board a cuttlefish and cockles to boot; i'faith, a jolly bout.

To't we went, and when things waxed warmer 'twas agreed we should toast every man his fancy; only we should give the name. But when we came to drink, the wench would not keep to the bond like the rest of us, for all I was there. How, think you, I liked of that? 'Wilt be mum?' says one, and in jest, 'Hast met a wolf?' 'O well said!' cries she, and falls a-blushing like fire; Lord! you might have lit a candle at her face. One Wolf there is, look you, master Wolf the son of neighbour Labas, one of your tall and sleek sort, in some folks' eyes a proper man. 'Twas he she made so brave a show of pining for out o' love. And I'd had wind o't too, mind you, softly, somehow, and so-to-speak; but there! I never raised inquiry for all my beard's so long.

Be that as it may, we four good men were well in, when he of Larissa, like the mischief he was, fell

---

"Cuttlefish": or perhaps 'onions and scallops'; for "cockles" the Greek has 'snails.' "Hast met a wolf?" the sight of a wolf was said proverbially to make a man dumb.

Θεσσαλικόν τι μέλισμα, κακαὶ φρένες· ἁ δὲ
    Κυνίσκα
ἔκλαεν ἐξαπίνας θαλερώτερον ἢ παρὰ ματρὶ
παρθένος ἑξαέτης κόλπῳ ἐπιθυμήσασα.[1]
τᾶμος ἐγών, τὸν ἴσαις τὺ Θυώνιχε, πὺξ ἐπὶ κόρρας
ἤλασα, κἄλλαν αὖθις. ἀνειρύσσασα δὲ πέπλως
ἔξω ἀπῴχετο θᾶσσον· 'ἐμὸν κακόν, οὔ τοι ἀρέσκω;
ἄλλος τοι γλυκίων ὑποκόλπιος; ἄλλον ἰοῖσα
θάλπε φίλον. τήνῳ τεὰ[2] δάκρυα μᾶλα ῥέοντι.'
μάστακα δοῖσα[3] τέκνοισιν ὑπωροφίοισι χελιδὼν
ἄψορρον ταχινὰ πέτεται βίον ἄλλον ἀγείρειν·
ὠκυτέρα μαλακᾶς ἀπὸ δίφρακος ἔδραμε τήνα
ἰθὺ δι' ἀμφιθύρω καὶ δικλίδος, ᾇ πόδες ἆγον·
αἰνός θην λέγεταί τις 'ἔβα κένταυρος[4] ἀν' ὕλαν.
    εἰκάδι·[5] ταὶ δ' ὀκτώ, ταὶ δ' ἐννέα, ταὶ δὲ δέκ'
    ἄλλαι,
σάμερον ἑνδεκάτα· ποτίθες δέκα, καὶ δύο[6] μῆνες,
ἐξ ᾧ ἀπ' ἀλλάλων· οὐδ' εἰ Θρᾳκιστὶ κέκαρμαι,
οἶδε. Λύκος νῦν πάντα,[7] Λύκῳ καὶ νυκτὸς ἀνῷκται·
ἄμμες δ' οὔτε λόγῳ τινὸς ἄξιοι οὔτ' ἀριθμητοί,
δύστηνοι Μεγαρῆες ἀτιμοτάτῃ ἐνὶ μοίρῃ.
κεἰ μὲν ἀποστέρξαιμι, τὰ πάντα κεν εἰς δέον
    ἔρποι.

---

[1] *P. Ant.* with Junt. ἐπιθυμήνασα   [2] τεὰ Ahrens: mss
τά or τὰ σά: cf. *Megara* 56   [3] δοῖσα Schol: mss δ'οἷα
[4] so *P. Ant.* and Sch: ἔβα καὶ ταῦρος some mss: others and
Sch. ἔβακεν ταῦρος   [5] εἰκάδι E: mss εἴκατι   [6] δέκα καὶ
δύο E: mss δύο καὶ δέκα or δύο καὶ δύο (following the corruption
εἴκατι above): with the passage cf. Ar. *Nub.* 1131   [7] *P. Ant.*
prob. ἁ δὲ Λύκῳ, or τῷ δὲ Λύκος, νῦν πάντα with some mss

a-singing a Thessalian catch beginning ' My friend the Wolf '; whereupon Cynisca bursts out a-weeping and a-wailing like a six-year-old maiden in want of a lap. Then—you know me, Thyonichus,—I up and fetched her a clout o' the ear, and again a clout. Whereat she catched up her skirts and was gone in a twink. ' Am I not good enough, my sweet mischief? Hast ever a better in thy lap? Go to, pack, and be warming another. Yon's he thou wee'pst apples over.' Now a swallow, mark you, that bringeth her young eaves-dwellers their pap, gives and is gone again to get her more ; so quickly that piece was up from her cushions and off through door-place and through door, howsoever her feet would carry her. Aye, 'tis an old story how the Centaur went through the wood.

Let me see, 'twas the twentieth o' the month. Eight, nine, ten; to-day's the eleventh. You've only to add ten days and 'twill be two months since we parted; and I may be Thracian-cropped for aught she knows. Ah! 'tis all Wolf nowadays ; Wolf hath the door left open for him o' nights; as for me, I forsooth am altogether beside the reckoning, like miserable Megara, last i' the list. 'Tis true, if I would but take my love off the wench, all would go well. But alack! how can that be? When

"Add ten days and 'twill be two months": the meaning is ' in another week it will be the 20th of the next month but one'; ten is a round number, for in Greece the weeks were of ten days, cf. σχεδόν 10. 12. The carouse took place, say, on the 20th April; in another 'week' it will be the 20th June. "Thracian-cropped": cf. l. 4: the Thracian barbarians wore their hair long. "Megara": the Megarians, upon asking the oracle which was the finest people in Greece, were told that Thrace had fine horses, Sparta fine women, and Syracuse fine men, but Argos surpassed them all ; and as for Megara, she was out of the reckoning altogether.

νῦν δὲ πόθεν; μῦς, φαντί, Θυώνιχε, γεύμεθα
πίσσας.
χὤτι τὸ φάρμακόν ἐστιν ἀμηχανέοντος ἔρωτος,
οὐκ οἶδα. πλὰν Σῖμος ὁ τᾶς ἐπιχάλκω[1]ἐρασθεὶς
ἐκπλεύσας ὑγιὴς ἐπανῆνθ᾽, ἐμὸς ἁλικιώτας.
πλευσοῦμαι κἠγὼν διαπόντιος· οὔτε κάκιστος
οὔτε πρᾶτος ἴσως, ὁμαλὸς δέ τις ὁ στρατιώτας.

ΘΥΩΝΙΧΟΣ

ὤφελε μὲν χωρεῖν κατὰ νῶν τεόν, ὧν ἐπεθύμεις
Αἰσχίνα. εἰ δ᾽ οὕτως ἄρα τοι δοκεῖ ὥστ᾽ ἀποδαμεῖν,
μισθοδότας Πτολεμαῖος ἐλευθέρῳ οἷος ἄριστος.

ΑΙΣΧΙΝΑΣ

τἆλλα δ᾽ ἀνὴρ ποῖός τις;

ΘΥΩΝΙΧΟΣ
⟨ἐνὶ πρά⟩τοισιν ἄριστος.[2]

εὐγνώμων, φιλόμουσος, ἐρωτικός, εἰς ἄκρον ἁδύς,
εἰδὼς τὸν φιλέοντα, τὸν οὐ φιλέοντ᾽ ἔτι μᾶλλον,
πολλοῖς πολλὰ διδούς, αἰτεύμενος οὐκ ἀνανεύων,
οἷα χρὴ βασιλῆ᾽· αἰτεῖν δὲ δεῖ οὐκ ἐπὶ παντί,
Αἰσχίνα. ὥστ᾽ εἴ τοι κατὰ δεξιὸν ὦμον ἀρέσκει
λῶπος ἄκρον περονᾶσθαι, ἐπ᾽ ἀμφοτέροις δὲ
βεβακὼς
τολμασεῖς ἐπιόντα μένειν θρασὺν ἀσπιδιώταν,
ᾇ τάχος εἰς Αἴγυπτον. ἀπὸ κροτάφων πελόμεσθα
πάντες γηραλέοι, καὶ ἐπισχερὼ ἐς γένυν ἕρπει
λευκαίνων ὁ χρόνος· ποιεῖν τι δεῖ, ἇς γόνυ χλωρόν.

---

[1] cf. Sophron 145 σκανάσῃ ἐν τᾷ ἐπιχάλκω (sc. ἀσπίδι)   [2] P.
Ant. restored by Hunt : mss ἐλευθέρῳ οἷος ἄριστος or omit

mouse tastes pitch, Thyonichus—; and what may be the medicine for a love there's no getting away from, 'faith, I know not—save that Simus that fell in love, as the saying is, with Mistress Brassbound and went overseas, he came home whole ; a mate of mine he was. Suppose I cross the water, like him ; your soldier's life, as 'tis not maybe o' the highest, so is it not o' the lowest, but 'tis e'en as good as another.

THYONICHUS

I would indeed thy desire had run smooth, Aeschinas. But if so be thy mind is made up to go thy ways abroad, I'll e'en tell thee the best pay-master a freeman can have ; King Ptolemy.

AESCHINAS

And what sort of man is he in other ways?

THYONICHUS

The pick o' the best : a kind heart, a man of parts, a true gallant, and the top o' good-fellowship ; knows well the colour of a friend, and still better the look of a foe ; like a true king, gives far and wide and says no man nay—albeit one should not be for ever asking, Aeschinas. (*in mock-heroic strain*) So an thou be'st minded to clasp the warrior's cloak about thee, and legs astride to abide the onset of the hardy foeman, to Egypt with thee. To judge by our noddles we're all waxing old, and old Time comes us grizzling line by line down the cheek. We must fain be up and doing while there's sap in our legs.

" When mouse tastes pitch " : the mouse that fell into the caldron of pitch was proverbial of those who find themselves in difficulties through their own folly. " Mistress Brass-bound " : contemporary slang for the soldier's shield.

XV.—THE WOMEN AT THE ADONIS-FESTIVAL

THE *scene of this mime is Alexandria, and the chief characters are two fellow-countrywomen of the author. Gorgo, paying a morning call, finds Praxinoa, with her two-year-old child, superintending the spinning of her maids, and asks her to come with her to the Festival of Adonis at the palace of Ptolemy II. Praxinoa makes some demur, but at last washes and dresses and sallies forth with her visitor and their two maids. After sundry encounters in the crowded streets, they enter the palace, and soon after, the* prima donna *begins the Dirge—which is really a wedding-song containing a forecast of a dirge—with an address to the bride Aphrodite and a reference to the deification of the queen of Ptolemy I. The song describes the scene—the offerings displayed about the marriage-bed, the two canopies of greenery above it, the bedstead with its representation of the Rape of Ganymede, the coverlets which enwrap the effigies of Adonis and Aphrodite, the image of the holy bridegroom himself—and ends with an anticipation of the choral dirge to be sung on the morrow at the funeral of Adonis.*

XV.—ΣΥΡΑΚΟΣΙΑΙ Η ΑΔΩΝΙΑΖΟΥΣΑΙ

ΓΟΡΓΩ

Ἔνδοι Πραξινόα;

ΠΡΑΞΙΝΟΑ

Γοργοῖ φίλα, ὡς χρόνῳ· ἔνδοι.
θαῦμ' ὅτι καὶ νῦν ἦνθες. ὅρη δρίφον[1] Εὐνόα αὐτᾷ.
ἔμβαλε καὶ ποτίκρανον.

ΓΟΡΓΩ

ἔχει κάλλιστα.

ΠΡΑΞΙΝΟΑ

καθίζευ.

ΓΟΡΓΩ

ὦ τᾶς ἀλεμάτω[1] ψυχᾶς· μόλις ὕμμιν ἐσώθην,
Πραξινόα, πολλῶ μὲν ὄχλω, πολλῶν δὲ τεθρίπ-
πων·
παντᾷ κρηπῖδες, παντᾷ χλαμυδηφόροι ἄνδρες·
ἁ δ' ὁδὸς ἄτρυτος· τὺ δ' ἑκαστάτω ὡς ἐναποικεῖς[2].

ΠΡΑΞΙΝΟΑ

ταῦθ' ὁ πάραρος τῆνος· ἐπ' ἔσχατα γᾶς ἔλαβ'
ἐνθὼν
ἱλεόν, οὐκ οἴκησιν, ὅπως μὴ γείτονες ὦμες
ἀλλάλαις, ποτ' ἔριν, φθονερὸν κακόν, αἰὲν ὁμοῖος.

---

[1] P. Ant., cf. Hesych. Et. M. 287. 50: mss δίφρον   [2] ἀλε-
μάτω Stephanus: mss ἀδεμάτω (so Greg. Cor.), ἀδειμά(ν)του,
ἀδαμά(ν)του   [3] ἑκαστάτω ὡς ἐναποικεῖς E, cf. l. 45 τυτθὸν
ὅσσον ἄπωθεν and ὡς 'where' i. 13: mss ἑκαστέρω (ἑκαστοτέρω)
ἔμ' ἀποικεῖς: Koennecke and Γ. Ant. ἑκαστέρω αἰὲν ἀποικεῖς

XV.—THE WOMEN AT THE ADONIS-FESTIVAL

GORGO (*with her maid Eutychis at the door, as the maid Eunoa opens it*)

Praxinoa at home?

PRAXINOA (*running forward*)

Dear Gorgo! at last! she *is* at home. I quite thought you'd forgotten me. (*to the maid*) Here, Eunoa, a chair for the lady, and a cushion in **it**.

GORGO (*refusing the cushion*)

No, thank you, really.

PRAXINOA

Do sit down.

GORGO (*sitting*)

O what a silly I was to come! What with the crush and the horses, Praxinoa, I've scarcely got here alive. It's all big boots and people in uniform. And the street was never-ending, and you can't think how far your house is along it.

PRAXINOA

That's my lunatic; came and took one at the end of the world, and more an animal's den, too, than a place for a human being to live in, just to prevent you and me being neighbours, out of sheer spite, the jealous old wretch! He's always the same.

" You can't think how far," etc.: or perhaps ' You always live too far away.'

ΓΟΡΓΩ

μὴ λέγε τὸν τεὸν ἄνδρα, φίλα, Δίνωνα τοιαῦτα
τῶ μικκῶ παρεόντος· ὅρη γύναι, ὡς ποθορῇ τυ.
θάρσει Ζωπυρίον, γλυκερὸν τέκος· οὐ λέγει ἀπφῦν.[1]

ΠΡΑΞΙΝΟΑ

αἰσθάνεται τὸ βρέφος, ναὶ τὰν πότνιαν.

ΓΟΡΓΩ

καλὸς ἀπφῦς.

ΠΡΑΞΙΝΟΑ

ἀπφῦς μὰν τῆνος τὰ πρόαν—λέγομες δὲ πρόαν θην
‘πάππα,[2] νίτρον καὶ φῦκος ἀπὸ σκανᾶς ἀγοράσ-
    δειν’—
ἵκτο[3] φέρων ἅλας ἄμμιν, ἀνὴρ τρισκαιδεκάπαχυς.

ΓΟΡΓΩ

χὠ μὸς ταὐτᾷ[3] ἔχει, φθόρος ἀργυρίω, Διοκλείδας·
ἑπταδράχμως κυνάδας, γραιᾶν ἀποτίλματα πηρᾶν,
πέντε πόκως ἔλαβ᾽ ἐχθές, ἅπαν ῥύπον, ἔργον ἐπ᾽
    ἔργῳ.
ἀλλ᾽ ἴθι τὠμπέχονον καὶ τὰν περονατρίδα λάζευ.
βᾶμες τῶ βασιλῆος ἐς ἀφνειῶ Πτολεμαίω
θασόμεναι τὸν Ἄδωνιν· ἀκούω χρῆμα καλόν τι
κοσμεῖν τὰν βασίλισσαν.

ΠΡΑΞΙΝΟΑ

ἐν ὀλβίω ὄλβια πάντα.

[1] Ζωπυρίον (diminutive of Ζώπυρος) Buecheler: mss -ίων
λέγει: mss also λέγω   [2] πάππα Wil. from *Et. Mag.*:
mss πάντα   ἀγοράσδειν Ahrens; baby-language, cf. Theophr.
Char. 7. 10: mss ἀγοράσδων   [3] so *P. Ant*: mss ἦνθε, ἦλθε,
κῆνθε   [4] ταὐτᾷ Ahrens: mss ταῦτ᾽ or ταύτά γ᾽

178

GORGO

My dear, pray don't call your good Dinon such names before Baby. See how he's staring at you. (*to the child*) It's all right, Zopy, my pet. It's not dad-dad she's talking about.

PRAXINOA

Upon my word, the child understands.

GORGO

Nice dad-dad.

PRAXINOA

And yet that dad-dad of his the other day—the other day, now, I tell him ' Daddy, get mother some soap and rouge from the shop,' and, would you believe it? back he came with a packet of salt, the great six feet of folly!

GORGO

Mine's just the same. Diocleidas is a perfect spendthrift. Yesterday he gave seven shillings apiece for mere bits of dog's hair, mere pluckings of old handbags, five of them, all filth, all work to be done over again. But come, my dear, get your cloak and gown. I want you to come with me (*grandly*) to call on our high and mighty Prince Ptolemy to see the Adonis. I hear the Queen's getting up something quite splendid this year.

PRAXINOA (*hesitating*)

Fine folks, fine ways.

ΓΟΡΓΩ

ὧν ἴδες, ὧν εἶπες καὶ ἰδοῖσα τὺ τῷ μὴ ἰδόντι.
ἕρπειν ὥρα κ' εἴη.

ΠΡΑΞΙΝΟΑ

ἀεργοῖς αἰὲν ἑορτά.

Εὐνόα, αἶρε τὸ νῆμα καὶ ἐς μέσον αἰνόδρυπτε
θές πάλιν· αἱ γαλέαι μαλακῶς χρήζοντι καθεύ-
    δειν.
κινεῦ δή, φέρε θᾶσσον ὕδωρ. ὕδατος πρότερον
    δεῖ,
ἃ δὲ σμᾶμα φέρει. δὸς ὅμως. μὴ δὴ πολύ,
    λαστρί·[1]
ἔγχει ὕδωρ. δύστανε, τί μευ τὸ χιτώνιον ἄρδεις;
παῦε· ὁκοῖα θεοῖς ἐδόκει, τοιαῦτα νένιμμαι.
ἁ κλᾳξ τᾶς μεγάλας πεῖ[2] λάρνακος; ὧδε φέρ'
    αὐτάν.

ΓΟΡΓΩ

Πραξινόα, μάλα τοι τὸ καταπτυχὲς ἐμπερόναμα
τοῦτο πρέπει· λέγε μοι, πόσσω κατέβα τοι ἀφ'
    ἱστῶ;

ΠΡΑΞΙΝΟΑ

μὴ μνάσῃς Γοργοῖ· πλέον ἀργυρίω καθαρῶ μνᾶν
ἢ δύο· τοῖς δ' ἔργοις καὶ τὰν ψυχὰν ποτέθηκα.

---

[1] δὲ σμᾶμα G. Hermann: mss δ' ἐς νᾶμα   λαστρί E.
Schwartz, cf. Herodas 6. 10: mss ἄπληστε   [2] Ahr. and
P. *Ant*: mss πῆ, πᾶ

GORGO

Yes; but sightseers make good gossips, you know, if you've been and other people haven't. It's time we were on the move.

PRAXINOA (*still hesitating*)

It's always holidays with people who've nothing to do. (*suddenly making up her mind*) Here, Eunoa, you scratch-face, take up the spinning and put it away with the rest. Cats always *will* lie soft. Come, bestir yourself. Quick, some water! (*to Gorgo*) Water's wanted first, and she brings the soap. (*to Eunoa*) Never mind; give it me. (*E. pours out the powdered soap*) Not all that, you wicked waste! Pour out the water. (*E. washes her mistress's hands and face*) Oh, you wretch! What do you mean by wetting my bodice like that? That's enough. (*to Gorgo*) I've got myself washed somehow, thank goodness. (*to Eunoa*) Now where's the key of the big cupboard? Bring it here. (*Takes out a Dorian pinner—a gown fastened with pins or brooches to the shoulders and reaching to the ground, with an overfold coming to the waist—and puts it on with Eunoa's aid over the inner garment with short sleeves which she wears indoors*)

GORGO (*referring to the style of the overfold*)

Praxinoa, that full gathering suits you really well. Do tell me what you gave for the material.

PRAXINOA

Don't speak of it, Gorgo; it was more than eight golden sovereigns, and I can tell you I put my very soul into making it up.

"Wicked waste": the Greek is "pirate-vessel."

THE BUCOLIC POETS

ΓΟΡΓΩ

ἀλλὰ κατὰ γνώμαν ἀπέβα τοι.

ΠΡΑΞΙΝΟΑ

τοῦτο κα εἴπαις.[1]

τὤμπέχονον φέρε μοι καὶ τὰν θολίαν κατὰ κόσμον
ἀμφίθες. οὐκ ἀξῶ τυ τέκνον. μορμὼ δάκνει ἵππος. 4
δάκρυ᾽, ὅσσα θέλεις, χωλὸν δ᾽ οὐ δεῖ τυ γενέσθαι.
ἔρπωμες. Φρυγία, τὸν μικκὸν παῖσδε λαβοῖσα,
τὰν κύν᾽ ἔσω κάλεσον, τὰν αὐλείαν ἀπόκλαξον.[2]

ΓΟΡΓΩ

ὦ θεοί, ὅσσος ὄχλος· πῶς καὶ πόκα τοῦτο
        περάσαι
χρὴ τὸ κακόν; μύρμακες ἀνάριθμοι καὶ ἄμετροι.

ΠΡΑΞΙΝΟΑ

πολλά τοι ὦ Πτολεμαῖε πεποίηται καλὰ ἔργα,
ἐξ ὦ ἐν ἀθανάτοις ὁ τεκών· οὐδεὶς κακοεργὸς
δαλεῖται τὸν ἰόντα παρέρπων Αἰγυπτιστί,
οἷα πρὶν ἐξ ἀπάτας κεκροτημένοι ἄνδρες ἔπαισδον
ἀλλάλοις γ᾽ ὁμαλοί, κακὰ παίχνια, πάντες ἐρειοί.[3] 5
    ἁδίστα Γοργοῖ, τί γενοίμεθα; τοὶ πολεμισταὶ
ἵπποι τῶ βασιλῆος. ἄνερ φίλε, μή με πατήσῃς.
ὀρθὸς ἀνέστα ὁ πυρρός· ἴδ᾽ ὡς ἄγριος. κυνοθαρσὴς
Εὐνόα, οὐ φευξῇ; διαχρησεῖται τὸν ἄγοντα.
ὠνάθην μεγάλως, ὅτι μοι τὸ βρέφος μένει ἔνδοι.[4]

---

[1] *P. Ant.* with some mss: others κεῦ (κάλ᾽) εἶπες (-ας): *O. P.*
1618 κατειπ[[2] *P. Ant.* ἐπικλαξον   [3] γ᾽ and παίχνια *P. Ant.*:
mss omit γ᾽ and read παίγνια   ἐρειοί: mss also ἐριοί, explained
by Hesych. as καινοί   [4] ἔνδοι Casaubon: mss ἔνδον

182

GORGO

Well, all I can say is, it's *most* successful.

PRAXINOA

I'm inclined to agree with you.[1] (*to Eunoa*) Come,
put on my cloak and hat for me, and mind you do
it properly. (*Eunoa puts her cloak about her head and
shoulders and pins the straw sun-hat to it*). (*taking
up the child*) No; I'm not going to take *you*, Baby.
Horse-bogey bites little boys. (*the child cries*) You
may cry as much as you like; I'm not going to
have you lamed for life. (*to Gorgo, giving the child to
the nurse*) Come along. Take Baby and amuse him,
Phrygia, and call the dog indoors and lock the
front-door.

(*in the street*) GORGO [2]

Heavens, what a crowd! How we're to get
through this awful crush and how long it's going
to take us, I can't imagine. Talk of an antheap!

PRAXINOA

I *must* say, you've done us many a good turn, my
good Ptolemy, since your father went to heaven.
We have no villains sneaking up to murder us in
the streets nowadays in the good old Egyptian
style. They don't play those awful games now—the
thorough-paced rogues, every one of them the same,
all queer!

Gorgo dearest! what *shall* we do? The Royal
Horse! Don't run me down, my good man. That
bay's rearing. Look, what temper! Stand back,
Eunoa, you reckless girl! He'll be the death of
that man. Thank goodness I left Baby at home!

---

[1] *lit.* 'you may say so.'   [2] so P. Ant: generally given
to Praxinoa

ΓΟΡΓΩ

θάρσει Πραξινόα· καὶ δὴ γεγενήμεθ' ὄπισθεν,
τοὶ δ' ἔβαν ἐς χώραν.

ΠΡΑΞΙΝΟΑ

καὐτὰ συναγείρομαι ἤδη. [1]
ἵππον καὶ τὸν ψυχρὸν ὄφιν τὰ μάλιστα δεδοίκω
ἐκ παιδός. σπεύδωμες· ὄχλος πολὺς ἄμμιν
ἐπιρρεῖ.

ΓΟΡΓΩ

ἐξ αὐλᾶς ὦ μᾶτερ;

ΓΡΑΥΣ

ἐγών, τέκνα.

ΓΟΡΓΩ

εἶτα παρενθεῖν
εὐμαρές;

ΓΡΑΥΣ

ἐς Τροίαν πειρώμενοι ἦνθον Ἀχαιοί,
καλλίστα παίδων· πείρᾳ θην πάντα τελεῖται.

ΓΟΡΓΩ

χρησμὼς ἁ πρεσβῦτις ἀπῷχετο θεσπίξασα.

ΠΡΑΞΙΝΟΑ

πάντα γυναῖκες ἴσαντι, καὶ ὡς Ζεὺς ἀγάγεθ' Ἥραν.

ΓΟΡΓΩ

θᾶσαι Πραξινόα, περὶ τὰς θύρας ὅσσος ὅμιλος·
θεσπέσιος. [2]

---

[1] Cf. Xen. *Cyr.* 4. 5. 37, where ἀσύντακτα εἶναι is opposed to χώραν λαβεῖν, ibid. 8. 6. 19 συναγείρειν στρατιάν, Plat. *Prot.* 328 d ἐμαυτὸν ὡσπερεὶ συναγείρας   [2] so *P. Ant.*: this word, generally given to Praxinoa, was given to Gorgo by Ameis, but without a stop before it

GORGO

It's all right, Praxinoa. We've got well behind them, you see. They're all where they ought to be, now.

PRAXINOA (*recovering*)

And fortunately I can say the same of my poor wits. Ever since I was a girl, two things have frightened me more than anything else, a horrid chilly snake and a horse. Let's get on. Here's ever such a crowd pouring after us.

GORGO (*to an Old Woman*)

Have you come from the palace, mother?

OLD WOMAN

Yes, my dears.

GORGO

Then we can get there all right, can we?

OLD WOMAN

Trying took Troy, my pretty; don't they say where there's a will there's a way?

GORGO

That old lady gave us some oracles, didn't she?

PRAXINOA (*mock-sententiously*)

My dear, women know everything. They know all about Zeus marrying Hera.[1]

GORGO

Do look, Praxinoa; what a crowd there is at the door! It's marvellous!

"I can say the same": the Greek has a pun on 'assembling' troops and 'collecting' one's wits. "Gave us some oracles": i.e. her sententious remarks were about as useful as oracles generally are. "My dear," etc. : P. Ant. gives this line to 'Some Man,' but we should expect his presence to be indicated in the dialogue.

ΠΡΑΞΙΝΟΑ

Γοργοῖ, δὸς τὰν χέρα μοι· λαβὲ καὶ τὺ
Εὐνόα Εὐτυχίδος· πότεχ᾽ αὖτα, μὴ ᾽ποπλαναθῇς.[1]
πᾶσαι ἅμ᾽ εἰσένθωμες· ἀπρὶξ ἔχευ Εὐνόα ἁμῶν.
οἴμοι δειλαία, δίχα μευ τὸ θερίστριον ἤδη
ἔσχισται, Γοργοῖ.   ποττῶ Διός, αἴ τι[2] γένοιο   7
εὐδαίμων ὤνθρωπε, φυλάσσεο τὠμπέχονόν μευ.

ΞΕΝΟΣ

οὐκ ἐπ᾽ ἐμὶν μέν, ὅμως δὲ φυλαξεῦμαι.

ΠΡΑΞΙΝΟΑ

ὄχλος ἄθρως·
ὠθεῦνθ᾽ ὥσπερ ὕες.

ΞΕΝΟΣ

θάρσει γύναι· ἐν καλῷ εἰμές.

ΠΡΑΞΙΝΟΑ

κῆς ὥρας κἤπειτα, φίλ᾽ ἀνδρῶν, ἐν καλῷ εἴης
ἄμμε περιστέλλων. χρηστῶ κοἰκτίρμονος ἀνδρός.
φλίβεται Εὐνόα ἄμμιν· ἄγ᾽ ὦ δειλὰ τὺ βιάζευ.

κάλλιστ᾽· ῾ἔνδοι πᾶσαι᾽ ὁ τὰν νυὸν εἶπ᾽ ἀπο-
κλάξας.

ΓΟΡΓΩ

Πραξινόα, πόταγ᾽ ὦδε. τὰ ποικίλα πρᾶτον ἄθρη-
σον,
λεπτὰ καὶ ὡς χαρίεντα· θεῶν περονάματα φασεῖς.

[1] Hunt: P. Ant. μη απoπλαγχθης (so O. P. 1618) corrected
to μη που πλανηθης: mss μή τι (τυ) πλανηθῇς   [2] P. Ant.
αιθε, O. P. 1618]μθε: mss εἴ τι
186

PRAXINOA

Give me your arm, Gorgo; and you take hold of
Eutychis' arm, Eunoa; and you take care, Eutychis,
not to get separated. We'll all go in together.
Mind you keep hold of me, Eunoa. Oh dear, oh
dear, Gorgo! my summer cloak's torn right in two.
(*to a stranger*) For Heaven's sake, as you wish to be
saved, mind my cloak, sir.

FIRST STRANGER

I really can't help what happens; but I'll do my
best.

PRAXINOA

The crowd's simply enormous; they're pushing
like a drove of pigs.

FIRST STRANGER

Don't be alarmed, madam; we're all right.

PRAXINOA

You deserve to be all right to the end of your
days, my dear sir, for the care you've been taking of
us. (*to Gorgo*) What a kind considerate man! Poor
Eunoa's getting squeezed. (*to Eunoa*) Push, you
coward, can't you? (*they pass in*)

That's all right. All inside, as the bridegroom
said when he shut the door.

GORGO (*referring, as they move forward towards the
daïs, to the draperies which hang between the pillars*)
Praxinoa, do come here. Before you do anything
else I insist upon your looking at the embroideries.
How delicate they are! and in such good taste!
They're really hardly human, are they?

" Summer cloak ": the festival was probably held upon
the longest day.

THE BUCOLIC POETS

ΠΡΑΞΙΝΟΑ

πότνι' Ἀθαναία· ποῖαί σφ' ἐπόνασαν ἔριθοι,
ποῖοι ζωγράφοι τἀκριβέα γράμματ' ἔγραψαν.
ὡς ἔτυμ' ἑστάκαντι, καὶ ὡς ἔτυμ' ἐνδινεῦντι·
ἔμψυχ', οὐκ ἐνυφαντά. σοφόν τοι[1] χρῆμ' ἄνθρωπος.
αὐτὸς δ' ὡς θαητὸς ἐπ' ἀργυρέας κατάκειται
ἁρμοῖ[2] πρᾶτον ἴουλον ἀπὸ κροτάφων κατα-
    βάλλων—
ὁ τριφίλητος Ἄδωνις, ὁ κἠν Ἀχέροντι φιλεῖται.[3]

ΕΤΕΡΟΣ ΞΕΝΟΣ

παύσασθ' ὦ δύστανοι, ἀνάνυτα κωτίλλοισαι
τρυγόνες· ἐκκναισεῦντι πλατειάσδοισαι ἅπαντα.

ΠΡΑΞΙΝΟΑ

μᾶ, πόθεν ὤνθρωπος; τί δὲ τίν, εἰ κωτίλαι εἰμές;
πασάμενος ἐπίτασσε.[4] Συρακοσίαις ἐπιτάσσεις.
ὡς εἰδῇς καὶ τοῦτο, Κορίνθιαι εἰμὲς ἄνωθεν,
ὡς καὶ ὁ Βελλεροφῶν· Πελοποννασιστὶ λαλεῦμες·[5]
Δωρίσδεν δ' ἔξεστι δοκῶ τοῖς Δωριέεσσι.
μὴ φύη, Μελιτῶδες, ὃς ἁμῶν καρτερὸς εἴη,
πλὰν ἑνός. οὐκ ἀλέγω. μή μοι κενεὰν ἀπομάξῃς.

ΓΟΡΓΩ

σίγη Πραξινόα· μέλλει τὸν Ἄδωνιν ἀείδειν
ἁ τᾶς Ἀργείας θυγάτηρ, πολύϊδρις ἀοιδός,
ἅτις καὶ πέρυσιν[6] τὸν ἰάλεμον ἀρίστευσε.

---

[1] τοι schol. on Soph. *Ant.* 349: mss τι   [2] ἁρμοῖ Kaibel,
cf. Callim. *fr.* 44, Ap. Rhod. i. 972: mss κλισμῶ: with *ἀργυρέας*
supply *κλίνας*   [3] *P. Ant.*, *O. P.* 1618 φιληθείς   [4] *P. Ant.*
with *Et. M.* ποτίτασσε   [5] *O.P.*1618 λαλ͵ευσαι   [6] so Reiske
with *O. P.* 1618, *P. Ant.*: mss πέρχην or σπέρχιν
188

PRAXINOA

Huswife Athena! the weavers that made that
material and the embroiderers who did that close
detailed work are simply marvels.   How realistically
the things all stand and move about in it! they're
living!   It *is* wonderful what people can do.   And
then the Holy Boy; how perfectly beautiful he looks
lying on his silver couch, with the down of manhood
just showing on his cheeks,—(*religioso*) the thrice-
beloved Adonis, beloved even down below!

SECOND STRANGER

Oh dear, oh dear, ladies! do stop that eternal
cooing.   (*to the bystanders*)   They'll weary me to
death with their ah-ah-ah-ing.

PRAXINOA

My word! where *does* that person come from?
What business is it of yours if we do coo?   Buy your
slaves before you order them about, pray.   You're
giving your orders to Syracusans.   If you *must* know,
we're Corinthians by extraction, like Bellerophon him-
self.   What *we* talk's Peloponnesian.   I suppose Dorians
may speak Doric, mayn't they?   Persephone! let's
have no more masters than the one we've got.   I shall
do just as I like.   Pray don't waste your breath.

GORGO

Be quiet, Praxinoa.   She's just going to begin the
song, that Argive person's daughter, you know, the
" accomplished vocalist " that was chosen to sing

" Don't waste your breath ": the Greek has 'don't scrape
the top of an empty measure.'   " Accomplished vocalist " :
the Greek phrase is Epic, perhaps a quotation from an
advertisement or the like.

THE BUCOLIC POETS

φθεγξεῖταί τι, σάφ' οἶδα, καλόν· διαθρύπτεται[1]
ἤδη.

ΓΥΝΗ ΑΟΙΔΟΣ

Δέσποιν', ἃ Γολγώς τε καὶ Ἰδάλιον ἐφίλησας,
αἰπεινόν τ' Ἔρυκα, χρυσωπίζοισ'[2] Ἀφροδίτα,
οἷόν τοι τὸν Ἄδωνιν ἀπ' ἀενάω Ἀχέροντος
μηνὶ δυωδεκάτῳ μαλακαίποδες[3] ἄγαγον Ὧραι,
βάρδισται μακάρων Ὧραι φίλαι, ἀλλὰ ποθειναὶ
ἔρχονται πάντεσσι βροτοῖς αἰεί τι φορεῦσαι.
Κύπρι Διωναία, τὺ μὲν ἀθανάταν ἀπὸ θνατᾶς,
ἀνθρώπων ὡς μῦθος, ἐποίησας Βερενίκαν
ἀμβροσίαν ἐς στῆθος ἀποστάξασα γυναικός·
τὶν δὲ χαριζομένα, πολυώνυμε καὶ πολύναε,
ἁ Βερενικεία θυγάτηρ Ἑλένᾳ εἰκυῖα
Ἀρσινόα πάντεσσι καλοῖς ἀτιτάλλει Ἄδωνιν.
πὰρ μὲν ὅσσ'[4] ὥρια κεῖται, ὅσα δρυὸς ἄκρα καλεῖται[5]
πὰρ δ' ἁπαλοὶ κᾶποι πεφυλαγμένοι ἐν ταλα-
    ρίσκοις
ἀργυρέοις, Συρίω δὲ μύρω χρύσει' ἀλάβαστρα·
εἴδατά θ' ὅσσα γυναῖκες ἐπὶ πλαθάνω πονέονται
ἄνθεα μίσγοισαι λευκῷ παντοῖα μαλεύρῳ,
ὅσσα τ' ἀπὸ γλυκερῶ μέλιτος τά τ' ἐν ὑγρῷ
    ἐλαίῳ,
πάντ' αὐτῷ πετεηνὰ καὶ ἑρπετὰ τεῖδε πάρεστι.

[1] P. Ant. διαχρέμπτεται "clearing her throat"   [2] χρυ-
σωπίζοισα Ludwich, cf. καλλωπίζω and χρυσῶπις: mss
χρυσῷ παίζοισα   [3] mss also μαλακαὶ πόδας   [4] Shackle: mss
πὰρ μέν οἱ contra metrum   [5] so P. Ant: mss φέροντ(α)ι

190

the dirge *last* year.   You may be sure *she*'ll give us
something good.   Look, she's making her bow.

The Dirge

Lover of Golgi and Idaly and Eryx' steepy hold,
O Lady Aphrodite with the face that beams like gold,
Twelve months are sped and soft-footéd Heav'n's
    pretty laggards, see,
Bring o'er the never-tarrying stream Adonis back to
    thee.
The Seasons, the Seasons, full slow they go and come,
But some sweet thing for all they bring, and so they
    are welcome home.
O Cypris, Dion's daughter, of thee anealed, 'tis said,
Our Queen that was born of woman is e'en immortal
    made ;
And now, sweet Lady of many names, of many shrines
    Ladye,
Thy guerdon's giv'n ; for the Queen's daughtér, as
    Helen fair to see,
Thy lad doth dight with all delight upon this holyday;
For there's not a fruit the orchard bears but is here
    for his hand to take,
And cresses trim all kept for him in many a silver tray,
And Syrian balm in vials of gold ; and O, there's
    every cake
That ever woman kneaded of bolted meal so fair
With blossoms blent of every scent or oil or honey
    rare—
Here's all outlaid in semblance made of every bird
    and beast.

"Last year": the day of the festival was apparently
regarded as the first day of Adonis' six months' stay upon
the earth, the other six being spent in Hades.   "Anealed":
'anointed.'

χλωρὰ δὲ σκιάδε μαλακῷ βρίθοντ᾽ ἀννήθῳ[1]
δέδμανθ᾽· οἱ δέ τε κῶροι ὑπερπωτῶνται Ἔρωτες,
οἷοι ἀηδονιδῆες ἀεξομενᾶν ἐπὶ δένδρῳ[2]
πωτῶνται πτερύγων πειρώμενοι ὄσδον ἀπ᾽ ὄσδω.
ὢ ἔβενος, ὢ χρυσός, ὢ ἐκ λευκῶ ἐλέφαντος
αἰετὼ οἰνοχόον Κρονίδᾳ Διὶ παῖδα φέροντε.[3]
πορφύρεοι δὲ τάπητες ἄνω μαλακώτεροι ὕπνω·
ἁ Μιλάτος ἐρεῖ χὠ τὰν Σαμίαν καταβόσκων
‘ ἔστρωται κλίνα τῷδώνιδι τῷ καλῷ ἁμά·[4]
τὸν μὲν Κύπρις ἔχει, τὸν δ᾽[5] ὁ ῥοδόπαχυς
    Ἄδωνις.’

ὀκτωκαιδεκέτης ἢ ἐννεακαίδεχ᾽ ὁ γαμβρός·
οὐ κεντεῖ τὸ φίλημ᾽, ἔτι οἱ περὶ χείλεα πυρρά.
νῦν μὲν Κύπρις ἔχοισα τὸν αὐτᾶς χαιρέτω
    ἄνδρα·
ἀῶθεν δ᾽ ἄμμες νιν ἅμα δρόσῳ ἀθρόαι ἔξω
οἰσεῦμες ποτὶ κύματ᾽ ἐπ᾽ ἀϊόνι πτύοντα,
λύσασαι δὲ κόμαν καὶ ἐπὶ σφυρὰ κόλπον ἀνεῖσαι
στήθεσι φαινομένοις λιγυρᾶς ἀρξεύμεθ᾽[6] ἀοιδᾶς·
‘ ἔρπεις, ὢ φίλ᾽ Ἄδωνι, καὶ ἐνθάδε κῆς Ἀχέροντα

---

[1] χλωρὰ δὲ σκιάδε μαλακῷ βρίθοντ᾽ (dual) ἀννήθῳ E, cf. i. 75,
18. 5, and Jebb on Soph. *O. C.* 1676: mss χλωραὶ δὲ σκιάδες
μαλακῷ βρίθοντες (-ουσαι) ἀνήθῳ   [2] ἀεξομενᾶν ἐπὶ δένδρῳ Ahr.
Wil: mss -νων ἐπὶ δένδρων   [3] some mss αἰετοὶ (*P. Ant.*), all
φέροντες   [4] Ahr: mss ἄλλα   [5] τὸν μὲν and τὸν δ᾽ E (there
were two coverlets, but one wedding-couch): mss τὰν μὲν and
τὰν δ᾽   [6] Kiessling, *P. Ant.* (-ουμ.): mss -ωμ.

Two testers green they have plight ye, with dainty
    dill well dressed,
Whereon, like puny nightingales that flit from bough
    to bough
Trying their waxing wings to spread, the Love-babes
    hovering go.
How fair the ebony and the gold, the ivory white
    how fair,
And eagles twain to Zeus on high bringing his cup-
    bearer !
Aye, and the coverlets spread for ye are softer spread
    than sleep—
Forsooth Miletus town may say, or the master of
    Samian sheep,
" The bridal bed for Adonis spread of my own
    making is ;
Cypris hath this for her wrapping, Adonis that for
    his."
  Of eighteen years or nineteen is turned the rose-
    limbed groom ;
His pretty lip is smooth to sip, for it bears but flaxen
    bloom.
And now she's in her husband's arms, and so we'll
    say good-night ;
But to-morrow we'll come wi' the dew, the dew, and
    take hands and bear him away
Where plashing wave the shore doth lave, and there
    with locks undight
And bosoms bare all shining fair will raise this
    shrilling lay :—
" O sweet Adonis, none but thee of the children of
    Gods and men

  " Miletus, Samian sheep": Milesian and Samian wool was
famous.

ἡμιθέων, ὡς φαντί, μονώτατος. οὔτ' Ἀγαμέμνων
τοῦτ' ἔπαθ', οὔτ' Αἴας ὁ μέγας, βαρυμάνιος ἥρως,
οὔθ' Ἕκτωρ Ἑκάβας ὁ γεραίτατος[1] εἴκατι
  παίδων,
οὐ Πατροκλῆς, οὐ Πύρρος ἀπὸ Τροίας ἐπαν-
  ενθών,
οὔθ' οἱ ἔτι πρότερον Λαπίθαι καὶ Δευκαλίωνες,
οὐ Πελοπηϊάδαι τε καὶ Ἄργεος ἄκρα Πελασγοί.
ἵλαθι νῦν, φίλ' Ἄδωνι, καὶ ἐς νέον·[2] εὐθυμεύσαις
καὶ νῦν ἦνθες, Ἄδωνι, καὶ ὅκκ' ἀφίκῃ, φίλος
  ἥξεῖς.

ΓΟΡΓΩ

Πραξινόα, τὸ χρῆμα σοφώτατον ἁ θήλεια·[3]
ὀλβία ὅσσα ἴσατι, πανολβία ὡς γλυκὺ φωνεῖ.
ὥρα ὅμως κῆς οἶκον. ἀνάριστος Διοκλείδας.
χὡνὴρ ὄξος ἅπαν, πεινᾶντι δὲ μηδὲ ποτένθῃς.
χαῖρε Ἄδων ἀγαπατὲ καὶ ἐς χαίροντας ἀφίκνευ.[4]

---

[1] mss also γεραίτερος   [2] mss also νέωτα (so P. Ant.) and
νέω   [3] σοφώτατον E with P. Ant: mss σοφώτερον   ἁ θήλεια
= τὸ θῆλυ; there is the common confusion in 146 between
general and particular   [4] mss ἀφίκευ, ἀφίκνευ, ἀφικνεῦ

'Twixt overworld and underworld doth pass and pass
    agen ;
That cannot Agamemnon, nor the Lord o' the
    Woeful Spleen,
Nor the first of the twice-ten children that came of
    the Troyan queen,
Nor Patroclus brave, nor Pyrrhus bold that home
    from the war did win,
Nor none o' the kith o' the old Lapíth nor of them
    of Deucalion's kin—
E'en Pelops line lacks fate so fine, and Pelasgian
    Argos' pride.
> Adonis sweet, Adonis dear,
> Be gracious for another year ;
> Thou'rt welcome to thine own alwáy,
> And welcome we'll both cry to-day
>   And next Adonis-tide."

GORGO

O Praxinoa ! what clever things we women are !
I do envy her knowing all that, and still more having
such a lovely voice. But I must be getting back.
It's Diocleidas' dinner-time, and that man's all
pepper ; I wouldn't advise anyone to come near him
even, when he's kept waiting for his food. Good-
bye, Adonis darling ; and I only trust you may find
us all thriving when you come next year.

"The Lord o' the Woeful Spleen": Ajax. "The first
of the twice-ten children": Hector. P. Ant. gives all
after "dinner-time" to Praxinoa, as though it were "*My*
husband, too*"; but this would require 'my' to be expressed.
"All pepper": in the Greek 'all vinegar.'

XVI.—THE CHARITES

THE *traditional name of this poem,* The Charites *or* Graces, *may have been really the title Theocritus had given to the whole volume of a small collection of poems, for which this poem was now written as a special dedication. In it he bewails the indifference of a money-loving age, and asks for the patronage of Hiero, then general-in-chief, afterwards king, of Syracuse, even as Simonides had the patronage—not of the first Hiero, as he would have said had this Hiero then been king, but—of the great lords of Thessaly.*

XVI.—ΧΑΡΙΤΕΣ Η ΙΕΡΩΝ

Αἰεὶ τοῦτο Διὸς κούραις μέλει, αἰὲν ἀοιδοῖς,
ὑμνεῖν ἀθανάτους, ὑμνεῖν ἀγαθῶν κλέα ἀνδρῶν.
Μοῦσαι μὲν θεαὶ ἐντί, θεοὺς θεαὶ ἀείδοντι·
ἄμμες δὲ βροτοὶ οἵδε, βροτοὺς βροτοὶ ἀείδωμεν.

τίς γὰρ τῶν ὁπόσοι γλαυκὰν ναίουσιν ὑπ' ἀῶ,
ἡμετέρας Χάριτας [1] πετάσας ὑποδέξεται οἴκῳ
ἀσπασίως, οὐδ' αὖθις ἀδωρήτους ἀποπέμψει,
αἱ δὲ σκυζόμεναι γυμνοῖς ποσὶν οἴκαδ' ἴασι,
πολλά με τωθάζοισαι, ὅτ' ἀλιθίαν ὁδὸν ἦνθον,
ὀκνηραὶ δὲ πάλιν κενεᾶς ἐν πυθμένι χηλοῦ
ψυχροῖς ἐν γονάτεσσι κάρη μίμνοντι βαλοῖσαι,
ἔνθ' αἰεί σφισιν ἕδραι, ἐπὴν ἄπρακτοι ἵκωνται;
τίς τῶν νῦν τοιόσδε; τίς εὖ εἰπόντα φιλήσει;
οὐκ οἶδ'· οὐ γὰρ ἔτ' ἄνδρες ἐπ' ἔργμασιν ὡς πάρος
    ἐσθλοῖς
αἰνεῖσθαι σπεύδοντι, νενίκηνται δ' ὑπὸ κερδέων·
πᾶς δ' ὑπὸ κόλπῳ χεῖρας ἔχων πόθεν οἴσεται ἀθρεῖ
ἄργυρον, οὐδέ κεν ἰὸν ἀποτρίψας τινὶ δοίη,
ἀλλ' εὐθὺς μυθεῖται· 'ἀπωτέρω ἢ γόνυ κνάμα·
αὐτῷ μοι τί γένοιτο [2]; θεοὶ τιμῶσιν ἀοιδούς.

---

[1] ἡμετέρας Χάριτας: schol. τὰ οἰκεῖα ποιήματα   [2] τί
γένοιτο; E, cf. Theophr. *Char.* 14. 2 λογισάμενος ταῖς ψήφοις
καὶ κεφάλαιον ποιήσας ἐρωτᾷν τὸν παρακαθήμενον· τί γίγνεται·
'what does it come to ?': mss τί or τι

XVI.—THE CHARITES

'Tis ever the care of Zeus' daughters and ever of the poets to magnify the Immortal Gods and eke to magnify the achievements of great men. But the Muses are Gods, and being Gods do sing of Gods, while as for us we are men, and being men let us sing of men.

Now who of all that dwell beneath the gray dawn, say who, will open his door to receive my pretty Graces gladly, and not rather send them away empty-handed, so that they get them home frowning and barefoot, there to fleer at me for sending them a fool's errand, there to shrink once again into the bottom of an empty press, and sinking their heads upon their chill knees to abide where they ever lodge when they return unsuccessful from abroad? Who, I say, in this present world will let them in, and who in the present days will love one that hath spoke him well? I cannot tell. The praise once sought for noble acts is sought no more; pelf reigns conqueror of every heart; and every man looks hand in pocket where he may get him silver; nay, he would not give another so much as the off-scrapings of the rust of it, but straightway cries "Charity begins at home. What comes thereout for

---

"Charity begins at home": in the Greek 'the knee lies nearer than the shin.'

τίς δέ κεν ἄλλου ἀκούσαι; ἅλις πάντεσσιν Ὅμηρος. 20
οὗτος ἀοιδῶν λῷστος, ὃς ἐξ ἐμεῦ οἴσεται οὐδέν.'

δαιμόνιοι, τί δὲ κέρδος ὁ μυρίος ἔνδοθι χρυσὸς
κείμενος; οὐχ ἅδε πλούτου φρονέουσιν ὄνασις,
ἀλλὰ τὸ μὲν ψυχᾷ, τὸ δέ πού τινι δοῦναι ἀοιδῶν·
πολλοὺς[1] εὖ ἔρξαι παῶν, πολλοὺς δὲ καὶ ἄλλων
ἀνθρώπων, αἰεὶ δὲ θεοῖς ἐπιβώμια ῥέζειν,
μηδὲ ξεινοδόκον κακὸν ἔμμεναι, ἀλλὰ τραπέζᾳ
μειλίξαντ' ἀποπέμψαι, ἐπὴν ἐθέλωντι[2] νέεσθαι,
Μουσάων δὲ μάλιστα τίειν ἱεροὺς ὑποφήτας,
ὄφρα καὶ εἰν Ἀΐδαο κεκρυμμένος ἐσθλὸς ἀκούσῃς, 30
μηδ' ἀκλεὴς μύρηαι ἐπὶ ψυχροῦ Ἀχέροντος,
ὡσεί τις μακέλᾳ τετυλωμένος ἔνδοθι χεῖρας
ἀχὴν ἐκ πατέρων πενίαν ἀκτήμονα κλαίων.

πολλοὶ ἐν Ἀντιόχοιο δόμοις καὶ ἄνακτος Ἀλεύα
ἁρμαλιὰν ἔμμηνον ἐμετρήσαντο πενέσται·
πολλοὶ δὲ Σκοπάδαισιν ἐλαυνόμενοι ποτὶ σακοὺς
μόσχοι σὺν κεραῇσιν ἐμυκήσαντο βόεσσι,
μυρία δ' ἂμ πεδίον Κρανώνιον ἐνδιάασκον
ποιμένες ἔκκριτα μῆλα φιλοξείνοισι Κρεώνδαις·
ἀλλ' οὔ σφιν τῶν ἧδος, ἐπεὶ γλυκὺν ἐξεκένωσαν 40
θυμὸν ἐς εὐρεῖαν σχεδίαν στυγνοῖο γέροντος,[3]
ἄμναστοι δὲ τὰ πολλὰ καὶ ὄλβια τῆνα λιπόντες

---

[1] πολλοὺς Wil: mss πολλοὺς δ'   [2] Mss ἐθέλοντι
[3] στυγνοῖο γέροντος Hemsterhuys from Propert. 3. 18. 24 :
mss στυγνοῦ ἀχέροντος

me? 'Tis the Gods that honour poets. Who would hear yet another? Homer is enough for all. Him rank I best of poets, who of me shall get nothing."

Poor simple fools! what profits it a man that he have thousands of gold laid by? To the wise the enjoyment of riches is not that, but rather to give first somewhat to his own soul, and then something, methinks, to one of the poets; to wit, it is first to do much good as well to other men as to his kinsfolk, to make offering of sacrifice unceasingly upon the altars of the Gods, and, like one hospitably minded, to send his guests, when go they will, kindly entreated away; and secondly and more than all, it is to bestow honour upon the holy interpreters of the Muses, that so you may rather be well spoken of even when you lie hid in Death, than, like some horny-handed delving son of a poor father bewailing his empty penury, make your moan beside chill Acheron's brink without either name or fame.

Many indeed were the bondmen earned their monthly meed in the houses of Antiochus and King Aleuas, many the calves that went lowing with the horned kine home to the byres of the Scopads, and ten thousand were the fine sheep that the shepherds of the plain of Crannon watched all night for the hospitable Creondae; but once all the sweet wine of their life was in the great cup, once they were embarked in the barge of the old man loathsome, the joyance and pleasure of those things was theirs no more: and though they left behind

THE BUCOLIC POETS

δειλοῖς ἐν νεκύεσσι μακροὺς αἰῶνας ἔκειντο,
εἰ μὴ θεῖος ἀοιδὸς ὁ Κήϊος αἰόλα φωνέων
βάρβιτον ἐς πολύχορδον ἐν ἀνδράσι θῆκ' ὀνο-
    μαστοὺς
ὁπλοτέροις, τιμᾶς δὲ καὶ ὠκέες ἔλλαχον ἵπποι,
οἵ σφισιν ἐξ ἱερῶν στεφανηφόροι ἦνθον ἀγώνων.

τίς δ' ἂν ἀριστῆας Λυκίων ποτέ, τίς κομόωντας
Πριαμίδας ἢ θῆλυν ἀπὸ χροιῆς Κύκνον ἔγνω,
εἰ μὴ φυλόπιδας προτέρων ὕμνησαν ἀοιδοί;
οὐδ' Ὀδυσεὺς ἑκατόν τε καὶ εἴκοσι μῆνας ἀλαθεὶς
πάντας ἐπ' ἀνθρώπους, Ἀΐδαν τ' εἰς ἔσχατον ἐνθὼν
ζωὸς καὶ σπήλυγγα φυγὼν ὀλοοῖο Κύκλωπος
δηναιὸν κλέος ἔσχεν, ἐσιγάθη δ' ἂν ὑφορβὸς
Εὔμαιος καὶ βουσὶ Φιλοίτιος ἀμφ' ἀγελαίαις
ἔργον ἔχων, αὐτός τε περίσπλαγχνος Λαέρτης,
εἰ μή σφεας ὤνασαν Ἰάονος ἀνδρὸς ἀοιδαί.

ἐκ Μοισᾶν ἀγαθὸν κλέος ἔρχεται ἀνθρώποισι,
χρήματα δὲ ζώοντες ἀμαλδύνουσι θανόντων.
ἀλλ' ἴσος γὰρ ὁ μόχθος ἐπ' ἀόνι κύματα μετρεῖν,
ὅσσ' ἄνεμος χέρσονδε κατὰ[1] γλαυκᾶς ἁλὸς ὠθεῖ,
ἢ ὕδατι νίζειν θολερὰν διαειδέι πλίνθον,
καὶ φιλοκερδείᾳ βεβλαμμένον ἄνδρα παρειπεῖν·[2]
χαιρέτω ὅστις τοῖος, ἀνάριθμος δέ οἱ εἴη
ἄργυρος, αἰεὶ δὲ πλεόνων ἔχοι ἵμερος αὐτόν.
αὐτὰρ ἐγὼ τιμάν τε καὶ ἀνθρώπων φιλότατα
πολλῶν ἡμιόνων τε καὶ ἵππων πρόσθεν ἑλοίμαν.

---

[1] κατὰ Buecheler : mss μετὰ   [2] παρειπεῖν : mss also
παρελθεῖν

them all that great and noble wealth, they had lain among the vile dead long ages unremembered, had not the great Ceian cried sweet varied lays to the strings and famoused them in posterity, and had not the coursers that came home to them victorious out of the Games achieved the honour and glory which called the poet to his task.

Then too the lords of the old Lycians, then the long-haired children of Priam or that Cycnus that was wan as a woman,—say who had known aught of them, had not poets hymned the battle-cries of an elder day? Moreover Odysseus had wandered his hundred months and twenty through all the world, come to uttermost Hades alive, and gone safe from out the cave of the fell Cyclops, and then had never enjoyed the long and lasting glory of it all; and as well great-heart Laertes himself as Eumaeus the hog-ward and Philoetius the keeper of herded kine, all alike had been under silence had it not profited them of the lays of a man of Ionia.

Yes; good fame men may get of the Muses, but riches be wasted of their posterity after they are dead. But seeing one may as well strive to wash clean in clear water a sun-dried brick, as well stand on the beach and number the waves driven shoreward of the wind from the blue sea, as seek to win by words one whose heart is wounded with the love of gain, I bid all such a very good day, and wish them silver beyond counting and long life to their craving for more. For myself, I would rather the esteem and friendship of my fellow-men than hundreds of mules and horses.

"The great Ceian": Simonides. "A man of Ionia": Homer. "Sun-dried brick": when wetted this becomes clay again.

δίζημαι δ', ὅτινι θνατῶν κεχαρισμένος ἔνθω
σὺν Μοίσαις· χαλεπαὶ γὰρ ὁδοὶ τελέθουσιν ἀοιδοῖς
κουράων ἀπάνευθε Διὸς μέγα βουλεύοντος.
οὔπω μῆνας ἄγων ἔκαμ' οὐρανὸς οὐδ' ἐνιαυτούς·
πολλοὶ κινήσουσιν ἔτι τροχὸν ἅματος[1] ἵπποι.
ἔσσεται οὗτος ἀνήρ, ὃς ἐμεῦ κεχρήσετ' ἀοιδοῦ
ῥέξας ἢ Ἀχιλεὺς ὅσσον μέγας ἢ βαρὺς Αἴας
ἐν πεδίῳ Σιμόεντος, ὅθι Φρυγὸς ἠρίον Ἴλου.

ἤδη νῦν Φοίνικες ὑπ' ἀελίῳ δύνοντι
οἰκεῦντες Λιλύβας[2] ἄκρον σφυρὸν ἐρρίγασιν·
ἤδη βαστάζουσι Συρακόσιοι μέσα δοῦρα
ἀχθόμενοι σακέεσσι βραχίονας ἰτεΐνοισιν·
ἐν δ' αὐτοῖς Ἱέρων προτέροις ἴσος ἡρώεσσι
ζώννυται, ἵππειαι δὲ κόρυν σκιάουσιν[3] ἔθειραι.
αἱ γὰρ Ζεῦ κύδιστε πάτερ καὶ πότνι' Ἀθάνα
κούρα θ', ἣ σὺν ματρὶ πολυκλάρων Ἐφυραίων
εἴληχας μέγα ἄστυ παρ' ὕδασι Λυσιμελείας,
ἐχθροὺς ἐκ νάσοιο κακαὶ πέμψειαν ἀνάγκαι
Σαρδόνιον κατὰ κῦμα φίλων μόρον ἀγγέλλοντας
τέκνοις ἠδ' ἀλόχοισιν ἀριθμητοὺς ἀπὸ πολλῶν·
ἄστεα δὲ προτέροισι πάλιν ναίοιτο πολίταις,
δυσμενέων ὅσα χεῖρες ἐλωβήσαντο κατ' ἄκρας,
ἀγροὶ δ' ἐργάζοιντο τεθαλότες,[4] αἱ δ' ἀνάριθμοι
μήλων χιλιάδες βοτάνᾳ διαπιανθεῖσαι
ἂμ πεδίον βλαχῶντο, βόες δ' ἀγελαδὸν ἐς αὖλιν

---

[1] ἅματος Wil : mss ἅρματος   [2] Λιλύβας Kuiper : mss
Λιβύας   [3] σκιάουσιν : mss also σκεπάουσιν   [4] ἀγροὶ δ'
ἐργάζοιντο (passive) τεθαλότες E : mss ἀγροὺς δ' ἐργ. τεθαλότας

And so now I am on my way to seek to whom in all the world I with the Muses may come and be welcome ;—with the Muses, for 'tis ill travelling for your poet if he have not with him the Daughters of the Great Counsellor. Not yet are the heavens wearied of bringing round the months nor the years ; many the horses yet will roll the wheel of the day ; and I shall yet find the man who therefore shall need me for his poet because he shall have done as doughtily as ever did great Achilles or dread Aias by the grave of Phrygian Ilus in Simoeis vale.

For lo ! the Phoenician dweller in the foot of Lilybè in the west shudders already and shakes ; the Syracusan hath already his spear by the middle and his wicker targe upon his arm ; and there like one of the olden heroes stands Hiero girding his loins among his men, a horse-hair plume waving on his crest. And I would to thee, renowned Father, and to thee, Lady Athena, I would to thee, Maiden who with thy Mother dost possess by Lysimeleia's side the great city of the rich Ephyreans, I would that evil necessities may clear our island of hostile folk and send them down the Sardinian wave with tidings of death to wives and children, a remnant easy to number of a mighty host ; and I pray that all the towns the hands of enemies have laid so utterly waste, may be inhabited again of their ancient peoples, and their fields laboured and made to bring forth abundantly, their lowlands filled with the bleating of fat flocks in their tens of thousands, and the twilight

"Lilybè" : the western angle of Sicily, the promontory of Lilybaeum. The reference to the coming campaign against the Carthaginians dates the poem in the year 274. "The Maiden" : the maiden is Persephone, the mother Demeter, and the city Syracuse.

ἐρχόμεναι σκνιφαῖον ἐπισπεύδοιεν ὁδίταν·
νειοὶ δ' ἐκπολέοιντο [1] ποτὶ σπόρον, ἀνίκα τέττιξ
ποιμένας ἐνδίους πεφυλαγμένος ὑψόθι δένδρων
ἀχεῖ ἐν ἀκρεμόνεσσιν· ἀράχνια δ' εἰς ὅπλ' ἀράχναι
λεπτὰ διαστάσαιντο, βοᾶς δ' ἔτι μηδ' ὄνομ' εἴη·
ὑψηλὸν δ' Ἱέρωνι κλέος φορέοιεν ἀοιδοὶ
καὶ πόντου Σκυθικοῖο πέραν καὶ ὅθι πλατὺ τεῖχος
ἀσφάλτῳ δήσασα Σεμίραμις ἐμβασίλευσεν.

εἷς μὲν ἐγώ, πολλοὺς δὲ Διὸς φιλέοντι καὶ ἄλλους
θυγατέρες, τοῖς πᾶσι μέλοι Σικελὰν Ἀρέθοισαν
ὑμνεῖν σὺν λαοῖσι καὶ αἰχμητὰν Ἱέρωνα.

ὦ Ἐτεόκλειοι Χάριτες θεαί, ὦ Μινύειον
Ὀρχομενὸν φιλέοισαι ἀπεχθόμενόν ποτε Θήβαις,
ἄκλητος μὲν ἔγωγε μένοιμί κεν, ἐς δὲ καλεύντων
θαρσήσας Μοίσαισι σὺν ἀμετέραισιν ἴοιμ' ἄν.[2]
καλλείψω δ' οὐδ' ὔμμε· τί γὰρ Χαρίτων ἀγαπατὸν
ἀνθρώποις ἀπάνευθεν; ἀεὶ Χαρίτεσσιν ἅμ' εἴην.

---

[1] ἐκπολέοιντο E, 'be ploughed not here and there only but throughout the landscape': mss ἐκπονέοιντο, ἐκπλέοιντο, ἐκτελέοιντο   [2] ἴοιμ' ἄν Wil: mss ἰοίμαν, ἰκοίμαν

"Eteocles": this early king of Orchomenus in Boeotia, was said to have been the first to offer sacrifice to the Graces, and Thebes had reason to hate the same Orchomenus because a

traveller warned to hasten his steps by the home-going of innumerable herds; and I pray likewise that against the time when the cricket is fain to sing high in the twigs overhead because of the noontide-resting shepherds, against that time, the time of sowing, none of the fallows be left unturned of the plough, and as for the weapons of war, may spiders weave over them their slender webs, and of the war-cry the very name be forgot. And the glory of Hiero, that may poets waft high both over the Scythian main and eke where Semiramis reigned within that broad wall she made with mortar of pitch; and of these poets I am one, one of the many beloved by the daughters of Zeus, which are concerned all of them to magnify Sicilian Arethuse with her people and her mighty man of war.

O holy Graces first adored of Eteocles, O lovers of that Minyan Orchomenus which Thebes had cause to hate of old, as, if I be called not, I will abide at home, so, if I be called, I will take heart and go with our Muses to the house of any that call. And you shall come too; for mortal man possesseth nothing desirable if he have not the Graces, and 'tis my prayer the Graces be with me evermore.

certain Erginus in revenge for the murder of his father had made Thebes tributary to Orchomenus; Theocritus hints at a wish that Hiero may follow the example of Eteocles in the matter of patronage, and Syracuse prevail over Carthage as Orchomenus did over Thebes. "The Graces": he plays on two meanings of the word *Charites*, thanks or gratitude or favour, and the Graces who were the spirits of beauty and excellence and handmaidens of the Muses.

XVII — THE PANEGYRIC OF PTOLEMY

A PANEGYRIC *of Ptolemy II, Philadelphus, who reigned from* 285 *to* 247. *The references to historical personages and events, coupled with a comparison with XVI, point to* 273 *as the date of the poem. The Ptolemies, like Alexander, traced their descent from Heracles. Ptolemy I, son of Lagus, was deified about* 283, *and his queen Berenice between* 279 *and* 275.

XVII.—ΕΓΚΩΜΙΟΝ ΕΙΣ ΠΤΟΛΕΜΑΙΟΝ

Ἐκ Διὸς ἀρχώμεσθα καὶ ἐς Δία λήγετε Μοῖσαι,
ἀθανάτων τὸν ἄριστον ἐπὴν αἴρωμεν[1] ἀοιδαῖς·
ἀνδρῶν δ' αὖ Πτολεμαῖος ἐνὶ πρώτοισι λεγέσθω
καὶ πύματος καὶ μέσσος· ὁ γὰρ προφερέστατος
    ἀνδρῶν.
ἥρωες, τοὶ πρόσθεν ἀφ' ἡμιθέων ἐγένοντο,
ῥέξαντες καλὰ ἔργα σοφῶν ἐκύρησαν ἀοιδῶν·
αὐτὰρ ἐγὼ Πτολεμαῖον ἐπιστάμενος καλὰ εἰπεῖν
ὑμνήσαιμ'· ὕμνοι δὲ καὶ ἀθανάτων γέρας αὐτῶν.
Ἴδαν ἐς πολύδενδρον ἀνὴρ ὑλατόμος ἐλθὼν
παπταίνει, παρεόντος ἄδην, πόθεν ἄρξεται ἔργου·
τί πρῶτον καταλέξω; ἐπεὶ πάρα μυρία εἰπεῖν,
οἷσι θεοὶ τὸν ἄριστον ἐτίμησαν βασιλήων.

    ἐκ πατέρων· οἷος μὲν ἔην τελέσαι μέγα ἔργον
Λαγείδας Πτολεμαῖος, ὅκα φρεσὶν ἐγκατάθοιτο
βουλάν, ἃν οὐκ ἄλλος ἀνὴρ οἷός τε νοῆσαι.
τῆνον καὶ μακάρεσσι πατὴρ ὁμότιμον ἔθηκεν
ἀθανάτοις, καί οἱ χρύσεος δόμος ἐν Διὸς οἴκῳ
δέδμηται· παρὰ δ' αὐτὸν Ἀλέξανδρος φίλα εἰδὼς
ἑδριάει, Πέρσαισι βαρὺς θεὸς αἰολομίτρας.

---

[1] Tucker: mss ἀείδωμεν or ἄδωμεν: P. Ant. αριστον [about 10 *letters*]εν αοιδης (= ἀοιδῆς?)

XVII.—THE PANEGYRIC OF PTOLEMY

With Zeus let us begin, Muses, and with Zeus I pray you end when the greatest of Immortals is exalted in our song: but for men first, midst and last be the name of Ptolemy; for he is of men the chiefest.

The heroes that came of demigods of yore found skilly singers of the glorious deeds which they did; and in like manner a cunning teller of praises shall raise the hymn to Ptolemy, seeing hymns make the meed even of the Gods above.

Now when the feller goes up to thick woody Ida he looks about him where to begin in all that plenty; and so I, where now shall I take up my tale when I might tell of ten thousand ways wherein the Gods have done honour to the greatest of kings?

'Twas in the blood. First what an achiever of mighty exploits was Ptolemy Lagid when his mind conceived a device such as no other mind could come by! Whom now the Father hath made of equal honour with the Blessed; a golden mansion is builded him in the house of Zeus, and seated friendly beside him is the Lord of the Glancing Baldric, that God of woe to the Persians, Alexander,

"'Twas in the blood": the Greek is ''twas from his fathers,' fathers meaning parents, as in Longus 4. 33; Theocritus deals first with his father Ptolemy Lagid and then with his mother Berenice.

ἀντία δ᾽ Ἡρακλῆος ἕδρα κενταυροφόνοιο[1]
ἵδρυται στερεοῖο τετυγμένα ἐξ ἀδάμαντος,
ἔνθα σὺν ἄλλοισιν θαλίας ἔχει Οὐρανίδαισι,
χαίρων υἱωνῶν περιώσιον υἱωνοῖσιν,
ὅττι σφεων Κρονίδας μελέων ἐξείλετο γῆρας,
ἀθάνατοι δὲ καλεῦνται ἑοὶ[2] νέποδες γεγαῶτες.
ἄμφω γὰρ πρόγονός σφιν ὁ καρτερὸς Ἡρακλείδας,
ἀμφότεροι δ᾽ ἀριθμεῦνται ἐς ἔσχατον Ἡρακλῆα.
τῷ καὶ ἐπεὶ δαίτηθεν ἴῃ κεκορημένος ἤδη
νέκταρος εὐόδμοιο φίλας ἐς δῶμ᾽ ἀλόχοιο,
τῷ μὲν τόξον ἔδωκεν ὑπωλένιόν τε φαρέτραν,
τῷ δὲ σιδάρειον σκύταλον κεχαραγμένον ὄζοις·
οἳ δ᾽ εἰς ἀμβρόσιον θάλαμον λευκοσφύρου Ἥβας
ὅπλα καὶ αὐτὸν ἄγουσι γενειήταν Διὸς υἱόν.

οἷα δ᾽ ἐν πινυταῖσι περικλειτὰ Βερενίκα
ἔπρεπε θηλυτέραις, ὄφελος μέγα γεινομένοισι.[3]
τᾷ μὲν Κύπρον ἔχοισα Διώνας πότνια κούρα
κόλπον ἐς εὐώδη ῥαδινὰς ἐσεμάξατο χεῖρας·
τῷ οὔπω τινὰ φαντὶ ἀδεῖν τόσον ἀνδρὶ γυναικῶν,
ὅσσον περ Πτολεμαῖος ἑὰν ἐφίλησεν ἄκοιτιν.
ἦ μὰν ἀντεφιλεῖτο πολὺ πλέον· ὧδέ κε παισὶ
θαρσήσας σφετέροισιν ἐπιτρέποι οἶκον ἅπαντα,
ὁππότε κεν φιλέων βαίνῃ λέχος ἐς φιλεοίσας,
ἀστόργου δὲ γυναικὸς ἐπ᾽ ἀλλοτρίῳ νόος αἰεί,
ῥαΐδιοι δὲ γοναί, τέκνα δ᾽ οὐ ποτεοικότα πατρί.

---

[1] ἕδρα κενταυροφόνοιο G. Kiessling : mss ἕδρακε ταυροφ.
[2] ἑοὶ Heinsius : mss θεοί   [3] γεινομένοισι E, generalising
plural : mss γειναμέναισι

while over against him is set the stark adamantine seat of Centaur-slayer Heracles, who taketh his meat with the other Sons of Heaven, rejoicing exceedingly that by grace of Zeus the children of his children's children have old age now lift from their limbs and they that were born his posterity are named and known of the Immortals. For unto either king the valiant founder of his race was a son of Heracles; both in the long last reckon Heracles of their line. And therefore now when the same Heracles hath had enough of the fragrant nectar and goes from table to the chamber of the wife he loves, he gives the one his bow and hanging quiver and the other his knaggy iron-hard club, to carry beside him as he goes, this bush-bearded son of Zeus, to the ambrosial chamber of the white-ankle Hebè.

Then secondly for his mother; how bright among dames discreet shone the fame of Berenicè, what a boon to her progeny was she! Of whom the lady possessor of Cyprus that is daughter of Dionè laid taper fingers upon the sweet soft bosom, and such, they say, did make her that never woman gave man so great delight as Ptolemy took in his love of that his wife. Aye, he got all as much as he gave and more; for while the wife that loves not sets her heart ever upon things alien, and has offspring indeed at her desire albeit the children favour not the father, 'tis when the love of the marriage-bed is each to each that with good courage one may leave, like Ptolemy, all his house to be ordered of his children. O Lady

"The wife that loves not": this refers to no definite woman, which would be not only in the worst taste but certain to defeat the object of the poem, the winning of Ptolemy's

κάλλει ἀριστεύουσα θεάων πότν' Ἀφροδίτα,
σοὶ τήνα μεμέλητο· σέθεν δ' ἕνεκεν Βερενίκα
εὐειδὴς Ἀχέροντα πολύστονον οὐκ ἐπέρασεν,
ἀλλά μιν ἁρπάξασα, πάροιθ' ἐπὶ νᾶα κατελθεῖν
κυανέαν καὶ στυγνὸν ἀεὶ πορθμῆα καμόντων,
ἐς ναὸν κατέθηκας, ἑᾶς δ' ἀπεδάσσαο τιμάς·
πᾶσιν δ' ἤπιος ἅδε βροτοῖς μαλακοὺς μὲν ἔρωτας
προσπνείει, κούφας δὲ διδοῖ ποθέοντι μερίμνας.

Ἀργεία κυάνοφρυ, σὺ λαοφόνον Διομήδεα
μισγομένα Τυδῆι τέκες, Καλυδωνίῳ ἀνδρί,[1]
ἀλλὰ Θέτις βαθύκολπος ἀκοντιστὰν Ἀχιλῆα
Αἰακίδα Πηλῆι, σὲ δ' αἰχμητὰ Πτολεμαῖε
αἰχμητᾷ Πτολεμαίῳ ἀρίζηλος Βερενίκα.

καί σε Κόως ἀτίταλλε βρέφος νεογιλλὸν ἐόντα,
δεξαμένα παρὰ ματρός, ὅτε πρώταν ἴδες ἀῶ.
ἔνθα γὰρ Εἰλείθυιαν ἐβώσατο λυσίζωνον
Ἀντιγόνας θυγάτηρ βεβαρημένα ὠδίνεσσιν·
ἃ δέ οἱ εὐμενέοισα παρίστατο, κὰδ δ' ἄρα πάντων
νωδυνίαν κατέχευε μελῶν· ὁ δὲ πατρὶ ἐοικὼς
παῖς ἀγαπατὸς ἔγεντο. Κόως δ' ὀλόλυξεν ἰδοῖσα,
φᾶ δὲ καθαπτομένα βρέφεος χείρεσσι φίλαισιν·
'ὄλβιε κοῦρε γένοιο, τίοις δέ με τόσσον, ὅσον περ
Δᾶλον ἐτίμασεν κυανάμπυκα Φοῖβος Ἀπόλλων·
ἐν δὲ μιᾷ τιμᾷ Τρίοπον[2] καταθεῖο κολώναν

---

[1] Hiller: mss Καλυδώνιον ἄνδρα
Stephanus perhaps rightly Τρίοπος

[2] Τρίοπον so mss:

214

Aphrodite, chiefest beauty of the Goddesses, as 'twas thou that hadst made her to be such, so 'twas of thee that the fair Berenicè passed not sad lamentable Acheron, but or e'er she reached the murky ship and that ever-sullen shipman the ferrier of the departed, was rapt away to be a Goddess in a temple, where now participating in thy great prerogatives, with a gentle breath she both inspires all mankind unto soft desires and lightens the cares of him that hath loved and lost.

Even as the dark-browed Argive maid did bear unto Tydeus of Calydon Diomed the slayer of peoples, but and even as deep-bosom'd Thetis bare unto Peleus Aeacid javelineer Achilles, in like manner, O my liege, did renowned Berenicè bear to warrior Ptolemy another warrior Ptolemy.

And when thou first saw'st the dawn, she that took thee from thy mother and dandled thee, poor babe, on her lap, was the good lady Cos; for there in Cos island had the daughter of Antigonè cried aloud to the Girdle-Looser in the oppression of pain, there had the Goddess stood by to comfort her and to shed immunity from grief upon all her limbs, and there was born in the likeness of his father the beloved son. And when she beheld him, good Cos broke into a cry of joy, and clasping the babe in her loving arms 'Heaven bless thee, boy,' said she, 'and grant I may have all as much honour of thee as blue-snooded Delos had of Phoebus Apollo; and not I only, but Heaven send thou assign equal privilege to

patronage. The phrase is simply a foil. Theocritus means that Ptolemy I would not have abdicated had he not had his wife's love and all that that entails.   " the Argive maid " : Deïpylè.

ἶσον Δωριέεσσι νέμων γέρας ἐγγὺς ἐοῦσιν·
ἶσον καὶ Ῥήναιαν ἄναξ ἐφίλησεν Ἀπόλλων.'
ὡς ἄρα νᾶσος ἔειπεν· ὃ δ' ὑψόθεν ἔκλαγε φωνᾷ
ἐς τρὶς ἀπὸ νεφέων μέγας αἰετὸς αἴσιος ὄρνις.
Ζηνός που τόδε σᾶμα. Διὶ Κρονίωνι μέλοντι
αἰδοῖοι βασιλῆες· ὃ δ' ἔξοχος, ὅν κε φιλήσῃ
γεινόμενον τὰ πρῶτα· πολὺς δέ οἱ ὄλβος ὀπαδεῖ·
πολλᾶς δὲ κρατέει γαίας, πολλᾶς δὲ θαλάσσας.

μυρίαι ἄπειροί τε καὶ ἔθνεα μυρία φωτῶν
λήϊον ἀλδήσκουσιν ὀφελλόμενον Διὸς ὄμβρῳ·
ἀλλ' οὔτις τόσα φύει ὅσα χθαμαλὰ Αἴγυπτος,
Νεῖλος ἀναβλύζων διερὰν ὅτε βῶλακα θρύπτει,
οὐδέ τις ἄστεα τόσσα βροτῶν ἔχει ἔργα δαέντων.
τρεῖς μέν οἱ πολίων ἑκατοντάδες ἐνδέδμηνται,
τρεῖς δ' ἄρα χιλιάδες τρισσαῖς ἐπὶ μυριάδεσσι,
δοιαὶ δὲ τριάδες, μετὰ δέ σφισιν ἐννεάδες τρεῖς·
τῶν πάντων Πτολεμαῖος ἀγήνωρ ἐμβασιλεύει.
καὶ μὰν Φοίνικας ἀποτέμνεται Ἀρραβίας τε
καὶ Συρίας Λιβύας τε κελαινῶν τ' Αἰθιοπήων·
Παμφύλοισι[1] τε πᾶσι καὶ αἰχμηταῖς Κιλίκεσσι
σαμαίνει, Λυκίοις τε φιλοπτολέμοισί τε Καρσί,
καὶ νάσοις Κυκλάδεσσιν· ἐπεί οἱ νᾶες ἄρισται[2]
πόντον ἐπιπλώοντι, θάλασσα δὲ πᾶσα καὶ αἶα
καὶ ποταμοὶ κελάδοντες ἀνάσσονται Πτολεμαίῳ,

---

[1] Παμφύλοισι Schrader : mss Παμφυλίοισι   [2] ἄρισται
Stephanus : mss ἄριστοι through misunderstanding οἱ

all the neighbour Dorian cities in the joint honour of the Triopian Hill; for Apollo gave Rheneia equal love with Delos.' Thus far the Island; and lo! from the clouds above came thrice over the boding croak of a great eagle. And 'faith, 'twas of Zeus that sign; for Zeus Cronion, as he watches over all reverend kings, so especially careth he for a king that he hath loved from his earliest hour. Such an one is attended of great good-fortune, and wins himself the mastery of much land and of many seas.

Ten thousand are the lands and ten thousand the nations that make the crops to spring under aid of the rain of Zeus, but there's no country so fruitful as the low-country of Egypt when Nile comes gushing up to soak the soil and break it, nor no country, neither, possessed of so many cities of men learned in labour. The cities builded therein are three hundreds and three thousands and three tens of thousands, and threes twain and nines three, and in them the lord and master of all is proud Ptolemy. Aye, and of Phoenicia and Arabia he taketh to him a hantle, and eke of Syria and Libya and of the swart Aethiop's country; and he giveth the word to all them of Pamphylia and all the warriors of Cilicia; and to the people of Lycia and warlike Caria and to the Cyclad Isles he giveth it; and this because he hath a noble navy sailing the main, so that all the sea, every land, and each of the sounding rivers doth acknowledge his dominion, and full many are the mighty warriors

"Rheneia": an island near Delos; Triopum is a promontory of Caria where the Dorian Pentapolis of Cos and the neighbouring cities celebrated a common worship of Apollo and other Gods. The Pentapolis was apparently asking Ptolemy for some privilege at this time.

πολλοὶ δ᾽ ἱππῆες, πολλοὶ δέ μιν ἀσπιδιῶται
χαλκῷ μαρμαίροντι σεσαγμένοι ἀμφαγέρονται.
ὄλβῳ μὲν πάντας κε καταβρίθοι βασιλῆας·
τόσσον ἐπ᾽ ἆμαρ ἕκαστον ἐς ἀφνεὸν ἔρχεται
    οἶκον
πάντοθε. λαοὶ δ᾽ ἔργα περιστέλλονται[1] ἕκηλοι.
οὐ γάρ τις δηίων πολυκήτεα Νεῖλον ὑπερβὰς
πεζὸς ἐν ἀλλοτρίαισι βοὰν ἐστάσατο κώμαις,
οὐδέ τις αἰγιαλόνδε θοᾶς ἐξάλατο ναὸς
θωρηχθεὶς ἐπὶ βουσὶν ἀνάρσιος Αἰγυπτίαισι·
τοῖος ἀνὴρ πλατέεσσιν ἐνίδρυται πεδίοισι
ξανθοκόμας Πτολεμαῖος, ἐπιστάμενος δόρυ
    πάλλειν,
ᾧ ἐπίπαγχυ μέλει πατρώια πάντα φυλάσσειν
οἷ᾽ ἀγαθῷ βασιλῆι, τὰ δὲ κτεατίζεται αὐτός.
οὐ μὰν ἀχρεῖός γε δόμῳ ἐνὶ πίονι χρυσὸς
μυρμάκων ἅτε πλοῦτος ἀεὶ κέχυται μογεόντων·
ἀλλὰ πολὺν μὲν ἔχοντι θεῶν ἐρικυδέες οἶκοι,
αἰὲν ἀπαρχομένοιο σὺν ἄλλοισιν γεράεσσι,
πολλὸν δ᾽ ἰφθίμοισι δεδώρηται βασιλεῦσι,
πολλὸν δὲ πτολίεσσι, πολὺν δ᾽ ἀγαθοῖσιν ἑταίροις.
οὐδὲ Διωνύσου τις ἀνὴρ ἱεροὺς κατ᾽ ἀγῶνας
ἵκετ᾽ ἐπιστάμενος λιγυρὰν ἀναμέλψαι ἀοιδάν,
ᾧ οὐ δωτίναν ἀντάξιον ὤπασε τέχνας.
    Μουσάων δ᾽ ὑποφῆται ἀείδοντι Πτολεμαῖον
ἀντ᾽ εὐεργεσίας. τί δὲ κάλλιον ἀνδρί κεν εἴη
ὀλβίῳ ἢ κλέος ἐσθλὸν ἐν ἀνθρώποισιν ἀρέσθαι;
τοῦτο καὶ Ἀτρείδαισι μένει· τὰ δὲ μυρία τῆνα,

---

[1] περιστέλλονται : mss also περιστέλλουσιν

a-horseback and full many the burnished brass-clad targeteers afoot that rally for the battle around his standard.

For wealth, his would outweigh the wealth of all the princes of the earth together,—so much comes into his rich habitation both day by day and from every quarter. And as for his peoples, they occupy their business without let or hindrance, seeing that no foeman hath crossed afoot that river of monsters to set up a cry in alien townships, nor none leapt from swift ship upon that beach all mailed to make havoc of the Egyptian kine,—of such noble sort is the flaxen-haired prince that is throned in these level plains, a prince who not only hath cunning to wield the spear, but, as a good king should, makes it his chiefest care both to keep all that he hath of his father and to add somewhat for himself. But not to no purpose doth his gold lie, like so much riches of the still-toiling emmet, in his opulent house ; much of it —for never makes he offerings of firstfruits but gold is one—is spent upon the splendid dwellings of the Gods, and much of it again is given in presents to cities, to stalwart kings, or to the good friends that bear him company. Nay, no cunning singer of tuneful song that hath sought part in Dionysus' holy contests but hath received of him a gift to the full worth of his skill.

But 'tis not for his wealth that the interpreters of the Muses sing praise of Ptolemy ; rather is it for his well-doing. And what can be finer for a wealthy and prosperous man than to earn a fair fame among his fellow-men ? This it is which endureth even to the sons of Atreus, albeit all those ten thousand

ὅσσα μέγαν Πριάμοιο δόμον κτεάτισσαν ἑλόντες
ἀέρι πᾳ κέκρυπται, ὅθεν πάλιν οὐκέτι νόστος.
μοῦνος ὅδε προτέρων τε καὶ ὧν[1] ἔτι θερμὰ κονία
στειβομένα καθύπερθε ποδῶν ἐκμάσσεται ἴχνη,
ματρὶ φίλᾳ καὶ πατρὶ θυώδεας εἴσατο ναούς·
ἐν δ' αὐτοὺς χρυσῷ περικαλλέας ἠδ' ἐλέφαντι
ἵδρυται πάντεσσιν ἐπιχθονίοισιν ἀρωγούς.
πολλὰ δὲ πιανθέντα βοῶν ὅγε μηρία καίει
μησὶ περιπλομένοισιν ἐρευθομένων ἐπὶ βωμῶν,
αὐτός τ' ἰφθίμα τ' ἄλοχος, τᾶς οὔτις ἀρείων
νυμφίον ἐν μεγάροισι γυνὰ περιβάλλετ' ἀγοστῷ,
ἐκ θυμοῦ στέργοισα κασίγνητόν τε πόσιν τε.
ὧδε καὶ ἀθανάτων ἱερὸς γάμος ἐξετελέσθη,
οὓς τέκετο κρείουσα Ῥέα βασιλῆας Ὀλύμπου·
ἐν δὲ λέχος[2] στόρνυσιν ἰαύειν Ζανὶ καὶ Ἥρᾳ
χεῖρας φοιβήσασα μύροις ἔτι[3] παρθένος Ἶρις.

χαῖρε ἄναξ Πτολεμαῖε· σέθεν δ' ἐγὼ ἶσα καὶ
    ἄλλων
μνάσομαι ἡμιθέων, δοκέω δ' ἔπος οὐκ ἀπόβλητον
φθέγξομαι ἐσσομένοις· ἀρετάν γε μὲν ἐκ Διὸς
    αἰτεῦ.[4]

---

[1] τε καὶ ὧν Briggs: mss τεκέων or τοκέων   [2] ἐν δὲ λέχος:
mss also ἁγνὸν δὲ (Ahr. ἅγνον δέ)   [3] ἔτι = ἀεὶ as in *Epig.* 20
and *Ep. Bion.* 92   [4] αἰτεῦ: mss also ἕξεις

possessions that fell to them when they took Priam's great house, they lie hid somewhere in that mist whence no return can be evermore. And this man hath done that which none before hath done, be he of them of old, be he of those whose footmarks are yet warm in the dust they trod ; he hath builded incense-fragrant temples to his mother and father dear, and hath set therein images of them in gold and ivory, very beautiful, to be the aid of all that live upon the earth. And many are the thighs of fatted oxen that as the months go round he consumes upon the reddening altars, he and that his fine noble spouse, who maketh him a better wife than ever clasped bridegroom under any roof, seeing that she loveth with her whole heart brother and husband in one. So too in heaven was the holy wedlock accomplished of those whom august Rhea bare to be rulers of Olympus, so too the myrrh-cleansed hands of the ever-maiden Iris lay but one couch for the slumbering of Zeus and Hera.

And now farewell, Lord Ptolemy ; and I will speak of thee as of other demi-gods, and methinks what I shall say will not be lost upon posterity ; 'tis this—excellence ask from none but Zeus.

XVIII.—THE EPITHALAMY OF HELEN

T<small>HIS</small> *is a short Epic piece of the same type as XIII. Both begin, as do XXV and Bion II, with a phrase suggesting that they are consequent upon something previous; but this, like the* ergo *or* igitur *of Propertius and Ovid, is no more than a recognised way of beginning a short poem. The introduction, unlike that of XIII, contains no dedication. The scholia tell us Theocritus here imitates certain passages of Stesichorus' first Epithalamy of Helen. He seems also to have had Sappho's book of Wedding-Songs before him.*

XVIII.—ΕΛΕΝΑΣ ΕΠΙΘΑΛΑΜΙΟΣ

Ἔν ποκ' ἄρα Σπάρτᾳ ξανθότριχι πὰρ Μενελάῳ
παρθενικαὶ θάλλοντα κόμαις ὑάκινθον ἔχοισαι
πρόσθε νεογράπτω θαλάμω χορὸν ἐστάσαντο,
δώδεκα ταὶ πρᾶται πόλιος, μέγα χρῆμα Λακαινᾶν,
ἁνίκα Τυνδαρίδᾳ κατεκλᾴζετο τὰν ἀγαπατὰν
μναστεύσας Ἑλέναν ὁ νεώτερος Ἀτρέος υἱῶν.
ἄειδον δ' ἄρα πᾶσαι ἐς ἓν μέλος ἐγκροτέοισαι
ποσσὶ περιπλίκτοις, ὑπὸ δ' ἴαχε δῶμ' ὑμεναίῳ.

Οὕτω δὴ πρώιζα κατέδραθες ὦ φίλε γαμβρέ;
ἦρά τις ἐσσὶ λίαν βαρυγώνατος, ἦρα φίλυπνος,
ἦρα πολύν τιν' ἔπινες, ὅκ'[1] εἰς εὐνὰν κατεβάλλευ;
εὕδειν μὰν σπεύδοντα καθ' ὥραν αὐτὸν ἐχρῆν
τυ,
παῖδα δ' ἐᾶν σὺν παισὶ φιλοστόργῳ παρὰ ματρὶ
παίσδειν ἐς βαθὺν ὄρθρον, ἐπεὶ καὶ ἔνας καὶ ἐς
ἀῶ
κῆς ἔτος ἐξ ἔτεος, Μενέλα, τεὰ ἁ[2] νυὸς ἄδε.

---

[1] ὅκ' Wil. with *P. Ant.*: mss ὅτ'   [2] Μενέλα τεὰ ἁ Meineke:
mss Μενέλαε τεά

224

XVIII.—THE EPITHALAMY OF HELEN

IT seems that once upon a time at the house of flaxen-haired Menelaus in Sparta, the first twelve maidens of the town, fine pieces all of Laconian womanhood, came crowned with fresh flowering luces, and before a new-painted chamber took up the dance, when the younger child of Atreus shut the wedding door upon the girl of his wooing, upon the daughter of Tyndareüs, to wit the beloved Helen. There with their pretty feet criss-crossing all to the time of one tune they sang till the palace rang again with the echoes of this wedding-song :—

What Bridegroom! dear Bridegroom! thus early
    abed and asleep?
        Wast born a man of sluggardye,
        Or is thy pillow sweet to thee,
        Or ere thou cam'st to bed maybe
            Didst drink a little deep?
If thou wert so fain to sleep betimes, 'twere better
    sleep alone,
        And leave a maid with maids to play
        By a fond mother's side till dawn of day,
        Sith for the morrow and its morn,
        For this and all the years unborn,
            This sweet bride is thine own.

ὄλβιε γάμβρ᾽, ἀγαθός τις ἐπέπταρεν ἐρχομένῳ
   τοι

ἐς Σπάρταν ἄπερ ὦλλοι ἀριστέες ὡς ἀνύσαιο.
μοῦνος ἐν ἡμιθέοις Κρονίδαν Δία πενθερὸν ἑξεῖς·
Ζανός τοι θυγάτηρ ὑπὸ τὰν μίαν ἵκετο χλαῖναν,
οἵα Ἀχαιιάδων γαῖαν πατεῖ οὐδεμί᾽ ἄλλα.
ἦ μέγα κά τι τέκοιτ᾽, εἰ ματέρι τίκτοι ὁμοῖον·
ἄμμες ταὶ[1] πᾶσαι συνομάλικες, αἷς δρόμος ωὑτὸς
χρισαμέναις ἀνδριστὶ παρ᾽ Εὐρώταο λοετροῖς,
τετράκις ἑξήκοντα κόραι, θῆλυς νεολαία—
τᾶν οὐδ᾽ ἦν[2] τις ἄμωμος, ἐπεὶ χ᾽ Ἑλένᾳ παρι-
   σωθῇ.

ἀὼς ἀντέλλοισα καλὸν διέφανε[3] πρόσωπον,
πότνια Νύξ, ἅτε λευκὸν ἔαρ χειμῶνος ἀνέντος·
ὧδε καὶ ἁ χρυσέα Ἑλένα διαφαίνετ᾽ ἐν ἁμῖν.
πιείρᾳ μέγα λᾷον[4] ἀνέδραμε κόσμος ἀρούρᾳ
ἢ κάπῳ κυπάρισσος ἢ ἅρματι Θεσσαλὶς[5] ἵππος·
ὧδε καὶ ἁ ῥοδόχρως Ἑλένα Λακεδαίμονι κόσμος.

---

[1] E: P. Ant. δε, mss δ᾽ αἱ or γὰρ   [2] E: mss ἂν (P. Ant.
τᾶν δ ουτ᾽ ἅτις)   [3] διέφανε Ahrens: mss διέφαινε   [4] μέγα
λᾷον Eichstaedt: mss μεγάλα ἅτ᾽   [5] mss also (with P. Ant.)
Θεσσαλὸς

When thou like others of high degree cam'st here
    thy suit a-pressing,
Sure some good body, well is thee, sneezed thee a
    proper blessing ;
For of all these lordings there's but one shall be son
    of the High Godheád,
        Aye, 'neath one coverlet with thee
        Great Zeus his daughter is come to be,
        A lady whose like is not to see
            Where Grecian women tread.
And if she bring a mother's bairn 'twill be of a
    wondrous grace ;
For sure all we which her fellows be, that ran with
    her race,
Anointed lasses like the lads, Eurótas' pools beside—
O' the four-times threescore maidens that were
    Sparta's flower and pride
There was none so fair as might compare with
    Menelaüs' bride.

O Lady Night, 'tis passing bright the face o' the
    rising day ;
        'Tis like the white spring o' the year
        When winter is no longer here ;
        But so shines golden Helen clear
            Among our meinie so gay.
And the crops that upstand in a fat ploughlánd do
    make it fair to see,
        And a cypress the garden where she grows,
        And a Thessaly steed the chariot he knows ;
        But so doth Helen red as the rose
            Make fair her dear countrye.

"The white spring": white with flowers.   "Meinie".
company.

οὔτε τις ἐκ ταλάρω πανίσδεται ἔργα τοιαῦτα,
οὔτ' ἐνὶ δαιδαλέῳ πυκινώτερον ἄτριον ἱστῷ
κερκίδι συμπλέξασα μακρῶν ἔταμ' ἐκ κελεόντων·
οὐ μὰν οὐδὲ λύραν¹ τις ἐπίσταται ὧδε κροτῆσαι
Ἄρτεμιν ἀείδοισα καὶ εὐρύστερνον Ἀθάναν,
ὡς Ἑλένα, τᾶς πάντες ἐπ' ὄμμασιν ἵμεροι ἐντί.

ὦ καλὰ ὦ χαρίεσσα κόρα, τὺ μὲν οἰκέτις ἤδη,
ἄμμες δ' ἐς δρόμον ἦρι καὶ ἐς λειμώνια φύλλα
ἑρψεῦμες στεφάνως δρεψεύμεναι ἁδὺ πνέοντας,
πολλὰ τεοῦς Ἑλένα μεμναμέναι ὡς γαλαθηναὶ
ἄρνες γεινομένας ὄϊος μαστὸν ποθέοισαι.
πράτᾳ² τοι στέφανον λωτῶ χαμαὶ αὐξομένοιο
πλέξασαι σκιερὰν καταθήσομες ἐς πλατάνιστον,
πράτᾳ² δ' ἀργυρέας ἐξ ὄλπιδος ὑγρὸν ἄλειφαρ
λαζύμεναι σταξεῦμες ὑπὸ σκιερὰν πλατάνιστον·
γράμματα δ' ἐν φλοιῷ γεγράψεται, ὡς παριών
            τις
ἀννείμῃ, Δωριστί· 'σέβευ μ', Ἑλένας φυτὸν
            ἐμμί.'³

χαίροις ὦ νύμφα, χαίροις εὐπένθερε γαμβρέ.
Λατὼ μὲν δοίη, Λατὼ κουροτρόφος ὔμμιν

---

¹ οὐδὲ λύραν : mss also οὐ κιθάραν   ² πράτᾳ Reiske :
mss πρᾶται   ³ σέβευ and ἐμμὶ Hermann : mss σέβου and
εἰμί

And **never** doth woman on bobbin wind such **thread**
    as her baskets teem,
Nor shuttlework so close and fine cuts from the
    weaver's beam,
Nor none hath skill to ply the quill to the Gods of
    Women above
As the maiden wise in whose bright eyes dwells all
    desire and love.

O maid of beauty, maid of grace, thou art a huswife
    now ;
But we shall betimes to the running-place i' the
    meads where flowers do blow,
And cropping garlands sweet and sweet about our
    brows to do,
Like lambs athirst for the mother's teat shall long,
    dear Helen, for you.
For you afore all shall a coronal of the gay ground-
    ling trefoil
Hang to a shady platan-tree, and a vial of running
    oil
His offering drip from a silver lip beneath the same
    platan-tree,
        And a Doric rede be writ i' the bark
        For him that passeth by to mark,
          ' I am Helen's ; worship me.'

And 'tis Bride farewell, and Groom farewell, that be
    son of a mighty sire,
And Leto, great Nurse Leto, grant children at your
    desire,

"Quill": the plectrum of the lyre. "The Gods of
Women" : the Greek has ' Artemis and Athena.'

εὐτεκνίαν, Κύπρις δέ, θεὰ Κύπρις ἶσον ἔρασθαι
ἀλλάλων, Ζεὺς δέ, Κρονίδας Ζεὺς ἄφθιτον
    ὄλβον,
ὡς ἐξ εὐπατριδᾶν εἰς εὐπατρίδας πάλιν ἔνθῃ.
εὔδετ' ἐς ἀλλάλων στέρνον φιλότατα πνέοντες[1]
καὶ πόθον· ἔγρεσθαι δὲ πρὸς ἀῶ μὴπιλάθησθε.
νεύμεθα κάμμες ἐς ὄρθρον, ἐπεί κα πρᾶτος
    ἀοιδὸς
ἐξ εὐνᾶς κελαδήσῃ ἀνασχὼν εὔτριχα δειράν.

    Ὑμὴν ὦ Ὑμέναιε, γάμῳ ἐπὶ τῷδε χαρείης.

----

[1] P. Ant. πνεοντε

And Cypris, holy Cypris, an equal love alwáy,
      And Zeus, high Zeus, prosperitye
      That drawn of parents of high degree
      Shall pass to a noble progenye
         For ever and a day.
Sleep on and rest, and on either breast may the
    love-breath playing go ;
      Sleep now, but when the day shall break
      Forget not from your sleep to wake ;
      For we shall come wi' the dawn along
      Soon as the first-waked master o' song
         Lift feathery neck to crow.

Sing Hey for the Wedding, sing Ho for the Wedder.
    and thanks to him that made it !

XIX.—THE HONEY-STEALER

THIS *little poem probably belongs to a later date than the Bucolic writers, and was brought into the collection merely owing to its resemblance to the* Runaway Love *of Moschus.*

XIX.—ΚΗΡΙΟΚΛΕΠΤΗΣ

Τὸν κλέπταν ποτ' Ἔρωτα κακὰ κένταϲε μέλιϲϲα
κηρίον ἐκ ϲίμβλων ϲυλεύμενον, ἄκρα δὲ χειρῶν
δάκτυλα πάνθ' ὑπένυξεν. ὃ δ' ἄλγεε καὶ χέρ'
    ἐφύϲη
καὶ τὰν γᾶν ἐπάταξε καὶ ἅλατο, τᾷ δ' Ἀφροδίτᾳ
δεῖξεν ἑὰν[1] ὀδύναν καὶ μέμφετο, ὅττι γε τυτθὸν
θηρίον ἐϲτὶ μέλιϲϲα καὶ ἁλίκα τραύματα ποιεῖ.
χἀ μάτηρ γελάϲαϲα· 'τί δ'; οὐκ ἴϲοϲ ἐϲϲὶ
    μελίϲϲαιϲ,
ὃϲ τυτθὸϲ μὲν ἔειϲ,[2] τὰ δὲ τραύματα ταλίκα[3]
    ποιεῖϲ;'

---

[1] ἑὰν Wil : mss τὰν   [2] ὃϲ Valckenaer : mss χὡ   ἔειϲ
Wil thinks probable : mss ἔηϲ   [3] ταλίκα Porson : mss
ἁλίκα

XIX.—THE HONEY-STEALER

WHEN the thievish Love one day was stealing honeycomb from the hive, a wicked bee stung him, and made all his finger-tips to smart. In pain and grief he blew on his hand and stamped and leapt upon the ground, and went and showed his hurt to Aphrodite, and made complaint that so a little a beast as a bee could make so great a wound. Whereat his mother laughing, 'What?' cries she, 'art not a match for a bee, and thou so little and yet able to make wounds so great?'

XX.—THE YOUNG COUNTRYMAN

A NEATHERD, *chafing because a city wench disdains him, protests that he is a handsome fellow, and that Gods have been known to make love to country-folk, and calls down upon her the curse of perpetual celibacy. This spirited poem is a monologue, but preserves the mime-form by means of dumb characters, the shepherds of line* 19. *Stylistic considerations belie the tradition which ascribes it to Theocritus.*

XX.—ΒΟΥΚΟΛΙΣΚΟΣ

Εὐνίκα μ' ἐγέλαξε θέλοντά μιν ἀδὺ φιλῆσαι,
καί μ' ἐπικερτομέοισα τάδ' ἔννεπεν ' ἔρρ' ἀπ' ἐμεῖο.
βουκόλος ὢν ἐθέλεις με κύσαι τάλαν; οὐ μεμάθηκα
ἀγροίκως φιλέειν, ἀλλ' ἀστικὰ χείλεα θλίβειν.
μὴ τύγε μευ κύσσῃς τὸ καλὸν στόμα μηδ' ἐν
    ὀνείροις.
οἷα βλέπεις, ὁπποῖα λαλεῖς, ὡς ἄγρια παίσδεις,
χείλεά τοι νοτέοντι,[1] χέρες δέ τοι εἰσὶ μέλαιναι,
καὶ κακὸν ἐξόσδεις. ἀπ' ἐμεῦ φύγε, μή με
    μολύνῃς.'
τοιάδε μυθίζοισα τρὶς εἰς ἑὸν ἔπτυσε κόλπον,
καί μ' ἀπὸ τᾶς κεφαλᾶς ποτὶ τὼ πόδε συνεχὲς
    εἶδε
χείλεσι μυχθίζοισα καὶ ὄμμασι λοξὰ βλέποισα,
καὶ πολὺ τᾷ μορφᾷ θηλύνετο, καί τι σεσαρὸς
καὶ σοβαρόν μ' ἐγέλαξεν. ἐμοὶ δ' ἄφαρ ἔζεσεν
    αἷμα,
καὶ χρόα φοινίχθην ὑπὸ τὤλγεος ὡς ῥόδον ἔρσα.
χἁ μὲν ἔβα με λιποῖσα· φέρω δ' ὑποκάρδιον
    ὀργάν,
ὅττι με τὸν χαρίεντα κακὰ μωμήσαθ' ἑταίρα.

---

[1] νοτέοντι Sauppe : mss νοσέοντι

7 ὡς τρυφερὸν καλέεις, ὡς κωτίλα ῥήματα φράσδεις·
ὡς μαλακὸν τὸ γένειον ἔχεις, ὡς ἀδέα χαίταν.
As Wil. sees, these lines cannot belong here.

XX.—THE YOUNG COUNTRYMAN

WHEN I would have kissed her sweetly, Eunica fleered at me and flouted me saying, 'Go with a mischief! What? kiss me a miserable clown like thee? I never learned your countrified bussing; my kissing is in the fashion o' the town. I will not have such as thee to kiss my pretty lips, nay, not in his dreams. Lord, how you look! Lord, how you talk! Lord, how you antic! Your lips are wet and your hands black, and you smell rank. Hold off and begone, or you'll befoul me!' Telling this tale she spit thrice in her bosom, and all the while eyed me from top to toe, and mowed at me and leered at me and made much she-play with her pretty looks, and anon did right broadly, scornfully, and disdainfully laugh at me. Trust me, my blood boiled up in a moment, and my face went as red with the anguish of it as the rose with the dewdrops. And so she up and left me, but it rankles in my heart that such a filthy drab should cavil at a well-favoured fellow like me.

ποιμένες, εἴπατέ μοι τὸ κρήγυον· οὐ καλὸς ἐμμί;
ἆρά τις ἐξαπίνας με θεὸς βροτὸν ἄλλον ἔτευξε;
καὶ γὰρ ἐμοὶ τὸ πάροιθεν ἐπάνθεεν ἁδύ τι κάλλος
ὡς κισσὸς ποτὶ πρέμνον, ἐμὰν δ’ ἐπύκαζεν
    ὑπήναν,
χαῖται δ’ οἷα σέλινα περὶ κροτάφοισι κέχυντο,
καὶ λευκὸν τὸ μέτωπον ἐπ’ ὀφρύσι λάμπε μελαί-
    ναις·
ὄμματά μοι γλαυκᾶς χαροπώτερα πολλὸν Ἀθάνας,
καὶ στόματ’ αὖ πακτᾶς γλαφυρώτερα, κήκ [1] στομά-
    των δὲ
ἔρρεέ μοι φωνὰ γλυκερωτέρα ἢ μελίκηρον· [2]
ἁδὺ δέ μοι τὸ μέλισμα, καὶ ἢν σύριγγι μελίσδω,
κἢν αὐλῷ λαλέω, κἢν δώνακι, κἢν πλαγιαύλῳ.
καὶ πᾶσαι καλόν με κατ’ ὤρεα φαντὶ γυναῖκες,
καὶ πᾶσαί με φιλεῦντι· τὰ δ’ ἀστικά μ’ οὐκ
    ἐφίλησεν,
ἀλλ’ ὅτι βουκόλος ἐμμί, παρέδραμε κοὐ ποτάκουε. [3]
  οὐ καλὸς Διόνυσος ἐν ἄγκεσι ταῦρον [4] ἐλαύνει;
οὐκ ἔγνω δ’, ὅτι Κύπρις ἐπ’ ἀνέρι μήνατο βούτα
καὶ Φρυγίοις ἐνόμευσεν ἐν ὤρεσιν; οὐ τὸν [5] Ἄδωνιν
ἐν δρυμοῖσι φίλησε καὶ ἐν δρυμοῖσιν ἔκλαυσεν;
Ἐνδυμίων δὲ τίς ἦν; οὐ βουκόλος; ὅν γε Σελάνα
βουκολέοντα φίλησεν, ἀπ’ Οὐλύμπω δὲ μολοῖσα
Λάτμιον ἂν νάπος ἦλθε καὶ εἰς ἑὰ παιδικὰ νεῦσε [6]·
καὶ τὺ Ῥέα κλαίεις τὸν βουκόλον. οὐχὶ δὲ καὶ τὺ

---

[1] στόματ’ αὖ πακτᾶς E : mss στόμα δ’ αὖ π. or στόμα ἢ καὶ ὑπ’ ἀκτᾶς   γλαφυρώτερα Wil (but -ρον) : mss γλυκερώτερον from below   κήκ E : mss ἐκ   [2] μελίκηρον E : mss μελι-κήρω or μέλι κηρῷ   [3] ποτάκουε Ziegler : mss -ακούει [4] οὐ E : mss ὁ or χὠ   ταῦρον E, cf. e.g. Gerhard *Auser-*

Tell me true, master Shepherds; see you not here
a proper man, or hath some power taken and trans-
mewed him? Marry, 'twas a sweet piece of ivy
bloomed ere now on this tree, and a sweet piece
of beauty put fringe to this lip; the hair o' these
temples lay lush as the parsley; this forehead did
shine me white above and these eyebrows black
below; these eyes were beamy as the Grey-eyed
Lady's, this mouth trim as a cream-cheese; and the
voice which came forth o' this mouth was even as
honeycomb. Sweet also is the music I make, be it
o' the pipe, be it o' the babbling hautboy, be it o'
the flute or the crossflute. And there's not a lass in
the uplands but says I am good to look to, not one
but kisses me, neither; but your city pieces, look
you, never a kiss got I o' them, but they ran me by
and would not listen because I herd cows.

Doth not the beautiful Dionysus ride a bull i' the
dells? Wist she not Cypris ran mad after a neatherd
and tended cattle i' th' Phrygian hills? And the same
Cypris, loved she not Adonis in the woods and in the
woods bewailed him? And what of Endymion? Was
it not a neatherd the Lady Moon loved when he was
at his labour, and came down from Olympus into
Latmos vale to bow herself over him of her choice?
Thou too, great Rhea, dost bewail a neatherd; and
didst not e'en thou, thou Son of Cronus, become a

<hr>

lesene Vasenbilder 47 : mss πόρτιν through misinterpretation
of ἐλαύνει, cf. 5. 116, Ar. *Eccl.* 39   [5] οὐ τὸν Is. Vossius:
mss αὐτὸν   [6] Λάτμιον Musurus: mss λάθριον   παιδικὰ
νεῦσε Wil: mss παιδὶ κάθευδε

ὦ Κρονίδα διὰ παῖδα βοηνόμον ὄρνις ἐπλάγχθης;
Εὐνίκα δὲ μόνα τὸν βουκόλον οὐκ ἐφίλασεν,
ἁ Κυβέλας κρέσσων καὶ Κύπριδος ἠδὲ Σελάνας.
μηκέτι μηδ᾽ ἅ,[1] Κύπρι, τὸν ἀδέα μήτε κατ᾽ ἄστυ
μήτ᾽ ἐν ὄρει φιλέοι, μώνα δ᾽ ἀνὰ νύκτα καθεύδοι.[2]

[1] μηδ᾽ ἅ Wil : mss μηδ᾽ ἁ or μηδὲ   [2] φιλέοι and καθεύδοι
Ahrens : mss φιλέοις and καθεύδοις

wandering bird for the sake of a lad o' the kine?
Nay, 'twas left to mistress Eunica to deny a neatherd
her love, this piece that is a greater than Cybelè and
Cypris and the Lady Moon! Wherefore I beseech
thee, sweet Cypris, the same may never more
whether in upland or in lowland come at the love of
her leman, but may lie lone and sleep sole for
the rest of her days.

XXI.—THE FISHERMEN

THE *poet begins with a dedication in the manner of XI,
and passes quickly to his story. Two fishermen lie awake
at night in their cabin on the shore, and one of them tells
a dream he has just had of the catching of a golden fish.
He asks his friend what the dream may mean, for he
fears he may have to break his dream-oath that he would
be a fisherman no longer. To this the friend replies that
it was no oath he took, and that the moral of the dream
is that his only wealth is of the sea. Many considerations
go to show that the traditional ascription of the poem to
Theocritus is mistaken.*

XXI.—ΑΛΙΕΙΣ

Ἀ πενία Διόφαντε μόνα τὰς τέχνας ἐγείρει·
αὔτα τῶ μόχθοιο διδάσκαλος· οὐδὲ γὰρ εὔδειν
ἀνδράσιν ἐργατίναισι κακαὶ παρέχοντι μέριμναι.
κἂν ὀλίγον νυκτός τις ἐπιβρίσσῃσι,[1] τὸν ὕπνον
αἰφνίδιον θορυβεῦσιν ἐφιστάμεναι μελεδῶναι.

ἰχθύος ἀγρευτῆρες ὁμῶς δύο κεῖντο γέροντες
στρωσάμενοι βρύον αὖον ὑπὸ πλεκταῖς καλύβαισι,
κεκλιμένοι τοίχῳ ποτὶ φυλλίνῳ· ἐγγύθι δ᾽ αὐτοῖν
κεῖτο τὰ τῶν χειρῶν[2] ἀθλήματα, τοὶ καλαθίσκοι,
τοὶ κάλαμοι, τἄγκιστρα, τὰ φυκιόεντά τε λῖνα,[3]
ὁρμιαὶ κύρτοι τε καὶ ἐκ σχοίνων λαβύρινθοι,
μήρινθοι κώπα[4] τε γέρων τ᾽ ἐπ᾽ ἐρείσμασι λέμβος·
νέρθεν τᾶς κεφαλᾶς φορμὸς βραχύς· εἴματα
   πύσσοι.[5]

οὗτος τοῖς ἁλιεῦσιν ὁ πᾶς πόρος,[6] οὗτος ὁ πλοῦτος·
οὐ κλεῖδ᾽, οὐχὶ θύραν ἔχον,[7] οὐ κύνα· πάντα περισσὰ
ταῦτ᾽ ἐδόκει τήνοις· ἁ γὰρ πενία σφας ἐτήρει.[8]
οὐδεὶς δ᾽ ἐν μέσσῳ γείτων πέλεν· ἁ[9] δὲ παρ᾽ αὐτὰν
θλιβομένα[10] καλύβαν τρυφερὸν προσέναχ᾽
   θάλασσα.

---

[1] ἐπιβρίσσῃσι Reiske : mss -βησέεισι   [2] τῶν χειρῶν
Musurus : mss ταῖν (or ταῖς) χεροῖν or ταῖς χείρεσσιν   [3] λίνε
E (already suspected by Wil), cf. Mosch. *fr.* 3. 7, Headlam
Journ. of Philol. 1907, p. 315 : others δελήτα : mss λῆγ·
[4] κώπα Stroth-Kiessling : mss κῶα   [5] πύσσοι 'thick
(coats),' cf. πυκνός, πύκα, ἄβυσσος, βύθος E : Fritzsche πύσσο·

XXI.—THE FISHERMEN

THERE's but one stirrer-up of the crafts, Diophantus, and her name is Poverty. She is the true teacher of labour; for a man of toil may not so much as sleep for the disquietude of his heart. Nay, if he nod ever so little o' nights, then is his slumber broke suddenly short by the cares that beset him.

One night against the leafy wall of a wattled cabin there lay together upon a bed of dry tangle two old catchers of fish. Beside them were laid the instruments of their calling: their creels, their rods, their hooks, their weedy nets and lines, their weels and rush-woven lobster-pots, some net-ropes, a pair of oars, and upon its props an aged coble. Beneath their heads lay a little mat, and for coverlets they had their jackets of frieze. This was all the means and all the riches of these poor fishermen. Key, door, watchdog, had they none; all such things were ill-store to the likes of them, seeing in that house kept Poverty watch and ward; neither dwelt there any neighbour at their gates, but the very cabin-walls were hemmed by the soft and delicate up-flowing of the sea.

Musurus πῖλοι: mss πύσοι ⁶ πόρος Koehler: mss πόνος from line 20 ⁷ οὐ κλεῖδ' Buecheler: mss οὐδεὶς δ' from below οὐχὶ θύραν Briggs: mss οὐ χύθραν ἔχον Kaibel: mss εἶχ' ⁸ ταῦτ' Wil: mss πάντ' ἀ γὰρ Reiske: mss ἄγρα ἐτήρει Ahrens: mss ἐτέρη ⁹ πέλεν· ἀ Reiske: mss πενία from above ¹⁰ θλιβομένα Reiske: mss -ναν

οὔπω τὸν μέσατον δρόμον ἄννεν ἅρμα Σελάνας,
τοὺς δ' ἁλιεῖς ἤγειρε φίλος πόνος, ἐκ βλεφάρων δὲ
ὕπνον ἀπωσάμενος σφετέραις φρεσὶν ἤρεθεν αὐδάν.[1]

ΑΣΦΑΛΙΩΝ

ψεύδοντ' ὦ φίλε πάντες, ὅσοι τὰς νύκτας ἔφασκον
τῶ θέρεος μινύθειν, ὅτε τἄματα μακρὰ φέρουσιν.
ἤδη μυρί' ἐσεῖδον ὀνείρατα, κοὐδέπω ἀώς.
ἢ λαθόμαν, τί τὸ χρῆμα χρόνου ταὶ[2] νύκτες ἔχοντι;

ΕΤΑΙΡΟΣ

'Ασφαλίων, μέμφῃ τὸ καλὸν θέρος· οὐ γὰρ ὁ καιρὸς
αὐτομάτως παρέβα τὸν ἑὸν δρόμον· ἀλλὰ τὸν ὕπνον
ἁ φροντὶς κόπτοισα μακρὰν τὰν νύκτα ποιεῖ τοι.[3]

ΑΣΦΑΛΙΩΝ

ἆρ' ἔμαθες κρίνειν πόκ' ἐνύπνια; χρηστὰ γὰρ εἶδον.
οὔ σε θέλω τὠμῶ φαντάσματος ἦμεν ἄμοιρον.

ΕΤΑΙΡΟΣ

ὡς καὶ τὰν ἄγραν, τὠνείρατα πάντα μερίζευ.
οὐ γάρ σ' εἰκάξω κατὰ τὸν λόγον,[4] οὗτος ἄριστος
ἐστὶν ὀνειροκρίτας, ὁ διδάσκαλός ἐστι παρ' ᾧ νοῦς;
ἄλλως[5] καὶ σχολά ἐντι· τί γὰρ ποιεῖν ἂν ἔχοι τις
κείμενος ἐν φύλλοις ποτὶ κύματι μηδὲ καθεύδων;
ἀλλ' ὄνος ἐν ῥάμνῳ τό τε λύχνιον ἐν πρυτανείῳ·
φαντὶ γὰρ ἀγρυπνίαν[6] τάδ' ἔχειν. λέγε· ὅπποτε
    νυκτὸς
ὄψιν πᾶς τις ἑῷ γε φιλεῖ[7] μανύεν ἑταίρῳ.

---

[1] ἀπωσάμενος and ἤρεθεν E : mss ἀπωσάμενοι and ἤρεθον
αὐδὰν I. H. Voss : mss ᾠδὰν   [2] ἦ E : mss μὴ   χρόνου ταὶ
Martin : mss χρόνον δ' αἱ   [3] ποιεῖ τοι Hermann : mss
ποιεῦντι   [4] σ' εἰκάξω E : mss νικάξῃ, a correction following
on the corruption of λόγον   λόγον E : mss νόον, originally
an incorrect gloss on λόγον   [5] ἄλλως Musurus : mss ἄλλος

Now or ever the chariot of the Moon was half-way of its course, the fishermen's labour and trouble did rouse them, and thrusting slumber from their eyelids stirred up speech in their hearts.

ASPHALION

It seems they speak not true, friend, that say the summer nights grow less when they bring us the long days. Already I have had a thousand dreams, and the dawn is not yet. Or am I wrong when I say how long the watches of these nights are?

FRIEND

Asphalion, the pretty summer deserves not thy fault-finding. 'Tis not that Time hath truly and in himself over-run his course, but Care makes thy night long by curtailing thy slumber.

ASPHALION

Hast ever learnt to interpret a dream? I've had a good one this night, and am fain thou go shares in't.

FRIEND

Aye, we share our catch, and e'en let's share all our dreams. For shall I not be making conjecture of thee according to the saying, the best interpreter of dreams is he that learns of understanding? And what's more, we have time and to spare, for there's little enough for a man to do lying sleepless in a greenbed beside the sea. 'Faith, 'tis the ass in the thorns and the lamp in the town-hall, and they are the morals for waking. Come, thy dream; for a friend, look you, is always told a man's dreams.

σχολά ἐντι Reiske: mss σχόλοντι   [6] ἀγρυπνίαν Reiske: mss ἄγραν   λέγε· ὅπποτε E, cf. 15. 32 and 24. 130: mss λέγεο (or λέγω) ποτε   [7] πᾶς τις ἐφ᾽ γε φιλεῖ E: mss τά τις ἔσσεο δὲ λέγει (from λέγειν originally a gloss on μάννεν)

"The morals for waking": *i.e.* 'proverbial for keeping awake.'

ΑΣΦΑΛΙΩΝ

δειλινὸν ὡς *κατέδαρθον* ἐπ᾽ εἰναλίοισι πόνοισιν
(οὐκ ἦν μὰν πολύσιτος, ἐπεὶ δειπνεῦντες ἐν ὥρᾳ,
εἰ μέμνῃ, τᾶς γαστρὸς ἐφειδόμεθ᾽) εἶδον ἐμαυτὸν
ἐν πέτρᾳ μεμαῶτα, καθεζόμενος δ᾽ ἐδόκευον
ἰχθύας, ἐκ καλάμω [1] δὲ πλάνον κατέσειον ἐδωδάν.
καί τις τῶν τραφερῶν ὠρέξατο· καὶ γὰρ ἐν ὕπνοις
πᾶσα κύων ἄρκον [2] μαντεύεται, ἰχθύα κἠγών.
χὠ μὲν τὠγκίστρῳ ποτεφύετο, καὶ ῥέεν αἷμα,
τὸν κάλαμον δ᾽ ὑπὸ τῶ κινήματος ἀγκύλον εἶχον
τᾷ χερὶ τεινόμενον, περικλώμενον, εὐρὺν ἀγῶνα, [3]
πῶς μελετῶ [4] μέγαν ἰχθὺν ἀφαυροτέροισι σιδάροις.
εἶθ᾽ ὑπομιμνάσκων τῶ τρώματος ἠρέμ᾽ [5] ἔνυξα,
καὶ νύξας ἐχάλαξα, καὶ οὐ φεύγοντος ἔτεινα.
ἤνυσα δ᾽ ὧν τὸν ἄεθλον. ἀνείλκυσα χρύσεον ἰχθύν,
πάντᾳ τοι χρυσῷ πεπυκασμένον· εἶχέ με δεῖμα, [6]
μήτι Ποσειδάωνι πέλει πεφιλημένος ἰχθὺς
ἢ τάχα τᾶς γλαυκᾶς κειμήλιον Ἀμφιτρίτας.
ἠρέμα δ᾽ αὐτὸν ἐγὼν ἐκ τὠγκίστρω ἀπέλυσα,
μή ποτε τῶ στόματος τἀγκίστρια χρυσὸν ἔχοιεν. [7]
τὸν μὲν ἐπιστὰς ᾆσα καλάγρετον ἀπειρώταν, [8]
ὤμοσα δ᾽ οὐκέτι λοιπὸν ὑπὲρ πελάγους πόδα θεῖναι,
ἀλλὰ μενεῖν ἐπὶ γᾶς καὶ τῷ χρυσῷ βασιλεύσειν.

---

[1] καλάμω Valckenaer : mss -ων   [2] ἄρκον = ἄρκτον E, cf.
Herwerden *Lex. Suppl.*: mss ἄρτον or ἄρτω   [3] τᾷ χερί E:
mss τὼ χέρε   For asyndeton cf. Longus 3. 34   εὐρὺν
ἀγῶνα: cf. *Il.* 25. 274 and 23. 258   [4] μελετῶ E, cf. Hipp.
e.g. 554. 31 to 'treat' a patient: mss μὲν ἕλω   [5] ἠρέμα
Eldik : mss ἄρ᾽ ἐμέ   [6] με Mus : mss δέ or σε   δεῖμα Mus :
mss σῆμα   [7] ἔχοιεν Mus : mss ἔχοντι or ἔχοισα

ASPHALION

When I fell asleep last night after my labours o'
the sea—and faith, 'twas not for fulness, if you mind,
seeing we supped early to give our bellies short
commons—I dreamt I was hard at my work upon a
rock, seated watching for the fish and dangling my
piece of deception from my rod's end, when there
rose me a right gallant fellow—for mark you, I
surmise a fish as a sleeping dog will a bear—, well
hooked too, for 'a showed blood, and my rod all
bended wi' the pull of him, bended straining and
bowing in my hand, insomuch that I questioned me
sore how I was to deal with so great a fish with
so weak tools to my hand. Howbeit I gently
pricked him to mind him o' the hook, and pricking
let him have line, and when he ran not away
showed him the butt. Now was the prize mine.
I drew up a golden fish, a fish smothered in gold,
such indeed that I feared me lest he were a fish
favoured of Poseidon, or mayhap a treasured pos-
session of sea-green Amphitritè ; aye, and unhooked
him very carefully and slow lest ever the tackle
should come away with gold from his mouth.
Then, standing over, I sang the praises of that my
glorious catch, my seaman made landsman, and sware
I'ld nevermore set foot o' the sea, but I would rest
ashore rather and king it there with my gold. And

---

[7] ἔχοιεν Mus : mss ἔχοντι or ἔχοισα   [8] τὸν μὲν ἐπιστὰς ᾆσα
E, cf. 12. 23: mss καὶ τὸν μὲν πιστεύσασα   καλάγρετον
Ribbeck : mss καλά γε τὸν   ἀπειρώταν Hermann ; cf. Timoth.
Pers. 44 νησιώτας : mss ἠπήρατον

" Let him have line " : not, of course, from a reel.

ταῦτά με κἀξήγειρε, τὺ δ' ὦ ξένε λοιπὸν ἔρειδε
τὰν γνώμαν· ὅρκον γὰρ ἐγὼ τὸν ἐπώμοσα—

ΕΤΑΙΡΟΣ

θάρρει,[1]

καὶ σύγε μὴ[2] τρέσσῃς· οὐκ ὤμοσας· οὐδὲ γὰρ
ἰχθὺν
χρύσεον ὡς ἴδες εἶδες· ἴσα δ' ἐν ψεύδεσι νῶσις·[3]
εἰ γὰρ μὴ κνώσσων τὺ τὰ χωρία ταῦτα[4] ματεύεις,
ἔλπις τῶν ὕπνων· ζάτει τὸν σάρκινον ἰχθύν,
μὴ σὺ θάνῃς λιμῷ καὶ χρυσείοισιν[5] ὀνείροις.

---

[1] θάρρει E: others, giving it to Asph., ταρβῶ: mss θαρρῶ
[2] σύγε μὴ Mus; cf. 10. 34: mss σύγε   [3] ἴδες εἶδες E: mss
εἶδες εὖρες   ἐν ψεύδεσι νῶσις E, cf. 25. 263 and 17. 60:
others ἦν (or ἐν) ψεύδεσιν ὄψις: mss ἐν ψεύδεσιν ἴψεις   [4] γὰρ
μὴ E: mss με γὰρ   τὺ τὰ Mus: mss τοῦτο or τούτου
[5] καὶ χρυσείοισιν E: mss καίτοι χρυσοῖσιν

with that I awoke.   And now, good friend, it remains
for you to lend me your understanding ; for troth,
that oath I sware—

Be of good cheer ; never you fear that.   'Twas no
swearing when you sware that oath any more than
'twas seeing when you saw the golden fish.   Howbeit
there's wisdom to be had of empty shows ; for if you
will make real and waking search in these places
there's hope of your sleep and your dreams.   Go
seek the fish of flesh and blood, or you'll die of
hunger and golden visions.

"There's hope of your dreams" : ' hope of your getting
some advantage from them.'

XXII.—THE DIOSCURI

This *hymn to Castor and Polydeuces consists, first, of a prelude common to both, and secondly, of two main parts concerned one with Polydeuces and the other with Castor. The first of these, in a combination of the Epic style with the dialogue, tells how Polydeuces fought fisticuffs with Amycus on his way to Colchis, and the second how, when the brothers carried off the daughters of Leucippus, Castor fought Lynceus with spear and sword.*

Ὑμνέομεν Λήδας τε καὶ αἰγιόχου Διὸς υἱώ,
Κάστορα καὶ φοβερὸν Πολυδεύκεα πὺξ ἐρεθίζειν
χεῖρας ἐπιζεύξαντα μέσας βοέοισιν ἱμᾶσιν.
ὑμνέομεν καὶ δὶς καὶ τὸ τρίτον ἄρσενα τέκνα
κούρης Θεστιάδος, Λακεδαιμονίους δύ᾽ ἀδελφούς,
ἀνθρώπων σωτῆρας ἐπὶ ξυροῦ ἤδη ἐόντων,
ἵππων θ᾽ αἱματόεντα ταρασσομένων καθ᾽ ὅμιλον,
νηῶν θ᾽, αἳ δύνοντα καὶ οὐρανὸν εἰσανιόντα[1]
ἄστρα βιαζόμεναι χαλεποῖς ἐνέκυρσαν ἀήταις·[2]
οἱ δέ σφεων κατὰ πρύμναν ἀείραντες μέγα κῦμα
ἠὲ καὶ ἐκ πρῴρηθεν, ὅπη ποτὲ[3] θυμὸς ἑκάστου,
ἐς κοίλην ἔρριψαν, ἀνέρρηξαν δ᾽ ἄρα τοίχους
ἀμφοτέρους· κρέμαται δὲ σὺν ἱστίῳ ἄρμενα πάντα
εἰκῆ ἀποκλασθέντα· πολὺς δ᾽ ἐξ οὐρανοῦ ὄμβρος
νυκτὸς ἐφερπούσης· παταγεῖ δ᾽ εὐρεῖα θάλασσα,
κοπτομένη πνοιαῖς τε καὶ ἀρρήκτοισι χαλάζαις.
ἀλλ᾽ ἔμπης ὑμεῖς γε καὶ ἐκ βυθοῦ ἕλκετε νῆας
αὐτοῖσιν ναύτῃσιν ὀιομένοις θανέεσθαι·
αἶψα δ᾽ ἀπολήγοντ᾽ ἄνεμοι, λιπαρὴ δὲ γαλήνη
ἀμ πέλαγος· νεφέλαι δὲ διέδραμον ἄλλυδις ἄλλαι·
ἐκ δ᾽ Ἄρκτοί τ᾽ ἐφάνησαν, Ὄνων τ᾽ ἀνὰ μέσσον
ἀμαυρὴ
Φάτνη σημαίνουσα τὰ πρὸς πλόον εὔδια πάντα.
ὦ ἄμφω θνητοῖσι βοηθόοι, ὦ φίλοι ἄμφω,

---

[1] so Meineke: mss οὐρανοῦ ἐξανιόντα   [2] P. Ant. ἐ]πε-
κυρ[σαν   [3] so P. Ant.: mss ἢ ὅππη (ὅπη, ὅππα)

XXII.—THE HYMN TO THE DIOSCURI

Our song is of the sons of Leda and the Aegis-
Bearer, Castor to wit and with him Polydeuces, that
dire wielder of the fist and of the wrist-harness of
the leathern thong.   Twice is our song and thrice
of the boys of Thestius' daughter, the two Spartan
brethren which wont to save both men that are come
upon the brink and horses that are beset in the
bloody press; aye, and ships also, that because they
sail in despite of rise or set of the stars do fall upon
evil gales, which, or fore or aft or where they list,
upraise a great surge, and both hurl it into the hold
and rive with it their timbers whether on this side
or on that.   Then hang sail and shroud by the
board; and night comes, and with it a great storm
from the sky, and the broad sea rattles and plashes
with the battery of the blast and of the irresistible
hail.   But for all that, ye, even ye, do draw both
ship and despairing shipmen from out the hell;
the winds abate, the sea puts on a shining calm, the
clouds run asunder this way and that way; till out
come the Bears peeping, and betwixt the Asses lo!
that Manger so dim, which betokens all fair for
voyaging on the sea.   O helpers twain of men, O
friends both of mortals, O horseman harpers, O

ἱππῆες κιθαρισταί, ἀεθλητῆρες ἀοιδοί·
Κάστορος ἢ πρώτου Πολυδεύκεος ἄρξομ' ἀείδειν ;
ἀμφοτέρους ὑμνέων Πολυδεύκεα πρῶτον ἀείσω.

ἢ μὲν ἄρα προφυγοῦσα πέτρας εἰς ἓν ξυνιούσας
Ἀργὼ καὶ νιφόεντος ἀταρτηρὸν στόμα Πόντου,
Βέβρυκας εἰσαφίκανε θεῶν φίλα τέκνα φέρουσα.
ἔνθα μιῆς πολλοὶ κατὰ κλίμακος ἀμφοτέρων ἐξ
τοίχων ἄνδρες ἔβαινον Ἰησονίης ἀπὸ νηός,
ἐκβάντες δ' ἐπὶ θῖνα βαθὺν καὶ ὑπήνεμον ἀκτὴν
εὐνάς τ' ἐστόρνυντο πυρεῖά τε χερσὶν ἐνώμων.
Κάστωρ δ' αἰολόπωλος ὅ τ' οἰνωπὸς Πολυδεύκης
ἄμφω ἐρημάζεσκον ἀποπλαγχθέντες ἑταίρων,
παντοίην ἐν ὄρει θηεύμενοι ἄγριον ὕλην.
εὗρον δ' ἀέναον κρήνην ὑπὸ λισσάδι πέτρῃ
ὕδατι πεπληθυῖαν ἀκηράτῳ· αἱ δ' ὑπένερθεν
λάλλαι [1] κρυστάλλῳ ἠδ' ἀργύρῳ ἰνδάλλοντο
ἐκ βυθοῦ· ὑψηλαὶ δὲ πεφύκεσαν ἀγχόθι πεῦκαι
λεῦκαί τε πλάτανοί τε καὶ ἀκρόκομοι κυπάρισσοι,
ἄνθεά τ' εὐώδη, λασίαις φίλα ἔργα μελίσσαις,
ὅσσ' ἔαρος λήγοντος ἐπιβρύει ἂν λειμῶνας.
ἔνθα δ' ἀνὴρ ὑπέροπλος ἐνήμενος ἐνδιάασκε,
δεινὸς ἰδεῖν, σκληρῆσι τεθλασμένος [2] οὔατα πυγ-
μαῖς·
στήθεα δ' ἐσφαίρωτο πελώρια καὶ πλατὺ νῶτον
σαρκὶ σιδηρείῃ σφυρήλατος οἷα κολοσσός.
ἐν δὲ μύες στερεοῖσι βραχίοσιν ἄκρον ὑπ' ὦμον
ἕστασαν ἠΰτε πέτροι ὀλοίτροχοι, οὕστε κυλίνδων
χειμάρρους ποταμὸς μεγάλαις περιέξεσε δίναις·
αὐτὰρ ὑπὲρ νώτοιο καὶ αὐχένος ἠωρεῖτο
ἄκρων δέρμα λέοντος ἀφημμένον ἐκ ποδεώνων.

[1] Ruhnken : mss ἄλλαι   [2] O.P. 1806 (c. A.D. 80) τεθραυσμένος

258

boxer bards, whether of Castor first or Polydeuces shall I sing? Be my song of both, and yet the beginning of it of Polydeuces.

The Together-coming Rocks were safely passed and the baleful mouth of the snowy Pontic entered, and Argo with the dear children of the Gods aboard her had made the country of the Bebrycians. Down the ladders on either side went crowding the men of Jason's ship, and soon as they were out upon the soft deep sand of that lee shore, set to making them greenbeds and rubbing fire-sticks for fire. Then went Castor of the nimble coursers and Polydeuces ruddy as the wine together wandering afield from the rest, for to see the wild woodland of all manner of trees among the hills. Now beneath a certain slabby rock they did find a freshet brimming ever with water pure and clear. The pebbles at the bottom of it were like to silver and crystal, and long and tall there grew beside it, as well firs and poplars and planes and spiry cypresses, as all fragrant flowers which abound in the meadows of outgoing spring to be loved and laboured of the shag bee. In that place there sat taking the air a man both huge and terrible. His ears were crushed shapeless by the hard fist, and his giant breast and great broad back were orbed with iron flesh like a sledge-wrought effigy; moreover the sinews upon his brawny arms upstood beside the shoulder like the boulder-stones some torrent hath rolled and rounded in his swirling eddies; and, to end all, over his neck and about his back there was hung by the claws a swinging lion-skin.

τὸν πρότερος προσέειπεν ἀεθλοφόρος Πολυδεύκης·
Χαῖρε ξεῖν', ὅτις ἐσσί. τίνες βροτοί, ὧν ὅδε
χῶρος;

ΑΜΥΚΟΣ

χαίρω πῶς, ὅτε τ' ἄνδρας ὁρῶ, τοὺς μὴ πρὶν
ὄπωπα;

ΠΟΛΥΔΕΥΚΗΣ

θάρσει. μήτ' ἀδίκους μήτ' ἐξ ἀδίκων φάθι λεύσ-
σειν.

ΑΜΥΚΟΣ

θαρσέω, κοὐκ ἐκ σεῦ με διδάσκεσθαι τόδ' ἔοικεν.

ΠΟΛΥΔΕΥΚΗΣ

ἄγριος εἶ πρὸς πάντα παλίγκοτος ἠδ'[1] ὑπερόπτης;

ΑΜΥΚΟΣ

τοιόσδ' οἷον ὁρᾷς· τῆς σῆς γέ μεν οὐκ ἐπιβαίνω.

ΠΟΛΥΔΕΥΚΗΣ

ἔλθοις, καὶ ξενίων κε[2] τυχὼν πάλιν οἴκαδ' ἱκάνοις.

ΑΜΥΚΟΣ

μήτε σύ με ξείνιζε, τά τ' ἐξ ἐμεῦ οὐκ ἐν ἑτοίμῳ.

ΠΟΛΥΔΕΥΚΗΣ

δαιμόνι', οὐδ' ἂν τοῦδε πιεῖν ὕδατος σύγε δοίης ;

ΑΜΥΚΟΣ

γνώσεαι, εὖτέ σε δίψος ἀνειμένα χείλεα τέρσῃ.[3]

---

[1] ἠδ' Hemsterhuys: mss ἤ   [2] κε Ahrens: mss γε   [3] εὖτέ
σε Wil: mss εἴ σου   τέρσῃ Wil: mss τέρσει, O.P. 1806 τέρσοι

First spoke the champion Polydeuces. 'Whoever you may be, Sir,' says he, 'I bid you good morrow. Pray tell me what people possesseth this country.'

AMYCUS

Is it good-morrow, quotha, when I see strangers before me?

POLYDEUCES

Be of good cheer.   Trust me, we be no evil men nor come we of evil stock.

AMYCUS

Of right good cheer am I, and knew it or ever I learnt it of you.

POLYDEUCES

Pray are you a man o' the wilds, a churl come what may, a mere piece of disdain?

AMYCUS

I am what you see; and that's no goer upon other's ground, when all's said.

POLYDEUCES

Come you upon my ground and welcome; you shall not go away empty.

AMYCUS

I'll none of your welcomes and you shall none of mine.

POLYDEUCES

Lord, man! would you have me denied even a drink of this water?

AMYCUS

That shall you know when there comes you the parching languor o' thirst on the lips.

ΠΟΛΥΔΕΥΚΗΣ

ἄργυρος ἢ τίς ὁ μισθός ; ἐρεῖς, ᾧ κέν σε πίθοιμεν.

ΑΜΥΚΟΣ

εἷς ἑνὶ χεῖρας ἄειρον ἐναντίος ἀνδρὶ καταστάς.

ΠΟΛΥΔΕΥΚΗΣ

πυγμάχος, ἢ καὶ ποσσὶ θένω σκέλος; ὄμματα δ'
  ὀρθά.[1]

ΑΜΥΚΟΣ

πὺξ διατεινάμενος σφετέρης μὴ φείδεο τέχνης·

ΠΟΛΥΔΕΥΚΗΣ

τίς γάρ, ὅτῳ χεῖρας καὶ ἐμοὺς συνερείσω ἱμάντας;

ΑΜΥΚΟΣ

ἐγγὺς ὁρᾷς· οὐ γύννις ἐὼν[2] κεκλήσεθ' ὁ πύκτης.

ΠΟΛΥΔΕΥΚΗΣ

ἦ καὶ ἄεθλον ἑτοῖμον, ἐφ' ᾧ δηρισόμεθ' ἄμφω;   7

ΑΜΥΚΟΣ

σὸς μὲν ἐγώ, σὺ δ' ἐμὸς κεκλήσεαι, αἴ κε κρατήσω.

ΠΟΛΥΔΕΥΚΗΣ

ὀρνίθων φοινικολόφων τοιοίδε κυδοιμοί.

ΑΜΥΚΟΣ

εἶτ' οὖν ὀρνίθεσσιν ἐοικότες εἴτε λέουσι
γινόμεθ', οὐκ ἄλλῳ κε μαχεσσαίμεσθ' ἐπ' ἀέθλῳ.

ἦ ῥ' Ἄμυκος, καὶ κόχλον ἑλὼν μυκήσατο κοῖλον
οἳ δὲ θοῶς συνάγερθεν ὑπὸ σκιερὰς πλατανίστους

---

[1] θένω Wil: mss θένων or θέων   Junt. ἄμματα   mss also
ὀρθὸς, O. P. 1806 -θοι   [2] γύννις ἐών: mss also σύ με ἀμὸς

POLYDEUCES

Would you silver or aught else for price? Say
what you'll take.

AMYCUS

Up hands and fight me man against man.

POLYDEUCES

Fisticuffs is 't? or feet and all? mind you, I have
a good eye.

AMYCUS

Fists be it, and you may do all your best and
cunningest.

POLYDEUCES

But who is he for whom I am to bind thong to
arm?

AMYCUS

You see him nigh; the man that shall fight you
may be called a woman, but 'faith, shall not deserve
the name.

POLYDEUCES

And pray is there a prize we may contend for in
this our match?

AMYCUS

Whethersoever shall win shall have the other to
his possession.

POLYDEUCES

But such be the mellays of the red-crested game-
cock.

AMYCUS

Whether we be like cock or lion there shall be no
fight betwixt us on any other stake.

With these words Amycus took and blared upon
his hollow shell, and quickly in answer to his call

"A good eye": reading and meaning doubtful.

κοχλου φυσηθέντος ἀλεῖ[1] Βέβρυκες κομόωντες.
ὡς δ' αὔτως ἥρωας ἰὼν ἐκαλέσσατο πάντας
Μαγνήσσης ἀπὸ νηὸς ὑπείροχος ἐν δαῒ Κάστωρ.
οἱ δ' ἐπεὶ οὖν σπείρῃσιν ἐκαρτύναντο βοείαις   8
χεῖρας καὶ περὶ γυῖα μακροὺς εἴλιξαν ἱμάντας,
ἐς μέσσον σύναγον φόνον ἀλλήλοισι πνέοντες.

ἔνθα πολύς σφισι μόχθος ἐπειγομένοισιν ἐτύχθη,
ὁππότερος κατὰ νῶτα λάβοι φάος ἠελίοιο·
ἰδρείῃ μέγαν ἄνδρα παρήλυθες ὦ Πολύδευκες,
βάλλετο δ' ἀκτίνεσσιν ἅπαν 'Αμύκοιο πρόσωπον.
αὐτὰρ ὅγ' ἐν θυμῷ κεχολωμένος ἵετο πρόσσω,
χερσὶ τιτυσκόμενος. τοῦ δ' ἄκρον τύψε γένειον
Τυνδαρίδης ἐπιόντος· ὀρίνθη δὲ πλέον ἢ πρίν,
σὺν δὲ μάχην ἐτάραξε,[2] πολὺς δ' ἐπέκειτο νενευκὼς   9
ἐς γαῖαν. Βέβρυκες δ' ἐπαύτεον, οἱ δ' ἑτέρωθεν
ἥρωες κρατερὸν Πολυδεύκεα θαρσύνεσκον,
δειδιότες μή πώς μιν ἐπιβρίσας δαμάσειε
χώρῳ ἔνι στεινῷ Τιτυῷ ἐναλίγκιος ἀνήρ.
ἤτοι ὅγ' ἔνθα καὶ ἔνθα παριστάμενος[3] Διὸς υἱὸς
ἀμφοτέρῃσιν ἔνυσσεν[4] ἀμοιβαδίς, ἔσχεθε δ' ὁρμῆς
παῖδα Ποσειδάωνος ὑπερφίαλόν περ ἐόντα.
ἔστη δὲ πληγαῖς μεθύων, ἐκ δ' ἔπτυσεν αἷμα
φοίνιον· οἱ δ' ἅμα πάντες ἀριστῆες κελάδησαν,
ὡς ἴδον ἕλκεα λυγρὰ περὶ στόμα τε γναθμούς τε·   1
ὄμματα δ' οἰδήσαντος ἀπεστείνωτο προσώπου.
τὸν μὲν ἄναξ ἐτάρασσεν ἐτώσια χερσὶ προδεικνὺς

[1] ἀλεῖ 'thickly' E, see *Class. Rev.* 1913, p. 5: mss ἀεὶ
[2] mss also ἐτίναξε   [3] mss also περιστ.   [4] ἔνυσσεν Herwerden : mss ἄμυσσεν or ἔτυψεν

came the thick-haired Bebrycians and gathered
themselves together beneath the shady platans.
And in like manner all the heroes of the ship of
Magnesia were fetched by Castor the peerless man-
o'-war. And so the twain braced their hands with
the leathern coils and twined the long straps about
their arms, and forth and entered the ring breathing
slaughter each against the other.

Now was there much ado which should have the sun-
shine at his back ; but the cunning of my Polydeuces
outwent a mighty man, and those beams did fall full
in Amycus his face. So goes master Amycus in high
dudgeon forward with many outs and levellings o's
fists. But the child of Tyndareüs was ready, and
catched him a blow on the point o' the chin ; the which
did the more prick him on and make him to betumble
his fighting, so that he went in head-down and full-tilt.
At that the Bebrycians holla'd him on, and they of
the other part cried cheerly unto the stalwart Poly-
deuces for fear this Tityus of a man should haply over-
peise him and so bear him down in that narrow room.
But the son of Zeus stood up to him first on this side
and then on that, and touched him left and right and
left again ; and for all his puissance the child of Po-
seidon was stayed in 's onset, insomuch that he stood
all drunken with his drubbing and spit out the crim-
son blood. Whereat all the mighty men gave joyful
tongue together by reason of the grievous bruises he
had both by cheek and jowl ; for his eyes were all-to-
straitened with the puffing of their sockets. Next did
my lord maze his man awhile with sundry feints and

πάντοθεν· ἀλλ' ὅτε δή μιν ἀμηχανέοντ' ἐνόησε,
μέσσης ῥινὸς ὕπερθε κατ' ὀφρύος ἤλασε πυγμῇ,[1]
πᾶν δ' ἀπέσυρε μέτωπον ἐς ὀστέον. αὐτὰρ ὁ
    πληγεὶς
ὕπτιος ἐν φύλλοισι τεθηλόσιν ἐξετανύσθη.

ἔνθα μάχη δριμεῖα πάλιν γένετ' ὀρθωθέντος·
ἀλλήλους δ' ὄλεκον στερεοῖς θείνοντες ἱμᾶσιν.
ἀλλ' ὁ μὲν ἐς στῆθός τε καὶ ἔξω χεῖρας ἐνώμα
αὐχένος ἀρχηγὸς Βεβρύκων· ὁ δ' ἀεικέσι πληγαῖς
πᾶν συνέφυρε πρόσωπον[2] ἀνίκητος Πολυδεύκης.
σάρκες τῷ[3] μὲν ἱδρῶτι συνίζανον, ἐκ μεγάλου δὲ
αἶψ' ὀλίγος γένετ' ἀνδρός· ὁ δ' αἰεὶ πάσσονα γυῖα
αὐξομένου[4] φορέεσκε πόνου καὶ χροιῇ ἀμείνω.

πῶς γὰρ δὴ Διὸς υἱὸς ἀδηφάγον ἄνδρα καθεῖλεν;
εἰπὲ θεά, σὺ γὰρ οἶσθα· ἐγὼ δ' ἑτέρων ὑποφήτης
φθέγξομαι ὅσσ'[5] ἐθέλεις σύ, καὶ ὅππως τοι φίλον
    αὐτῇ.

ἤτοι ὅγε ῥέξαι τι λιλαιόμενος μέγα ἔργον
σκαιῇ μὲν σκαιὴν Πολυδεύκεος ἔλλαβε χεῖρα,
δοχμὸς ἀπὸ προβολῆς κλινθείς, ἑτέρῃ δ' ἐπιβαίνων
δεξιτερῆς ἤνεγκεν ἀπὸ λαγόνος πλατὺ γυῖον.
καί κε τυχὼν ἔβλαψεν Ἀμυκλαίων βασιλῆα·
ἀλλ' ὅγ' ὑπεξανέδυ κεφαλῇ,[6] στιβαρῇ δ' ἅμα χειρὶ
πλῆξεν ὑπὸ σκαιὸν κρόταφον καὶ ἐπέμπεσεν ὤμῳ·
ἐκ δ' ἐχύθη μέλαν αἷμα θοῶς κροτάφοιο χανόντος·
λαιῇ δὲ στόμα κόψε, πυκνοὶ δ' ἀράβησαν ὀδόντες·

---

[1] mss also πυγμὴν   [2] mss also μέτωπον   [3] τῷ Meineke:
mss δ' αἱ or δ' οἱ   [4] αὐξομένου Mein: mss ἀπτ.   ἀμείνω
Toup: mss -ων   [5] ὅσσ': mss also ὥς   [6] mss also κεφαλὴν

divers passes all about, and then, so soon as he had him all abroad, let drive at the very middle of his nose, flattened the face of him to the bone, and laid him flatlong amid the springing flowers.

His rising was the renewing of the fray, and a bitter one; aye, now were those swingeing iron gloves to fight unto death. The high lord of Bebrycia, he was all for the chest and none for the head; but as for the never-to-be-beaten Polydeuces, he was for pounding and braying the face with ugly shameful blows: and lo! the flesh of the one began to shrink with the sweating, and eftsoons was a great man made a little; but even as the other's labour increased, so waxed his limbs ever more full and round and his colour ever better.

Now Muse, I pray thee tell—for thou knowest it— how the child of Zeus destroyed that glutton; and he that plays thy interpreter will say what thou willest and even as thou choosest.

Then did Amycus, as who should achieve some great thing, come from his ward and with his left hand grasp Polydeuces' left, and going in with the other, drive the flat of his hand from his right flank. And had the blow come home, he had wrought harm to the king of Amyclae. But lo! my lord slips his head aside and the same moment struck out forth-right from the shoulder and smote him under the left temple; and from that gaping temple the red blood came spirting. Then his left hand did beat him in the mouth, so that the rows of teeth in 't

---

'The flat of the hand': or 'his great fist.'

αἰεὶ δ' ὀξυτέρῳ πιτύλῳ δηλεῖτο πρόσωπον,
μέχρι συνηλοίησε παρήϊα. πᾶς δ' ἐπὶ γαίῃ [1]
κεῖτ' ἀλλοφρονέων, καὶ ἀνέσχεθε νεῖκος ἀπαυδῶν
ἀμφοτέρας ἅμα χεῖρας, ἐπεὶ θανάτου σχεδὸν ἦεν.
τὸν μὲν ἄρα κρατέων περ ἀτάσθαλον οὐδὲν ἔρεξας,
ὦ πύκτη Πολύδευκες· ὄμοσσε δέ τοι μέγαν ὅρκον,
ὃν πατέρ' ἐκ πόντοιο Ποσειδάωνα κικλήσκων,
μήποτ' ἔτι ξείνοισιν ἑκὼν ἀνιηρὸς ἔσεσθαι.

  καὶ σὺ μὲν ὕμνησαί μοι ἄναξ. σὲ δὲ Κάστορ
    ἀείσω,
Τυνδαρίδη ταχύπωλε δορυσσόε χαλκεοθώρηξ.

  τὼ μὲν ἀναρπάξαντε δύω φερέτην Διὸς υἱὼ
δοιὰς Λευκίπποιο κόρας· δισσὼ δ' ἄρα τώγε
ἐσσυμένως ἐδίωκον ἀδελφεὼ υἷ' Ἀφαρῆος,
γαμβρὼ μελλογάμω, Λυγκεὺς καὶ ὁ καρτερὸς Ἴδας. [1]
ἀλλ' ὅτε τύμβον ἵκανον ἀποφθιμένου Ἀφαρῆος,
ἐκ δίφρων ἄρα βάντες ἐπ' ἀλλήλοισιν ὄρουσαν,
ἔγχεσι καὶ κοίλοισι βαρυνόμενοι σακέεσσι.
Λυγκεὺς δ' αὖ μετέειπεν ὑπὲκ κόρυθος μέγ' ἀΰσας·
  'δαιμόνιοι, τί μάχης ἱμείρετε; πῶς δ' ἐπὶ
    νύμφαις
ἀλλοτρίαις χαλεποί, γυμναὶ δ' ἐν χερσὶ μάχαιραι;
ἡμῖν τοι Λεύκιππος ἑὰς ἔδνωσε θύγατρας
τάσδε πολὺ προτέροις· ἡμῖν γάμος οὗτος ἐν ὅρκῳ·
ὑμεῖς δ' οὐ κατὰ κόσμον ἐπ' ἀλλοτρίοισι λέχεσσι
βουσὶ καὶ ἡμιόνοισι καὶ ἄλλοισι κτεάτεσσιν [1]

---

[1] ἐπὶ γαίῃ Ahrens : mss ἐνὶ γαίῃ or ἐπὶ γαῖαν

crackled again; aye, and an ever livelier patter o'
the fists did maul the face of him till his visage was
all one mash. Then down went he in a heap and
lay like to swoon upon the ground; and up with
both his hands for to cry the battle off, because he
was nigh unto death. But thou, good boxer
Polydeuces, for all thy victory didst nothing pre-
sumptuous. Only wouldst thou have him swear a
great oath by the name of his father Poseidon in the
sea, that he would nevermore do annoyance unto
strangers.

The tale of thy praise, great Lord, is told; and
now of thee, good my Castor, will I sing, Castor the
Tyndarid, lord of coursers, wielder of spears, knight
of the corslet of brass.

The twin children of Zeus were up and away with
the daughters twain of Leucippus, and the two sons
of Aphareus were hotfoot upon their track, Lynceus
to wit and doughty Idas, the bridegrooms that were
to be. But when they were got to the grave of
Aphareus dead, they lighted all from their chariots
together and made at one another in the accoutre-
ment of spear and shield. Then up spake Lynceus
and cried aloud from beneath his casque, saying:
'Sirs, why so desirous of battle? How come you so
unkind concerning other men's brides? and where-
fore these naked weapons in your hands? These
daughters of Leucippus were plighted to us, to us
long ere you came; we have his oath to it. But as
for you, you have prevailed on him unseemly for
other men's wives with cattle and mules and what

ἄνδρα παρετρέψασθε, γάμον δ' ἐκκλέπτετε[1] δώροις
ἦ μὴν πολλάκις ὕμμιν ἐνώπιον ἀμφοτέροισιν
αὐτὸς ἐγὼ τάδ' ἔειπα καὶ οὐ πολύμυθος ἐὼν περ·
"οὐχ οὕτω, φίλοι ἄνδρες, ἀριστήεσσιν ἔοικε
μνηστεύειν ἀλόχους, αἷς νυμφίοι ἤδη ἕτοιμοι.
πολλή τοι Σπάρτη, πολλὴ δ' ἱππήλατος Ἧλις,
Ἀρκαδίη τ' εὔμηλος Ἀχαιῶν τε πτολίεθρα,
Μεσσήνη τε καὶ Ἄργος ἅπασά τε Σισυφὶς ἀκτή·
ἔνθα κόραι τοκέεσσιν ὑπὸ σφετέροισι τρέφονται
μυρίαι οὔτε φυῆς ἐπιδευέες οὔτε νόοιο,
τάων εὐμαρὲς ὕμμιν ὀπυίεμεν[2] ἅς κ' ἐθέλητε·
ὡς ἀγαθοῖς πολέες βούλοιντό κε πενθεροὶ εἶναι,
ὑμεῖς δ' ἐν πάντεσσι διάκριτοι ἡρώεσσι,
καὶ πατέρες καὶ ἄνωθεν ἅπαν πατρώιον[3] αἷμα.
ἀλλὰ φίλοι τοῦτον μὲν ἐάσατε πρὸς τέλος ἐλθεῖν
ἄμμι γάμον· σφῶν δ' ἄλλον ἐπιφραζώμεθα πάντες."
ἴσκον τοιάδε πολλά, τὰ δ' εἰς ὑγρὸν ᾤχετο κῦμα
πνοιῇ ἔχουσ' ἀνέμοιο, χάρις δ' οὐχ ἕσπετο μύθοις
σφῶ γὰρ ἀκηλήτω καὶ ἀπηνέες. ἀλλ' ἔτι καὶ νῦν
πείθεσθ'· ἄμφω δ' ἄμμιν ἀνεψιὼ ἐκ πατρὸς ἐστόν.

'εἰ δ' ὑμῖν κραδίη πόλεμον ποθεῖ, αἵματι δὲ χρὴ
νεῖκος ἀναρρήξαντας ὁμοίιον ἔχθεα λῦσαι,[4]
Ἴδας μὲν καὶ ὅμαιμος ἐμός, κρατερὸς Πολυδεύκης,
χεῖρας ἐρωήσουσιν ἀπεχθομένης ὑσμίνης,
νῶι δ', ἐγὼ Λυγκεύς[5] τε, διακρινώμεθ' Ἄρηι
ὁπλοτέρω γεγαῶτε· γονεῦσι δὲ μὴ πολὺ πένθος
ἡμετέροισι λίπωμεν. ἅλις νέκυς ἐξ ἑνὸς οἴκου

---

[1] ἐκκλέπτετε E: mss ἐκλέπτετε or ἐκλέψατε   [2] ὀπυίεμεν
Wil: mss ὀπυίειν   [3] πατρώιον: mss also μητρώιον   [4] mss
also ἔγχεα λοῦσαι   [5] Λυγκεὺς: mss also Κάστωρ

270

not; ye be stealing bridal with a gift. Yet time and again, God wot, albeit I am no man of many words, I have myself spoke to your face and said: "It ill becometh princes, good friends, to go a-wooing such as be betrothed already. Sparta is wide, and so is Elis o' the coursers; wide likewise the sheep-walks of Arcady and the holds of Achaea; Messenè also and Argos and all the seaboard of Sisyphus: there's ten thousand maidens do dwell in them at the houses of their fathers, wanting nothing in beauty or in parts, of the which you may take whomso you will to your wives. For many there be would fain be made wife's father unto a good man and true, and you are men of mark among all heroes, you and your fathers and all your fathers' blood of yore. Nay then, my friends, suffer us to bring this marriage to fulfilment, and we'll all devise other espousal for you." Such was my often rede, but the wind's breath was ever away with it unto the wet sea-wave, and no favour followed upon my words; for ye are hard men both and relentless. Yet even at this hour I pray you give heed, seeing ye be our kin by the father.'

(*The beginning of Castor's reply is lost*)

'. . . But and if your heart would have war, if kindred strife must needs break forth and hate make an end in blood, then shall Idas and my doughty Polydeuces stand aside from the abhorrèd fray, and let you and me, Lynceus, that are the younger men, fight this matter out. So shall we leave our fathers the less sorrow, seeing one is enough dead of one household,

"The seaboard of Sisyphus": the district of Corinth.

εἰς· ἀτὰρ ὦλλοι πάντας [1] εὐφρανέουσιν ἑταίρους
νυμφίοι ἀντὶ νεκρῶν, ὑμεναιώσουσι δὲ κούρας
τάσδ'· ὀλίγῳ τοι ἔοικε κακῷ μέγα νεῖκος ἀναιρεῖν.'
   εἶπε, τὰ δ' οὐκ ἄρ' ἔμελλε θεὸς μεταμώνια θήσειν.
τὼ μὲν γὰρ ποτὶ γαῖαν ἀπ' ὤμων τεύχε' ἔθεντο,
ὣ γενεῇ προφέρεσκον· ὁ δ' ἐς μέσον ἤλυθε Λυγκεύς,
σείων καρτερὸν ἔγχος ὑπ' ἀσπίδος ἄντυγα πρώτην·
ὣς δ' αὔτως ἄκρας ἐτινάξατο δούρατος ἀκμὰς
Κάστωρ· ἀμφοτέροις δὲ λόφων ἐπένευον ἔθειραι.
ἔγχεσι μὲν πρώτιστα τιτυσκόμενοι πόνον [2] εἶχον
ἀλλήλων, εἴ πού τι χροὸς γυμνωθὲν ἴδοιεν.
ἀλλ' ἤτοι τὰ μὲν ἄκρα πάρος τινὰ δηλήσασθαι
δοῦρ' ἐάγη, σακέεσσιν ἔνι δεινοῖσι παγέντα.
τὼ δ' ἄορ ἐκ κολεοῖο ἐρυσσαμένω φόνον αὖτις
τεῦχον ἐπ' ἀλλήλοισι· μάχης δ' οὐ γίνετ' ἐρωή.
πολλὰ μὲν ἐς σάκος εὐρὺ καὶ ἱππόκομον τρυφά-
        λειαν
Κάστωρ, πολλὰ δ' ἔνυξεν ἀκριβὴς ὄμμασι Λυγκεύς
τοῖο σάκος, φοίνικα δ' ὅσον λόφον ἵκετ' ἀκωκή.
τοῦ μὲν ἄκρην ἐκόλουσεν ἐπὶ σκαιὸν γόνυ χεῖρα
φάσγανον ὀξὺ φέροντος ὑπεξαναβὰς ποδὶ Κάστωρ
σκαιῷ· ὁ δὲ πληγεὶς ξίφος ἔκβαλεν, αἶψα δὲ
        φεύγειν
ὡρμήθη ποτὶ σῆμα πατρός, τόθι καρτερὸς Ἴδας
κεκλιμένος θηεῖτο μάχην ἐμφύλιον ἀνδρῶν.
ἀλλὰ μεταΐξας πλατὺ φάσγανον ὦσε διαπρὸ
Τυνδαρίδης λαγόνος τε καὶ ὀμφαλοῦ· ἔγκατα δ' εἴσω
χαλκὸς ἄφαρ διέχευεν· ὁ δ' ἐς στόμα [3] κεῖτο νενευκὼς
Λυγκεύς, κὰδ δ' ἄρα οἱ βλεφάρων βαρὺς ἔδραμεν
        ὕπνος.

---

[1] mss also πάντες   [2] πόνον; mss also πόθον   [3] στόμα:
mss also χθόνα

and the two that be left shall glad all their friends as bridegrooms instead of men slain, and their wedding-song shall be of these maidens. And in such sort, I ween, a great strife is like to end in but little loss.'

So he spake and, it seems, God was not to make his speaking vain. For the two that were the elder did off their armour and laid it upon the ground; but Lynceus, he stepped forth with his stout lance a-quiver hard beneath the target's rim, and Castor, he levelled the point of his spear even in the same manner as Lynceus, the plumes nodding the while upon either's crest. First made they play with the tilting of the lance, if haply they might spy a naked spot; but or ever one of them was wounded the lance-point stuck fast in the trusty buckler and was knapped in twain. Then drew they sword to make havoc of each other; for there was no surcease of battle. Many a time did Castor prick the broad buckler or horse-haired casque; many a time did the quick-eyed Lynceus come at the other's targe or graze with the blade his scarlet crest. But soon, Lynceus making at his left knee, Castor back with his left foot and had off his fingers, so that his falchion dropped to the ground and he went scurrying towards his father's grave, where stout Idas lay watching the kindred fray. Howbeit the son of Tyndareüs was after him in a trice and drave his good sword clean through flank and navel, so that the bowels were presently scattered of the brass, and Lynceus bowed himself and fell upon his face, and lo! there sped down upon his eyelids profoundest sleep.

οὐ μὰν οὐδὲ τὸν ἄλλον ἐφ' ἑστίῃ εἶδε πατρώῃ
παίδων Λαοκόωσα φίλον γάμον ἐκτελέσαντα.
ἦ γὰρ ὅγε στήλην Ἀφαρηίου ἐξανέχουσαν
τύμβου ἀναρπάξας¹ ταχέως Μεσσήνιος Ἴδας
μέλλε κασιγνήτοιο βαλεῖν σφετέροιο φονῆα·
ἀλλὰ Ζεὺς ἐπάμυνε, χερῶν δέ οἱ ἔκβαλε τυκτὴν
μάρμαρον, αὐτὸν δὲ φλογέῳ συνέφλεξε κεραυνῷ.
οὕτω Τυνδαρίδαις πολεμιζέμεν οὐκ ἐν ἐλαφρῷ·
αὐτοί τε κρατέουσι καὶ ἐκ κρατέοντος ἔφυσαν.

χαίρετε Λήδας τέκνα, καὶ ἡμετέροις κλέος ὕμνοις
ἐσθλὸν ἀεὶ πέμποιτε. φίλοι δέ τε πάντες ἀοιδοὶ
Τυνδαρίδαις Ἑλένῃ τε καὶ ἄλλοις ἡρώεσσιν,
Ἴλιον οἳ διέπερσαν ἀρήγοντες Μενελάῳ.
ὑμῖν κῦδος ἄνακτες ἐμήσατο Χῖος ἀοιδός,
ὑμνήσας Πριάμοιο πόλιν καὶ νῆας Ἀχαιῶν
Ἰλιάδας τε μάχας Ἀχιλῆά τε πύργον αὐτῆς·
ὑμῖν αὖ καὶ ἐγὼ λιγεῶν μειλίγματα Μουσέων,
οἷ' αὐταὶ παρέχουσι καὶ ὡς ἐμὸς οἶκος ὑπάρχει,
τοῖα φέρω. γεράων δὲ θεοῖς κάλλιστον ἀοιδαί.²

¹ ἀναρπάξας E, cf. Pind. _N_. 10. 60: mss ἀναρρήξας   ² mss also ἀοιδὴ

But neither was the other of Laocoösa's children to be seen of his mother a wedded man at the hearth of his fathers. For Idas of Messenè, he up with the standing stone from the grave of Aphareus and would have hurled it upon the slayer of his brother, but Zeus was Castor's defence, and made the wrought marble to fall from his enemy's hands; for he consumed him with the flame of his levin-bolt. Ah! 'tis no child's-play to fight with the sons of Tyndareus; they prevail even as he that begat them prevaileth.

Fare you well, ye children of Leda; we pray you may ever send our hymns a goodly fame. For all singers are dear unto the sons of Tyndareus and unto Helen and unto other the heroes who were Menelaüs' helpfellows at the sacking of Troy. Your renown, O ye princes, is the work of the singer of Chios, when he sang of Priam's town and of the Achaean ships, of Troyan frays and of that tower of the war-cry Achilles; and here do I also bring your souls such offerings of propitiation as the melodious Muses do provide and my household is able to afford. And of all a God's prerogatives song is the fairest.

XXIII.—THE LOVER

THIS *poem, known to the Latin poets, cannot be ascribed to Theocritus. It was apparently sent by a lover to his neglectful beloved. The author tells how in a like case unrequited friendship led to the suicide of the one, and to the death of the other at the hands of an effigy of Love. The actual death of a boy through the accidental falling of a statue probably gave rise to a folk-tale which is here put into literary shape.*

XXIII.—ΕΡΑΣΤΗΣ

Ἀνήρ τις πολύφιλτρος ἀπηνέος ἤρατ᾽ ἐφάβω
τὰν μορφὰν ἀγαθῶ, τὸν δὲ τρόπον οὐκέθ᾽ ὁμοίω·
μίσει τὸν φιλέοντα καὶ οὐδὲ ἓν ἄμερον εἶχε,
κοὐκ ἤδει τὸν Ἔρωτα, τίς ὢν [1] θεὸς ἁλίκα τόξα
χερσὶ κρατεῖ, πῶς πικρὰ βέλη ποτὶ παίχνια
        βάλλει·
πάντα δὲ κἂν μύθοισι καὶ ἐν προσόδοισιν ἀτειρής.
οὐδέ τι τῶν πυρσῶν παραμύθιον, οὐκ ἀμάρυγμα
χείλεος, οὐκ ὄσσων λιπαρὸν σέλας, οὐ ῥοδόμαλον,
οὐ λόγος, οὐχὶ φίλαμα τὸ κουφίξον [3] τὸν ἔρωτα.
οἷα δὲ θὴρ ὑλαῖος ὑποπτεύῃσι κυνάγως,
οὕτως πάντ᾽ ἐποπώπει ἐπὶ [4] βροτόν· ἄγρια δ᾽
        αὐτῷ
χείλεα καὶ κῶραι δεινὸν βλέπος εἶχον ἀνάγκας· [5]
τᾷ δὲ χολᾷ τὸ πρόσωπον ἀμείβετο, φεῦγε δ᾽ ἀπὸ
        χρώς
ὁ πρὶν ταῖς ὀργαῖς περικείμενον. [6]   ἀλλὰ καὶ οὕτως
ἦν καλός· ἐξ ὀργᾶς [7] ἐρεθίζετο μᾶλλον ἐραστάς.
    λοίσθιον οὐκ ἤνεικε τόσαν φλόγα τᾶς [8] Κυθερείας,
ἀλλ᾽ ἐλθὼν ἔκλαιε ποτὶ στυγνοῖσι μελάθροις,

----

[1] ὢν Mein: mss ἦν   [2] ποτὶ παίχνια E, the *saevus iocus* of
Hor. *C.* i. 33. 12, cf. πρὸς ἡδονὴν and Mosch. i. 11: Steph.
ποτικάρδια, Ahr. ποτὶ καὶ Δία (see *C.R.* 1913, p. 5): mss ποτ
παιδία   [3] κουφίξον E: mss -ζον, -ζειν, -ζοι, -ζει   [4] ἐποπώπε
ἐπὶ E: cf. 4. 7: mss ἐποίει ποτὶ τὸν   [5] βλέπος ε. ἀνάγκα

278

XXIII.—THE LOVER

THERE was once a heart-sick swain had a cruel
fere, the face of the fere goodly but his ways not
like to it; for he hated him that loved him, and had
for him never a whit of kindness, and as for Love,
what manner of God he might be or what manner of
bow and arrows carry, or how keen and bitter were
the shafts he shot for his delectation, these things
wist he not at all, but both in his talk and conversa-
tion knew no yielding. And he gave no comfort
against those burning fires, not a twist of his lip, not
a flash of his eye, not the gift of a hip from the hedge-
row, not a word, not a kiss, to lighten the load of de-
sire. But he eyed every man even as a beast of the field
that suspects the hunter, and his lips were hard and
cruel and his eyes looked the dread look of fate. In-
deed his angry humour made change of his face, and
the colour of his cheeks fled away because he was a
prey to wrathful imaginings. But even so he was fair
to view ; his wrath served only to prick his lover the
more.

At last the poor man would bear no more so fierce
a flame of the Cytherean, but went and wept before

Meineke : mss βλέπον ε. ἀνάγκαν   ⁶ ὁ πρὶν Ahrens : mss
ὕβριν   ταῖς ὀργαῖς E : mss τᾶς ὀργᾶς   περικείμενον Wake-
field : mss ποτικείμενος   ⁷ ἦν Heinsius : mss ἡ   ἐξ ὀργᾶς
Steph. : mss δ' ἐξόρπασ'   ⁸ φλόγα τᾶς Eldik : mss φαότατος

καὶ κύσε τὰν φλιάν, οὕτω δ' ἀντέλλετο φωνᾷ·[1]
  "ἄγριε παῖ καὶ στυγνέ, κακᾶς ἀνάθρεμμα
    λεαίνας,
λάϊνε παῖ καὶ ἔρωτος ἀνάξιε, δῶρά τοι ἦλθον
λοίσθια ταῦτα φέρων, τὸν ἐμὸν βρόχον· οὐκέτι
    γάρ σε
κῶρε θέλω λυπεῖν ποθορώμενος,[2] ἀλλὰ βαδίζω,
ἔνθα τύ μευ κατέκρινας, ὅπῃ λόγος ἦμεν ἀταρπὸν
ξυνὰν[3] τοῖσιν ἐρῶσι, τὸ φάρμακον ἔνθα τὸ λάθους.[4]
ἀλλὰ καὶ ἢν ὅλον αὐτὸ λαβὼν ποτὶ χεῖλος
    ἀμέλξω,
οὐδ' οὕτως σβέσσω τὸν ἐμὸν πόθον.[5]

                    ἄρτι δὲ χαίρειν
τοῖσι τεοῖς προθύροις ἐπιτέλλομαι.[6] οἶδα τὸ μέλ-
    λον·
καὶ τὸ ῥόδον καλόν ἐστι, καὶ ὁ χρόνος αὐτὸ
    μαραίνει·
καὶ τὸ ἴον καλόν ἐστιν ἐν εἴαρι, καὶ ταχὺ γηρᾷ·
λευκὸν τὸ κρίνον ἐστί, μαραίνεται ἁνίκ' ἀπανθεῖ·[7]
ἁ δὲ χιὼν λευκά, κατατάκεται ἁνίκ' ἐπιπνεῖ·[8]
καὶ κάλλος καλόν ἐστι τὸ παιδικόν, ἀλλ' ὀλίγον
    ζῇ.
ἥξει καιρὸς ἐκεῖνος, ὁπάνικα καὶ τὺ φιλάσεις,
ἁνίκα τὰν κραδίαν ὀπτεύμενος ἁλμυρὰ κλαύσεις.
ἀλλὰ τὺ παῖ καὶ τοῦτο πανύστατον ἁδύ τι ῥέξον·
ὁππόταν ἐξελθὼν ἀρταμένον ἐν προθύροισι
τοῖσι τεοῖσιν ἴδῃς τὸν τλάμονα, μή με παρέλθῃς,
στᾶθι δὲ καὶ βραχὺ κλαῦσον, ἐπισπείσας δὲ τὸ
    δάκρυ

---

[1] ἀντέλλετο φωνᾷ E: mss ἀντέλοντο φωναὶ   [2] ποθορώμενος
E: mss ποχολώμενος(λ corr. to ρ)   [3] ἀταρπὸν ξυνὰν Toup: mss
ἀταρπῶν ξυνὸν   [4] λάθους E: mss λᾶθος   [5] πόθον Mus:

280

that sullen house, and kissed the doorpost of it, and
lifted up his voice saying " O cruel, O sullen child,
that wast nursed of an evil she-lion ; O boy of stone
which art all unworthy to be loved ; lo ! here am I
come with the last of my gifts, even this my halter.
No longer will I vex you with the sight of me ; but
here go I whither you have condemned me, where
they say the path lies all lovers must travel, where
is the sweet physic of oblivion. Yet if so be I take
and drink that physic up, every drop, yet shall I not
quench the fever of my desire.

And lo ! now I bid this thy door farewell or ever
I go. I know what is to be. The rose is fair
and Time withers it, the violet is fair in the year's
spring and it quickly groweth old ; the lily is
white,—it fades when its flowering's done ; and
white the snow,—it melts all away when the wind
blows warm : and even so, the beauty of a child
is beautiful indeed, but it liveth not for long. The
day will come when you shall love like me, when
your heart shall burn like mine, and your eyes weep
brinish tears. So I pray you, child, do me this one
last courtesy : when you shall come and find a poor
man hanging at your door, pass him not by ; but
stay you first and weep awhile for a libation upon

mss χόλον   [6] ἐπιτέλλομαι Reiske : mss -βάλλομαι   [7] ἀνίκ'
ἀπανθεῖ E : mss ἀν. πίπτη (see on l. 32)   [8] κατατάκεται Wil :
mss καὶ τ.   ἐπιπνεῖ E, impersonal ; see C.R. 1913, p. 6 : mss
παχθῇ

λῦσον τᾶς σχοίνω με καὶ ἀμφίθες ἐκ ῥεθέων σῶν
εἵματα καὶ κρύψον με, τὸ δ᾽ αὖ πύματόν με
    φίλασον·
κἂν νεκρῷ χαρίσαιτο σὰ χείλεα. μή με φοβαθῇς·
οὐ δύναμαι σίνειν [1] σε· διαλλάξεις με φιλάσας.
χῶμα δέ μοι κοίλου τι,[2] τό μευ κρύψει τὸν ἔρωτα,
χὢτ᾽ ἀπίῃς, τόδε μοι τρὶς ἐπαῦσον· 'ὦ φίλε κεῖσο.' [3]
ἢν δὲ θέλῃς, καὶ τοῦτο· 'καλὸς δέ μοι ὤλεθ᾽
    ἑταῖρος.'
γράψον καὶ τόδε γράμμα, τὸ σοῖς τοίχοισι
    χαράσσω.[4]
'τοῦτον ἔρως ἔκτεινεν. ὁδοιπόρε, μὴ παροδεύσῃς,
ἀλλὰ στὰς τόδε λέξον· ἀπηνέα εἶχεν ἑταῖρον.'"
    ὧδ᾽ εἰπὼν λίθον εἶλεν, ἐρεισάμενος δ᾽ ἐπὶ τοίχῳ
ἄχρι μέσων οὐδῶν φοβερὸν λίθον ἅπτετ᾽ ἐπι-
    στὰς [5]   5
τὰν λεπτὰν σχοινίδα, βρόχον δ᾽ ἐνέβαλλε [6] τρα-
    χήλῳ,
τὰν ἕδραν δ᾽ ἐκύλισεν ἀπαὶ ποδός, ἠδ᾽ ἐκρεμάσθη
νεκρός.
    ὃ δ᾽ αὖτ᾽ ὦιξε θύρας καὶ τὸν νεκρὸν εἶδεν
αὐλᾶς ἐξ ἰδίας ἀρταμένον, οὐδ᾽ ἐλυγίχθη
τὰν ψυχάν· οὐ κλαῦσε νέον φόνον, οὐδ᾽ [7] ἐπὶ νεκρῷ
εἵματα πάντ᾽ ἐμίαινεν ἐφαβικά, βαῖνε δ᾽ ἐς ἆθλα [8]
γυμναστῶν, καὶ ἔκηλα [9] φίλων ἐπεμαίετο λουτρῶν.
καὶ ποτὶ τὸν θεὸν ἦλθε, τὸν ὕβρισε· λαΐνεος [10] δὲ

[1] σίνειν Ahrens: mss εἶν   [2] μοι (Mus.) κοίλου τι E: mss
μευ κοῖλον τι or τὸ   [3] χὢτ᾽ E: mss κἂν corr. from χῶμ᾽ due
to confusion with l. 44   κεῖσο E: mss κεῖσαι   [4] χαράσσω
Wil: mss χαράξω   [5] ἅπτετ᾽ Mus: mss ὁπότ᾽   ἐπιστὰς

him, and then loosing him from the rope, put
about him some covering from your own shoulders;
and give him one last kiss, for your lips will be wel-
come even to the dead. And never fear me; I
cannot do thee any mischief; thou shalt kiss and
there an end. Then pray thee make a hole in some
earthy bank for to hide all my love of thee; and ere
thou turn thee to go thy ways, cry over me three
times 'Rest, my friend,' and if it seem thee good
cry also 'My fair companion's dead.' And for
epitaph write the words I here inscribe upon thy
wall:

> *Here's one that died of love; good wayfarer,*
> *Stay thee and say: his was a cruel fere."*

This said, he took a stone and set it up, that
dreadful stone, against the wall in the midst of the
doorway; then tied that slender string unto the
porch above, put the noose about his neck, rolled
that footing from beneath his feet, and lo! he hung
a corpse.

Soon that other, he opened the door and espied
the dead hanging to his own doorway; and his
stubborn heart was not bended. The new-done
murder moved him not unto tears, nor would he be
defiling all his young lad's garments with a dead
corpse; but went his ways to the wrestling-bouts and
betook himself light of heart to his beloved bath.
And so came he unto the God he had slighted. For

Legrand : mss ἀπ'αὐτοῦ, -τῶν   ⁶ ἐνέβλλεα or ἔμβαλλε Mus :
mss ἔβαλλε   ⁷ οὐδ' E : mss ἀλλ'   ⁸ ἐμίαινεν E : mss ἐμίανεν
ἆθλα Ahrens : mss ἄθλω   ⁹ ἔκηλα Wil : mss λε   ¹⁰ λαίνεος
E : mss λαινέας

283

ἵστατ' ἀπὸ κρηπῖδος ἐς ὕδατα· τῷ δ' ἐφύπερθεν
ἅλατο καὶ τὦγαλμα, κακὸν δ' ἔκτεινεν ἔφαβον·
νᾶμα[1] δ' ἐφοινίχθη· παιδὸς δ' ἐπενάχετο φωνά·
" χαίρετε τοὶ φιλέοντες· ὁ γὰρ μισῶν ἐφονεύθη.
στέργετε δ' οἱ μισεῦντες· ὁ γὰρ θεὸς οἶδε δικάζειν."

[1] νᾶμα Reiske : mss ἅμα

there stood an image of him upon the margin looking towards the water.   And lo! even the graven image leapt down upon him and slew that wicked lad ; and the water went all red, and on the water floated the voice of a child saying " Rejoice ye that love, for he that did hate is slain ; and love ye that hate, for the God knoweth how to judge."

XXIV.—THE LITTLE HERACLES

THIS *Epic poem, unlike the Hylas, is not an artistic whole.*[1]
*It tells first how the infant Heracles killed the two snakes
sent by the outraged Hera to devour him, and next of the
rites which the seer Teiresias advised his mother Alcmena
to perform in order to avert her wrath. We are then
told of the education of Heracles, and the poem breaks
off abruptly in the MSS. after an account of his diet and
clothing. Such a poem would doubtless be acceptable at
the Alexandrian court in the early years of the child who
was afterwards Ptolemy III. For the Ptolemies claimed
descent from Heracles.*

[1] It is now known for certain that this may well be
untrue. The Antinoë Papyrus has the remains of 32 lines
after l. 140, ending, as we learn from a marginal paraphrase,
with a request for the poet's victory in the competition.

XXIV.—ΗΡΑΚΛΙΣΚΟΣ

Ἡρακλέα δεκάμηνον ἐόντα πόχ' ἁ Μιδεᾶτις
Ἀλκμήνα καὶ νυκτὶ νεώτερον Ἰφικλῆα
ἀμφοτέρους λούσασα καὶ ἐμπλήσασα γάλακτος,
χαλκείαν κατέθηκεν ἐς ἀσπίδα, τὰν Πτερελάου
Ἀμφιτρύων καλὸν ὅπλον ἀπεσκύλευσε πεσόντος.
ἁπτομένα δὲ γυνὰ κεφαλᾶς μυθήσατο παίδων·
" εὕδετ' ἐμὰ βρέφεα γλυκερὸν καὶ ἐγέρσιμον ὕπνον,
εὕδετ' ἐμὰ ψυχά, δύ' ἀδελφεοί, εὔσοα τέκνα·
ὄλβιοι εὐνάζοισθε καὶ ὄλβιοι ἀῶ ἵκοισθε." [1]
ὣς φαμένα δίνησε σάκος μέγα· τοὺς δ' ἔλαβ' ὕπνος. [2]

ἆμος δὲ στρέφεται μεσονύκτιον ἐς δύσιν Ἄρκτος
Ὠρίωνα κατ' αὐτόν, ὃ δ' ἀμφαίνει μέγαν ὦμον,
τᾶμος ἄρ' αἰνὰ πέλωρα δύω πολυμήχανος Ἥρα
κυανέαις φρίσσοντας ὑπὸ σπείραισι δράκοντας
ὦρσεν ἐπὶ πλατὺν οὐδόν, ὅθι σταθμὰ κοῖλα θυράων
οἴκου, ἀπειλήσασα φαγεῖν βρέφος Ἡρακλῆα.
τὼ δ' ἐξειλυσθέντες ἐπὶ χθονὶ γαστέρας ἄμφω
αἱμοβόρους ἐκύλιον· ἀπ' ὀφθαλμῶν δὲ κακὸν πῦρ
ἐρχομένοις λάμπεσκε, βαρὺν δ' ἐξέπτυον ἰόν.
ἀλλ' ὅτε δὴ παίδων λιχμώμενοι ἐγγύθεν ἦλθον,
καὶ τότ' ἄρ' ἐξέγροντο, Διὸς νοέοντος ἅπαντα,
Ἀλκμήνας φίλα τέκνα, φάος δ' ἀνὰ οἶκον ἐτύχθη.
ἤτοι ὅγ' εὐθὺς ἄϋσεν, ὅπως κακὰ θηρί' ἀνέγνω

---

[1] ἵκοισθε : mss also ἴδοιτε   [2] for ἔλαβ' P. Ant. has ἕλεν

XXIV.—THE LITTLE HERACLES

ONCE upon a time when the little Heracles was ten months old, Alcmena of Midea took him and Iphicles that was his younger by a night, and laid them, washed both and suckled full, in the fine brazen buckler Amphitryon had gotten in spoil of Pterelaüs, and setting her hand upon their heads said "Sleep my babes, sleep sweetly and light; sleep, sweethearts, brothers twain, goodly children. Heaven prosper your slumbering now and your awakening to-morrow." And as she spake, she rocked the great targe till they fell asleep.

But what time the Bear swings low towards her midnight place over against the uplifted shoulder of mighty Orion, then sent the wily Hera two dire monsters of serpents, bridling and bristling and with azure coils, to go upon the broad threshold of the hollow doorway of the house, with intent they should devour the child Heracles. And there on the ground they both untwined their ravening bellies and went writhing forward, while an evil fire shined forth of their eyes and a grievous venom was spued out of their mouth. But when with tongues flickering they were come where the children lay, on a sudden Alcmena's little ones (for Zeus knew all) awoke, and there was made a light in the house. Iphicles, he straightway cried out when he espied the evil beasts and their pitiless fangs

κοίλου ὑπὲρ σάκεος καὶ ἀναιδέας εἶδεν ὀδόντας,
Ἰφικλέης, οὔλαν δὲ ποσὶν διελάκτισε χλαῖναν,
φευγέμεν ὁρμαίνων· ὁ δ᾽ ἐναντίος ἵετο [1] χερσὶν
Ἡρακλέης, ἄμφω δὲ βαρεῖ ἐνεδήσατο δεσμῷ,
δραξάμενος φάρυγος, τόθι φάρμακα λυγρὰ τέτυκται [2]
οὐλομένοις ὀφίεσσι, τὰ καὶ θεοὶ ἐχθαίροντι.
τὼ δ᾽ αὖτε σπείραισιν ἑλισσέσθην περὶ παῖδα
ὀψίγονον γαλαθηνὸν ὑπὸ τροφῷ αἰὲν ἄδακρυν·
ἂψ δὲ πάλιν διέλυον, ἐπεὶ μογέοιεν ἀκάνθας,
δεσμοῦ ἀναγκαίου πειρώμενοι ἔκλυσιν εὑρεῖν.

Ἀλκμήνα δ᾽ ἐσάκουσε βοᾶς καὶ ἐπέγρετο [3] πράτα·
"ἄνσταθ᾽ Ἀμφιτρύων· ἐμὲ γὰρ δέος ἴσχει ὀκνηρόν·
ἄνστα, μηδὲ πόδεσσι τεοῖς ὑπὸ σάνδαλα θείης.
οὐκ ἀίεις, παίδων ὁ νεώτερος ὅσσον ἀυτεῖ;
ἢ οὐ νοέεις, ὅτι νυκτὸς ἀωρί που, οἱ δέ τε τοῖχοι
πάντες ἀριφραδέες καθαρᾶς ἅπερ [4] ἠριγενείας;
ἔστι τί μοι κατὰ δῶμα νεώτερον, ἔστι φίλ᾽ ἀνδρῶν."
ὣς φάθ᾽. ὁ δ᾽ ἐξ εὐνᾶς ἀλόχῳ κατέβαινε πιθήσας·
δαιδάλεον δ᾽ ὥρμασε μετὰ ξίφος, ὅ οἱ ὕπερθεν
κλιντῆρος κεδρίνου περὶ πασσάλῳ αἰὲν ἄωρτο.
ἤτοι ὅγ᾽ ὠριγνᾶτο νεοκλώστου τελαμῶνος,
κουφίζων ἑτέρᾳ κολεόν, μέγα λώτινον ἔργον.
ἀμφιλαφὴς δ᾽ ἄρα παστὰς ἐνεπλήσθη πάλιν
ὄρφνας·
δμῶας δὴ τότ᾽ ἄυσεν ὕπνον βαρὺν ἐκφυσῶντας·
"οἴσετε πῦρ ὅτι θᾶσσον ἀπ᾽ ἐσχαρεῶνος ἑλόντες,
δμῶες ἐμοί·" στιβαροὺς δὲ θυρᾶν ἀνεκόψατ᾽ [5] ὀχῆας.

[1] ἵετο Meineke : mss εἴχετο   [2] mss also κέκρυπται   [3] P.
Ant. ἄκουσε ἐπέγρετο : mss also ἐπέδραμε   [4] ἅπερ Briggs :
mss ἄτερ   [5] ἀνεκόψατ᾽ Blass : mss ἀνακ.

above the target's rim, and kicked away the woollen
coverlet in an agony to flee; but Heracles made
against them with his hands, and griping them where
lies a baneful snake's fell poison hated even of the
Gods, held them both fast bound in a sure bondage
by the throat.   For a while thereat they two wound
their coils about that young child, that suckling babe
at nurse which never knew tears; but soon they
relaxed their knots and loosed their weary spines and
only strove to find enlargement from out those
irresistible bonds.

Alcmena was the first to hear the cry and awake.
"Arise, Amphitryon," quoth she; "for as for me
I cannot arise for fear.   Up then you, and tarry
not even till you be shod.   Hear you not how
the little one cries? and mark you not that all
the chamber-walls are bright as at the pure day-
spring hour, though sure 'tis the dead of night?
Troth, something, dear lord, is amiss with us."   At
these her words he up and got him down from the
bed, and leapt for the damasked brand which ever
hung to a peg above his cedarn couch, and so reached
out after his new-spun baldric even as with the
other hand he took up his great scabbard of lotus-
wood.   Now was the ample bower filled full again
of darkness, and the master cried upon his bond-
servants that lay breathing slumber so deep and loud,
saying "Quick, my bondservants! bring lights, bring
lights from the brazier," and so thrust his stout
door-pins back.   Then "Rouse ye," quoth the

" ἄνστατε δμῶες **ταλασίφρονες**. αὐτὸς ἀϋτεῖ."
ἦ ῥα γυνὰ Φοίνισσα μύλαις ἔπι κοῖτον ἔχουσα.
οἳ δ' αἶψα προγένοντο λύχνοις ἅμα δαιομένοισι
δμῶες· ἐνεπλήσθη δὲ δόμος σπεύδοντος ἑκάστου.
ἤτοι ἄρ' ὡς εἶδοντ' ἐπιτίτθιον[1] Ἡρακλῆα
θῆρε δύω χείρεσσιν ἀπρὶξ ἀπαλαῖσιν ἔχοντα,
συμπλήγδην ἰάχησαν· ὃ δ' ἐς πατέρ' Ἀμφιτρύωνα
ἑρπετὰ δεικανάασκεν, ἐπάλλετο δ' ὑψόθι χαίρων
κουροσύνᾳ,[2] γελάσας δὲ πάρος κατέθηκε ποδοῖν
πατρὸς ἑοῦ θανάτῳ κεκαρωμένα δεινὰ πέλωρα.
Ἀλκμήνα μὲν ἔπειτα ποτὶ σφέτερον βάλε κόλπον
ξηρὸν ὑπαὶ δείους ἀκρόχλοον Ἰφικλῆα·
Ἀμφιτρύων δὲ τὸν ἄλλον ὑπ' ἀμνείαν θέτο χλαῖναν
παῖδα, πάλιν δ' ἐς λέκτρον ἰὼν ἐμνάσατο κοίτου.

ὄρνιθες τρίτον ἄρτι τὸν ἔσχατον ὄρθρον ἄειδον,
Τειρεσίαν τόκα μάντιν ἀλαθέα πάντα λέγοντα
Ἀλκμήνα καλέσασα τέρας[3] κατέλεξε νεοχμόν,
καί νιν ὑποκρίνεσθαι, ὅπως τελέεσθαι ἔμελλεν,
ἠνώγει· " μηδ' εἴ τι θεοὶ νοέοντι πονηρόν,
αἰδόμενος ἐμὲ κρύπτε· καὶ ὡς οὐκ ἔστιν ἀλύξαι
ἀνθρώποις, ὅτι Μοῖρα κατὰ κλωστῆρος ἐπείγει.
ἀλλ'[4] Εὐηρείδα μάλα σε φρονέοντα διδάσκω."
τόσσ' ἔλεγεν βασίλεια· ὃ δ' ἀνταμείβετο τοίοις·[5]
" θάρσει ἀριστοτόκεια γύναι, Περσήϊον αἷμα,
θάρσει· μελλόντων δὲ τὸ λώϊον ἐν φρεσὶ θέσσο.[6]
ναὶ γὰρ ἐμῶν[7] γλυκὺ φέγγος ἀποιχόμενον πάλαι
    ὄσσων,

---

[1] P. Ant. υποτι[[2] P. Ant. γηθοσύναι   [3] P. Ant: mss
also χρέος   [4] ἀλλ' Ahr: mss μάντι (P. Ant.) or μάντιν   [5] τοίοις
Briggs: mss τοίως or τοῖος   [6] θέσσο E, cf. Sappho 78 and
Nicias A.P. 9. 564: mss θέσθαι or omit   [7] ἐμῶν E: mss ἐμὸν

Phoenician woman that had her sleeping over the mill, " rouse ye, strong-heart bondservants ; the master cries : " and quickly forth came those bond-servants with lamps burning every one, and lo ! all the house was filled full of their bustling. And when they espied the suckling Heracles with the two beasts in the clutch of his soft little fingers, they clapped their hands and shouted aloud. There he was, showing the creeping things to his father Amphitryon and capering in his pretty childish glee ; then laughing laid the dire monsters before his father's feet all sunken in the slumber of death. Then was Iphicles clipped aghast and palsied with fright to Alcmena's bosom, and the other child did Amphitryon lay again beneath the lamb's-wool coverlet, and so gat him back to bed and took up his rest.

The cocks at third crow were carolling the break of day, when he that never lied, the seer Teiresias, was called of Alcmena and all the strange thing told him. And she bade him give answer how it should turn out, and said " Even though the Gods devise us ill, I pray you hide it not from me in pity ; for not even thus may man escape what the spindle of Fate drives upon him. But enough, son of Eueres ; verily I teach the wise." At that he made the queen this answer : " Be of good cheer, O seed of Perseus, thou mother of noblest offspring ; be of good cheer and lay up in thy heart the best hope of that which is to come. For I swear to you by the dear sweet light that is so long gone from my eyes, many the

---

"At that he made," etc.: P. Ant. has for l. 72 ταν δ' Ευηρειτας τοιωδ' απαμ[είβετο μύθῳ]

πολλαὶ ᾿Αχαιιάδων μαλακὸν περὶ γούνατι νῆμα
χειρὶ κατατρίψουσιν ἀκρέσπερον ἀείδουσαι
᾿Αλκμήναν ὀνομαστί, σέβας δ᾿ ἔσῃ ᾿Αργείαισι.
τοῖος ἀνὴρ ὅδε μέλλει ἐς οὐρανὸν ἄστρα φέροντα
ἀμβαίνειν τεὸς υἱός, ἀπὸ στέρνων πλατὺς ἥρως,
οὗ καὶ θηρία πάντα καὶ ἀνέρες ἥσσονες ἄλλοι.
δώδεκά οἱ τελέσαντι πεπρωμένον ἐν Διὸς οἰκεῖν [1]
μόχθους, θνητὰ δὲ πάντα πυρὰ Τραχίνιος ἕξει·
γαμβρὸς δ᾿ ἀθανάτων κεκλήσεται, οἳ τάδ᾿ ἐπῶρσαν
κνώδαλα φωλεύοντα βρέφος διαδηλήσασθαι.
ἀλλὰ γύναι πῦρ μέν τοι ὑπὸ σποδοῦ εὔτυκον ἔστω,
κάγκανα δ᾿ ἀσπαλάθου ξύλ᾿ ἑτοιμάσατ᾿ ἢ παλι-
        ούρου
ἢ βάτου ἢ ἀνέμῳ δεδονημένον αὖον ἄχερδον·
καῖε δὲ τώδ᾿ ἀγρίαισιν ἐπὶ σχίζαισι δράκοντε
νυκτὶ μέσᾳ, ὅκα παῖδα κανεῖν τεὸν ἤθελον αὐτοί.
ἦρι δὲ συλλέξασα κόνιν πυρὸς ἀμφιπόλων τις
ῥιψάτω εὖ μάλα πᾶσαν ὑπὲρ ποταμοῖο φέρουσα
ῥωγάδας ἐς πέτρας ὑπερούριον, ἂψ δὲ νεέσθω [2]
ἄστρεπτος· καθαρῷ δὲ πυρώσατε δῶμα θεείῳ
πρᾶτον, ἔπειτα δ᾿ ἅλεσσι μεμιγμένον, ὡς νενό-
        μισται,
θαλλῷ ἐπιρραίνειν ἐστεμμένῳ [3] ἀβλαβὲς ὕδωρ·
Ζηνὶ δ᾿ ἐπιρρέξαι καθυπερτέρῳ ἄρσενα χοῖρον,
δυσμενέων αἰεὶ καθυπέρτεροι ὡς τελέθοιτε."

¹ οἰκεῖν Mus, P. Ant. οικην: mss οἰκῇς   ² so Herm, P.
Ant: mss νέεσθαι   ³ ἐστεμμένῳ Schaefer: mss -ον

294

Achaean women that as they card the soft wool
about their knees at even, shall sing hereafter of the
name of Alcmena, and the dames of Argos shall do
her honour of worship.   So mighty a man shall in
this your son rise to the star-laden heavens, to wit a
Hero broad of breast, that shall surpass all flesh, be
they man or be they beast.   And 'tis decreed that
having accomplished labours twelve, albeit all his
mortal part shall fall to a pyre of Trachis, he shall go
to dwell with Zeus, and shall be called in his
marriage a son of the Immortals, even of them who
despatched those venomous beasts of the earth to
make an end of him in his cradle.   But now, my
lady, let there be fire ready for thee beneath the
embers, and prepare ye dry sticks of bramble, brier,
or thorn, or else of the wind-fallen twigs of the wild
pear-tree ; and with that fuel of wild wood consume
thou this pair of serpents at midnight, even at the
hour they chose themselves for to slay thy son.
And betimes in the morning let one of thy hand-
maids gather up the dust of the fire and take it to
the river-cliff, and cast it, every whit and very
carefully, out upon the river to be beyond your
borders ; and on her homeward way look she never
behind her : next, for the cleansing of your house,
first burn ye therein sulphur pure, and then sprinkle
about it with a wool-wound branch innocent water
mingled, as the custom is, with salt : and for an end
offer ye a boar pig to Zeus pre-eminent, that so ye
may ever remain pre-eminent above your enemies."

86 ἔσται δὴ τοῦτ' ἆμαρ, ὁπηνίκα νεβρὸν ἐν εὐνᾷ
   καρχαρόδων σίνεσθαι ἰδὼν λύκος οὐκ ἐθελήσει.

These lines, rightly omitted by Briggs as due to a Christian
interpolator, occur in P. Ant. (c. A.D. 500).

φᾶ, καὶ ἐρωήσας ἐλεφάντινον ᾤχετο δίφρον
Τειρεσίας πολλοῖσι βαρύς περ ἐὼν ἐνιαυτοῖς.

'Ηρακλέης δ' ὑπὸ ματρὶ νέον φυτὸν ὡς ἐν ἀλωᾷ
ἐτρέφετ' 'Αργείου κεκλημένος 'Αμφιτρύωνος.
γράμματα μὲν τὸν παῖδα γέρων Λίνος ἐξεδίδαξεν,
υἱὸς 'Απόλλωνος μελεδωνεὺς ἄγρυπνος ἥρως,
τόξον δ' ἐντανύσαι καὶ ἐπὶ σκοπὸν εἶναι ὀϊστὸν
Εὔρυτος ἐκ πατέρων μεγάλαις ἀφνειὸς ἀρούραις.
αὐτὰρ ἀοιδὸν ἔθηκε καὶ ἄμφω χεῖρας ἔπλασσε
πυξίνα ἐν φόρμιγγι Φιλαμμονίδας Εὔμολπος.
ὅσσα δ' ἀπὸ σκελέων ἑδροστρόφοι 'Αργόθεν ἄνδρες
ἀλλάλους σφάλλοντι παλαίσμασιν, ὅσσά τε
    πύκται
δεινοὶ ἐν ἱμάντεσσιν, ἅ τ' ἐς γαῖαν προπεσόντες
πάμμαχοι ἐξεύροντο σοφίσματα [1] σύμφορα τέχνᾳ,
πάντ' ἔμαθ' 'Ερμείαο διδασκόμενος παρὰ παιδὶ
'Αρπαλύκῳ Φανοτῆϊ, τὸν οὐδ' ἂν τηλόθε λεύσσων
θαρσαλέως τις ἔμεινεν ἀεθλεύοντ' ἐν ἀγῶνι·
τοῖον ἐπισκύνιον βλοσυρῷ ἐπέκειτο προσώπῳ.

ἵππους δ' ἐξελάσασθαι ὑφ' ἅρματι, καὶ περὶ
    νύσσαν
ἀσφαλέως κάμπτοντα τροχοῦ σύριγγα φυλάξαι,
'Αμφιτρύων ὃν παῖδα φίλα φρονέων ἐδίδαξεν
αὐτός, ἐπεὶ μάλα πολλὰ θοῶν ἐξ ἦρατ' ἀγώνων
"Αργει ἐν ἱπποβότῳ κειμήλια, καὶ οἱ ἀαγεῖς
δίφροι, ἐφ' ὧν ἐπέβαινε, χρόνῳ διέλυσαν ἱμάντας.
δούρατι δὲ προβολαίῳ ὑπ' ἀσπίδι νῶτον ἔχοντα
ἀνδρὸς ὀρέξασθαι ξιφέων τ' ἀνέχεσθαι ἀμυχμόν,
κοσμῆσαί τε φάλαγγα λόχον τ' ἀναμετρήσασθαι
δυσμενέων ἐπιόντα καὶ ἱππήεσσι κελεῦσαι

----

[1] σοφίσματα Meineke : mss παλαίσματα

296

So spake Teiresias, and despite the weight of his many years, pushed back the ivory chair and was gone.

And Heracles, called now the son of Amphitryon of Argos, waxed under his mother's eye like a sapling set in a vineyard. Letters learned he of a sleepless guardian, a Hero, son of Apollo, aged Linus ; and to bend a bow and shoot arrows at the mark, of one that was born to wealth of great domains, Eurytus ; and he that made of him a singer and shaped his hand to the box-wood lyre, was Eumolpus, the son of Philammon. Aye, and all the tricks and falls both of the cross-buttockers of Argos, and of boxers skilly with the hand-strap, and eke all the cunning inventions of the catch-as-catch-can men that roll upon the ground, all these things learnt he at the feet of a son of Hermes, Harpalycus of Phanotè, whom no man could abide confidently in the ring even so much as to look upon him from aloof, so dread and horrible was the frown that sat on his grim visage.

But to drive horses in a chariot and guide the nave of his wheel safely about the turnpost, that did Amphitryon in all kindness teach his son himself; for he had carried off a multitude of precious things from swift races in the Argive grazing-land of steeds, and Time alone had loosed the harness from his chariots, seeing he kept them ever unbroken. And how to abide the cut and thrust of the sword or to lunge lance in rest and shield swung over back, how to marshal a company, measure an advancing squadron of the foe, or give the word to a troop of

Κάστωρ ἱππελάτας δέδαεν, φυγὰς Ἄργεος ἐλθών,[1]
ἧ[2] ποκα κλᾶρον ἄπαντα καὶ οἰνόπεδον μέγα Τυδεὺς 13
ναῖε, παρ᾿ Ἀδρήστοιο λαβὼν ἱππήλατον Ἄργος.
Κάστορι δ᾿ οὔτις ὁμοῖος ἐν ἡμιθέοις πολεμιστὴς
ἄλλος ἔην πρὶν γῆρας ἀποτρῖψαι νεότητα.

   ὧδε μὲν Ἡρακλῆα φίλα παιδεύσατο μάτηρ.
εὐνὰ δ᾿ ἧς τῷ παιδὶ τετυγμένα ἀγχόθι πατρὸς
δέρμα λεόντειον μάλα οἱ κεχαρισμένον αὐτῷ,
δεῖπνον δὲ κρέατ᾿[3] ὀπτά, καὶ ἐν κανέῳ μέγας ἄρτος
Δωρικός· ἀσφαλέως κε φυτοσκάφον ἄνδρα κορέσ-
      σαι·
αὐτὰρ ἐπ᾿ ἄματι τυννὸν ἄνευ πυρὸς αἴνυτο δόρπον.
εἵματα δ᾿ οὐκ ἀσκητὰ μέσας ὑπὲρ ἔννυτο κνάμας . . .

---

[1] ἱππελάτας E: mss ἱππαλίδας   for Ἄργεος P. Ant. has
Ἀργόθεν   [2] so P. Ant. (corrected to ᾠ): mss ὦ ποκα   [3] κρέατ᾿
E: cf. Il. 12. 311: mss κρέα τ᾿ (P. Ant. κρεατ might be either)

horse—all such lore had he of horseman Castor, when he came an outlaw from Argos, where Tydeus had received that land of horsemen from Adrastus and held all Castor's estate and his great vineyard.   And till such time as age had worn away his youth, Castor had no equal in war among all the demigods.

While Heracles' dear mother thus ordered his upbringing, the lad's bed was made him hard by his father's, and a lion-skin it was and gave him great delight ; for meals, his breakfast was roast flesh, and in his basket he carried a great Dorian loaf such as might surely satisfy a delving man, but after the day's work he would make his supper sparely and without fire ; and for his clothing he wore plain and simple attire that fell but a little below the knee. . . .[1]

[1] See p. 287 n.

XXV.—HOW HERACLES SLEW THE LION

THIS *Epic poem comprises three distinct parts, one of which still bears its separate title. It is not really a fragment, but pretends by a literary convention to be three "books" taken from an* Odyssey, *or rather* Heracleia, *in little. The first part, which bears the traditional stage-direction* Heracles to the Husbandman, *is concerned first with a description of the great farm of Augeias or Augeas, king of the Epeians of Elis—the same whose stables Heracles at another time cleaned out—put into the mouth of a garrulous old ploughman of whom Heracles has asked where he can find the king ; then the old man undertakes to show the mysterious stranger the way, and as they draw near the homestead they have a Homeric meeting with the barking dogs. The second part bears the title* The Visitation. *In it we are told how the enormous herd of cattle given by the Sun to his child Augeas returned in the evening from pasture, how the king and his son Phyleus took Heracles to see the busy scene in the farmyard, and how Heracles encountered*

300

the finest bull in the whole herd. In the third part, which has no traditional title, Heracles, accompanied by the king's son, is on his way to the town, and their conversation leads to Heracles' telling how he slew the Nemean lion. It has been doubted whether the poem is by Theocritus.

XXV.—[ΗΡΑΚΛΗΣ ΛΕΟΝΤΟΦΟΝΟΣ]

Τὸν δ' ὁ γέρων προσέειπε βοῶν ἐπίουρος ἀροτρεὺς
παυσάμενος ἔργοιο, τό οἱ μετὰ χερσὶν ἔκειτο·
'ἔκ τοι ξεῖνε πρόφρων μυθήσομαι ὅσσ' ἐρεείνεις,
Ἑρμέω ἁζόμενος δεινὴν ὄπιν εἰνοδίοιο·
τὸν γάρ φασι μέγιστον ἐπουρανίων κεχολῶσθαι,
εἴ κεν ὁδοῦ ζαχρεῖον ἀνήνηταί τις ὁδίτην.
    ποίμναι μὲν βασιλῆος ἐΰτριχες Αὐγείαο
οὐ πᾶσαι βόσκονται ἴαν βόσιν οὐδ' ἕνα χῶρον·
ἀλλ' αἱ μέν ῥα νέμονται ἐπ' ὄχθαις Εἰλίσσοντος,[1]
αἱ δ' ἱερὸν θείοιο παρὰ ῥόον Ἀλφειοῖο,
αἱ δ' ἐπὶ Βουπρασίου πολυβότρυος, αἱ δὲ καὶ ὧδε·
χωρὶς δὲ σηκοὶ σφι τετυγμένοι εἰσὶν ἑκάσταις.
αὐτὰρ βουκολίοισι περιπληθούσί περ ἔμπης
πάντεσσιν νομοὶ ὧδε τεθηλότες αἰὲν ἔασι
Μηνίου ἂμ μέγα τῖφος, ἐπεὶ μελιηδέα ποίην
λειμῶνες θαλέθουσιν ὑπόδροσοι εἰαμεναί τε
εἰς ἅλις, ἥ ῥα βόεσσι μένος κεραῇσιν ἀέξει.
αὖλις δέ σφισιν ἥδε τεῆς ἐπὶ δεξιὰ χειρὸς
φαίνεται εὖ μάλα πᾶσα πέρην ποταμοῖο ῥέοντος
κείνη, ὅθι πλατάνιστοι ἐπηετανοὶ πεφύασι
χλωρή τ' ἀγριέλαιος, Ἀπόλλωνος νομίοιο
ἱερὸν ἁγνόν, ξεῖνε, τελειοτάτοιο θεοῖο.
εὐθὺς δὲ σταθμοὶ περιμήκεες ἀγροιώταις

---

[1] Εἰλίσσοντος Meineke : mss ἀμφ' ἑλισοῦντος

XXV.—[HOW HERACLES SLEW THE LION]

And the old ploughman that was set over the kine ceased from the work he had in hand, and answered him, saying : " Sir, I will gladly tell you all you ask of me.   Trust me, I hold the vengeance of Hermes o' the Ways in mickle awe and dread ; for they say he be the wrathfullest God in Heaven an you deny a traveller guidance that hath true need of it.

King Augeas' fleecy flocks, good Sir, feed not all of one pasture nor all upon one spot, but some of them be tended along Heilisson, others beside divine Alpheüs' sacred stream, others again by the fair vineyards of Buprasium, and yet others, look you, hereabout ; and each flock hath his several fold builded.   But the herds, mark you, for all their exceeding number, find all of them their fodder sprouting ever around this great mere of river Menius ; for your watery leas and fenny flats furnish honey-sweet grass in plenty, and that is it which swells the strength of the horned kine.   Their steading is all one, and 'tis there upon your right hand beyond where the river goes running again ; there where the outspreading platans and the fresh green wild-olive, Sir, make a right pure and holy sanctuary of one that is graciousest of all Gods, Apollo o' the Pastures.   Hard by that spot there are builded rare and roomy quarters for us swains that

' goes running again ' : after leaving the mere.

δέδμηνθ᾽, οἳ βασιλῆι πολὺν καὶ ἀθέσφατον ὄλβον
ῥύομεθ᾽ ἐνδυκέως, τριπόλοις σπόρον ἐν νειοῖσιν
ἔσθ᾽ ὅτε βάλλοντες καὶ τετραπόλοισιν ὁμοίως.

οὔρους μὴν ἴσασι φυτοσκάφοι ἀμπελοεργοί,[1]
ἐς ληνοὺς δ᾽ ἱκνεῦνται, ἐπὴν θέρος ὥριον ἔλθῃ.
πᾶν γὰρ δὴ πεδίον τόδ᾽ ἐπίφρονος Αὐγείαο,
πυροφόροι τε γύαι καὶ ἀλωαὶ δενδρήεσσαι,
μέχρις ἐπ᾽ ἐσχατιὰς πολυπίδακος Ἀκρωρείης,
ἃς ἡμεῖς ἔργοισιν ἐποιχόμεθα πρόπαν ἦμαρ,
ἣ δίκη οἰκήων, οἷσιν βίος ἔπλετ᾽ ἐπ᾽ ἀγροῦ.

ἀλλὰ σύ πέρ μοι ἔνισπε, τό τοι καὶ κέρδιον αὐτῷ
ἔσσεται, οὗτινος ὧδε κεχρημένος εἰλήλουθας.
ἠέ τι Αὐγείην ἢ καὶ δμώων τινὰ κείνου
δίζεαι, οἵ οἱ ἔασιν; ἐγὼ δέ κέ τοι σάφα εἰδὼς
πάντα μάλ᾽ ἐξείποιμ᾽,[2] ἐπεὶ οὐ σέγε φημι κακῶν ἒξ
ἔμμεναι οὐδὲ κακοῖσιν ἐοικότα φύμεναι αὐτόν,
οἷόν τοι μέγα εἶδος ἐπιπρέπει. ἦ ῥά νυ παῖδες
ἀθανάτων τοιοίδε μετὰ θνητοῖσιν ἔασι.᾽

τὸν δ᾽ ἀπαμειβόμενος προσέφη Διὸς ἄ᾽ κιμος
υἱός·

᾽ ναὶ γέρον Αὐγείην ἐθέλοιμί κεν ἀρχὸν Ἐπειῶν
εἰσιδέειν· τοῦ γάρ με καὶ ἤγαγεν ἐνθάδε χρειώ.
εἰ δ᾽ ὃ μὲν ἀρ κατὰ ἄστυ μένει παρὰ οἷσι πολίταις
δήμου κηδόμενος, διὰ δὲ κρίνουσι θέμιστας,
δμώων δή τινα πρέσβυ σύ μοι φράσον ἡγεμονεύσας,
ὅστις ἐπ᾽ ἀγρῶν τῶνδε γεραίτερος αἰσυμνήτης,
ᾧ κε τὸ μὲν εἴποιμι, τὸ δ᾽ ἐκ φαμένοιο πυθοίμην.
ἄλλου δ᾽ ἄλλον ἔθηκε θεὸς ἐπιδευέα φωτῶν.᾽

τὸν δ᾽ ὁ γέρων ἐξαῦτις ἀμείβετο δῖος ἀροτρεύς,
᾽ ἀθανάτων ὦ ξεῖνε φραδῇ τινος ἐνθάδ᾽ ἱκάνεις,

---

[1] ἀμπελοεργοί Wil : mss οἱ πολύεργοι   [2] mss also ἀτρεκέως
εἴποιμ᾽

keep close watch over the king's so much and so marvellous prosperity; aye, we often turn the same fallows for the sowing three and four times in the year.

And as for the skirts of this domain, they are the familiar place of the busy vine-planters, who come hither to the vintage-home when the summer draweth to its end. Yea, the whole plain belongeth unto sapient Augeas, alike fat wheatfield and bosky vineyard, until thou come to the uplands of Acroreia and all his fountains; and in this plain we go to and fro about our labour all the day long as behoveth bondsmen whose life is upon the glebe.

But now pray tell me you, Sir,—as 'faith, it shall be to your profit—what it is hath brought you hither. Is your suit of Augeas himself, or of one of the bondsmen that serve him? I may tell you, even I, all you be fain to know, seeing none, I trow, can be of ill seeming or come of ill stock that makes so fine a figure of a man as you. Marry, the children of the Immortals are of such sort among mortal men."

To this the stalwart child of Zeus answered, saying: "Yea verily, gaffer, I would look upon Augeas the king of the Epeians; that which brings me hither is need of him. And so, if so be that caring for his people he abideth with them at the town to give judgment there, pray, father, carry me to one of the bondsmen that is elder and set in authority over these estates, unto whom I may tell what my suit is and have my answer of him. For 'tis God's will that one man have need of another."

And the gallant old ploughman answered him again: "Sure one of the Immortals, Sir," saith he,

ὥς τοι πᾶν ὃ θέλεις αἶψα χρέος ἐκτετέλεσται.
ὧδε γὰρ Αὐγείης, υἱὸς φίλος Ἠελίοιο,
σφωϊτέρῳ σὺν παιδί, βίῃ Φυλῆος ἀγαυοῦ·
χθιζός γ᾽ εἰλήλουθεν ἀπ᾽ ἄστεος, ἤμασι πολλοῖς
κτῆσιν ἐποψόμενος, ἥ οἱ νήριθμος ἐπ᾽ ἀγρῶν·
ὥς που καὶ βασιλεῦσιν ἐείδεται ἐν φρεσὶν ᾖσιν
αὐτοῖς κηδομένοισι σαώτερος ἔμμεναι οἶκος.
ἀλλ᾽ ἴομεν μάλα πρός μιν· ἐγὼ δέ τοι ἡγεμονεύσω
αὖλιν ἔφ᾽ ἡμετέρην, ἵνα κεν τέτμοιμεν ἄνακτα.᾽

    ὣς εἰπὼν ἡγεῖτο, νόῳ δ᾽ ὅγε πόλλ᾽ ἐμενοίνα,
δέρμα τε θηρὸς ὁρῶν χειροπληθῆ τε κορύνην,
ὁππόθεν ὁ ξεῖνος· μεμόνει ¹ δέ μιν αἰὲν ἔρεσθαι·
ἂψ δ᾽ ὄκνῳ ποτὶ χεῖλος ἐλάμβανε μῦθον ἰόντα,
μή τί οἱ οὐ κατὰ καιρὸν ἔπος προτιμυθήσαιτο
σπερχομένου· χαλεπὸν δ᾽ ἑτέρου νόον ἴδμεναι
    ἀνδρός.

    τοὺς δὲ κύνες προσιόντας ἀπόπροθεν αἶψ᾽
    ἐνόησαν,
ἀμφότερον ὀδμῇ τε χροὸς δούπῳ τε ποδοῖιν.
θεσπέσιον δ᾽ ὑλάοντες ἐπέδραμον ἄλλοθεν ἄλλος
Ἀμφιτρυωνιάδῃ Ἡρακλέι· τὸν δὲ γέροντα
ἀχρεῖον κλάζον τε περίσσαινόν θ᾽ ἑτέρωθεν.
τοὺς μὲν ὅγε λάεσσιν ἀπὸ χθονὸς ὅσσον ἀείρων
φευγέμεν ἂψ ὀπίσω δειδίσσετο, τρηχὺ δὲ φωνῇ
ἠπείλει μάλα πᾶσιν, ἐρητύσασκε δ᾽ ὑλαγμοῦ,
χαίρων ἐν φρεσὶν ᾖσιν, ὁθούνεκεν αὖλιν ἔρυντο
αὐτοῦ γ᾽ οὐ παρεόντος· ἔπος δ᾽ ὅγε τοῖον ἔειπεν·

---

¹ μεμόνει Buttmann: mss μέμοινε, μέμονε, μέμαεν

"hath sent you this way, so quickly come you by all you would. Augeas child of the Sun is here, and that piece of strength, his son the noble Phyleus, with him. 'Twas only yesterday he came from the town for to view after many days the possessions he hath without number upon the land. For in their hearts, 'faith, your kings are like to other men; they wot well their substance be surer if they see to it themselves. But enough; go we along to him. I will show you the way to our steading, and there it is like we find him."

With this he led on, musing as well he might concerning the skin of a beast he saw the stranger clad in, and the great club that filled his grasp, and whence he might be come; aye, and was minded and minded again to ask him right out, but ever took back the words that were even upon his tongue, for fear he should say him somewhat out of season, he being in that haste; for 'tis ill reading the mind of another man.

Now or ever they were come nigh, the dogs were quickly aware of their coming, as well by the scent of them as by the sound of their footfalls, and made at Heracles Amphitryoniad from this, that, and every side with a marvellous great clamour; and the old man, they bayed him likewise, but 'twas for baying's sake, and they fawned him about on the further side. Then did gaffer with the mere lifting stones from off the ground fray them back again and bespake them roughly and threateningly, every one, to make them give over their clamour, howbeit rejoicing in his heart that the steading should have so good defenders when he was away; and so upspake and

307

‘ ὦ πόποι, οἷον τοῦτο θεοὶ ποίησαν ἄνακτες
θηρίον ἀνθρώποισι μετέμμεναι, ὡς ἐπιμηθές.[1]
εἴ οἱ καὶ φρένες ὧδε νοήμονες ἔνδοθεν ἦσαν,
ᾔδει δ’, ᾧ τε χρὴ χαλεπαινέμεν ᾧ τε καὶ οὐκί,
οὐκ ἄν οἱ θηρῶν τις ἐδήρισεν περὶ τιμῆς·
νῦν δὲ λίην ζάκοτόν τε καὶ ἀρρηνὲς γένετ’ αὔτως.’
ἦ ῥα, καὶ ἐσσυμένως ποτὶ τωὔλίον ἷξον ἰόντες.

ΕΠΙΠΩΛΗΣΙΣ

Ἥλιος μὲν ἔπειτα ποτὶ ζόφον ἔτραπεν[2] ἵππους
δείελον ἦμαρ ἄγων· τὰ δ’ ἐπήλυθε πίονα μῆλα
ἐκ βοτάνης ἀνιόντα μετ’ αὔλιά τε σηκούς τε.
αὐτὰρ ἔπειτα βόες μάλα μυρίαι ἄλλαι ἐπ’ ἄλλαις
ἐρχόμεναι φαίνονθ’ ὡσεὶ νέφη ὑδατόεντα,
ἄσσα τ’ ἐν οὐρανῷ εἰσιν ἐλαυνόμενα προτέρωσε
ἠὲ νότοιο βίῃ ἠὲ Θρηκὸς βορέαο·
τῶν μέν τ’ οὔτις ἀριθμὸς ἐν ἠέρι γίνετ’ ἰόντων,
οὐδ’ ἄνυσις· τόσα γάρ τε μετὰ προτέροισι κυλίνδει
ἲς ἀνέμου, τὰ δέ τ’ ἄλλα κορύσσεται αὖτις ἐπ’
    ἄλλοις·
τόσσ’ αἰεὶ μετόπισθε βοῶν ἐπὶ βουκόλι’ ἤει.
πᾶν δ’ ἄρ’ ἐνεπλήσθη πεδίον, πᾶσαι δὲ κέλευθοι
ληΐδος ἐρχομένης, στείνοντο δὲ πίονες ἀγροὶ
μυκηθμῷ· σηκοὶ δὲ βοῶν ῥεῖα πλῆσθησαν
εἰλιπόδων, ὄϊες δὲ κατ’ αὐλὰς[3] ηὐλίζοντο.
    ἔνθα μὲν οὔτις ἔκηλος ἀπειρεσίων περ ἐόντων
εἱστήκει παρὰ βουσὶν ἀνὴρ κεχρημένος ἔργου·

---

[1] ἐπιμηθές Musurus: mss -θεὺς   [2] ἔτραπεν Mus: mss
ἤγαγεν   [3] Wil. αὔλιας

said : " Lord ! what a fiery inconsiderate beast is here made by the high Gods to be with man ! If there were but as great understanding within him, and he knew with whom to be angered and whom to forbear, there's no brute thing might claim such honour as he ; but it may not be, and he's nought but a blusterer, wild and uncouth." This said, they quickened their steps and passed on and came to the steading.

THE VISITATION

Now had the sun turned his steeds westward and brought evening on, and the fat flocks had left the pastures and were come up among the farmyards and folds. Then it was that the cows came thousand upon thousand, came even as the watery clouds which, be it of the Southwind or the Northwind out of Thrace, come driving forward through the welkin, till there's no numbering them aloft nor no end to their coming on, so many new doth the power of the wind roll up to join the old, row after row rearing crest ever upon crest—in like multitude now came those herds of kine still up and on, up and on. Aye, all the plain was filled, and all the paths of it, with the moving cattle ; the fat fields were thronged and choked with their lowing, and right readily were the byres made full of shambling kine, while the sheep settled themselves for the night in the yards.

Then of a truth, for all there were hinds without number, stood there no man beside those cattle idle for want of aught to do ; but here was one took

" fiery inconsiderate ": the Greek word means 'one that acts first and thinks afterwards'; see *Class. Rev.* 1913. 73.

ἀλλ' ὃ μὲν ἀμφὶ πόδεσσιν ἐϋτμήτοισιν ἱμᾶσι
καλοπέδιλ' ἀράρισκε παρασταδὸν ἐγγὺς ἀμέλγειν,
ἄλλος δ' αὖ νέα τέκνα φίλας ὑπὸ μητέρας [1] ἵει
πινέμεναι λιαροῖο μεμαότα πάγχυ γάλακτος,
ἄλλος ἀμόλγιον εἶχ', ἄλλος τρέφε πίονα τυρόν,
ἄλλος ἐσῆγεν ἔσω ταύρους δίχα θηλειάων.
Αὐγείης δ' ἐπὶ πάντας ἰὼν θηεῖτο βοαύλους,
ἥντινά οἱ κτεάνων κομιδὴν ἐτίθεντο νομῆες,
σὺν δ' υἱός τε βίη τε βαρύφρονος Ἡρακλῆος
ὡμάρτευν βασιλῆι διερχομένῳ μέγαν ὄλβον.

ἔνθα καὶ ἄρρηκτόν περ ἔχων ἐν στήθεσι θυμὸν
Ἀμφιτρυωνιάδης καὶ ἀρηρότα νωλεμὲς αἰεὶ
ἐκπάγλως θαύμαζε θεοῦ [2] τόγε μυρίον ἔδνον
εἰσορόων. οὐ γάρ κεν ἔφασκέ τις οὐδὲ ἐώλπει
ἀνδρὸς ληίδ' ἑνὸς τόσσην ἔμεν οὐδὲ δέκ' ἄλλων,
οἵτε πολύρρηνες πάντων[3] ἔσαν ἐκ βασιλήων.
Ἥλιος δ' ᾧ παιδὶ τόγ' ἔξοχον ὤπασε δῶρον,
ἀφνειὸν μήλοις περὶ πάντων ἔμμεναι ἀνδρῶν,
καί ῥά οἱ αὐτὸς ὄφελλε διαμπερέως βοτὰ πάντα
ἐς τέλος· οὐ μὲν γάρ τις ἐπήλυθε νοῦσος ἐκείνου
βουκολίοις, αἵτ' ἔργα καταφθείρουσι[4] νομήων,
αἰεὶ δὲ πλέονες κερααὶ βόες, αἰὲν ἀμείνους
ἐξ ἔτεος γίνοντο μάλ' εἰς ἔτος· ἦ γὰρ ἅπασαι
ζωοτόκοι τ' ἦσαν περιώσια θηλυτόκοι τε.

ταῖς δὲ τριηκόσιοι ταῦροι συνάμ' ἐστιχόωντο
κνήμαργοί θ' ἕλικές τε, διηκόσιοι γέ μεν ἄλλοι

---

[1] thus Mus: mss φίλαις ὑπὸ μητράσιν   [2] θεοῦ Wil: mss
θεῶν   [3] Knox πάππων   [4] καταφθείρουσι Mus: mss -φθίνουσι

thongs cut straight and true and had their feet to
the hobbles for to come at the milking; here was
another took thirsty yeanlings and put them to drink
of their dams' sweet warm milk; this again held the
milking-pail, and that did curd the milk for a good
fat cheese, and yonder was one a-bringing in the bulls
apart from the heifers.   Meanwhile King Augeas
went his rounds of the byres to see what care his
herdsmen might have of his goods; and through all
that great wealth of his there went with him his son
also, and grave-minded Heracles in his might.

And now, albeit he was possessed within him of a
heart of iron ever and without ceasing unmoved, the
child of Amphitryon fell marvellously a-wondering,
as well he might, when he saw the unnumbered
bride-gift of the God.   Indeed, no man would have
said, nay, nor thought, that so many cattle could
belong to ten men, let alone one; and those ten
must needs have been rich in sheep and oxen beyond
any kings.[1] For the Sun did give him that was his
child a most excellent gift, to wit to be the greatest
master of flocks in the world; and what is more,
himself did make them all to thrive and prosper
unceasingly without end, for of all the distempers
that destroy the labours of a keeper of oxen never
came there one upon that man's herds, but rather
did his horned dams wax ever year in year out both
more in number and better in kind, being never
known to cast their young and all passing good
bringers of cow-calves.

Moreover there went with them three hundred
bulls, white-shanked and crump-horned, and other

---

[1] *or* by inheritance from kingly grandsires

φοίνικες· πάντες δ' ἐπιβήτορες οἵγ' ἔσαν ἤδη.
ἄλλοι δ' αὖ μετὰ τοῖσι δυώδεκα βουκολέοντο
ἱεροὶ Ἠελίοιο· χρόην δ' ἔσαν ἠΰτε κύκνοι
ἀργησταί, πᾶσιν δὲ μετέπρεπον εἰλιπόδεσσιν·
οἳ καὶ ἀτιμαγέλαι βόσκοντ' ἐριθηλέα ποίην
ἐν νομῷ, ὧδ' ἔκπαγλον ἐπὶ σφίσι γαυριόωντο.[1]
καί ῥ' ὁπότ' ἐκ λασίοιο θοοὶ προγενοίατο θῆρες
ἐς πεδίον δρυμοῖο βοῶν ἕνεκ' ἀγρομενάων,[2]
πρῶτοι τοίγε μάχηνδε κατὰ χροὸς ᾔεσαν ὀδμήν,
δεινὸν δ' ἐβρυχῶντο φόνον λεῦσσόν τε προσώπῳ.

τῶν μέν τε προφέρεσκε βίηφί τε καὶ σθένεϊ ᾧ
ἠδ' ὑπεροπλίῃ Φαέθων μέγας, ὅν ῥα βοτῆρες
ἀστέρι πάντες ἔϊσκον, ὁθούνεκα πολλὸν ἐν ἄλλοις
βουσὶν ἰὼν λάμπεσκεν, ἀρίζηλος δ' ἐτέτυκτο.
ὃς δή τοι σκύλος αὖον ἰδὼν χαροποῖο λέοντος
αὐτῷ ἔπειτ' ἐπόρουσεν ἐΰσκόπῳ Ἡρακλῆι
χρίμψασθαι ποτὶ πλευρὰ κάρη στιβαρόν τε
    μέτωπον.
τοῦ μὲν ἄναξ προσιόντος ἐδράξατο χειρὶ παχείῃ
σκαιοῦ ἄφαρ κέραος, κατὰ δ' αὐχένα νέρθ' ἐπὶ γαίης
κλάσσε βαρύν περ ἐόντα, πάλιν δέ μιν ὦσεν ὀπίσσω
ὤμῳ ἐπιβρίσας· ὁ δέ οἱ περὶ νεῦρα τανυσθεὶς
μυῶν ἐξ ὑπάτοιο βραχίονος ὀρθὸς ἀνέστη.
θαύμαζεν δ' αὐτός τε ἄναξ υἱός τε δαΐφρων
Φυλεύς οἵ τ' ἐπὶ βουσὶ κορωνίσι βουκόλοι ἄνδρες,
Ἀμφιτρυωνιάδαο βίην ὑπέροπλον ἰδόντες.

Τὼ δ' εἰς ἄστυ λιπόντε κατ' αὐτόθι πίονας ἀγροὺς
ἐστιχέτην, Φυλεύς τε βίη θ' Ἡρακληείη.

___

[1] mss also γαυριόωντες [2] ἀγρομενάων E, opposed to ἀτι-
μαγέλαι (l. 132); cf. Od. 16. 3 which the writer had before

two hundred dun, and all leapers grown ; and over and above these, there was a herd of twelve sacred to the Sun, and the colour of them glistering white like a swan, so that they did outshine all shambling things ; and what is more, they were lone-grazers all in the springing pastures, so marvellous proud were they and haughty ; and the same, when swift beasts of the field came forth of the shag forest after the kine that went in herds, ever at the smell of them would out the first to battle, bellowing dreadfully and glancing death.

Now of these twelve the highest and mightiest both for strength and mettle was the great Lucifer, whom all the herdsmen likened to that star, for that going among the other cattle he shined exceeding bright and conspicuous ; and this fellow, when he espied that tanned skin of a grim lion, came at the watchful wearer of it for to have at his sides with his great sturdy front. But my lord up with a strong hand and clutched him by the left horn and bowed that his heavy neck suddenly downward, and putting his shoulder to't had him back again ; and the muscle of his upper arm was drawn above the sinews till it stood on a heap. And the king marvelled, both he and his son the warlike Phyleus, and the hinds also that were set over the crump-horned kine, when they beheld the mettlesome might of the child of Amphitryon.

Then did Phyleus and Heracles the mighty leave the fat fields behind them and set out for the town.

him at ll. 68 ff: mss ἀγροτεράων (or προτεράων), but the cattle were not wild.

λαοφόρου δ' ἐπέβησαν ὅθι πρώτιστα κελεύθου,
λεπτὴν καρπαλίμοισι τρίβον ποσὶν ἐξανύσαντες,
ἥ ῥα δι' ἀμπελεῶνος ἀπὸ σταθμῶν τετάνυστο
οὔτι λίην ἀρίσημος ἐν ὕλῃ χλωρᾷ ἰοῦσα,[1]
τῇ μιν ἄρα προσέειπε Διὸς γόνον ὑψίστοιο
Αὐγείω φίλος υἱὸς ἕθεν μετόπισθεν ἰόντα,[2]
ἧκα παρακλίνας κεφαλὴν κατὰ δεξιὸν ὦμον·
'ξεῖνε, πάλαι τινὰ πάγχυ σέθεν πέρι μῦθον
       ἀκούσας
ὥς, εἴπερ,[3] σφετέρῃσιν ἐνὶ φρεσὶ βάλλομαι ἄρτι.
ἤλυθε γὰρ στείχων τις ἀπ' Ἄργεος ὡς νέον ἀκμὴν[4]
ἐνθάδ' Ἀχαιὸς ἀνὴρ Ἑλίκης ἐξ ἀγχιάλοιο,
ὃς δή τοι μυθεῖτο καὶ ἐν πλεόνεσσιν Ἐπειῶν,
οὕνεκεν Ἀργείων τις ἕθεν παρεόντος ὄλεσσε
θηρίον, αἰνολέοντα, κακὸν τέρας ἀγροιώταις,
κοίλην αὖλιν ἔχοντα Διὸς Νεμέοιο παρ' ἄλσος—
οὐκ οἶδ' ἀτρεκέως ἢ Ἄργεος ἐξ ἱεροῖο
αὐτόθεν ἢ Τίρυνθα νέμων πόλιν ἠὲ Μυκήνην.
ὣς κεῖνός γ' ἀγόρευε· γένος δέ μιν εἶναι ἔφασκεν,
εἰ ἐτεόν περ ἐγὼ μιμνήσκομαι, ἐκ Περσῆος.

ἔλπομαι οὐχ ἕτερον τόδε τλήμεναι αἰγιαλήων
ἠὲ σέ, δέρμα δὲ θηρός, ὅ τοι περὶ πλευρὰ καλύπτει,[5]
χειρῶν καρτερὸν ἔργον ἀριφραδέως ἀγορεύει.[5]
εἴπ' ἄγε νῦν μοι πρῶτον, ἵνα γνώω κατὰ θυμόν,
ἥρως, εἴτ' ἐτύμως μαντεύομαι εἴτε καὶ οὐκί,
εἰ σύγ' ἐκεῖνος, ὃν ἧμιν ἀκουόντεσσιν ἔειπεν
οὑξ Ἑλίκηθεν Ἀχαιός, ἐγὼ δέ σε φράζομαι ὀρθῶς·
εἰπὲ δ' ὅπως ὀλοὸν τόδε θηρίον αὐτὸς ἔπεφνες,

---

[1] ἰοῦσα E : mss ἐοῦσῃ by confusion with the corrupt end of
l. 160   [2] mss also ἐόντα   [3] εἴπερ elliptical as in Plat.
Rep. 497 e   [4] νέον ἀκμὴν E 'still (cf. 4. 60) recently (cf.

314

Their swift feet were gotten to the end of the little
path which stretched from the farmsteads through
the vineyard and ran not over-clearly in the midst of
the fresh greenery, and they were just come to the
people's highway, when the dear son of Augeas up
and spake to the child of most high Zeus that
was following behind him, and with a little turn of
his head over his right shoulder, "Sir," says he,
"there's somewhat I had heard of you, and O how
late am I, if of you it were, to bethink me on't but
now! 'Tis not long since there came hither from
Argos an Achaean of Helicè-by-the-sea, who told a
tale, look you, unto more than one of us Epeians,
how that he had seen an Argive slay a beast of the
field, to wit a lion dire that was the dread of the
countryside and had the den of his lying beside the
grove of Zeus of Nemea—yet he knew not for sure,
he said, whether the man was truly of sacred Argos
itself or was a dweller in Tiryns town or in Mycenae.
Howbeit, such was his tale, and he said also, if
I remember true, that for his lineage the man was of
Perseus.

Now methinks there is but one of those men-
o'-the-shore could do a deed like that, and you
are he; moreover the wild-beast-skin your frame is
clad in signifieth clearly enough the prowess of your
hands. Come on, my lord, have me well to wit, first
whether my boding be true or no, whether you be
he the Achaean of Helicè told us of, and I know you
for what you are; and then tell me, pray, how
yourself destroyed that same pestilent beast and how

Hom.),' *i.e.* it is a thing that can be still called recent : mss
νέος ἀκμὴν or μέσος ἀκμῆς   [b] Meineke thus transposes the
latter halves of 175 and 176

ὅππως τ' εὔυδρον Νεμέης εἰσήλυθε χῶρον·
οὐ μὲν γάρ κε τοσόνδε κατ' Ἀπίδα κνώδαλον
    εὕροις
ἱμείρων ἰδέειν, ἐπεὶ οὐ μάλα τηλίκα βόσκε,
ἀλλ' ἄρκτους τε σύας τε λύκων τ' ὀλοφώιον ἔθνος.
τῶ καὶ θαυμάζεσκον ἀκούοντες τότε μῦθον·
οἳ δέ νυ καὶ ψεύδεσθαι ὁδοιπόρον ἀνέρ' ἔφαντο
γλώσσης μαψιδίοιο χαριζόμενον παρεοῦσιν."

    ὣς εἰπὼν μέσσης ἐξηρώησε κελεύθου
Φυλεύς, ὄφρα κιοῦσιν ἅμα σφισὶν ἄρκιος εἴη,
καί ῥά τε ῥηίτερον φαμένου κλύοι Ἡρακλῆος·
ὅς μιν ὁμαρτήσας τοίῳ προσελέξατο μύθῳ·
    "ὦ Αὐγηιάδη, τὸ μὲν ὅττι με πρῶτον ἀνήρευ,
αὐτὸς καὶ μάλα ῥεῖα κατὰ στάθμην ἐνόησας.
ἀμφὶ δέ σοι τὰ ἕκαστα λέγοιμί κε τοῦδε πελώρου
ὅππως ἐκράανθεν, ἐπεὶ λελίησαι ἀκούειν,
νόσφιν γ' ἢ ὅθεν ἦλθε· τὸ γὰρ πολέων περ ἐόντων
Ἀργείων οὐδείς κεν ἔχοι σάφα μυθήσασθαι·
οἷον δ' ἀθανάτων τίν' ἐίσκομεν ἀνδράσι πῆμα
ἱρῶν μηνίσαντα Φορωνήεσσιν ἐφεῖναι.
πάντας γὰρ πίσηας ἐπικλύζων ποταμὸς ὣς
λῖς ἄμοτον κεράιζε, μάλιστα δὲ Βεμβιναίους
οἳ ἕθεν ἀγχόμοροι προσναῖον ἀτλητοπαθεῦντες.[1]
    τὸν μὲν ἐμοὶ πρώτιστα τελεῖν ἐπέταξεν ἄεθλον
Εὐρυσθεύς, κτεῖναι δέ μ' ἐφίετο θηρίον αἰνόν.
αὐτὰρ ἐγὼ κέρας ὑγρὸν ἑλὼν κοίλην τε φαρέτρην
ἰῶν ἐμπλείην νεόμην, ἑτέρηφι δὲ βάκτρον
εὐπαγὲς αὐτόφλοιον ἐπηρεφέος κοτίνοιο
ἔμμητρον, τὸ μὲν αὐτὸς ὑπὸ ζαθέῳ Ἑλικῶνι

---

[1] προσναῖον: mss also ναῖον   ἀτλητοπαθεῦντες E: mss
ἄτλητα παθέοντες or παθῦντες

he came to be dwelling in the well-watered vale of Nemea; for I ween you shall not find such a creature as that if you would, the Apian lands around, seeing they breed not anything so huge, but only the bear and the boar and the fell wolf. Therefore, also did they wonder that heard that tale; indeed they said the traveller lied with intent to pleasure the company with an idle tongue."

With these words Phyleus bent him sidelong from the midst of the road both to make room enough for them twain to go together, and that he might the easier hear what Heracles had to say. Who now came abreast of him, and "Son of Augeas" quoth he, "your former question you have answered yourself, readily and aright; but of this monster, being you so desire it, I will tell you how it all fell out every whit, save whence he came; for not one man in all Argos can speak certainly to that; only were we persuaded it was some God sent him to vex the children of Phoroneus because he was wroth concerning some sacrifices. For all the lowlanders were whelmed with him as he had been a river in flood; he plundered them all without cloy or surfeit, but most of all the people of Bembina, whose borders to their very great and intolerable misfortune marched with his.

Now this did Eurystheus make my very first task; he charged me to slay that direful beast. So I took with me my supple bow and a good quiverful of arrows, and in the other hand a stout cudgel, made, without peeling or pithing, of a shady wild-olive which myself had found under holy Helicon and torn up

"the Apian lands" : the Peloponnese.

εὑρὼν σὺν πυκινῇσιν ὁλοσχερὲς ἔσπασα ῥίζαις.
αὐτὰρ ἐπεὶ τὸν χῶρον, ὅθι λῖς ἦεν, ἵκανον,
δὴ τότε τόξον ἑλὼν στρεπτὴν ἐπέλασσα κορώνῃ
νευρείην, περὶ δ᾽ ἰὸν ἐχέστονον εἶθαρ ἔβησα.
πάντῃ δ᾽ ὄσσε φέρων ὀλοὸν τέρας ἐσκοπίαζον,
εἴ μιν ἐσαθρήσαιμι πάρος τί με κεῖνον ἰδέσθαι.
ἤματος ἦν τὸ μεσηγύ, καὶ οὐδέπῃ ἴχνια τοῖο[1]
φρασθῆναι δυνάμην οὐδ᾽ ὠρυγμοῖο πυθέσθαι.
οὐδὲ μὲν ἀνθρώπων τις ἔην ἐπὶ βουσὶ καὶ ἔργοις
φαινόμενος σπορίμοιο δι᾽ αὔλακος, ὅντιν᾽ ἐροίμην·
ἀλλὰ κατὰ σταθμοὺς χλωρὸν δέος εἶχεν ἕκαστον.
οὐ μὴν πρὶν πόδας ἔσχον ὄρος τανύφυλλον ἐρευνῶν,
πρὶν ἰδέειν ἀλκῆς τε μεταυτίκα πειρηθῆναι.

ἤτοι ὃ μὲν σήραγγά προδείελος ἔστιχεν εἰς ἥν,
βεβρωκὼς κρειῶν τε καὶ αἵματος, ἀμφὶ δὲ χαίτας
αὐχμηρὰς πεπάλακτο φόνῳ χαροπόν τε πρόσωπον
στήθεά τε, γλώσσῃ δὲ περιλιχμᾶτο γένειον.
αὐτὰρ ἐγὼ θάμνοισιν ἄφαρ σκιεροῖσιν ἐκρύφθην
ἐν τρίβῳ ὑλήεντι δεδεγμένος ὁππόθ᾽ ἵκοιτο,
καὶ βάλον ἆσσον ἰόντος ἀριστερὸν ἐς κενεῶνα
τηϋσίως· οὐ γάρ τι βέλος διὰ σαρκὸς ὄλισθεν
ὀκριόεν, χλωρῇ δὲ παλίσσυτον ἔμπεσε ποίῃ.
αὐτὰρ ὃ κρᾶτα δαφοινὸν ἀπὸ χθονὸς ὦκ᾽ ἐπάειρε
θαμβήσας, πάντῃ δὲ διέδρακεν ὀφθαλμοῖσι
σκεπτόμενος, λαμυροὺς δὲ χανὼν ὑπέδειξεν ὀδόν-
        τας.[2]
τῷ δ᾽ ἐγὼ ἄλλον ὀϊστὸν ἀπὸ νευρῆς προΐαλλον
ἀσχαλόων, ὅ μοι ὁ[3] πρὶν ἐτώσιος ἔκφυγε χειρός·
μεσσηγὺς δ᾽ ἔβαλον στηθέων, ὅθι πνεύμονος ἕδρη.

---

[1] οὐδέπῃ Cholmeley : mss οὐδ᾽ ὅπῃ or οὐδενὸς   mss also
τοῖα   [2] mss also ὑπ᾽ ὀδόντας ἔφαινε   [3] ὃ Hermann : mss
ὅτι, ὡς, ὃς   ὁ added by Hermann

318

whole and complete with all her branching roots; and
so forth and made for those parts where the lion was.
Whither when I was come, I took and tipped my
string, and straightway notched a bearer of pain and
grief, and fell a-looking this way and that way after
the pestilent monster, if so be I might espy him ere
he should espy me. 'Twas midday now, yet could I
nowhere mark his track nor hear his roaring;
neither was there any man set over a plough-team
and the toil of the seed-furrow that I could see and
ask of him, seeing pale wan fear kept every man at
the farmstead. Howbeit, I never gave over to
search the leafy uplands till I should behold him and
put my strength speedily to the test.

Now towards evening he came his ways unto his
den full fed both of flesh and gore, his tangled mane,
his grim visage and all his chest spattered with blood,
and his tongue licking his chaps. To waylay him I
hid myself quickly in a brake beside the woody path,
and when he came near let fly at his left flank. But
it availed me not; the barbèd shaft could not pass
the flesh, but glanced and fell on the fresh green sward.
Astonied, the beast lift suddenly up his gory head,
and looked about him and about, opening his mouth
and showing his gluttonous teeth; whereupon I sped
another shaft from the string (for I took it ill
that the first had left my hand to no purpose), and
smote him clean in the middle of the chest where

ἀλλ' οὐδ' ὡς ὑπὸ βύρσαν ἔδυ πολυώδυνος ἰός,
ἀλλ' ἔπεσε προπάροιθε ποδῶν ἀνεμώλιος αὕτως.
    τὸ τρίτον αὖ μέλλεσκον ἀσώμενος ἐν φρεσὶν
        αἰνῶς
ἀερύειν· ὁ δέ μ' εἶδε περιγληνώμενος ὄσσοις
θὴρ ἄμοτος, μακρὴν δὲ περ' ἰγνύῃσιν ἕλιξε
κέρκον, ἄφαρ δὲ μάχης ἐμνήσατο· πᾶς δέ οἱ αὐχὴν
θυμοῦ ἐνεπλήσθη, πυρσαὶ δ' ἔφριξαν ἔθειραι
σκυζομένῳ, κυρτὴ δὲ ῥάχις γένετ' ἠΰτε τόξον,
πάντοθεν εἰλυθέντος ὑπὸ λαγόνας τε καὶ ἰξύν.
ὡς δ' ὅταν ἁρματοπηγὸς ἀνὴρ πολέων ἴδρις ἔργων
ὄρπηκας κάμπτῃσιν ἐρινεοῦ εὐκεάτοιο,[1]
θάλψας ἐν πυρὶ πρῶτον, ἐπαξονίῳ κύκλα δίφρῳ,
τοῦ μὲν ὑπὲκ χειρῶν ἔφυγεν τανύφλοιος ἐρινεὸς
καμπτόμενος, τηλοῦ δὲ μιῇ πήδησε σὺν ὁρμῇ·
ὣς ἐπ' ἐμοὶ λῖς αἰνὸς ἀπόπροθεν ἀθρόος ἆλτο
μαιμώων χροὸς ἆσαι· ἐγὼ δ' ἑτέρῃφι βέλεμνα
χειρὶ προεσχεθόμην καὶ ἀπ' ὤμων δίπλακα λώπην,
τῇ δ' ἑτέρῃ ῥόπαλον κόρσης ὕπερ αὖον ἀείρας
ἤλασα κὰκ κεφαλῆς, διὰ δ' ἄνδιχα τρηχὺν ἔαξα
αὐτοῦ ἐπὶ λασίοιο καρήατος ἀγριέλαιον
θηρὸς ἀμαιμακέτοιο· πέσεν δ' ὅγε πρὶν ἔμ' ἱκέσθαι
ὑψόθεν ἐν γαίῃ, καὶ ἐπὶ τρομεροῖς ποσὶν ἔστη
νευστάζων κεφαλῇ· περὶ γὰρ σκότος ὄσσε οἱ ἄμφω
ἦλθε, βίῃ σεισθέντος ἐν ὀστέῳ ἐγκεφάλοιο.
    τὸν μὲν ἐγὼν ὀδύνῃσι παραφρονέοντα βαρείαις
νωσάμενος, πρὶν αὖτις ὑπότροπον ἀμπνυνθῆναι,
αὐχένος ἀρρήκτοιο παρ' ἰνίον ἤλασα[2] προφθάς,
ῥίψας τόξον ἔραζε πολύρραπτόν τε φαρέτρην·

---

[1] mss also εὐκάμπτοιο   [2] ἤλασα : mss also ἔφθασα

the lungs do lie. But nay; not even so was the hide of him to be pierced by the sore grievous arrow; there it fell vain and frustrate at his feet.

At this I waxed exceeding distempered and made to draw for the third time. But, ere that, the ravening beast rolled around his eyes and beheld me, and lashing all his tail about his hinder parts bethought him quickly of battle. Now was his neck brimming with ire, his tawny tresses an-end for wrath, his chine arched like a bow, as he gathered him up all together unto flank and loin. Then even as, when a wainwright, cunning man, takes the seasoned wild-fig boughs he hath warmed at the fire and bends them into wheels for an axled chariot, the thin-rinded figwood escapes at the bending from his grasp and leaps at one bound afar, even so did that direful lion from a great way off spring upon me, panting to be at my flesh. Then it was that with the one hand I thrust before me the cloak from my shoulders folded about my bunched arrows, and with the other lift my good sound staff above my head and down with it on his crown, and lo! my hard wild-olive was broke clean in twain on the mere shaggy pate of that unvanquishable beast. Yet as for him, or ever he could reach me he was fallen from the midst of his spring, and so stood with trembling feet and wagging head, his two eyes being covered in darkness because the brains were all-to-shaken in the skull of him.

Perceiving now that he was all abroad with the pain and grief of it, ere he might recover his wits I cast my bow and my broidered quiver upon the ground and let drive at the nape of that massy

ἤγχον δ᾽ ἐγκρατέως στιβαρὰς σὺν χεῖρας ἐρείσας
ἐξόπιθεν, μὴ σάρκας ἀποδρύψῃ ὀνύχεσσι,
πρὸς δ᾽ οὐδας πτέρνῃσι πόδας στερεῶς ἐπίεζον
οὐραίους[1] ἐπιβάς, πλευρῇσί τε μῆρ᾽ ἐφύλασσον,
μέχρις οὗ ἐξετάνυσσα βραχίονος[2] ὀρθὸν ἀείρας
ἄπνευστον, ψυχὴν δὲ πελώριος ἔλλαβεν[3] Ἄιδης.

καὶ τότε δὴ βούλευον, ὅπως λασιαύχενα βύρσαν
θηρὸς τεθνειῶτος ἀπὸ μελέων ἐρυσαίμην,
ἀργαλέον μάλα μόχθον, ἐπεὶ οὐκ ἦν οὔτε[4] σιδήρῳ
οὔτε λίθοις τμητὴ[5] πειρωμένῳ οὐδέ μεν ὕλῃ.
ἔνθα μοι ἀθανάτων τις ἐπὶ φρεσὶ θῆκε νοῆσαι
αὐτοῖς δέρμα λέοντος ἀνασχίζειν ὀνύχεσσι.
τοῖσι θοῶς ἀπέδειρα, καὶ ἀμφεθέμην μελέεσσιν
ἔρκος ἐνναλίου ταμεσίχροος ἰωχμοῖο.

οὗτός τοι Νεμέου γένετ᾽ ὦ φίλε θηρὸς ὄλεθρος,
πολλὰ πάρος μήλοις τε καὶ ἀνδράσι κήδεα θέντος."

---

[1] mss also οὐραίου and οὐραίη   [2] mss also μέχρι   οὗ E :
mss οἷ   mss and Musurus also βραχίονας and -να   [3] mss
also ἔλλαχεν   [4] ἦν οὔτε Wil : mss ἔσκε   [5] thus Meineke:
mss τμητὴ οὐδὲ λίθοις

neck. Then from the rear, lest he should tear me with his talons, I gat my arms about his throat, and treading his hind-paws hard into the ground for to keep the legs of them from my sides, held on with might and main till at length I could rear him backward by the foreleg, and so stretched him strangled on the ground, and vasty Hades received his spirit.

That done, I fell a-pondering how I might flay me off the dead beast's shag-neckèd skin. 'What a task!' thought I; for there was no cutting that, neither with wood nor with stone nor yet with iron. At that moment one of the Immortals did mind me I should cut up the lion's skin with the lion's talons. So I to it, and had him flayed in a trice, and cast the skin about me for a defence against the havoc of gashing war.

Such, good friend, was the slaying of the Lion of Nemea, that had brought so much and sore trouble both upon man and beast."

XXVI.—THE BACCHANALS

THIS *poem was probably written in honour of the
initiation of a boy of nine into the mysteries of Dionysus
by a mock slaying-rite. That young children were
initiated into these mysteries is clear from a poem of
Antistius in the Anthology, which may have been written
for a similar occasion ; and in Callimachus Artemis asks
that her maiden attendants shall be nine years old.*[1] *In
this poem the father describes the slaying of Pentheus by
his mother, and takes credit to himself for following her
example. The slaying of the boy is the bringing of him
to Dionysus, even as the eagles made Ganymede immortal
by bringing him to Zeus. The poem is almost certainly
not by Theocritus, but such poems may well have figured
in the competitions mentioned in line* 112 *of the* Ptolemy.

[1] Antist. *Anth. Pal.* 11. 40, Callim. 3. 14, quoted by
Cholmeley.

XXVI.—ΛΗΝΑΙ Η ΒΑΚΧΑΙ

Ἰνὼ κΑὐτονόα χὰ μαλοπάρανος Ἀγαύα
τρεῖς θιάσως ἐς ὄρος τρεῖς ἄγαγον αὐταὶ ἐοῖσαι.
χαὶ μὲν ἀμερξάμεναι λασίας δρυὸς ἄγρια φύλλα
κισσόν τε ζώοντα καὶ ἀσφόδελον τὸν ὑπὲρ γᾶς
ἐν καθαρῷ λειμῶνι κάμον δυοκαίδεκα βωμώς,
τὼς τρεῖς τᾷ Σεμέλᾳ, τὼς ἐννέα τῷ Διονύσῳ.
ἱερὰ δ' ἐκ κίστας πεπονάμενα [1] χερσὶν ἑλοῖσαι
εὐφάμως κατέθεντο νεοδρέπτων ἐπὶ βωμῶν,
ὡς ἐδίδαξ',[2] ὡς αὐτὸς ἐθυμάρει Διόνυσος.
Πενθεὺς δ' ἀλιβάτω πέτρας ἄπο πάντ' ἐθεώρει,
σχῖνον ἐς ἀρχαίαν καταδύς, ἐπιχώριον ἔρνος.
Αὐτονόα πράτα νιν ἀνέκραγε δεινὸν ἰδοῖσα,
σὺν δ' ἐτάραξε ποσὶν μανιώδεος ὄργια Βάκχῳ,
ἐξαπίνας ἐπιοῖσα· τὰ δ' οὐχ ὁρέοντι βέβαλοι.
μαίνετο μέν θ' αὔτα, μαίνοντο δ' ἄρ' εὐθὺ καὶ
        ἄλλαι.[3]
Πενθεὺς μὲν φεῦγεν πεφοβημένος, αἱ δ' ἐδίωκον,
πέπλως ἐκ ζωστῆρος ἐς ἰγνύαν ἐρύσαισαι.
Πενθεὺς μὲν τόδ' ἔειπε 'τίνος κέχρησθε γυναῖκες;'
Αὐτονόα τόδ' ἔειπε 'τάχα γνώσῃ πρὶν ἀκοῦσαι.'
μάτηρ τὰν κεφαλὰν μυκήσατο παιδὸς ἑλοῖσα,
ὅσσον περ τοκάδος τελέθει μύκημα λεαίνας·
Ἰνὼ δ' ἐξέρρηξε σὺν ὠμοπλάτᾳ μέγαν ὦμον

---

[1] Wordsworth ποπανεύματα   [2] so P. Ant. : mss impf.
[3] ἄλλαι Ahrens : mss ἄλλαι

XXVI.—THE BACCHANALS

THREE dames led three meinies to the mountain,
Ino, Autonoë, and apple-cheeked Agavè, and gather-
ing there wild leaves of the shag-haired oak, and
living ivy and groundling asphodel, wrought in a
lawn of the forest twelve altars, unto Semelè three
and unto Dionysus nine. Then took they from a
box offerings made of their hands and laid them in
holy silence upon those altars of their gathering, as
was at once the precept and the pleasure of the
great Dionysus. Meanwhile Pentheus spied upon
all they did from a steepy crag, being crept into an
ancient mastich-tree such as grow in that country.
Autonoe saw him first and gave a horrible shriek,
and made quick confusion of the sacred things of the
madding Bacchus with her feet, for these things are
not to be seen of the profane. Mad was she now,
and the others were straightway mad also. Pentheus,
he fled afraid, and the women, girding their kirtles
up about their thighs, they went in hot pursuit.
Pentheus, he cried " What would you, ye women? "
Autonoe, she cried " That shall you know ere you
hear it." Then took off the mother the head of her
child and roared even as the roar of a milch lioness,
while Ino setting foot upon his belly wrenched
shoulder and shoulder-blade from the one side of

"meinies": companies.   "apple-cheeked": the Greek
may also mean 'white-faced.'   "offerings made of their
hands": or perhaps 'sacrificial cakes.'

λὰξ ἐπὶ γαστέρα βᾶσα, καὶ Αὐτονόας ῥυθμὸς
   ωὑτός·
αἱ δ' ἄλλαι τὰ περισσὰ κρεανομέοντο γυναῖκες.
ἐς Θήβας δ' ἀφίκοντο πεφυρμέναι αἵματι πᾶσαι,
ἐξ ὄρεος πένθημα καὶ οὐ Πενθῆα φέροισαι.
   οὐκ ἀλέγω, μηδ' ὅστις ἀπεχθόμενος [1] Διονύσῳ
ἄλλος ἔοι,[2] μηδ' εἰ χαλεπώτερα τῶνδε μογήσαι,[3]
εἴη δ' ἐνναέτης ἢ καὶ δεκάτῳ ἐπιβαίνοι·
αὐτὸς δ' εὐαγέοιμι καὶ εὐαγέεσσιν ἄδοιμι.
ἐκ Διὸς αἰγιόχω τιμὰν ἔχει αἰετὸς οὕτως.
εὐσεβέων παίδεσσι[4]τὰ λώϊα, δυσσεβέων δ' οὔ.
   χαίροι μὲν Διόνυσος, ὃν ἐν Δρακάνῳ νιφόεντι
Ζεὺς ὕπατος μεγάλαν ἐπιγωνίδα κάτθετο λύσας·
χαίροι δ' εὐειδὴς Σεμέλα καὶ ἀδελφεαὶ αὐτᾶς
Καδμεῖαι πολλοῖς μεμελημέναι ἡρωῖναι,[5]
αἳ τόδε ἔργον ἔρεξαν ὀρίναντος Διονύσου
οὐκ ἐπιμωματόν.   μηδεὶς τὰ θεῶν ὀνόσαιτο.

---

[1] so P. Ant.: mss μηδ' ἄλλος (Junt. -ον) ἀπεχθόμεναι (Mus.
-έμεναι)   [2] lost from P. Ant, which has schol. ὁ μεμιστημένος
τῷ Διονύσῳ μὴ ἐμοὶ μέλοι: suppl. E, sc. ἀλέγοιμι: mss φροντίζοι
[3] -δε μογήσαι Ahr. with P. Ant: mss δ' ἐμόγησε   [4] P. Ant.
μεν παισι   [5] thus Graefe: mss πολλαῖς and ἡρωίναις, P. Ant.
]ιναις

him, and Autonoe made the other side like unto it; and the other women wrought out the rest of the butchery. And so bedabbled all with blood they carried with them into Thebes in the stead of a kindred wight a kindred woe.

And I care not if they did, and may I take thought for no other that is hated of Dionysus, nay, not if such an one suffer a worse fate than Pentheus and be but a child nine years old or going ten years. As for me, may I be pure and do the will of them that are pure. Thus hath the eagle honour of the Aegis-Bearer. To the children of pious fathers belong the good things rather than to those that come of impious men.

All hail to Dionysus, whom most high Zeus took forth from his mighty thigh and laid down in snowy Dracanus; and all hail to beauteous Semele and her heroine sisters, the far-honoured daughters of Cadmus who did at Dionysus' bidding this deed that none may blame. Where 'tis a God's will let no man cavil.

"Made the other side like unto it": the Greek is 'Autonoe's rhythm was the same,' *i.e.* 'Autonoe followed suit.' "Kindred wight"; the Greek has a grim pun upon *Pentheus* and *penthēma* (woe).

XXVII.—THE LOVERS' TALK

THIS *poem in its complete form was a match between a shepherd and another whom he had challenged, the stake being the shepherd's pipe. The missing part comprised the lines introducing the match, the whole of the rival's piece, and the prelude of the shepherd's piece. What is left is the main part of the shepherd's piece, its epilogue, and the award of the umpire. The umpire returns the shepherd his pipe, and adds a compliment in the form of a request that now he will play him another of his tunes, as, not having lost his pipe in the match, he will still be able to do. In the dialogue supposed to be recited, or perhaps to be sung, by the shepherd, one speaker answers the other speaker line for line except in two places where the same speaker has two lines. These exceptions, necessary in order to shift the rôle of answerer, have brought about a wrong arrangement of lines 9 and 19 in the manuscripts. The poem may be ascribed to an imitator of Theocritus. Line 4 he has taken bodily from him.*

XXVII.—[ΟΑΡΙΣΤΥΣ]

. . . . . .

ΑΚΡΟΤΙΜΗ
Τὰν πινυτὰν Ἑλέναν Πάρις ἥρπασε βουκόλος
  ἄλλος.

ΔΑΦΝΙΣ
μᾶλλον ἑκοῖσ᾽ Ἑλένα τὸν βουκόλον ἐσσὶ[1] φιλεῦσα.

ΑΚΡΟΤΙΜΗ
μὴ[2] καυχῶ σατυρίσκε· κενὸν τὸ φίλαμα λέγουσιν.

ΔΑΦΝΙΣ
ἔστι καὶ ἐν κενεοῖσι φιλάμασιν ἀδέα τέρψις.

ΑΚΡΟΤΙΜΗ
τὸ στόμα μευ πλύνω καὶ ἀποπτύω τὸ φίλαμα.

ΔΑΦΝΙΣ
πλύνεις χείλεα σεῖο; δίδου πάλιν, ὄφρα φιλάσω.

ΑΚΡΟΤΙΜΗ
καλόν σοι δαμάλας φιλέειν, οὐκ ἄζυγα κώραν.

---

[1] ἑκοῖσ᾽ Ahrens : mss ἐδοῖσ᾽   ἐσσὶ E : mss ἐστὶ   [2] μὴ
Musurus : mss omit

XXVII.—[THE LOVERS' TALK]

(*The Shepherd tells of the conversation between Daphnis and Acrotimè*)

. . . . . .

ACROTIME

'Twas a neatherd like you carried off the wise Helen.

DAPHNIS

Helen is more willing now, for she kisses her neatherd.

ACROTIME

Soft, my satyr-boy, be not so sure; there's a saying "nought goes to a kiss."

DAPHNIS

Even in an empty kiss there's a sweet delight.

ACROTIME

Look ye, I wipe my mouth o' your kiss and spit it from me.

DAPHNIS

Wipe thy lips, quotha? then give them hither again and have thee another.

ACROTIME

'Twere rather becoming you to kiss your heifers than a maiden woman like me.

ΔΑΦΝΙΣ

μὴ καυχῶ· τάχα γάρ σε παρέρχεται ὡς ὄναρ ἥβη. 8

ΑΚΡΟΤΙΜΗ

ἁ σταφυλὶς σταφίς ἐστι καὶ οὐ ῥόδον αὖον ὀλεῖται.

ΔΑΦΝΙΣ

ἦδε τί γηράσκῃ; τόδε που μέλι καὶ γάλα πίνω.[1]
δεῦρ᾽ ὑπὸ τὰς κοτίνους, ἵνα σοί τινα μῦθον ἐνέψω.

ΑΚΡΟΤΙΜΗ

οὐκ ἐθέλω· καὶ πρίν με παρήπαφες ἀδέϊ μύθῳ.

ΔΑΦΝΙΣ

δεῦρ᾽ ὑπὸ τὰς πτελέας, ἵν᾽ ἐμᾶς σύριγγος ἀκούσῃς.

ΑΚΡΟΤΙΜΗ

τὴν σαυτοῦ φρένα τέρψον· ὀϊζύον οὐδὲν ἀρέσκει.

ΔΑΦΝΙΣ

φεῦ φεῦ τᾶς Παφίας χόλον ἅζεο καὶ σύγε κώρα.

ΑΚΡΟΤΙΜΗ

χαιρέτω ἁ Παφία· μόνον ἵλαος Ἄρτεμις εἴη.

ΔΑΦΝΙΣ

μὴ λέγε, μὴ βάλλῃ σε καὶ ἐς λίνον ἄλλυτον[2] ἔνθῃς.

ΑΚΡΟΤΙΜΗ

βαλλέτω ὡς ἐθέλῃ· πάλιν Ἄρτεμις ἄμμιν ἀρήξει.[3]

---

[1] this line is omitted in some mss : γηράσκῃ E : mss -σκω
[2] ἄλλυτον Mus (?) : mss ἄκλιτον   [3] ἐθέλῃ E : mss ἐθέλῃς
    ἀρήξει E : mss ἀρήγῃ

DAPHNIS

Soft you, be not so sure ; your youth passes you by like a dream.

ACROTIME

But the grape's in the raisin, and dry rose-leaves may live.

DAPHNIS (*kissing her cheek*)

Shall *this* be suffered to grow old, that is my milk and honey ? Pray you come hither under those wild-olives ; I would fain tell you a tale.

ACROTIME

Nay, I thank you ; you beguiled me before with your pretty tales.

DAPHNIS

Then pray you come hither under those elms and let me play you my pipe.

ACROTIME

Nay ; that way you may pleasure yourself; scant joy comes of a sorry thing.

DAPHNIS

Alackaday ! you likewise, honey, must e'en fear the wrath of Dame Paphian.

ACROTIME

Dame Paphian may go hang for me ; my prayers are to Artemis.

DAPHNIS

Hist ! or she'll have at thee, and then thou'lt be in the trap.

ACROTIME

Let her have at me ; Artemis will help me out.

335

THE BUCOLIC POETS

ΔΑΦΝΙΣ

οὐ φεύγεις τὸν Ἔρωτα, τὸν οὐ φύγε παρθένος ἄλλη.

ΑΚΡΟΤΙΜΗ

φεύγω ναὶ τὸν Πᾶνα· σὺ δὲ ζυγὸν αἰὲν ἀείραις.[1]
μήπιβάλῃς τὴν χεῖρα· καὶ εἰσέτι χεῖλος ἀμύξω.[2]

ΔΑΦΝΙΣ

δειμαίνω, μὴ δή σε κακωτέρῳ ἀνέρι δώσω.

ΑΚΡΟΤΙΜΗ

πολλοί μ' ἐμνώοντο, νόῳ δ' ἐμῷ οὔτις ἔαδε.[3]

ΔΑΦΝΙΣ

εἷς καὶ ἐγὼ πολλῶν μνηστὴρ τεὸς ἐνθάδ' ἱκάνω.

ΑΚΡΟΤΙΜΗ

καὶ τί φίλος ῥέξαιμι; γάμοι πλήθουσιν ἀνίας.

ΔΑΦΝΙΣ

οὐκ ὀδύνην, οὐκ ἄλγος ἔχει γάμος, ἀλλὰ χορείην.

ΑΚΡΟΤΙΜΗ

ναὶ μάν ϝασι γυναῖκας ἑοὺς τρομέειν παρακοίτας.

ΔΑΦΝΙΣ

μᾶλλον ἀεὶ κρατέουσι· τί καὶ [4] τρομέουσι γυναῖκες;

ΑΚΡΟΤΙΜΗ

ὠδίνειν τρομέω· χαλεπὸν βέλος Εἰλειθυίης.

---

[1] ἀείραις Ahr : mss ἄειρες   [2] this line is before 18 in
some mss, after it in others   [3] ἔαδε (perf.) Fritzsche :
mss ἀείδει, Mus. ἔαδε   [4] τί καὶ Wil : mss τίνα

DAPHNIS

No other maiden escapes Love, nor dost thou escape him.

ACROTIME

'Fore Pan, that do I ; as for you, I only pray you may ever bear his yoke. (*he puts his arm about her and makes to kiss her again*) Unhand me, man ; i'll bite thy lip yet.

DAPHNIS

But I fear if I let thee go a worser man will have thee.

ACROTIME

Many the wooers have been after me, but never a one have I had to my mind.

DAPHNIS

Well, here am I come to add one more to those many.

ACROTIME

O friend, what is to do? marriage is all woe.

DAPHNIS

Nay ; a marriage is a thing neither of pain nor grief but rather of dancing.

ACROTIME

Aye, but I'm told the wives do fear their bed-fellows.

DAPHNIS

Nay ; rather have they ever the upper hand ; what should wives fear?

ACROTIME

'Tis the throes I fear ; the stroke of Eileithyia is hard to bear.

THE BUCOLIC POETS

ΔΑΦΝΙΣ

ἀλλὰ τεὴ βασίλεια μογοστόκος Ἄρτεμίς ἐστιν.

ΑΚΡΟΤΙΜΗ

ἀλλὰ τεκεῖν τρομέω, μὴ καὶ χρόα καλὸν ὀλέσσω.

ΔΑΦΝΙΣ

ἢν δὲ τέκῃς φίλα τέκνα, νέον φάος ὄψεαι υἷας.

ΑΚΡΟΤΙΜΗ

καὶ τί μοι ἕδνον ἄγεις γάμου ἄξιον, ἢν ἐπινεύσω;

ΔΑΦΝΙΣ

πᾶσαν τὰν ἀγέλαν, πάντ' ἄλσεα καὶ νομὸν ἕξεις.

ΑΚΡΟΤΙΜΗ

ὄμνυε μὴ μετὰ λέκτρα λιπὼν ἀέκουσαν ἀπενθεῖν.[1]

ΔΑΦΝΙΣ

οὐ μαὐτὸν τὸν Πᾶνα, καὶ ἢν ἐθέλῃς με διῶξαι.

ΑΚΡΟΤΙΜΗ

τεύχεις μοι θαλάμους, τεύχεις καὶ δῶμα καὶ αὐλάς;

ΔΑΦΝΙΣ

τεύχω σοι θαλάμους· τὰ δὲ πώεα καλὰ νομεύω.

ΑΚΡΟΤΙΜΗ

πατρὶ δὲ γηραλέῳ τίνα μάν,[2] τίνα μῦθον ἐνέψω;

ΔΑΦΝΙΣ

αἰνήσει σέο λέκτρον, ἐπὴν ἐμὸν οὔνομ' ἀκούσῃ.

---

[1] ἀπενθεῖν Reiske : mss ἀπένθῃς   [2] μάν Ahr : mss κεν

DAPHNIS

But thou hast Artemis to thy queen, and she lightens the labour.

ACROTIME

Ah! but I fear lest the childbirth lose me my pretty face.

DAPHNIS

But if thou bear sweet children, thou'lt see a new light in thy sons.

ACROTIME

And if I say thee yea, what gift bring'st thou with thee worthy the marriage?

DAPHNIS

Thou shalt have all my herd and all the planting and pasture I possess.

ACROTIME

Swear thou'lt never thereafter leave me all forlorn.

DAPHNIS

Before great Pan I swear it, even if thou choose to send me packing.

ACROTIME

Buildest me a bower and a house and a farmstead?

DAPHNIS

Yea, I build thee a house, and the flocks I feed are fine flocks.

ACROTIME

But then my gray-headed father, O what can I say to him?

DAPHNIS

He'll think well o' thy wedlock when he hears my name.

THE BUCOLIC POETS

ΑΚΡΟΤΙΜΗ

οὔνομα σὸν λέγε τῆνο· καὶ οὔνομα πολλάκι τέρπει.

ΔΑΦΝΙΣ

Δάφνις ἐγώ, Λυκίδας δε πατήρ, μήτηρ δὲ Νομαίη.

ΑΚΡΟΤΙΜΗ

ἐξ εὐηγενέων· ἀλλ' οὐ σέθεν εἰμὶ χερείων.

ΔΑΦΝΙΣ

οἶδ', Ἀκροτίμη ἐσσί,[1] πατὴρ δέ τοί ἐστι Μενάλκας.

ΑΚΡΟΤΙΜΗ

δεῖξον ἐμοὶ τεὸν ἄλσος, ὅπη σέθεν ἵσταται αὐλά.[2]

ΔΑΦΝΙΣ

δεῦρ' ἴδε, πῶς ἀνθεῦσιν ἐμαὶ ῥαδιναὶ κυπάρισσοι.

ΑΚΡΟΤΙΜΗ

αἶγες ἐμαὶ βόσκεσθε· τὰ βουκόλω ἔργα νοήσω.

ΔΑΦΝΙΣ

ταῦροι καλὰ νέμεσθ', ἵνα παρθένῳ ἄλσεα δείξω.

ΑΚΡΟΤΙΜΗ

τί ῥέζεις σατυρίσκε; τί δ' ἔνδοθεν ἅψαο μαζῶν;

ΔΑΦΝΙΣ

μᾶλα τεὰ πράτιστα τάδε χνοάοντα διδάξω.

ΑΚΡΟΤΙΜΗ

ναρκῶ ναὶ τὸν Πᾶνα. τεὴν πάλιν ἔξελε χεῖρα.

---

[1] οἶδ' Jacobs : mss οὐδ'   Ἀκροτίμη ἐσσί E : mss ἄκρα
τιμήεσσι, Mus. ἄ. τιμήεσσα   [2] τεὸν Wil : mss ἔθον, Mus.
ἔθεν   αὐλά E : mss α or αια, Mus. αὐλις

340

ACROTIME

Then tell me that name o' thine; there's often joy in a name.

DAPHNIS

'Tis Daphnis, mine, and my father's Lycidas and my mother's Nomaeë.

ACROTIME

Thou com'st of good stock; and yet methinks I am as good as thou.

DAPHNIS

Aye, I know it; thou art Acrotimè and thy father Menalcas.

ACROTIME

Come, show me thy planting, show me where thy farmstead is.

DAPHNIS

Lo! this way it is; look how tall and slender my cypress-trees spring!

ACROTIME

Graze on, my goats; I go to see the neatherd's labours.

DAPHNIS

Feed you well, my bulls; I would fain show the maid my planting.

ACROTIME

What art thou at, satyr-boy? why hast put thy hand inside on my breasts?

DAPHNIS

I am fain to give thy ripe pippins their first lesson.

ACROTIME

'Fore Pan, I shall swoon; take back thy hand.

ΔΑΦΝΙΣ

θάρσει κῶρα φίλα. τί μοι ἔτρεμες; ὡς μάλα δειλά.

ΑΚΡΟΤΙΜΗ

βάλλεις εἰς ἀμάραν με καὶ εἵματα καλὰ μιαίνεις.

ΔΑΦΝΙΣ

ἀλλ᾽ ὑπὸ σοὺς πέπλους ἁπαλὸν νάκος ἠνίδε βάλλω.

ΑΚΡΟΤΙΜΗ

φεῦ φεῦ καὶ τὰν μίτραν ἀπέσχισας·[1] ἐς τί δ᾽
ἔλυσας;

ΔΑΦΝΙΣ

τᾷ Παφίᾳ πράτιστον ἐγὼ τόδε δῶρον ὀπάσσω.[2]

ΑΚΡΟΤΙΜΗ

μίμνε τάλαν· τάχα τίς τοι ἐπέρχεται· ἦχον ἀκούω.

ΔΑΦΝΙΣ

ἀλλήλαις λαλέουσι τεὸν γάμον αἱ κυπάρισσοι.

ΑΚΡΟΤΙΜΗ

ἀμπεχόνην ποίησας ἐμὴν ῥάκος·[3] εἰμὶ δὲ γυμνά.

ΔΑΦΝΙΣ

ἄλλην ἀμπεχόνην τῆς σῆς τοι μείζονα δώσω.

ΑΚΡΟΤΙΜΗ

φῇς μοι πάντα δόμεν· τάχα δ᾽ ὕστερον οὐδ᾽ ἅλα
δοίης.

ΔΑΦΝΙΣ

αἴθ᾽ αὐτὰν δυνάμαν καὶ τὰν ψυχὰν ἐπιβάλλειν.

---

[1] μίτραν Winsem: mss μικρὰν   ἀπέσχισας Scaliger: mss
ἀπέστιχες   [2] ὀπάσσω E, cf l. 64; he cannot be said to
give it on the spot: mss ὀπάζω   [3] ἀμπεχόνην Ahr: mss

DAPHNIS

Never thou mind, sweet; what hadst thou to fear, little coward?

ACROTIME

Thou thrustest me into the water-conduit and soilest my pretty clothes.

DAPHNIS

Nay; look ye there! I cast my soft sheepskin under thy cloak.

ACROTIME

Out, alack! thou hast torn off my girdle, too. Why didst loose that?

DAPHNIS

This shall be my firstlings to our Lady of Paphos.

ACROTIME

Hold, ah hold! sure somebody's e'en coming. There's a noise.

DAPHNIS

Aye, the cypress-trees talking together of thy bridal.

ACROTIME

Thou hast torn my mantle and left me in the nude.

DAPHNIS

I'll give thee another mantle, and an ampler.

ACROTIME

You say you'll give me anything I may ask, who soon mayhap will deny me salt.

DAPHNIS

Would I could give thee my very soul to boot!

τὰμπεχόνην, Mus. τἀμπέχονον   ἐμὴν Hermann : mss ἐμὸν
ῥάκος Mus (?) : mss ῥάγος

THE BUCOLIC POETS

ΑΚΡΟΤΙΜΗ

Ἄρτεμι, μὴ νεμέσα σοῖς ῥήμασιν[1] οὐκέτι πιστῇ.

ΔΑΦΝΙΣ

ῥέξω[2] πόρτιν Ἔρωτι καὶ αὐτᾷ βῶν Ἀφροδίτᾳ.

ΑΚΡΟΤΙΜΗ

παρθένος ἔνθα βέβηκα, γυνὴ δ᾽ εἰς οἶκον ἀφέρπω.

ΔΑΦΝΙΣ

ἀλλὰ γυνὴ μήτηρ τεκέων τροφός, οὐκέτι κώρα.

ὡς οἱ μὲν χλοεροῖσιν ἰαινόμενοι μελέεσσιν
ἀλλήλοις ψιθύριζον. ἀνέστατο[3] φώριος εὐνή.
χἢ μὲν ἀνεγρομένη πάλιν ἔστιχε[4] μᾶλα νομεύειν
ὄμμασιν αἰδομένοις,[5] κραδίη δέ οἱ ἔνδον ἰάνθη,
ὃς δ᾽ ἐπὶ ταυρείας ἀγέλας κεχαρημένος εὐνᾶς.

ΚΡΙΤΗΣ

δέχνυσο τὰν σύριγγα τεὰν πάλιν, ὄλβιε ποίμαν·[6]
τᾷ καὶ ποιμναγῶν[7] ἑτέραν σκεψώμεθα μολπάν.

---

[1] σοῖς ῥήμασιν Ahr: mss σοι ἔρημας   [2] ῥέξω Mus: mss ῥέζω   [3] so E, cf. ἐκκλησίαν ἀναστῆσαι: mss ἀνίστατο (ἀνίστα) [4] πάλιν ἔστιχε Wil: mss γε διέστ.   [5] αἰδομένοις Herm: mss -οι, Mus. -η   [6] Lines 72–3 are omitted by Mus.   τεὰν Ahr: mss τεῶν   [7] ποιμναγῶν E, cf. κυναγὸς: mss ποιμαιγνίων

344

ACROTIME

O Artemis, be not wroth with a transgressor of
thy word.

DAPHNIS

Love shall have a heifer of me, and great
Aphrodite a cow.

ACROTIME

Lo, I came hither a maid and I go home a
woman.

DAPHNIS

Aye, a mother and a nursing-mother, maiden no
more.

Thus they prattled in the joy of their fresh young
limbs. The secret bridal over, she rose and went
her ways for to feed her sheep, her look shamefast
but her heart glad within her; while as for him, he
betook himself to his herds of bulls rejoicing in his
wedlock.

THE UMPIRE

Here, take the pipe, thou happy shepherd; 'tis
thine once more; and so let's hear and consider
another of the tunes of the leaders o' sheep.

XXVIII.—THE DISTAFF

THE DISTAFF *is an occasional poem in the Aeolic dialect and the Asclepiad metre, and was almost certainly modelled upon Sappho or Alcaeus. It was written by Theocritus before or during a voyage from Syracuse to Miletus, and presented with the gift of a carved ivory distaff to the wife of his friend the poet-physician Nicias.*

XXVIII.—ΗΛΑΚΑΤΗ

Γλαύκας ὦ φιλέριθ' ἀλακάτα δῶρον 'Αθανάας
γύναιξιν, νόος οἰκωφελίας αἶσιν ἐπάβολος,
θάρσεισ' ἄμμιν ὑμάρτη πόλιν ἐς Νείλεος ἀγλάαν,
ὄππα Κύπριδος ἶρον καλάμῳ χλῶρον ὑπ' ἀπάλῳ.
τυῖδε γὰρ πλόον εὐάνεμον αἰτήμεθα πὰρ Δίος,
ὅππως ξέννον ἔμον τέρψομ' ἴδων κἀντιφιλήσομαι[1]
Νικίαν, Χαρίτων ἰμεροφώνων ἵερον φύτον,
καὶ σὲ τὰν ἐλέφαντος πολυμόχθω γεγενημέναν
δῶρον Νικίας εἰς ἀλόχω[2] χέρρας ὀπάσσομεν,
σὺν τᾷ πόλλα μὲν ἔρρ'[3] ἐκτελέσεις ἀνδρείοις
     πέπλοις,
πόλλα δ' οἶα γύναικες φορέοισ' ὑδάτινα βράκη.
δὶς γὰρ μάτερες ἄρνων μαλάκοις ἐν βοτάνᾳ πόκοις
πέξαιντ' αὐτοέτει, Θευγένιδός γ' ἔννεκ' εὐσφύρω·
οὕτως ἀνυσίεργος, φιλέει δ' ὄσσα σαόφρονες.
οὐ γὰρ εἰς ἀκίρας οὐδ' ἐς ἀέργω κεν ἐβολλόμαν
ὄπασσαί σε δόμοις ἀμμετέρας ἔσσαν ἀπὺ χθόνος.

The Aeolic forms and accents are in many cases the restoration of Ahrens, but a few undoubted traces of them remain in the mss   [1] κἀντιφιλήσομαι Musurus: mss -ήσω   [2] ἀλόχω: mss also ὀλόχω perhaps rightly   [3] ἔρρ(α) = ἔρια Buecheler: mss ἐργ'

XXVIII.—THE DISTAFF

Distaff, friend of them that weave and spin, gift of the Grey-eyed Huswife above to all good huswives here below, come away, come away to Neleus' town so bright and fair, where the Cyprian's precinct lies fresh and green among the tall soft reeds; for 'tis thither bound I ask of Zeus fair passage, with intent both to glad my eyes with the sight and my heart with the love of a dear good child of the Ladies o' the Voice of Delight, by name Nicias, and to give you, my pretty offspring of laboured ivory, into the hands of the goodwife of the same, to be her helpmate in the making of much wool into clothes, whether the coats of men or those translucent robes the women do wear. For the fleecy mothers o' flocks might well get them shorn afield twice in one year for aught Mistress Pretty-toes would care, so busy a little body is she and enamoured of all that delighteth the discreet. Trust me, I would never have given a fellow-countryman into the house of a do-nought or a sloven. And fellow-countryman it is, seeing you

"Neleus' town": Miletus was founded by Neleus, and a temple of Aphrodite-in-the Marsh seems to have been one of its outstanding features.   "Tall soft reeds": Simias ap. Powell, *Coll. Alex.* 109, speaks of 'islands roofed with high-tressed reeds.'

349

καὶ γάρ τοι πάτρις, ἂν ὠξ Ἐφύρας κτίσσε ποτ᾽
   Ἀρχίας
νάσω Τρινακρίας μύελον, ἄνδρων δοκίμων πόλιν.

  νῦν μὰν οἶκον ἔχοισ᾽ ἄνερος, ὃς πόλλ᾽ ἐδάη σόφα
ἀνθρώποισι νόσοις φάρμακα λύγραις ἀπαλάλκεμεν, 2
οἰκήσεις κατὰ Μίλλατον ἐράνναν πεδ᾽ Ἰαόνων,
ὡς εὐαλάκατος Θεύγενις ἐν δαμότισιν πέλη,
καί οἱ μνᾶστιν ἄει τῶ φιλαοίδω παρέχης ξένω·
κῆνο γάρ τις ἔρει τὤπος ἴδων σ᾽· ‘ἦ μεγάλα χάρις
δώρῳ σὺν ὀλίγῳ· πάντα δὲ τίματα τὰ πὰρ φίλων.’

hail from the town old Archias founded out of Ephyra, the sap and savour of the Isle o' Three Capes, the birthplace of good men and true.

But now you are to lodge at a wiseacre's deep-learned in the lore of such spells as defend us of the flesh from woeful ills ; now you are to dwell among an Ionian people in Miletus the delectable, to the end that Theugenis' neighbours may be jealous of her and her distaff, and so you may serve always to mind her of her friend the lover of song. For at the sight of you it shall be said, " Great love goes here with a little gift, and all is precious that comes of a friend."

"Ephyra": an old name for Corinth, the mother city of Syracuse.

XXIX–XXX. —THE AEOLIC LOVE-POEMS

THESE *two poems are inspired, like XII, by a passionate friendship. The first line of No. 1 contains a quotation from Alcaeus, and in both poems metre and dialect point to him or Sappho as the model. The metre in the one case is the fourteen-syllable Sapphic Pentameter, and in the other the Greater Asclepiad. As in XII, there is much here that is reminiscent to us of some of the Elizabethan love-poetry.*[1]

[1] The Antinoë Papyrus has the remains of what appears to be a third Aeolic Love-Poem of about 33 lines, but they are too fragmentary to be given here ; Hunt calls it XXXI.

XXIX.—ΠΑΙΔΙΚΟΝ ΑΙΟΛΙΚΟΝ a'

'Οἶνος' ὦ φίλε παῖ λέγεται 'καὶ ἀλάθεα·'
κἄμμε[1] χρῆ μεθύοντας ἀλαθέας ἔμμεναι.
κἠγὼ μὲν ἐρέω τὰ φρένων κέατ'[2] ἐν μύχῳ·
οὐκ ὅλας σε φίλην[3] με θέλεισθ' ἀπὺ καρδίας·
γινώσκω· τὸ γὰρ αἴμισυ[4]τᾶς ζοίας ἔχω
ζὰ τὰν σὰν ἰδέαν, τὸ δὲ λοῖπον ἀπώλετο,
κὤτα μὲν σὺ θέλεις, μακάρεσσιν ἴσαν ἄγω
ἀμέραν· ὅτα δ' οὐκὶ θέλεις τύ, μάλ' ἐν σκότῳ.
πῶς ταῦτ' ἄρμενα, τὸν φιλέοντ' ὀνίαις δίδων;
ἀλλ' εἴ μοί τι πίθοιο νέος προγενεστέρῳ,
τῷ κε λώιον αὐτὸς ἔχων ἔμ' ἐπαινέσαις.
ποίησαι καλιὰν μίαν ἐνν[5] ἔνι δενδρίῳ,
ὅππα[6] μηδὲν ἀπίξεται ἄγριον ὄρπετον.
νῦν δὲ τῷδε μὲν ἄματος ἄλλον ἔχεις κλάδον,
ἄλλον δ' αὔριον, ἐξ ἐτέρω δ' ἔτερον μάτης.
καὶ μέν σευ τὸ κάλον τις ἴδων ῥέθος αἰνέσαι,
τῷ δ' εὐθὺς πλέον ἢ τριέτης ἐγένευ φίλος,
τὸν πρῶτον δὲ φίλεντα[7] τρίταιον ἐθήκαο
ἀνδρῶν, τῶν ὑπὲρ ἀνορέαν[8] δοκέεις πνέην·
φίλη δ', ἆς κε ζόης, τὸν ὕμοιον[9] ἔχην ἄι.
αἰ γὰρ ὦδε πόης, ἄγαθος μὲν ἀκούσεαι
ἐξ ἄστων· ὁ δέ τοι κ' Ἔρος οὐ χαλέπως ἔχοι,
ὃς ἀνδρῶν φρένας εὐμαρέως ὑπαδάμναται,
κἤμε μάλθακον ἐξ ἐπόησε σιδαρίω.

---

[1] κἄμμε Brunck : mss κἄμμες   [2] E: mss, P. Ant. τὰ φρένων
ἐρέω κέατ'   [3] σε φίλην E: mss φιλέειν   [4] αἴμισυ Hoffmann,
P. Ant.: mss ἄμισυ   [5] ἐνν Wil: mss εἰν   [6] mss ὄπη or ὄππη

354

XXIX.—The First Love-Poem

In sack, out sooth goes the saying, lad, and now
that you and I are a-drinking we must fain be men
of truth. I for one will tell what doth lie in my
mind's hold, and it is that you will not that I should
love you with my whole heart. I know it; for such
is the power of your beauty that there's but half
a living left me to love you withal, seeing my day is
spent like as a God's or in very darkness according
as you do choose. What righteousness is here, to
deliver one that loves you over unto woe? Trust
me, if you 'ld only hearken to your elder 'twould be
profit unto you and thanks unto me. Listen then :
one tree should hold one nest, and that where no
noisome beast may come at it; but you, you do
possess one bough to-day and another to-morrow,
seeking ever from this unto that; and if one but see
and praise your fair face, straightway are you more
than a three years' friend to him, and as for him
that first loved you, in three days, lad, you reckon
him of those men whose very manhood you seem to
disdain. Choose rather to be friends with the same
body so long as you shall live ; for if so you do,
you will have both honour of the world and kind-
ness of that Love who doth so easily vanquish the
mind of man and hath melted in me a heart of
very iron.

[7] φίλεντα Hoffm. : mss φιλεῦντα   [8] mss ὑπερανορέων   [9] τὸν
ὕμοιον = the same, cf. *Meg.* 33.

ἀλλὰ πὲρρ[1] ἀπάλω στύματός σε πεδέρχομαι
ὀμνάσθην, ὅτι πέρρυσιν ἦσθα νεώτερος,
κὤτι γηραλέοι πέλομεν πρὶν ἀπόπτυσαι
καὶ ῥύσσοι, νεότατα δ' ἔχην παλινάγρετον
οὐκ ἔστι· πτέρυγας γὰρ ἐπομμαδίαις φόρη,
κἄμμες βαρδύτεροι τὰ ποτήμενα συλλάβην.
ταῦτα χρῆ σε νόεντα πέλην προτιμώτερον[2],
καί μοι τὠραμένῳ συνέραν ἀδόλως σέθεν,
ὅππως, ἄνικα τὰν γένυν ἀνδρεῖαν ἔχης,
ἀλλάλοισι πελώμεθ' Ἀχιλλέϊοι φίλοι.
αἰ δὲ ταῦτα φέρην ἀνέμοισιν ἐπιτρόπης,
ἐν θύμῳ δὲ λέγης ' τί με δαιμόνι' ἐννόχλης;
νῦν μὲν κἠπὶ τὰ χρύσια μᾶλ' ἔνεκεν σέθεν
βαίην καὶ φύλακον νεκύων πεδὰ Κέρβερον,
τότα δ' οὐδὲ κάλεντος[3] ἐπ' αὐλείαις θύραις
προμόλοιμί κε παυσάμενος χαλέπω μόνω.[4]

---

[1] πὲρρ Wil: Ahr πὲρ: mss περὶ   [2] σε νόεντα Buecheler:
mss νοέοντα   mss προτιμότερον and ποτιμότερον, *P. Ant.*
]τιμωτερον: = kinder E   [3] κάλεντος E: mss καλεῦντος
[4] μόνω E = madness: mss πόθω and μούνῳ (?)

O by those soft lips I beseech you remember that you were younger a year agone, and as we men wax old and wrinkled sooner than one may spit, so there's no re-taking of Youth once she be fled, seeing she hath wings to her shoulders, and for us 'tis ill catching winged beasts. Come then, think on these things and be the kinder for't, and give love for love where true loving is; and so when Time shall bring thee a beard we'll be Achilles and his friend. But if so be you cast me these words to the winds, and say, and say in your heart, "Peace, man; begone," then, for all I would go now for your sake and get the Golden Apples or fetch you the Watch-dog o' the Dead, I would not come forth, no, not if you should stand at my very door and call me, for the pain of my woodness would be overpast.

"Achilles and his friend": Patroclus. "Golden Apples": of the Hesperides; the fetching of these and of Cerberus were two of the Labours of Heracles. "woodness": madness.

XXX.—ΠΑΙΔΙΚΟΝ ΑΙΟΛΙΚΟΝ β'

Ὤιαι τῶ χαλέπω καὶνομόρω τῶδε νοσήματος·
τετόρταιος ἔχει παῖδος ἔρος μῆνά με[1] δεύτερον,
κάλω μὲν μετρίως, ἀλλ' ὅποσον τῷ πόδι περρέχει
τὰς γᾶς, τοῦτο χάρις, ταῖς δὲ παραύϜαις γλύκυ 5
    μειδία[2].
καὶ νῦν μὲν τὸ κάκον ταῖς μὲν ἔχει, ταῖσι δέ μ'οὐκ
    ἔχει[3].   4
τάχα δ' οὐδ' ὅσον ὕπνω 'πιτύχην ἔσσετ' ἐρωΐα.
ἔχθες γὰρ παρίων ἔδρακε λέπτ' ἄμμε δι' ὀφρύγων[4]
αἰδέσθεις προτίδην[5] ἄντιος, ἠρεύθετο δὲ χρόα,
ἔμεθεν δὲ πλέον τᾶς κραδίας ὦρος ἐδράξατο·
εἰς οἶκον δ' ἀπέβαν ἔλκος ἔχων καὶ τὸ <κέαρ
    δάκων>[6]   1
πόλλα δ' εἰσκαλέσαις θῦμον ἐμαύτῳ διελεξάμαν[7]
'τί δὴ ταῦτ' ἐπόης; ἀλοσύνας τί ἔσχατον ἔσσεται;
λευκὰς οὐκὶ Ϝίσαισθ' ὅττι φόρης ἐν κροτάφοις
    τρίας[8];
ὦρά τοι φρονέην, μὴ ωὐκὶ[9] νέος τὰν ἰδέαν πέλη
πάντ' ἔρδη ὅσσαπερ οἱ τῶν ἐτέων ἄρτια γεύμενοι.[10]
καὶ μὰν ἄλλα σε λάθει· τὸ δ' ἄρ' ἦς λῶϊον, ἔμμεναι

---

[1] μῆνά με Bergk : ms μῆνα   4, 5 transp. Fritzsche, *P. Ant.*
[2] παραύϜαις (Ϝ E) γλύκυ μειδία Bgk : ms παραύλαις γλ. μειδίαμα,
P. Ant. παραυ[[3] Bgk : ms ταῖς μὲν ἔχει ταῖς δ' οὔ   [4] λέπτ'
ἄμμε Schwabe : δι' ὀφρύγων Bgk-Herw. (ὀφρύϜων? E): ms λεπτὰ
μελίφρυγων   [5] προτίδην E : ms ποτίδην   [6] κέαρ δάκων sup-

388

XXX.—The Second Love-Poem

Ayе me, the pain and the grief of it! I have been sick of Love's quartan now a month and more. He's not so fair, I own, but all the ground his pretty foot covers is grace, and the smile of his face is very sweetness. 'Tis true the ague takes me now but day on day off, but soon there'll be no respite, no not for a wink of sleep. When we met yesterday he gave me a sidelong glance, afeared to look me in the face, and blushed crimson; at that, Love gripped my reins still the more, till I gat me wounded and heartsore home, there to arraign my soul at bar and hold with myself this parlance: " What wast after, doing so? whither away this fond folly? know'st thou not there's three gray hairs on thy brow? Be wise in time, or one that is no youth in's looks shall play new-taster o' the years. Other toys thou forgettest; 'twere better, sure, at thy time o' life to know no

plied by Fritzsche   7 διελεξάμαν Bgk : ms διέλυξε   8 οὐκὶ Fίσαισθ᾽ E : ms οὐκ ἐπῖσθης θ᾽   φόρης and τρίας Bgk : ms φόροις and τρία   9 φρονέην Bgk : ms φρονέσιν   μὴ ωὐκὶ νέος E: ms μὴ . . . ινέος : see Class. Rev. 1911 p. 67   10 γεύμενοι Kreissler : ms γεγεύμ.

ξέννον τῶν χαλέπων παῖδος <ἔρων ἢ τόον ἔντ’>[1]
ἔραν.

τῷ μὲν γὰρ βίος ἔρπει Fίσα γόννοις ἐλάφω θόας
τελάσσαι δ’ ἀτέρα ποντοπόρην ᾆ αὔριον ἀμέραν,[2]
οὐδ’[3] αὔτω γλυκέρας ἄνθεμον ἄβας πεδ’ ὑμαλίκω   2
μένει· τῷ δ’ ὁ πόθος καὶ τὸν ἔσω μύελον ἐσθίει
ὀμμιμνασκομένῳ, πόλλα δ’ ὄρη νύκτος ἐνύπνια,
παύσασθαι δ’ ἐνιαυτὸς χαλέπας οὐκ ἴ<κονος
δύας—.>’[4]
    ταῦτα κἄτερα πόλλα προτ’ ἔμον[5] θῦμον ἐμεμ-
        ψάμαν·
ὁ δὲ τοῦτ’ ἔφατ’· ‘ὄττις δοκίμοι[6] τὸν δολομάχανον
νικάσην Ἔρον, οὗτος δοκίμοι τοὶς ὑπὲρ ἀμμέων
εὔρην βραϊδίως ἄστερας, ὁππόσσακιν ἔννεα·
καὶ νῦν, εἴτε θέλω, χρή με μάκρον σχόντα τὸν
        ἄμφενα
ἔλκην τὸν ζύγον, εἴτ’ οὐκὶ θέλω· ταῦτα γάρ, ὦγαθε,
βόλλεται θέος ὃς καὶ Δίος ἔσφαλε μέγαν νόον   3
καὔτας Κυπρογενήας· ἔμε μάν, φύλλον[7] ἐπάμερον
σμίκρας δεύμενον αὔρας, ὀνέλων ᾆ κε φόρη φόρη.’[8]

---

[1] ἔρων ἢ τόον ἔντ’ supplied by E   ἔρπει Fίσα E: ms
ἔρπε ρωϊσα   [2] τελάσσαι = τολμῆσαι E from Hesych: ms
δλάσει   ᾆ αὔριον ἀμέραν = ταύτῃ τῶν ἡμερῶν ἢ αὔριόν ἐστι E:
ms αὔριον ἀμ.   [3] P. Ant. τωδ[[4] χαλέπας Bgk: ms χαλε-
παὶ suppl. E: ms οὐκὶ   for the aposiopesis cf. Il. 23.
319 ff.   [5] προτ’ Bgk: ms ποτ’   [6] δοκίμοι Bgk: ms δοκεῖ μοι

more such loves as this. For whom Life carries swift and easy as hoof doth hind, and might endure to cross and cross the sea every day's morrow that is, can he and the flower o' sweet Youth abide ever of one date? How much less he that hath yearnful remembrance gnawing at his heart's core, and dreams often o' nights and taketh whole years to cure his lovesickness!"

Such lesson and more read I unto my soul, and thus she answered me again: "Whoso thinketh to outvie yon cozening Love, as soon might he think to tell how-many-times-nine stars be i' th' skies above us; and so I too, willy-nilly, must fain stretch my neck beneath the yoke and pull, seeing such, my lord, is the will of a God that hath betrayed ev'n the mickle mind of Zeus, and beguiled ev'n the Cyprus-born, and catcheth up and carrieth whithersoever he list (as well he may) a poor mortal leaf like me that needs but a puff of air to lift it."

---

[7] φύλλον Fritzsche : ms φίλον   [8] δεύμενον Bgk : ms δευό-
μενον   ὀνέλων Ahr : ms ὁ μέλλων   ᾷ κε Wil : ms αἴκα   φόρη
φόρη E : cf. Stob. Floril. 28. 18fin. οἷς ἐπισφαλὴς ὀπηδεῖ (mss
ὅπη δὴ) παντοίη τύχη φορῇ (mss φορὴ) πνεύματος αἰωρουμένη, and
see Class. Rev. 1911, p. 65 : ms φορεῖ

THE INSCRIPTIONS

THESE *little poems are all, with the exception of IV,
actual inscriptions, and would seem to have been collected
from the works of art upon which they were inscribed.
XII and XXIII are in all probability by other hands,
and there is some doubt of the genuineness of XXIV ;
but the rest are not only ascribed to Theocritus in the best
manuscripts, but are fully worthy of him.*

ΕΠΙΓΡΑΜΜΑΤΑ

I

Τὰ ῥόδα τὰ δροσόεντα καὶ ἁ κατάπυκνος ἐκείνα
ἔρπυλλος κεῖται ταῖς Ἑλικωνιάσι,
ταὶ δὲ μελάμφυλλοι δάφναι τὶν Πύθιε Παιάν,
Δελφὶς ἐπεὶ πέτρα τοῦτό τοι ἀγλάϊσε·
βωμὸν δ' αἱμάξει κεραὸς τράγος οὗτος ὁ μαλός,
τερμίνθου τρώγων ἔσχατον ἀκρεμόνα.

II

Δάφνις ὁ λευκόχρως, ὁ καλᾷ σύριγγι μελίσδων
βουκολικοὺς ὕμνους, ἄνθετο Πανὶ τάδε,
τοὺς τρητοὺς δόνακας, τὸ λαγωβόλον, ὀξὺν ἄκοντα,
νεβρίδα, τὰν πήραν, ᾇ ποκ' ἐμαλοφόρει.

III

Εὕδεις φυλλοστρῶτι πέδῳ Δάφνι σῶμα κεκμακὸς
ἀμπαύων, στάλικες δ' ἀρτιπαγεῖς ἀν' ὄρη·
ἀγρεύει δέ τυ Πὰν καὶ ὁ τὸν κροκόεντα Πρίηπος
κισσὸν ἐφ' ἱμερτῷ κρατὶ καθαπτόμενος,
ἄντρου ἔσω στείχοντες ὁμόρροθοι. ἀλλὰ τὺ φεῦγε,
φεῦγε μεθεὶς ὕπνου κῶμα καταρρύμενον.[1]

---

[1] καταρρύμενον E: cf. Sappho fr. 4 κῶμα κατάρρει, and
χύμενος: mss καταγρόμενον or καταγόμενον

364

THE INSCRIPTIONS

I.—[AN INSCRIPTION FOR A PICTURE]

THOSE dewy roses and that thick bushy thyme are an offering to the Ladies of Helicon, and since 'tis the Delphian Rock hath made it honoured, the dark-leaved bay, Pythian Healer, is for thee ; and yon horny white he-goat that crops the outmost sprays of the terebinth-tree is to be the blood-offering upon the altar.

II.—[FOR A PICTURE]

THESE stopped reeds, this hurl-bat, this sharp javelin, this fawnskin, and this wallet he used to carry apples in, are an offering unto Pan from the fair-skinned Daphnis, who piped the music o' the country upon this pretty flute.

III.—[FOR A PICTURE]

YOU sleep there upon the leaf-strown earth, good Daphnis, and rest your weary frame, while your netting-stakes are left planted on the hillside. But Pan is after you, and Priapus also, with the yellow ivy about his jolly head ; they are going side by side into your cave. Quick then, put off the lethargy that is shed of sleep, and up with you and away.

IV

Τήναν τὰν λαύραν, τόθι ταὶ δρύες, αἰπόλε κάμψας
  σύκινον εὑρήσεις ἀρτιγλυφὲς ξόανον
ἀσκελὲς[1] αὐτόφλοιον ἀνούατον, ἀλλὰ φάλητι
  παιδογόνῳ δυνατὸν Κύπριδος ἔργα τελεῖν.
σακὸς δ’ εὐίερος περιδέδρομεν, ἀέναον δὲ
  ῥεῖθρον ἀπὸ σπιλάδων πάντοσε τηλεθάει
δάφναις καὶ μύρτοισι καὶ εὐώδει κυπαρίσσῳ,
  ἔνθα πέριξ κέχυται βοτρυόπαις ἕλικι
ἄμπελος, εἰαρινοὶ δὲ λιγυφθόγγοισιν ἀοιδαῖς
  κόσσυφοι ἀχεῦσιν ποικιλότραυλα μέλη,
ξουθαὶ δ’ ἀδονίδες μινυρίσμασιν ἀνταχεῦσι[2]
  μέλπουσαι στόμασιν τὰν μελίγαρυν ὄπα.
ἕζεο δὴ τηνεῖ καὶ τῷ χαρίεντι Πριήπῳ
  εὖχε’ ἀποστέρξαι τοὺς Δάφνιδός με πόθους,
κεὐθὺς ἐπιρρέξειν χίμαρον καλόν. ἢν δ’ ἀνανεύσῃ,
  τοῦδε τυχὼν ἐθέλω τρισσὰ θύη τελέσαι·
ῥέξω γὰρ δαμάλαν, λάσιον τράγον, ἄρνα τὸν ἴσχω
  σακίταν. ἄιοι δ’ εὐμενέως ὁ θεός.

V

Λῇς ποτὶ τᾶν Νυμφᾶν διδύμοις αὐλοῖσιν ἀεῖσαι
  ἁδύ τί μοι; κἠγὼ πακτίδ’ ἀειράμενος
ἀρξεῦμαί τι κρέκειν, ὁ δὲ βουκόλος ἄμμιγα θελξεῖ
  Δάφνις, κηροδέτῳ πνεύματι μελπόμενος.

---

[1] ἀσκελὲς Jahn, *i.e.* a herm, cf. *A.P.* 10. 8, 6. 20 ; mss
τρισκελὲς   [2] ἀνταχεῦσι Scaliger : mss ἀντιαχεῦσι

IV.—[A LOVE-POEM IN THE FORM OF A WAYSIDE INSCRIPTION]

WHEN you turn the corner of yonder lane, sweet Goatherd, where the oak-trees are, you'll find a new-carved effigy of fig-wood, without legs or ears and the bark still upon it, but nevertheless an able servant of the Cyprian. There's a brave little sacrificial close runs round it, and a never-ceasing freshet that springs from the rocks there is greened all about with bays and myrtles and fragrant cypress, among which the mother o' grapes doth spread and twine, and in spring the blackbirds cry their lisping medleys of clear-toned song, and the babbling nightingales cry them back their warblings with the honey voice that sings from their tuneful throats. Thither go, and sit you down and pray that pretty fellow to make cease my love of Daphnis, and I'll straightway offer him a fat young goat; but should he say me nay, then I'll make him three sacrifices if he'll win me his love, a heifer, a shaggy buck-goat, and a pet lamb I am rearing; and may the God hear and heed your prayer.

V.—[AN INSCRIPTION FOR A PICTURE]

'FORE the Nymphs I pray you play me some sweet thing upon the double pipe, and I will take my viol and strike up likewise, and neatherd Daphnis shall join with us and make charming music with the

ἐγγὺς δὲ στάντες λασίας δρυὸς ἄντρου ὄπισθεν[1]
Πᾶνα τὸν αἰγιβάταν ὀρφανίσωμες ὕπνου.

VI

'Α δείλαιε τὺ Θύρσι, τί τὸ πλέον, εἰ καταταξεῖς
δάκρυσι διγλήνους ὦπας ὀδυρόμενος;
οἴχεται ἁ χίμαρος, τὸ καλὸν τέκος, οἴχετ' ἐς Ἄιδαν·
τραχὺς γὰρ χαλαῖς ἀμφεπίαξε λύκος.
αἱ δὲ κύνες κλαγγεῦντι· τί τὸ πλέον, ἁνίκα τήνας
ὄστιον οὐδὲ τέφρα λείπεται οἰχομένας;

VII

Νήπιον υἱὸν ἔλειπες, ἐν ἁλικίᾳ δὲ καὶ αὐτός,
Εὐρύμεδον, τύμβου τοῦδε θανὼν ἔτυχες.
σοὶ μὲν ἕδρα θείοισι μετ' ἀνδράσι· τὸν δὲ πολῖται
τιμασεῦντι, πατρὸς μνώμενοι ὡς ἀγαθῶ.

VIII

'Ηλθε καὶ ἐς Μίλητον ὁ τοῦ Παιήονος υἱός,
ἰητῆρι νόσων ἀνδρὶ συνεσσόμενος
Νικίᾳ, ὅς μιν ἐπ' ἦμαρ ἀεὶ θυέεσσιν ἱκνεῖται,
καὶ τόδ' ἀπ' εὐώδους γλύψατ' ἄγαλμα κέδρου,
'Ηετίωνι χάριν γλαφυρᾶς χερὸς ἄκρον ὑποστὰς
μισθόν· ὁ δ' εἰς ἔργον πᾶσαν ἀφῆκε τέχνην.

---

[1] mss also λασιαύχενος ἐγγύθεν ἄντρου

notes of his wax-bound breath ; and so standing beside the shaggy oak behind the cave, let's rob yon goat-foot Pan of his slumber.

VI.—[FOR A PICTURE]

WELL-A-DAY, you poor Thyrsis! what boots it if you cry your two eyes out of their sockets ? Your kid's gone, the pretty babe, dead and gone, all crushed in the talons of the great rough wolf. True, the dogs are baying him ; but to what end, when there's neither ash nor bone of the poor dead left ?

VII.—[FOR THE GRAVE OF A YOUNG FATHER]

HERE are you, Eurymedon, come in your prime to the grave ; but you left a little son behind you, and though your dwelling henceforth is with the great o' the earth, you may trust your countrymen to honour the child for the sake of the father.

VIII.—[FOR NICIAS' NEW STATUE OF ASCLEPIUS]

THE Great Healer's son is come to Miletus now, to live with his fellow-craftsman Nicias, who both maketh sacrifice before him every day, and hath now made carve this statue of fragrant cedar-wood ; he promised Eëtion a round price for the finished cunning of his hand, and Eëtion hath put forth all his art to the making of the work.

IX

Ξεῖνε, Συρακόσιός τοι ἀνὴρ τόδ' ἐφίεται "Ορθων·
    χειμερίας μεθύων μηδαμὰ νυκτὸς ἴοις.
καὶ γὰρ ἐγὼ τοιοῦτον ἔχον πότμον,[1] ἀντὶ δὲ πολλᾶς
    πατρίδος ὀθνείαν κεῖμαι ἀφεστάμενος.[2]

X

Ὑμῖν τοῦτο θεαὶ κεχαρισμένον ἐννέα πάσαις
    τὤγαλμα Ξενοκλῆς θῆκε τὸ μαρμάρινον,
μουσικός· οὐχ ἑτέρως τις ἐρεῖ. σοφίῃ δ' ἐπὶ τῇδε
    αἶνον ἔχων Μουσέων οὐκ ἐπιλανθάνεται.

XI

Εὐσθένεος τὸ μνῆμα, φυσιγνώμων ὃς ἄριστος,[3]
    δεινὸς ἀπ' ὀφθαλμοῦ καὶ τὸ νόημα μαθεῖν.
εὖ μιν ἔθαψαν ἑταῖροι ἐπὶ ξείνης ξένον ὄντα,
    χὠ ὑμνοθέτης αὐτῷ δαιμονίως φίλος ἦν.
πάντων ὧν ἐπέοικεν ἔχει τεθνεὼς ὁ σοφιστής·
    καίπερ ἄκικυς ἐὼν εἶχ' ἄρα κηδεμόνας.

---

[1] πότμον: mss also μόρον   [2] mss also ὀθνείων ἀφεστάμενος E, cf. ἀποστησάσθων C.I.A. 1. 32. 18: mss ἐφέσσ. and ἐρέσσ.   [3] ὃς ἄριστος E, for the more usual attracted form φυσιγνώμονος οὗ (or οἵου) ἀρίστου, cf. xiv. 59 : mss ὁ σοφιστὴς from below

IX.—[FOR THE GRAVE OF A LANDED GENTLEMAN]

THIS, good Stranger, is the behest of Orthon of Syracuse: Go you never abroad drunk of a stormy night; for that was my fate to do, and so it is I lie here, and there's weighed me out a foreign country in exchange for much native-land.

X.—[FOR AN ALTAR WITH A FRIEZE OF THE MUSES]

THIS carved work of marble, sweet Goddesses, is set up for the nine of you by the true musician—as all must name him—Xenocles, who having much credit of his art forgets not the Muses whose it is.

XI.—[FOR THE GRAVE OF A STROLLING PHYSIOGNOMIST]

HERE lies Strong-i'-th'-arm the great physiognomist, the man who could read the mind by the eye. And so, for all he is a stranger in a strange land, he has had friends to give him decent burial, and the dirge-writer has been kindness itself. The dead philosopher has all he could have wished; and thus, weakling wight though he be, there is after all somebody that cares for him.

"Weakling wight": an Epic word to point the play upon the name.

XII

Δημομέλης ὁ χορηγός, ὁ τὸν τρίποδ' ὦ Διόνυσε
καὶ σὲ τὸν ἥδιστον θεῶν μακάρων ἀναθείς,
μέτριος ἦν ἐν πᾶσι, χορῷ δ' ἐκτήσατο νίκην
ἀνδρῶν, καὶ τὸ καλὸν καὶ τὸ προσῆκον ὁρῶν.

XIII

Ἡ Κύπρις οὐ πάνδημος. ἱλάσκεο τὴν θεὸν εἰπὼν
οὐρανίην, ἁγνῆς ἄνθεμα Χρυσογόνης
οἴκῳ ἐν Ἀμφικλέους,[1] ᾧ καὶ τέκνα καὶ βίον εἶχε
ξυνόν. ἀεὶ δέ σφιν λῷον εἰς ἔτος ἦν
ἐκ σέθεν ἀρχομένοις ὦ πότνια· κηδόμενοι γὰρ
ἀθανάτων αὐτοὶ πλεῖον ἔχουσι βροτοί.

XIV

Ἀστοῖς καὶ ξείνοισιν ἴσον νέμει ἥδε τράπεζα·
θεὶς ἀνελοῦ ψήφου πρὸς λόγον ἑλκομένης.[2]
ἄλλος τις πρόφασιν λεγέτω· τὰ δ' ὀθνεῖα Κάϊκος
χρήματα καὶ νυκτὸς βουλομένοις ἀριθμεῖ.

[1] Ἀμφικλέους : a Coan name   [2] ἑλκομένης, cf. *Hibeh Papp.* 1. p. 65, Theophr. *Char.* 24 : mss also ἀρχομένης

XII.—[FOR A PRIZE TRIPOD]

CHOIR-MASTER Demomeles, who set up this tripod and this effigy, Dionysus, of the sweetest God in heaven, had always been a decent fellow, and he won the victory with his men's-chorus because he knew beauty and seemliness when he saw them.

XIII.—[FOR A COAN LADY'S NEW STATUE OF APHRODITE]

THIS is not the People's Cyprian, but pray when you propitiate this Goddess do so by the name of Heavenly; for this is the offering of a chaste woman, to wit of Chrysogonè, in the house of Amphicles, whose children and whose life she shared; so that beginning, Great Lady, with worship of thee, they ever increased their happiness with the years. For any that have a care for the Immortals are the better off for it themselves.

XIV.—[FOR THE TABLE OF A BARBARIAN MONEY-CHANGER]

THIS table makes no distinction of native and foreigner. You pay in and you receive out in strict accordance with the lie of the counters. If you want shifts and shuffles go elsewhere. Caïcus pays out deposits even after dark.

XV

Γνώσομαι, εἴ τι νέμεις ἀγαθοῖς πλέον, ἢ καὶ ὁ δειλὸς
  ἐκ σέθεν ὡσαύτως ἶσον, ὁδοιπόρ᾽, ἔχει.
‘χαιρέτω οὗτος ὁ τύμβος’ ἐρεῖς ‘ἐπεὶ Εὐρυμέ-
    δοντος
  κεῖται τῆς ἱερῆς κοῦφος ὑπὲρ κεφαλῆς.’

XVI

Ἡ παῖς ᾤχετ᾽ ἄωρος ἐν ἑβδόμῳ ἥδ᾽ ἐνιαυτῷ
  εἰς Ἀΐδην πολλῆς ἡλικίης προτέρη,
δειλαίη, ποθέουσα τὸν εἰκοσάμηνον ἀδελφόν,
  νήπιον ἀστόργου γευσάμενον θανάτου.
αἰαῖ ἐλεινὰ παθοῦσα Περιστέρη, ὡς ἐν ἑτοίμῳ
  ἀνθρώποις δαίμων θῆκε τὰ λυγρότατα.

XVII

Θᾶσαι τὸν ἀνδριάντα τοῦτον ὦ ξένε
  σπουδᾷ, καὶ λέγ᾽ ἐπὰν ἐς οἶκον ἔνθῃς·
‘Ἀνακρέοντος εἰκόν᾽ εἶδον ἐν Τέῳ
  τῶν πρόσθ᾽ εἴ τι περισσὸν ᾠδοποιῶν’
προσθεὶς δὲ χὤτι ‘τοῖς νέοισιν ἄδετο,’
  ἐρεῖς ἀτρεκέως ὅλον τὸν ἄνδρα.

XVIII

Ἅ τε φωνὰ Δώριος χὠνὴρ ὁ τὰν κωμῳδίαν
  εὑρὼν Ἐπίχαρμος.
ὦ Βάκχε χάλκεόν νιν ἀντ᾽ ἀλαθινοῦ
  τὶν ὧδ᾽ ἀνέθηκαν,
τοὶ Συρακόσσαις ἐνίδρυνται πελωρίστᾳ πόλει,
  οἷ᾽ ἄνδρα πολίταν,[1]

[1] Gow: mss ἀνδρὶ πολίτᾳ (πολῖται)

374

XV.—[FOR THE GRAVE OF A BRAVE MAN]

I sHALL know, master Wayfarer, whether you
prefer the valiant or esteem him even as the craven;
for you will say: " Blest be this tomb for lying so
light above the sacred head of Eurymedon."

XVI.—[FOR THE GRAVE OF TWO LITTLE CHILDREN]

THIS little maid was taken untimely, seven years
old and her life before her, and 'twas for grief, the
poor child, that her brother of twenty months should
have tasted, pretty babe, the unkindness of Death ;
O Peristerè, the pity of it ! how near to man and
ready hath God set what is woefullest !

XVII.—[FOR A STATUE OF ANACREON AT TEOS]

Look well upon this statue, good Stranger, and·
when you return home say " I saw at Teos a likeness
of Anacreon, the very greatest of the old makers of
songs "; and you will describe him to the letter if
you say also " He delighted in the young."

XVIII.—[FOR A STATUE OF EPICHARMUS IN THE THEATRE AT SYRACUSE]

THE speech is the Dorian, and the theme the
inventor of comedy, Epicharmus. They that have
their habitation in the most mighty city of Syracuse
have set him up here, as became fellow-townsmen,
unto thee, good Bacchus, in bronze in the stead of

375

σωροῦ τὸν εἶκε ῥημάτων μεμναμένοι[1]
  τελεῖν ἐπίχειρα.
πολλὰ γὰρ ποττὰν ζόαν τοῖς παισὶν εἶπε χρήσιμα·
  μεγάλα χάρις αὐτῷ.

XIX

Ὁ μουσοποιὸς ἐνθάδ᾽ Ἱππῶναξ κεῖται.
κεἰ μὲν πονηρός, μὴ ποτέρχευ τῷ τύμβῳ·
εἰ δ᾽ ἐσσὶ κρήγυός τε καὶ παρὰ χρηστῶν,
θαρσέων καθίζευ, κἢν θέλῃς ἀπόβριξον.

XX

Ὁ μικκὸς τόδ᾽ ἔτευξε τᾷ Θραΐσσᾳ
Μήδειος τὸ μνᾶμ᾽ ἐπὶ τᾷ ὁδῷ κἠπέγραψε Κλείτας.
ἔχει τὰν χάριν ἁ γυνὰ ἀντὶ τήνων,[2]
ὧν τὸν κοῦρον ἔθρεψε· τί μάν; ὅτι χρησίμα καλεῖται.

XXI

Ἀρχίλοχον καὶ στᾶθι καὶ εἴσιδε τὸν πάλαι ποιητὰν
  τὸν τῶν ἰάμβων, οὗ τὸ μυρίον κλέος
  διῆλθε κἠπὶ νύκτα καὶ ποτ᾽ ἀῶ.
ἠρά νιν αἱ Μοῖσαι καὶ ὁ Δάλιος ἠγάπευν Ἀπόλλων,
  ὡς ἐμμελής τ᾽ ἐγένετο κἠπιδέξιος
  ἔπεά τε ποιεῖν πρὸς λύραν τ᾽ ἀείδειν.

---

[1] thus E, εἶκε from ἵζω, cf. Hom. εἶσα: mss σωρὸν (or σ.
γὰρ) εἶχε ῥημάτων (or χρημάτων) μεμναμένους   [2] for ἔχει mss
have ἑξεῖ

the flesh; and thus have remembered to pay him his wages for the great heap of words he hath builded. For many are the things he hath told their children profitable unto life. He hath their hearty thanks.

XIX.—[A NEW INSCRIPTION FOR THE GRAVE OF HIPPONAX]

HERE lies the bard Hipponax. If you are a rascal, go not nigh his tomb; but if you are a true man of good stock, sit you down and welcome, and if you choose to drop off to sleep you shall.

XX.—[AN INSCRIPTION FOR THE GRAVE OF A NURSE]

THIS memorial the little Medeius hath builded by the wayside to his Thracian nurse, and written her name upon it, "Cleita." She hath her reward for the child's good upbringing, and what is it? to be called "a good servant" evermore.

XXI.—[FOR A STATUE OF ARCHILOCHUS]

STAND and look at Archilochus, the old maker of iambic verse, whose infinite renown hath spread both to utmost east and furthest west. Sure the Muses and Delian Apollo liked him well, such taste and skill had he to bring both to the framing of the words and to the setting of them to the lyre.

XXII

Τὸν τῶ Ζανὸς ὅδ᾽ ὑμιν υἱὸν ὠνὴρ
τὸν λεοντομάχαν, τὸν ὀξύχειρα,
πρᾶτος τῶν ἐπάνωθε μωσοποιῶν
Πείσανδρος συνέγραψεν οὐκ Καμίρω,
χὥσσους ἐξεπόνασεν εἶπ᾽ ἀέθλους.
τοῦτον δ᾽ αὐτὸν ὁ δᾶμος, ὡς σάφ᾽ εἰδῆς,
ἔστασ᾽ ἐνθάδε χάλκεον ποήσας
πολλοῖς μησὶν ὄπισθε κἠνιαυτοῖς.

XXIII

Αὐδήσει τὸ γράμμα, τί σᾶμά τε καὶ τίς ὑπ᾽ αὐτῷ·
Γλαύκης εἰμὶ τάφος τῆς ὀνομαζομένης.

XXIV

Ἀρχαῖα τὠπόλλωνι τἀναθήματα
ὑπῆρχεν· ἡ βάσις δὲ τοῦ μὲν εἴκοσι,
τοῦ[1] δ᾽ ἑπτά, τοῦ δὲ πέντε, τοῦ δὲ δώδεκα,
τοῦ δὲ διηκοσίοισι νεωτέρη ἤδ᾽ ἐνιαυτοῖς·
τοσσόσδε γὰρ τὶν[2] ἐξέβη μετρούμενος.

---

[1] here and below τοῦ Wil: mss τοῖς   [2] τὶν E, supply
ἀριθμὸς : mss νιν

XXII.—[FOR A STATUE OF PEISANDER AT CAMIRUS]

THIS is Peisander of Camirus, the bard of old time who first wrote you of the lion-fighting quick-o'-th'-hand son of Zeus and told of all the labours he wrought. That you may know this for certain, the people have made his likeness in bronze and set it here after many months and many years.

XXIII.—[FOR THE GRAVE OF ONE GLAUCÈ]

THE writing will say what the tomb is and who lies beneath it : "I am the grave of one that was called Glaucè."

XXIV.—[FOR A NEW BASE TO SOME OLD OFFERINGS]

THESE offerings Apollo had possessed before ; but the base you see below them is younger, than this by twenty years and that by seven, this by five and that by twelve, and this again by two hundred. For when you reckon them that is what it comes to,

ΘΕΟΚΡΙΤΟΥ ΑΠΟΣΠΑΣΜΑΤΑ

I

Eustath. ad *Iliad.* 5. 905, p. 620, 29 Ἀδελφὴ δέ
ἐστιν Ἄρεως ἡ Ἥβη, ὡς καὶ Θεόκριτος μυθολογεῖ.

II

Etym. Magn., p. 290, 53 δυσὶν ἀντιφέρεσθαι,
ὡς παρὰ Θεοκρίτῳ.

III

Athen. 7, 284 ᴀ Θεόκριτος δ' ὁ Συρακόσιος ἐν
τῇ ἐπιγραφομένῃ Βερενίκῃ τὸν λευκὸν ἐπονομα-
ζόμενον ἰχθὺν ἱερὸν καλεῖ διὰ τούτων·

. . . καί τις ἀνὴρ αἰτεῖται ἐπαγροσύνην τε καὶ
    ὄλβον,
ἐξ ἁλὸς ᾧ ζωή, τὰ δὲ δίκτυα κείνῳ ἄροτρα,
σφάζων ἀκρόνυχος ταύτῃ θεῷ ἱερὸν ἰχθύν,
ὃν λεῦκον καλέουσιν, ὁ γάρ θ' ἱερώτατος ἄλλων,
καί κε λίνα στήσαιτο καὶ ἐξερύσαιτο θαλάσσης
ἔμπλεα . . .

THE FRAGMENTS

THREE *fragments of Theocritus have been preserved in quotations.*

I

Eustathius commenting upon Iliad 5. 905 *says :—*

Hebe is the sister of Ares, as Theocritus tells us.

II

In the Etymologicum Magnum *we read :—*

To fight against two, as in Theocritus.

III

The third passage is quoted by Athenaeus (7. 284A) *from a poem in honour of Berenicè, the queen either of Ptolemy I or of Ptolemy III ; it is also referred to by Eustathius upon* Iliad 16. 407 (1067. 43) :—

. . . And if a man whose living is of the deep, a man whose ploughshares are his nets, prayeth for luck and lucre with an evening sacrifice unto this Goddess of one of the noble fishes which being noblest of all they call Leucus, then when he shall set his trammels he shall draw them from out the sea full to the brim . . .

II

THE POEMS AND FRAGMENTS
OF BION

I.—THE LAMENT FOR ADONIS

LIKE *all the so-called songs in this book, this poem is lyric only in spirit. It is not one of the actual songs sung at the Adonis-festival, but, like the song in Theocritus XV, a conventional book-representation of them written for recitation. The suggestion here and there of a refrain is intended primarily to aid the illusion, but also serves the purpose sometimes of paragraphing the poem. The poem belongs to the second part of the festival; it is the dirge proper As in XV the wedding-song refers to the coming dirge, so here the dirge refers to the past wedding-song. The* Lament for Adonis *is generally believed to be the work of Bion.*

ΒΙΩΝΟΣ

I.—ΑΔΩΝΙΔΟΣ ΕΠΙΤΑΦΙΟΣ

Αἰάζω τὸν Ἄδωνιν· ‘ἀπώλετο καλὸς Ἄδωνις·’
‘ὤλετο καλὸς Ἄδωνις’ ἐπαιάζουσιν Ἔρωτες.

μηκέτι πορφυρέοις ἐνὶ φάρεσι Κύπρι κάθευδε·
ἔγρεο δειλαία, κυανόστολα[1] καὶ πλατάγησον
στήθεα καὶ λέγε πᾶσιν ‘ἀπώλετο καλὸς Ἄδωνις.’
αἰάζω τὸν Ἄδωνιν· ἐπαιάζουσιν Ἔρωτες.

κεῖται καλὸς Ἄδωνις ἐν ὤρεσι μηρὸν ὀδόντι,
λευκῷ λευκὸν ὀδόντι τυπείς, καὶ Κύπριν ἀνιῇ
λεπτὸν ἀποψύχων· τὸ δέ οἱ μέλαν εἴβεται αἷμα
χιονέας κατὰ σαρκός, ὑπ’ ὀφρύσι δ’ ὄμματα ναρκῇ,
καὶ τὸ ῥόδον φεύγει τῶ χείλεος· ἀμφὶ δὲ τήνῳ
θνάσκει καὶ τὸ φίλημα, τὸ μήποτε Κύπρις ἀνοίσει.
Κύπριδι μὲν τὸ φίλημα καὶ οὐ ζώοντος ἀρέσκει,
ἀλλ’ οὐκ οἶδεν Ἄδωνις, ὅ νιν θνάσκοντ’ ἐφίλησεν.
αἰάζω τὸν Ἄδωνιν· ἐπαιάζουσιν Ἔρωτες.

ἄγριον ἄγριον ἕλκος ἔχει κατὰ μηρὸν Ἄδωνις·
μεῖζον δ’ ἀ Κυθέρεια φέρει ποτικάρδιον ἕλκος.

---

[1] κυανόστολα Wil : mss κυανοστόλε

THE POEMS AND FRAGMENTS
OF BION

I.—THE LAMENT FOR ADONIS

I cry woe for Adonis and say *The beauteous Adonis is dead;* and the Loves cry me woe again and say *The beauteous Adonis is dead.*

Sleep no more, Cypris, beneath thy purple coverlet, but awake to thy misery; put on the sable robe and fall to beating thy breast, and tell it to the world, *The beauteous Adonis is dead.*

Woe I cry for Adonis and the Loves cry woe again.

The beauteous Adonis lieth low in the hills, his thigh pierced with the tusk, the white with the white, and Cypris is sore vexed at the gentle passing of his breath; for the red blood drips down his snow-white flesh, and the eyes beneath his brow wax dim; the rose departs from his lip, and the kiss that Cypris shall never have so again, that kiss dies upon it and is gone. Cypris is fain enough now of the kiss of the dead; but Adonis, he knows not that she hath kissed him.

Woe I cry for Adonis and the Loves cry woe again.

Cruel, O cruel the wound in the thigh of him, but greater the wound in the heart of her. Loud did

τῆνον[1] μὲν περὶ παῖδα φίλοι κύνες ὠδύραντο
καὶ Νύμφαι κλαίουσιν ὀρειάδες· ἁ δ᾽ Ἀφροδίτα
λυσαμένα πλοκαμῖδας ἀνὰ δρυμὼς ἀλάληται
πενθαλέα νήπλεκτος ἀσάνδαλος· αἱ δὲ βάτοι νιν
ἐρχομέναν κείροντι καὶ ἱερὸν αἷμα δρέπονται·
ὀξὺ δὲ κωκύουσα δι᾽ ἄγκεα μακρὰ φορεῖται
Ἀσσύριον βοόωσα πόσιν καὶ παῖδα καλεῦσα.
ἀμφὶ δέ νιν μέλαν αἷμα παρ᾽ ὀμφαλὸν ἀωρεῖτο,
στήθεα δ᾽ ἐκ μηρῶν φοινίσσετο, τοὶ δ᾽[2] ὑπὸ μαζοὶ
χιόνεοι τὸ πάροιθεν Ἀδώνιδι πορφύροντο.
'αἰαῖ τὰν Κυθέρειαν' ἐπαιάζουσιν Ἔρωτες.
    ὤλεσε τὸν καλὸν ἄνδρα, συνώλεσεν ἱερὸν εἶδος.
Κύπριδι μὲν καλὸν εἶδος, ὅτε ζώεσκεν Ἄδωνις·
κάτθανε δ᾽ ἁ μορφὰ σὺν Ἀδώνιδι. 'τὰν Κύπριν
    αἰαῖ'
ὤρεα πάντα λέγοντι, καὶ αἱ δρύες 'αἱ τὸν Ἄδωνιν.'
καὶ ποταμοὶ κλαίοντι τὰ πένθεα τᾶς Ἀφροδίτας,
καὶ παγαὶ τὸν Ἄδωνιν ἐν ὤρεσι δακρύοντι,
ἄνθεα δ᾽ ἐξ ὀδύνας ἐρυθαίνεται· ἁ δὲ Κυθήρα
πάντας ἀνὰ κναμὼς, ἀνὰ πᾶν νάπος οἰκτρὸν ἀείδει
'αἰαῖ τὰν Κυθέρειαν, ἀπώλετο καλὸς Ἄδωνις.'
Ἀχὼ δ᾽ ἀντεβόασεν 'ἀπώλετο καλὸς Ἄδωνις.'
Κύπριδος αἰνὸν ἔρωτα τίς οὐκ ἔκλαυσεν ἂν αἰαῖ;
    ὡς ἴδεν, ὡς ἐνόησεν Ἀδώνιδος ἄσχετον ἕλκος,
ὡς ἴδε φοίνιον αἷμα μαραινομένῳ περὶ μηρῷ,
πάχεας ἀμπετάσασα κινύρετο· 'μεῖνον Ἄδωνι,
δύσποτμε μεῖνον Ἄδωνι, πανύστατον ὥς σε κιχείω,
ὥς σε περιπτύξω καὶ χείλεα χείλεσι μίξω.
ἔγρεο τυτθὸν Ἄδωνι, τὸ δ᾽ αὖ πύματόν με φίλησον,
τοσσοῦτόν με φίλησον, ὅσον ζώῃ τὸ φίλημα,

wail his familiar hounds, and loud now weep the
Nymphs of the hill; and Aphrodite, she unbraids
her tresses and goes wandering distraught, unkempt,
unslippered in the wild wood, and for all the briers
may tear and rend her and cull her hallowed blood,
she flies through the long glades shrieking amain,
crying upon her Assyrian lord, calling upon the lad
of her love. Meantime the red blood floated in a
pool about his navel, his breast took on the purple
that came of his thighs, and the paps thereof that
had been as the snow waxed now incarnadine.

The Loves cry woe again saying "Woe for Cytherea."
Lost is her lovely lord, and with him lost her
hallowed beauty. When Adonis yet lived Cypris
was beautiful to see to, but when Adonis died her
loveliness died also. With all the hills 'tis *Woe for
Cypris* and with the vales 'tis *Woe for Adonis;* the
rivers weep the sorrows of Aphrodite, the wells of
the mountains shed tears for Adonis; the flowerets
flush red for grief, and Cythera's isle over every
foothill and every glen of it sings pitifully *Woe for
Cytherea, the beauteous Adonis is dead,* and Echo ever
cries her back again, *The beauteous Adonis is dead.*
Who would not have wept his woe over the dire tale
of Cypris' love?

She saw, she marked his irresistible wound, she
saw his thigh fading in a welter of blood, she lift her
hands and put up the voice of lamentation saying
"Stay, Adonis mine, stay, hapless Adonis, till I come
at thee for the last time, till I clip thee about and
mingle lip with lip. Awake Adonis, awake for a
little while, and give me one latest kiss; kiss me all
so long as ever the kiss be alive, till thou give up

389

ἄχρις ἀποψύχῃς ἐς ἐμὸν στόμα κεἰς ἐμὸν ἧπαρ
πνεῦμα τεὸν ῥεύσῃ, τὸ δέ σευ γλυκὺ φίλτρον
  ἀμέλξω,
ἐκ δὲ πίω τὸν ἔρωτα, φίλημα δὲ τοῦτο φυλάξω
ὡς¹ αὐτὸν τὸν Ἄδωνιν, ἐπεὶ σύ με δύσμορε φεύγεις,
φεύγεις μακρὸν Ἄδωνι, καὶ ἔρχεαι εἰς Ἀχέροντα
πὰρ στυγνὸν βασιλῆα καὶ ἄγριον, ἁ δὲ τάλαινα
ζώω καὶ θεὸς ἐμμὶ καὶ οὐ δύναμαί σε διώκειν.
λάμβανε Περσεφόνα τὸν ἐμὸν πόσιν· ἐσσὶ γὰρ αὐτὰ
πολλὸν ἐμεῦ κρέσσων, τὸ δὲ πᾶν καλὸν ἐς σὲ
  καταρρεῖ·²
ἐμμὶ δ' ἐγὼ πανάποτμος, ἔχω δ' ἀκόρεστον ἀνίαν,
καὶ κλαίω τὸν Ἄδωνιν, ὅ μοι θάνε, καί σε φοβεῦμαι.
θνάσκεις ὦ τριπόθητε, πόθος δέ μοι ὡς ὄναρ ἔπτα,
χήρα δ' ἁ Κυθέρεια, κενοὶ δ' ἀνὰ δώματ' Ἔρωτες.
σοὶ δ' ἅμα κεστὸς ὄλωλε. τί γὰρ τολμηρὲ κυνάγεις;
καλὸς ἐὼν τοσσοῦτον ἐμήναο θηρὶ παλαίειν;'
ὧδ' ὀλοφύρατο Κύπρις· ἐπαιάζουσιν Ἔρωτες
'αἰαῖ τὰν Κυθέρειαν, ἀπώλετο καλὸς Ἄδωνις.'

  δάκρυον ἁ Παφία τόσσον χέει, ὅσσον Ἄδωνις
αἷμα χέει· τὰ δὲ πάντα ποτὶ χθονὶ γίνεται ἄνθη.
αἷμα ῥόδον τίκτει, τὰ δὲ δάκρυα τὰν ἀνεμώναν.
αἰάζω τὸν Ἄδωνιν, ἀπώλετο καλὸς Ἄδωνις.

  μηκέτ' ἐνὶ δρυμοῖσι τὸν ἀνέρα μύρεο Κύπρι.
οὐκ ἀγαθὰ στιβάς ἐστιν Ἀδώνιδι φυλλὰς ἐρήμα·
λέκτρον ἔχοι Κυθέρεια τὸ σὸν καὶ³ νεκρὸς Ἄδωνις.

---

¹ ὡς Mus: mss ὥς σ'   ² καταρρεῖ Stephanus: mss καὶ
ἄρρει   ³ ἔχοι Valckenaer: mss ἔχει   καὶ E: mss νῦν δὲ
or τὸ δὲ due to taking καὶ as "and"

390

thy breath into my mouth and thy spirit pass into
my heart, till I have drawn the sweet milk of thy
love-potion and I have drunk up all thy love; and
that kiss of Adonis I will keep as it were he that
gave it, now that thou fliest me, poor miserable, fliest
me far and long, Adonis, and goest where is Acheron
and the cruel sullen king, while I alas! live and am
a God and may not go after thee.   O Persephone,
take thou my husband, take him if thou wilt; for
thou art far stronger than I, and gettest to thy share
all that is beautiful; but as for me, 'tis all ill and
for ever, 'tis pain and grief without cloy, and I
weep that my Adonis is dead and I fear me what
thou wilt do.   O dearest and sweetest and best,
thou diest, and my dear love is sped like a dream;
widowed now is Cytherea, the Loves are left idle
in her bower, and the girdle of the Love-Lady is
lost along with her beloved.   O rash and overbold [1]
why didst go a-hunting?   Wast thou so wooed to
pit thee against a wild beast and thou so fair?"
This was the wail of Cypris, and now the Loves cry
her woe again, saying *Woe for Cytherea, the beauteous
Adonis is dead.*

The Paphian weeps and Adonis bleeds, drop for
drop, and the blood and tears become flowers upon
the ground.   Of the blood comes the rose, and of
the tears the windflower.

I cry woe for Adonis, the beauteous Adonis is dead.

Mourn thy husband no more in the woods, sweet
Cypris; the lonely leaves make no good lying for
such as he: rather let Adonis have thy couch as in
life so in death; for being dead, Cytherea, he is yet

"wood": mad.

καὶ νέκυς ὢν καλός ἐστι, καλὸς νέκυς, οἷα καθεύδων.
κάτθεό νιν μαλακοῖς ἐνὶ φάρεσιν οἷς[1] ἐνίαυεν,
ᾧ μετὰ τεῦς[2] ἀνὰ νύκτα τὸν ἱερὸν ὕπνον ἐμόχθει
παγχρυσέῳ κλιντῆρι· ποθεῖ καὶ στυμνὸν[3] Ἄδωνιν.
βάλλε δέ νιν στεφάνοισι καὶ ἄνθεσι· πάντα σὺν
αὐτῷ,
ὡς τῆνος τέθνακε καὶ ἄνθεα πάντα θανόντων.[4]
ῥαῖνε δέ νιν Συρίοισιν[5] ἀλείφασι, ῥαῖνε μύροισιν·
ὀλλύσθω μύρα πάντα· τὸ σὸν μύρον ὤλετ' Ἄδωνις.

κέκλιται ἁβρὸς Ἄδωνις ἐν εἵμασι πορφυρέοισιν·
ἀμφὶ δέ νιν κλαίοντες ἀναστενάχουσιν Ἔρωτες   8(
κειράμενοι χαίτας ἐπ' Ἀδώνιδι· χὠ μὲν ὀϊστώς,
ὃς δ' ἐπὶ τόξον ἔβαλλεν, ὃ[6] δὲ πτερόν, ὃς δὲ φαρέ-
τραν·
χὠ μὲν ἔλυσε πέδιλον Ἀδώνιδος, οἳ δὲ λέβητι
χρυσείῳ φορέουσιν ὕδωρ, ὃ δὲ μηρία λούει,
ὃς δ' ὄπιθεν πτερύγεσσιν ἀναψύχει τὸν Ἄδωνιν.
'αἰαῖ[7] τὰν Κυθέρειαν' ἐπαιάζουσιν Ἔρωτες.

ἔσβεσε λαμπάδα πᾶσαν ἐπὶ φλιαῖς Ὑμέναιος,
καὶ στέφος ἐξεπέτασσε γαμήλιον· οὐκέτι δ' Ὑμήν,
'Ὑμὴν οὐκέτ' ἀείδει ἑὸν μέλος, ἀλλ' ἐπαείδει[8]
'αἰαῖ' καὶ 'τὸν Ἄδωνιν' ἔτι πλέον ἢ Ὑμέναιον.   9(
αἱ Χάριτες κλαίοντι τὸν υἱέα τῶ Κινύραο,
'ὤλετο καλὸς Ἄδωνις' ἐν ἀλλάλαισι λέγοισαι.
'αἰαῖ' δ' ὀξὺ λέγοντι πολὺ πλέον ἢ Παιῶνα.[9]
χαὶ[10] Μοῖραι τὸν Ἄδωνιν ἀνακλείουσιν 'Ἄδωνιν,'

---

[1] οἷς Steph.: mss οἱ   [2] ᾧ E: mss τοῖς   τεῦς Wil: mss σεῦ
[3] E, see *C. R.* 1913. 76, Alex. 197 K: mss στυγνόν   [4] πάντα
θανόντων E, cf. 78: mss πάντ' ἐμαράνθη emended from *Epit.
Bion.* 69 after πάντα σὺν αὐτῷ had come in from above

392

lovely, lovely in death as he were asleep. Lay him down in the soft coverlets wherein he used to slumber, upon that couch of solid gold whereon he used to pass the nights in sacred sleep with thee ; for the very couch longs for Adonis, Adonis all dishevelled. Fling garlands also and flowers upon him ; now that he is dead let them die too, let every flower die. Pour out upon him unguents of Syria, perfumes of Syria ; perish now all perfumes, for he that was thy perfume is perished and gone.

There he lies, the delicate Adonis, in purple wrappings, and the weeping Loves lift up their voices in lamentation ; they have shorn their locks for Adonis' sake. This flung upon him arrows, that a bow, this a feather, that a quiver. One hath done off Adonis' shoe, others fetch water in a golden basin, another washes the thighs of him, and again another stands behind and fans him with his wings.

The Loves cry woe again saying " Woe for Cytherea."

The Wedding-God hath put out every torch before the door, and scattered the bridal garland upon the ground ; the burden of his song is no more " Ho for the Wedding ;" there's more of "Woe" and "Adonis" to it than ever there was of the wedding-cry. The Graces weep the son of Cinyras, saying one to another, *The beauteous Adonis is dead*, and when they cry woe 'tis a shriller cry than ever the cry of thanksgiving. Nay, even the Fates weep and wail for Adonis, calling upon his name ; and more-

⁵ Συρίοισιν Ruhnken : mss μύροισι   ⁶ ἔβαλλεν ὃ Wil : mss ἔβαιν' ὃς   ⁷ αἰαῖ Lennep : mss αὐτὰν   ⁸ thus Ahr : mss ἀειδονέος μέλος ἄλλεται αἲ αἲ   ⁹ αἰαῖ Pierson : mss αὐταὶ
    Παιῶνα Ahr : mss τὺ Διῶνα   ¹⁰ χαὶ Meineke : mss καὶ

καί νιν ἐπαείδουσιν· ὁ δέ σφισιν οὐχ ὑπακούει·
οὐ μὰν οὐκ ἐθέλει, Κώρα δέ νιν οὐκ ἀπολύει.

λῆγε γόων Κυθέρεια τὸ σάμερον, ἴσχεο κομμῶν·[1]
δεῖ σε πάλιν κλαῦσαι, πάλιν εἰς ἔτος ἄλλο
    δακρῦσαι.

---

[1] κομμῶν Barth : mss κώμων

over they sing a spell upon him to bring him back again, but he payeth no heed to it; yet 'tis not from lack of the will, but rather that the Maiden will not let him go.

Give over thy wailing for to-day, Cytherea, and beat not now thy breast any more; thou needs wilt wail again and weep again, come another year.

II.—MYRSON AND LYCIDAS

THIS *fragmentary shepherd-mime is probably to be ascribed to an imitator of Bion. At Myrson's request, Lycidas sings him the tale of Achilles at Scyros.*

II.—[ΜΥΡΣΩΝ ΚΑΙ ΛΥΚΙΔΑΣ]

ΜΥΡΣΩΝ

Λῆς νύ τί μοι Λυκίδα Σικελὸν μέλος ἁδὺ λιγαίνειν,
ἱμερόεν γλυκύθυμον ἐρωτικόν, οἷον ὁ Κύκλωψ
ἄεισεν Πολύφαμος ἐπᾳονίᾳ[1] Γαλατείᾳ;

ΛΥΚΙΔΑΣ

κἠμοὶ[2] συρίσδεν, Μύρσων, φίλον· ἀλλὰ τί μέλψω;

ΜΥΡΣΩΝ

Σκύριον ὦ Λυκίδα ζαλώμενον[3] ἁδὺν ἔρωτα,
λάθρια Πηλείδαο φιλάματα, λάθριον εὐνάν,
πῶς παῖς ἔσσατο φᾶρος, ὅπως δ᾽ ἐψεύσατο[4] μορφὰν
κἠν κώραισιν ὅπως[5] Λυκομηδίσιν ἀπαλέγοισα
ἠείδη κατὰ[6] παστὸν Ἀχιλλέα Δηϊδάμεια.

ΛΥΚΙΔΑΣ

Ἅρπασε τὰν Ἑλέναν πόθ᾽ ὁ βουκόλος, ἆγε δ᾽ ἐς
Ἴδαν,
Οἰνώνᾳ κακὸν ἄλγος. ἐχώσατο δ᾽ ἁ Λακεδαίμων,

---

[1] ἐπᾳονίᾳ E, cf. Theocr. 25. 249 : mss ἐπ᾽ ἠϊόνι   [2] κἠμοὶ
Brunck : mss κἤν μοι   [3] ζαλώμενον Wil : mss ζαλῶν μένος
[4] ἐψεύσατο Canter, cf. Nonn. Dion. 44. 289 : mss ἐγεύσατο
[5] thus Wil : mss κἤν ὅπως ἐν κώραις   [6] ἠείδη (from οἶδα) κατὰ
E, cf. Moero ap. Athen. 491 B : mss ἀηδήνεα τὰ

II.—MYRSON AND LYCIDAS

MYRSON

THEN prithee, Lycidas, wilt thou chant me some pretty lay of Sicily, some delightful sweetheart song of love such as the Cyclops sang to Galatea of the sea-beaches ?

LYCIDAS

I myself should like to make some music, Myrson; so what shall it be ?

MYRSON

The sweet and enviable love-tale of Scyros, Lycidas, the stolen kisses of the child of Peleus and the stolen espousal of the same, how a lad donned women's weeds and played the knave with his outward seeming, and how in the women's chamber the reckless Deïdameia found out Achilles among the daughters of Lycomedes.

LYCIDAS (*sings*)

Once on a day, and a woeful day for the wife that loved him well,
The neatherd stole fair Helen and bare her to Ida fell.

"The wife that loved him well": Oenōnè, wife of Paris.

πάντα δὲ λαὸν ἄγειρεν Ἀχαϊκόν, οὐδέ τις Ἕλλην
οὔτε Μυκηναίων οὔτ' Ἤλιδος οὔτε Λακώνων,
μεῖνεν ἑὸν κατὰ δῶμα φυγὼν δύστανον Ἄρηα.[1]
λάνθανε δ' ἐν κώραις Λυκομηδίσι μοῦνος Ἀχιλλεύς,
εἴρια δ' ἀνθ' ὅπλων ἐδιδάσκετο, καὶ χερὶ λευκᾷ
παρθενικὸν κόπον[2] εἶχεν, ἐφαίνετο δ' ἠΰτε κώρα·
καὶ γὰρ ἴσον τήναις θηλύνετο, καὶ τόσον ἄνθος
χιονέαις πόρφυρε παρηΐσι, καὶ τὸ βάδισμα
παρθενικῆς ἐβάδιζε, κόμας δ' ἐπύκαζε καλύπτρᾳ.
θυμὸν δ' ἀνέρος[3] εἶχε, καὶ ἀνέρος εἶχεν ἔρωτα·
ἐξ ἀοῦς δ' ἐπὶ νύκτα παρίζετο[4] Δηϊδαμείᾳ,
καὶ ποτὲ μὲν τήνας ἐφίλει χέρα, πολλάκι δ' αὐτᾶς
στάμονα καλὸν ἄειρε, τὰ δαίδαλα δ' ἄτρι'[5] ἐπήνει·
ἤσθιε δ' οὐκ ἄλλα σὺν ὁμάλικι, πάντα δ' ἐποίει
σπεύδων κοινὸν ἐς ὕπνον. ἔλεξέ νυ καὶ λόγον αὐτᾷ·
'ἄλλαι[6] μὲν κνώσσουσι σὺν ἀλλάλαισιν ἀδελφαί,
αὐτὰρ ἐγὼ μώνα, μώνα[7] δὲ σὺ νύμφα καθεύδεις.
αἱ δύο παρθενικαὶ[8] συνομάλικες, αἱ δύο καλαί·
ἀλλὰ μόναι κατὰ[9] λέκτρα καθεύδομες· ἁ δὲ πονηρὰ
Νυσαία[10] δολία με κακῶς ἀπὸ σεῖο μερίσδει.
οὐ γὰρ ἐγὼ σέο . . . .'

[1] φυγὼν δύστανον Bentley: mss φέρων δισσὶ ἀνὰν or δισσὶν
ἀνὰν or δυσὶν ἁγνὸν Ἄρηα Scaliger: mss ἄρηα [2] κόπον Scal.:
mss κόπον or χορὸν [3] δ' ἀνέρος Lennep: mss δ' Ἄρεος
[4] παρίζετο Canter: mss μερίζ. [5] στάμονα Scal: mss στόμ'
ἀνὰ δαίδαλα δ' ἄτρι' Len: mss δ' ἀδέα δάκρυ' [6] ἄλλαι E:
mss ἄλλαι [7] μώνα μώνα Len: mss μώνα μίμνω [8] αἱ δύο π.

400

Sparta was wroth and roused to arms Achaea wide
    and far;
    Mycenae, Elis, Sparta-land—
    No Greek but scorned at home to stand
        For all the woes of war.
Yet one lay hid the maids amid, Achilles was he hight;
    Instead of arms he learnt to spin
    And with wan hand his rest to win,
    His cheeks were snow-white freakt with red,
    He wore a kerchief on his head,
    And woman-lightsome was his tread,
        All maiden to the sight.
Yet man was he in his heart, and man was he in
    his love;
    From dawn to dark he'ld sit him by
    A maid yclept Deïdamy,
    And oft would kiss her hand, and oft
    Would set her weaver's-beam aloft
        And praise the web she wove.
Come dinner-time, he'd go to board that only maid
    beside,
And do his best of deed and word to win her for his
    bride;
"The others share both board and bed," such wont
    his words to be,
"I sleep alone and you alone; though we be maidens
    free,
Maidens and fair maidens, we sleep on pallets two;
'Tis that cruel crafty Nysa that is parting me and
    you. . . ."

"with wan hand": the un-sunburnt hand of an indoor-
living person.

Salmasius: mss αἱ δ᾽ ὑπὸ π.   9 κατὰ Scal: mss καὶ
  10 Νυσαία Wil: mss Νύσσα or Νύσσα γὰρ

III–XVIII

THE *remaining poems and fragments are preserved in quotations made by Stobaeus, with the exception of the last, which is quoted by the grammarian Orion* (Anth. 5, 4).

III.—[ΚΛΕΟΔΑΜΟΣ ΚΑΙ ΜΥΡΣΩΝ]

ΚΛΕΟΔΑΜΟΣ

Εἴαρος ὦ Μύρσων ἢ χείματος ἢ φθινοπώρω
ἢ θέρεος τί τοι ἁδύ; τί δὲ πλέον εὔχεαι ἐλθεῖν;
ἢ θέρος, ἁνίκα πάντα τελείεται ὅσσα μογεῦμες;
ἢ γλυκερὸν φθινόπωρον, ὅτ᾽ ἀνδράσι λιμὸς ἐλαφρά;
ἢ καὶ χεῖμα δύσεργον; ἐπεὶ καὶ χείματι πολλοὶ
θαλπόμενοι θέλγονται[1] ἀεργείᾳ τε καὶ ὄκνῳ·
ἦ τοι καλὸν ἔαρ πλέον εὔαδεν; εἰπέ, τί τοι φρήν
αἱρεῖται; λαλέειν γὰρ ἐπέτραπεν ἁ σχολὰ ἄμμιν.

ΜΥΡΣΩΝ

κρίνειν οὐκ ἐπέοικε θεήια ἔργα βροτοῖσι·
πάντα γὰρ ἱερὰ ταῦτα καὶ ἁδέα· σεῦ δὲ ἕκατι
ἐξερέω Κλεόδαμε, τό μοι πέλεν ἅδιον ἄλλων.
οὐκ ἐθέλω θέρος ἦμεν, ἐπεὶ τόκα μ᾽ ἅλιος ὀπτῇ.
οὐκ ἐθέλω φθινόπωρον, ἐπεὶ νόσον ὥρια τίκτει.
οὖλον χεῖμα φέρειν νιφετὸν κρυμώς τε φοβεῦμαι.
εἶαρ ἐμοὶ τριπόθητον ὅλῳ λυκάβαντι παρείη,
ἁνίκα μήτε κρύος μήθ᾽ ἅλιος ἄμμε βαρύνει.
εἴαρι πάντα κύει, πάντ᾽ εἴαρος ἁδέα βλαστεῖ,
χἀ νὺξ ἀνθρώποισιν ἴσα καὶ ὁμοῖος ἀώς...

---

[1] θέλγονται Ursinus : mss θάλποντας

III.—[FROM A SHEPHERD-MIME]

CLEODAMUS

WHICH will you have is sweetest, Myrson, spring, winter, autumn, or summer? which are you fainest should come? Summer, when all our labours are fulfilled, or sweet autumn when our hunger is least and lightest, or the winter when no man can work—for winter also hath delights for many with her warm firesides and leisure hours—or doth the pretty spring-time please you best? Say, where is the choice of your heart? To be sure, we have time and to spare for talking.

MYRSON

'Tis unseemly for mortal men to judge of the works of Heaven, and all these four are sacred, and every one of them sweet. But since you ask me, Cleodamus, I will tell you which I hold to be sweeter than the rest. I will not have your summer, for then the sun burns me; I will not have your autumn, neither, for that time o' year breeds disease; and as for your winter, he is intolerable; I cannot away with frost and snow. For my part, give me all the year round the dear delightful spring, when cold doth not chill nor sun burn. In the spring the world's a-breeding, in the spring the world's all sweet buds, and our days are as long as our nights and our nights as our days. . . .

IV

Ἰξευτὰς ἔτι κῶρος ἐν ἄλσεϊ δενδράεντι
ὄρνεα θηρεύων τὸν ἀπότροπον εἶδεν Ἔρωτα
ἐσδόμενον πύξοιο ποτὶ κλάδον· ὡς δ' ἐνόησε,
χαίρων ὥνεκα δὴ μέγα φαίνετο τὤρνεον αὐτῷ,
τὼς καλάμως ἅμα πάντας ἐπ' ἀλλάλοισι συνάπτων
τᾷ καὶ τᾷ τὸν Ἔρωτα μετάλμενον ἀμφεδόκευε.
χὠ παῖς ἀσχαλάων, ὅκα¹ οἱ τέλος οὐδὲν ἀπάντη,
τὼς καλάμως ῥίψας ποτ' ἀροτρέα πρέσβυν ἵκανεν,
ὅς νιν τάνδε τέχναν ἐδιδάξατο, καὶ λέγεν αὐτῷ,
καί οἱ δεῖξεν Ἔρωτα καθήμενον. αὐτὰρ ὁ πρέσβυς
μειδιάων κίνησε κάρη καὶ ἀμείβετο παῖδα
'φείδεο τᾶς θήρας, μηδ' ἐς τόδ' ἔτ' ὄρνεον ἔρχευ.
φεῦγε μακράν. κακόν ἐστι τὸ θηρίον. ὄλβιος ἐσσῇ,
εἰσόκα μή νιν ἕλῃς· ἢν δ' ἀνέρος ἐς μέτρον ἔλθῃς,
οὗτος ὁ νῦν φεύγων καὶ ἀπάλμενος αὐτὸς ἀφ' αὑτῶ
ἐλθὼν ἐξαπίνας κεφαλὰν ἔπι σεῖο καθιξεῖ.'

V

Ἁ μεγάλα μοι Κύπρις ἔθ' ὑπνώοντι παρέστα,
νηπίαχον τὸν Ἔρωτα καλᾶς ἐκ χειρὸς ἄγοισα
ἐς χθόνα νευστάζοντα, τόσον δέ μοι ἔφρασε μῦθον·
'μέλπειν μοι φίλε βοῦτα λαβὼν τὸν Ἔρωτα
      δίδασκε.'
ὣς λέγε· χἁ μὲν ἀπῆνθεν, ἐγὼ δ' ὅσα βουκολίασδον,
νήπιος ὡς ἐθέλοντα μαθεῖν τὸν Ἔρωτα δίδασκον,
ὡς εὗρε πλαγίαυλον ὁ Πάν, ὡς αὐλὸν Ἀθάνα,
ὡς χέλυν Ἑρμάων, κίθαριν ὡς ἁδὺς Ἀπόλλων.

¹ ὅκα Porson : mss οὕνεχα

IV.—[LOVE AND THE FOWLER]

ONE day a fowler-lad was out after birds in a coppice, when he espied perching upon a box-tree bough the shy retiring Love. Rejoicing that he had found what seemed him so fine a bird, he fits all his lime-rods together and lies in wait for that hipping-hopping quarry. But soon finding that there was no end to it, he flew into a rage, cast down his rods, and sought the old ploughman who had taught him his trade; and both told him what had happened and showed him where young Love did sit. At that the old man smiled and wagged his wise head, and answered: "Withhold thy hand, my lad, and go not after this bird; flee him far; 'tis evil game. Thou shalt be happy so long as thou catch him not, but so sure as thou shalt come to the stature of a man, he that hoppeth and scapeth thee now will come suddenly of himself and light upon thy head."

V.—[LOVE'S SCHOOLING]

I DREAMED and lo! the great Cyprian stood before me. Her fair hand did lead, with head hanging, the little silly Love, and she said to me: "Pray you, sweet Shepherd, take and teach me this child to sing and play," and so was gone. So I fell to teaching master Love, fool that I was, as one willing to learn; and taught him all my lore of country-music, to wit how Pan did invent the cross-flute and Athena the flute, Hermes the lyre and sweet Apollo the harp.

ταῦτά νιν ἐξεδίδασκον· ὁ δ' οὐκ ἐμπάζετο μύθων,
ἀλλά μοι αὐτὸς ἄειδεν ἐρωτύλα, καί μ' ἐδίδασκε
θνατῶν ἀθανάτων τε πόθως καὶ ματέρος ἔργα.
κἠγὼν ἐκλαθόμαν μὲν ὅσων τὸν Ἔρωτ' ἐδίδασκον,
ὅσσα δ' Ἔρως μ' ἐδίδαξεν ἐρωτύλα πάντ' ἐδιδάχθην.

VI

Ταὶ Μοῖσαι τὸν Ἔρωτα τὸν ἄγριον οὐ φοβέονται
ἐκ θυμῶ δὲ φιλεῦντι καὶ ἐκ ποδὸς αὐτῷ ἕπονται.
κἠν μὲν ἄρα ψυχάν τις ἔχων ἀνέραστον ἀείδῃ,
τῆνον ὑπεκφεύγοντι καὶ οὐκ ἐθέλοντι διδάσκειν·
ἢν δὲ νόον τις [1] Ἔρωτι δονεύμενος ἁδὺ μελίσδῃ,
ἐς τῆνον μάλα πᾶσαι ἐπειγόμεναι προρέοντι.
μάρτυς ἐγών, ὅτι μῦθος ὅδ' ἔπλετο πᾶσιν ἀλαθής.
ἢν μὲν γὰρ βροτὸν ἄλλον ἢ ἀθανάτων τινὰ μέλπω,
βαμβαίνει μοι γλῶσσα καὶ ὡς πάρος οὐκέτ' ἀείδει·
ἢν δ' αὖτ' ἐς τὸν Ἔρωτα καὶ ἐς Λυκίδαν τι μελίσδω,
καὶ τόκα μοι χαίροισα διὰ στόματος ῥέει αὐδά.

VII

... Οὐκ οἶδ', οὐδ' ἐπέοικεν ἃ μὴ μάθομες πονέ-
εσθαι.
εἴ μοι καλὰ πέλει τὰ μελύδρια, καὶ τάδε μῶνα
κῦδος ἐμοὶ θήσοντι, τά μοι πάρος ὤπασε Μοῖρα·
εἰ δ' οὐχ ἁδέα ταῦτα, τί μοι ποτὶ [2] πλείονα μοχθεῖν;
εἰ μὲν γὰρ βιότω διπλόον χρόνον ἄμμιν ἔδωκεν
ἢ Κρονίδας ἢ Μοῖρα πολύτροπος, ὥστ' ἀνύεσθαι

[1] τις Brunck : mss τῷ   [2] ποτὶ Ahr : mss πολὺ

408

But nay, the child would give no heed to aught I might say ; rather would he be singing love-songs of his own, and taught me of the doings of his mother and the desires of Gods and men. And as for all the lore I had been teaching master Love, I clean forgot it, but the love-songs master Love taught me, I learnt them every one.

VI.—[A LOVE POEM]

THE Muses know no fear of the cruel Love ; rather do their hearts befriend him greatly and their footsteps follow him close. And let one that hath not love in his soul sing a song, and they forthwith slink away and will not teach him ; but if sweet music be made by him that hath, then fly they all unto him hot-foot. And if you ask me how I know that this is very truth, I tell you I may sing praise of any other, be he God or man, and my tongue will wag falteringly and refuse me her best ; but if my music be of love and Lycidas, then my voice floweth from my lips rejoicing.

VII.—[THE POET'S PHILOSOPHY OF LIFE]

. . . I know not, and 'tis unseemly to labour aught we wot not of. If my poor songs are good, I shall have fame out of such things as Fate hath bestowed upon me already—they will be enough ; but if they are bad, what boots it me to go toiling on ? If we men were given, be it of the Son of Cronus or of fickle Fate, two lives, the one for pleasuring and mirth and

τὸν μὲν ἐς εὐφροσύναν καὶ χάρματα, τὸν δ' ἐπὶ[1]
    μόχθῳ,
ἢν τάχα μοχθήσαντι μεθύστερον[2] ἐσθλὰ δέχεσθαι.
εἰ δὲ θεοὶ κατένευσαν ἕνα χρόνον ἐς βίον ἐλθεῖν
ἀνθρώποις, καὶ τόνδε βραχὺν καὶ μείονα πάντων,   10
ἐς πόσον ἃ δειλοὶ καματώδε' ἐς[3] ἔργα πονεύμες,
ψυχὰν δ' ἄχρι τίνος ποτὶ κέρδεα καὶ ποτὶ τέχνας
βάλλομες, ἱμείροντες ἀεὶ πολὺ πλείονος ὄλβω;
λαθόμεθ' ἢ ἄρα[4] πάντες, ὅτι θνατοὶ γενόμεσθα,
χὡς βραχὺν ἐκ Μοίρας λάχομες χρόνον; . . .

VIII

Ὄλβιοι οἱ φιλέοντες, ἐπὴν ἴσον ἀντεράωνται.
ὄλβιος ἦν Θησεὺς τῷ Πειριθόῳ παρεόντος,
εἰ καὶ ἀμειλίκτοιο κατήλυθεν εἰς Ἀΐδαο.
ὄλβιος ἦν χαλεποῖσιν ἐν Ἀξείνοισιν Ὀρέστας,
ὥνεκά οἱ ξυνὰς Πυλάδας ἄρητο[5] κελεύθως.
ἦν μάκαρ Αἰακίδας ἑτάρῳ ζώοντος Ἀχιλλεύς·
ὄλβιος ἦν θνάσκων, ὅτι οἱ μόρον αἰνὸν ἄμυνεν.

IX

Ἔσπερε, τᾶς ἐρατᾶς χρύσεον φάος Ἀφρογενείας,
Ἔσπερε κυανέας ἱερὸν φίλε νυκτὸς ἄγαλμα,
τόσσον ἀφαυρότερος μήνας, ὅσον ἔξοχος ἄστρων,
χαῖρε φίλος, καί μοι ποτὶ ποιμένα κῶμον ἄγοντι
ἀντὶ σελαναίας τὺ δίδου φάος, ὥνεκα τήνα

---

¹ ἐπὶ Wil: mss ἐνὶ   ² Mein: mss ποθ' ὕστερον   Legrand:
mss καμάτως κεῖς   ⁴ cf. Mosch. 2. 140   ⁵ ἄρητο Grotius:
mss ἄροιτο or ἄρκτο

the other for toil, then perhaps might one do the toiling first and get the good things afterward. But seeing Heaven's decree is, man shall live but once, and that for too brief a while to do all he would, then O how long shall we go thus miserably toiling and moiling, and how long shall we lavish our life upon getting and making, in the consuming desire for more wealth and yet more? Is it that we all forget that we are mortal and Fate hath allotted us so brief a span? . . . .

VIII.—[REQUITED LOVE]

HAPPY are lovers when their love is requited. Theseus, for all he found Hades at the last implacable, was happy because Perithoüs went with him; and happy Orestes among the cruel Inhospitables, because Pylades had chosen to share his wanderings; happy also lived Achilles Aeacid while his dear comrade was alive, and died happy, seeing he so avenged his dreadful fate.

IX.—[TO HESPERUS]

EVENING Star, which art the golden light of the lovely Child o' the Foam, dear Evening Star, which art the holy jewel of the blue blue Night, even so much dimmer than the Moon as brighter than any other star that shines, hail, gentle friend, and while I go a-serenading my shepherd love shew me a light instead of the Moon, for that she being new but

---

"Inhospitables": the barbarous inhabitants of the shores of the Black Sea.   "his dear comrade": Patroclus. "Child o' the Foam": Aphrodite.

σάμερον ἀρχομένα τάχιον δύεν. οὐκ ἐπὶ φωρὰν
ἔρχομαι, οὐδ᾽ ἵνα νυκτὸς ὁδοιπορέοντας ἐνοχλέω·
ἀλλ᾽ ἐράω· καλὸν δέ τ᾽ ἐρασσαμένῳ συναρέσθαι.

X

Ἄμερε Κυπρογένεια, Διὸς τέκος ἠὲ θαλάσσας,
τίπτε τόσον θνατοῖσι καὶ ἀθανάτοισι χάλεπτες;[1]
τυτθὸν ἔφαν· τί νυ τόσσον ἀπήχθεο καὶ τεῖν[2]
        αὐτᾷ,
ταλίκον ὡς πάντεσσι κακὸν τὸν Ἔρωτα τεκέσθαι,[3]
ἄγριον, ἄστοργον, μορφᾷ νόον οὐδὲν ὁμοῖον;
ἐς τί δέ νιν πτανὸν καὶ ἑκαβόλον ὤπασας ἦμεν,
ὡς μὴ πικρὸν ἐόντα δυναίμεθα τῆνον ἀλύξαι;

XI—ΕΙΣ ΤΟΝ ΥΑΚΙΝΘΟΝ

. . . ἀμφασία τὸν Φοῖβον ἔλεν τὸ σὸν ἄλγος ὁρῶντα.[4]
δίζετο φάρμακα πάντα, σοφὰν δ᾽ ἐπεμαίετο[5]
        τέχναν,
χρῖεν δ᾽ ἀμβροσίᾳ καὶ νέκταρι, χρῖεν ἄπασαν
ὠτειλάν· Μοίραισι δ᾽ ἀναλθέα φάρμακα πάντα . . .

XII

. . . αὐτὰρ ἐγὼν βασεῦμαι ἐμὰν ὁδὸν ἐς τὸ κάταντες
τῆνο ποτὶ ψάμαθόν τε καὶ ἀϊόνα ψιθυρίσδων,
λισσόμενος Γαλάτειαν ἀπηνέα· τὰς δὲ γλυκείας
ἐλπίδας ὑστατίῳ μέχρι γήραος οὐκ ἀπολείψω . . .

---

[1] χάλεπτες E = you were troublesome : mss χαλέπτεις
[2] τεῖν Hermann : mss τὶν   [3] τεκέσθαι Herm : mss τέκηαι

yesterday is too quickly set. I be no thief nor highwayman—'tis not for that I'm abroad at night—, but a lover; and lovers deserve all aid.

X.—[TO APHRODITE]

GENTLE Dame of Cyprus, be'st thou child of Zeus, or child of the sea, pray tell me why wast so unkind alike unto Gods and men—nay, I'll say more, why so hateful unto thyself, as to bring forth so great and universal a mischief as this Love, so cruel, so heartless, so all unlike in ways and looks? and wherefore also these wings and archeries that we may not escape him when he oppresseth us?

XI.—OF HYACINTHUS

... When he beheld thy agony Phoebus was dumb. He sought every remedy, he had recourse to cunning arts, he anointed all the wound, anointed it with ambrosia and with nectar; but all remedies are powerless to heal the wounds of Fate ...

XII.—[GALATEA'S LOVER]

. . But I will go my way to yonder hillside, singing low to sand and shore my supplication of the cruel Galatea; for I will not give over my sweet hopes till I come unto uttermost old age ...

---

⁴ δρῶντα Usener: mss ἔχοντα   ⁵ ἐπεμαίετο Vulcanius: mss ἐπεβαίνετο or ἐπεβώσατο

XIII

... οὐ καλὸν ὦ φίλε πάντα λόγον ποτὶ τέκτονα
    φοιτᾶν,
μηδ' ἐπὶ πάντ' ἄλλω[1] χρέος ἰσχέμεν· ἀλλὰ καὶ
    αὐτὸς
τεχνᾶσθαι σύριγγα· πέλει δέ τοι εὐμαρὲς ἔργον ...

XIV

Μοίσας Ἔρως καλέοι, Μοῖσαι τὸν Ἔρωτα φέροιεν.
μολπὰν ταὶ Μοῖσαί μοι ἀεὶ ποθέοντι διδοῖεν,
τὰν γλυκερὰν μολπάν, τᾶς φάρμακον ἅδιον
    οὐδέν.

XV

... ἐκ θαμινᾶς ῥαθάμιγγος, ὅπως λόγος, αἰὲς
    ἰοίσας
χὰ λίθος ἐς ῥωχμὸν κοιλαίνεται. ...

XVI

... μηδὲ λίπῃς μ' ἀγέραστον, ἐπεὶ χὠ Φοῖβος
    ἀείδων
μισθοδοκεῖ.[2] τιμὰ δὲ τὰ πράγματα κρέσσονα
    ποιεῖ ...

[1] μηδ' ἐπὶ Grotius : mss μηδέ τοι   ἄλλω Salmasius : mss
ἄλλο   [2] ἀείδων μισθοδοκεῖ E : mss ἀείδειν μισθὸν ἔδωκε

XIII.—[DO IT YOURSELF]

... It is not well, friend, to go to a crafts-man upon all matters, nor to resort unto another man in every business, but rather to make you a pipe yourself; and 'faith, 'tis not so hard, neither ...

XIV.—[LOVE AND SONG]

MAY Love call the Muses, and the Muses bring Love; and may the Muses ever give me song at my desire, dear melodious song, the sweetest physic in the world.[1]

XV.—[PERSISTENCE]

... 'Tis said a continual dripping will e'en wear a hollow in a stone ...

XVI.—[WORTHY OF HIS HIRE]

... I pray you leave me not without some reward; for even Phoebus is paid for his music, and a meed maketh things better ...

[1] Better perhaps regarded as two fragments, the first ending "bring Love"; the following "and" is not in the Greek.

XVII

... μορφὰ θηλυτέραισι πέλει καλόν, ἀνέρι δ᾽
ἀλκά ...

XVIII

πάντα θεοῦ γ᾽ ἐθέλοντος ἀνύσιμα, πάντα βροτοῖσιν
ἐκ μακάρων ῥᾶϊστα καὶ οὐκ ἀτέλεστα γένοντο.[1]

[1] ῥᾶϊστα Ahr : mss γὰρ ῥάστα   γένοντο Ahr : mss γένοιτο

XVII.—[AFTER THEIR KIND]

. . . The woman's glory is her beauty, the man's his strength . . .

XVIII.—[GOD WILLING]

. . . All things may be achieved if Heav'n will ; all is possible, nay, all is very easy if the Blessed make it so . . .

III

THE POEMS OF MOSCHUS

I.—THE RUNAWAY LOVE

CYPRIS *has lost her boy Love, and cries him in the streets*

ΜΟΣΧΟΥ ΣΙΚΕΛΙΩΤΟΥ

I.—ΕΡΩΣ ΔΡΑΠΕΤΗΣ

Ἁ Κύπρις τὸν Ἔρωτα τὸν υἱέα μακρὸν ἐβώστρει·
" ὅστις ἐνὶ τριόδοισι πλανώμενον εἶδεν Ἔρωτα,
δραπετίδας ἐμός ἐστιν· ὁ μανύσας γέρας ἑξεῖ·
μισθός[1] τοι τὸ φίλημα τὸ Κύπριδος· ἢν δ᾽ ἀγάγῃ
νιν,
οὐ γυμνὸν τὸ φίλημα, τὺ δ᾽ ὦ ξένε καὶ πλέον ἑξεῖς.
ἔστι δ᾽ ὁ παῖς περίσαμος· ἐν εἴκοσι παισὶ[2] μάθοις
νιν.
χρῶτα μὲν οὐ λευκός, πυρὶ δ᾽ εἴκελος· ὄμματα δ᾽
αὐτῷ
δριμύλα καὶ φλογόεντα· κακαὶ φρένες, ἁδὺ λάλημα·
οὐ γὰρ ἴσον νοέει καὶ φθέγγεται· ὡς μέλι φωνά,
ὡς δὲ χολὰ νόος ἐστίν· ἀνάμερος, ἠπεροπευτάς,
οὐδὲν ἀλαθεύων, δόλιον βρέφος, ἄγρια παίσδων.
εὐπλόκαμον τὸ κάρανον, ἔχει δ᾽ ἰταμὸν τὸ μέτωπον.
μικκύλα μὲν τήνῳ τὰ χερύδρια, μακρὰ δὲ βάλλει.
βάλλει κεἰς Ἀχέροντα καὶ εἰς Ἀΐδα βασίλεια.
γυμνὸς ὅλος τό γε σῶμα, νόος δέ οἱ εὖ πεπύκασται.
καὶ πτερόεις ὡς ὄρνις ἐφίπταται ἄλλον ἐπ᾽ ἄλλῳ,
ἀνέρας ἠδὲ γυναῖκας, ἐπὶ σπλάγχνοις δὲ κάθηται.
τόξον ἔχει μάλα βαιόν, ὑπὲρ τόξω δὲ βέλεμνον,

---

[1] μισθός : mss μισθόν   [2] παισὶ Heinsius : mss πᾶσι

THE POEMS OF MOSCHUS

I.—THE RUNAWAY LOVE

Cypris one day made hue and cry after her son Love and said: " Whosoever hath seen one Love loitering at the street-corners, know that he is my runaway, and any that shall bring me word of him shall have a reward; and the reward shall be the kiss of Cypris; and if he bring her runaway with him, the kiss shall not be all. He is a notable lad; he shall be known among twenty: complexion not white but rather like to fire; eyes keen and beamy; of an ill disposition but fair spoken, for he means not what he says—'tis voice of honey, heart of gall; froward, cozening, a ne'er-say-troth; a wily brat; makes cruel play. His hair is plenty, his forehead bold; his baby hands tiny but can shoot a long way, aye, e'en across Acheron into the dominions of Death. All naked his body, but well covered his mind. He's winged like a bird and flies from one to another, women as well as men, and alights upon their hearts. He hath a very little bow and upon it an arrow; 'tis

τυτθὸν μὲν τὸ βέλεμνον, ἐς αἰθέρα δ' ἄχρι φορεῖται.
καὶ χρύσεον περὶ νῶτα φαρέτριον, ἔνδοθι δ' ἐντὶ
τοὶ πικροὶ κάλαμοι, τοῖς πολλάκι κἀμὲ τιτρώσκει.
πάντα μὲν ἄγρια ταῦτα· πολὺ πλέον ἀ δαῒς [1] αὐτῷ·
βαιὰ λαμπὰς ἐοῖσα τὸν ἅλιον αὐτὸν ἀναίθει.

ἤν τύ γ' ἕλῃς τῆνον, δήσας ἄγε μηδ' ἐλεήσῃς.
κἢν ποτίδῃς κλαίοντα, φυλάσσεο μή σε πλανάσῃ.
κἢν γελάῃ, τύ νιν ἕλκε. καὶ ἢν ἐθέλῃ σε φιλῆσαι,
φεῦγε· κακὸν τὸ φίλαμα, τὰ χείλεα φάρμακον ἐντί.
ἢν δὲ λέγῃ 'λάβε ταῦτα, χαρίζομαι ὅσσα μοι ὅπλα,'
μὴ τὺ θίγῃς πλάνα δῶρα· τὰ γὰρ πυρὶ πάντα
    βέβαπται."

---

[1] πλέον ἀ δαῒς W.il : mss πλέον δ' ἀεὶ or πλεῖον δέ οἱ

30 αἰαῖ καὶ τὸ σίδαρον, ὃ τὸν πυρόεντα καθέξει. This line,
which can hardly belong here, is omitted by some of the mss.

but a small arrow but carries even to the sky. And at his back is a little golden quiver, but in it lie the keen shafts with which he ofttimes woundeth e'en me. And cruel though all this equipage be, he hath something crueller far, his torch; 'tis a little light, but can set the very Sun afire.

Let any that shall take him bind and bring him and never pity. If he see him weeping, let him have a care lest he be deceived; if laughing, let him still hale him along; but if making to kiss him, let him flee him, for his kiss is an ill kiss and his lips poison; and if he say 'Here, take these things, you are welcome to all my armour,' then let him not touch those mischievous gifts, for they are all dipped in fire."

II.—EUROPA

MOSCHUS *tells in Epic verse how the virgin Europa, after dreaming of a struggle between the two continents for the possession of her, was carried off from among her companions by Zeus in the form of a bull, and borne across the sea from Tyre to Crete, there to become his bride. The earlier half of the poem contains a description of Europa's flower-basket. It bears three pictures in inlaid metal—Io crossing the sea to Egypt in the shape of a heifer, Zeus restoring her there by a touch to human form, and the birth of the peacock from the blood of Argus slain.*

II.—ΕΥΡΩΠΗ

Εὐρώπῃ ποτὲ Κύπρις ἐπὶ γλυκὺν ἧκεν ὄνειρον,
νυκτὸς ὅτε τρίτατον [1] λάχος ἵσταται, ἐγγύθι δ' ἠώς,
ὕπνος ὅτε γλυκίων μέλιτος βλεφάροισιν ἐφίζων
λυσιμελὴς πεδάᾳ μαλακῷ κατὰ φάεα δεσμῷ,
εὖτε καὶ ἀτρεκέων ποιμαίνεται ἔθνος ὀνείρων·
τῆμος ὑπωροφίοισιν ἐνὶ κνώσσουσα δόμοισι
Φοίνικος θυγάτηρ ἔτι παρθένος Εὐρώπεια
ὠίσατ' ἠπείρους δοιὰς περὶ εἷο μάχεσθαι,
ἄσσιον [2] ἀντιπέρην τε· φυὴν δ' ἔχον οἷα γυναῖκες.
τῶν δ' ἡ μὲν ξείνης μορφὴν ἔχεν, ἡ δ' ἄρ' ἐῴκει
ἐνδαπίῃ, καὶ μᾶλλον ἑῆς περιίσχετο κούρης,
φάσκεν δ' ὥς μιν ἔτικτε καὶ ὡς ἀτίτηλέ μιν αὐτή.
ἡ δ' ἑτέρη κρατερῇσι βιωομένη παλάμῃσιν
εἴρυεν οὐκ ἀέκουσαν, ἐπεὶ φάτο μόρσιμον εἷο [3]
ἐκ Διὸς αἰγιόχου γέρας ἔμμεναι Εὐρώπειαν.
ἡ δ' ἀπὸ μὲν στρωτῶν λεχέων θόρε δειμαίνουσα,
παλλομένη κραδίην· τὸ γὰρ ὡς ὕπαρ εἶδεν ὄνειρον.
ἑζομένη δ' ἐπὶ δηρὸν ἀκὴν ἔχεν, ἀμφοτέρας δὲ
εἰσέτι πεπταμένοισιν ἐν ὄμμασιν εἶχε γυναῖκας.
ὀψὲ δὲ δειμαλέην ἀνενείκατο παρθένον [4] αὐδήν·
'τίς μοι τοιάδε φάσματ' ἐπουρανίων προΐηλεν;

---

[1] τρίτατον Musurus : mss τρίτον   [2] ἄσσιον = ἆσσον, called
Doric by Eustath. 1643. 32 ; ἀντιπέρην cannot = τὴν ἀντ. E :

428

II.—EUROPA

ONCE upon a time Europa had of the Cyprian a
delightful dream. 'Twas the third watch o' the
night when 'tis nigh dawn and the Looser of Limbs
is come down honey-sweet upon the eyelids for to
hold our twin light in gentle bondage, 'twas at that
hour which is the outgoing time of the flock of true
dreams, that whenas Phoenix' daughter the maid
Europa slept in her bower under the roof, she dreamt
that two lands near and far strove with one
another for the possession of her. Their guise was
the guise of women, and the one had the look of an
outland wife and the other was like to the dames of
her own country. Now this other clave very ve-
hemently to her damsel, saying she was the mother
that bare and nursed her, but the outland woman
laid violent hands upon her and haled her away ; nor
went she altogether unwilling, for she that haled her
said : "The Aegis-Bearer hath ordained thee to be
mine." Then leapt Europa in fear from the bed of
her lying, and her heart went pit-a-pat ; for she had
had a dream as it were a waking vision. And sitting
down she was long silent, the two women yet before
her waking eyes. At last she raised her maiden voice
in accents of terror, saying : "Who of the People of
Heaven did send me forth such phantoms as these ?

mss ἄσσαν, ἀσίδα τ', ἄσσαδ', ἀσιάδ'   ³ εἶο Ahr : mss εἶναι
⁴ δειμαλέην : mss also δὴ μάλ' ἔπειτ'   παρθένον : mss also -os

429

ποῖοί με στρωτῶν λεχέων ὕπερ ἐν θαλάμοισιν
ἡδὺ μάλα κνώσσουσαν ἀνεπτοίησαν ὄνειροι,
τίς δ᾽ ἦν ἡ ξείνη, τὴν εἴσιδον ὑπνώουσα;
ὥς μ᾽ ἔλαβε κραδίην κείνης πόθος, ὥς με καὶ αὐτὴ
ἀσπασίως ὑπέδεκτο καὶ ὡς σφετέρην ἴδε παῖδα.
ἀλλά μοι εἰς ἀγαθὸν μάκαρες κρήνειαν[1] ὄνειρον.᾽

ὣς εἰποῦσ᾽ ἀνόρουσε, φίλας δ᾽ ἐπεδίζεθ᾽ ἑταίρας
ἥλικας οἰέτεας θυμήρεας εὐπατερείας,
τῇσιν ἀεὶ συνάθυρεν, ὅτ᾽ ἐς χορὸν ἐντύνοιτο,[2]
ἢ ὅτε φαιδρύνοιτο[3] χρόα προχοῇσιν ἀναύρων,
ἢ ὁπότ᾽ ἐκ λειμῶνος ἐΰπνοα λείρι᾽ ἀμέργοι.
αἲ δέ οἱ αἶψα φάανθεν· ἔχον δ᾽ ἐν χερσὶν ἑκάστη
ἀνθοδόκον τάλαρον· ποτὶ δὲ λειμῶνας ἔβαινον
ἀγχιάλους, ὅθι τ᾽ αἰὲν ὁμιλαδὸν ἠγερέθοντο
τερπόμεναι ῥοδέῃ τε φυῇ καὶ κύματος ἠχῇ.

αὐτὴ δὲ χρύσεον τάλαρον φέρεν Εὐρώπεια,
θηητόν, μέγα θαῦμα, μέγαν πόνον Ἡφαίστοιο,
ὃν Λιβύῃ πόρε δῶρον, ὅτ᾽ ἐς λέχος Ἐννοσιγαίου
ἤϊεν· ἣ δὲ πόρεν περικαλλέϊ Τηλεφαάσσῃ,
ἥτε οἱ αἵματος ἔσκεν· ἀνύμφῳ δ᾽ Εὐρωπείῃ
μήτηρ Τηλεφάασσα περικλυτὸν ὤπασε δῶρον.

ἐν τῷ δαίδαλα πολλὰ τετεύχατο μαρμαίροντα.
ἐν μὲν ἔην χρυσοῖο τετυγμένη Ἰναχὶς Ἰώ,
εἰσέτι πόρτις ἐοῦσα, φυὴν δ᾽ οὐκ εἶχε γυναίην.
φοιταλέη δὲ πόδεσσιν ἐφ᾽ ἁλμυρὰ βαῖνε κέλευθα,
νηχομένη ἰκέλη· κυάνου[4] δ᾽ ἐτέτυκτο θάλασσα.
δοιοῦ[5] δ᾽ ἕστασαν ὑψοῦ ἐπ᾽ ὀφρύος αἰγιαλοῖο

---

[1] so Wakefield: mss κρίνειαν   [2] so Wil: mss -οντο, -αιντο
-αιτο   [3] mss also φαιδρύνοιτο   [4] so Mein: mss -νὴ, -νῇ
[5] Herm: mss -οὶ

What meant the strange dreams that did affray me in that most sweet slumber I had upon the bed in my chamber? And who was the outland wife I did behold in my sleep? O how did desire possess my heart for her, and how gladly likewise did she take me to her arms and look upon me as I had been her child! I only pray the Blessed may send the dream turn out well."

So speaking she up and sought the companions that were of like age with her, born the same year and of high degree, the maidens she delighted in and was wont to play with, whether there were dancing afoot or the washing of a bright fair body at the outpourings of the water-brooks, or the cropping of odorous lily-flowers in the mead. Forthwith were they before her sight, bound flower-baskets in hand for the longshore meadows, there to foregather as was their wont and take their pleasure with the springing roses and the sound of the waves.

Now Europa's basket was of gold, an admirable thing, a great marvel and a great work of Hephaestus, given of him unto Libya the day the Earth-Shaker took her to his bed, and given of Libya unto the fair beauteous Telephassa because she was one of her own blood; and so the virgin Europa came to possess the renownèd gift, being Telephassa was her mother.

And in this basket were wrought many shining pieces of cunning work. Therein first was wrought the daughter of Inachus, in the guise of a heifer yet, passing wide over the briny ways by labour of her feet like one swimming; and the sea was wrought of blue lacquer; and high on either cliff-brow stood

"daughter of Inachus": Io.
"either cliff-brow": Greece and Egypt (Gow).

φῶτες ἀολλήδην, θηεῦντο δὲ ποντοπόρον βοῦν.
ἐν δ᾽ ἦν Ζεὺς Κρονίδης ἐπαφώμενος ἠρέμα χερσὶ [1]
πόρτιος Ἰναχίης, τὴν [2] δ᾽ ἑπταπόρῳ παρὰ Νείλῳ
ἐκ βοὸς εὐκεράοιο πάλιν μετάμειβε γυναῖκα.
ἀργύρεος μὲν ἔην Νείλου ῥόος, ἡ δ᾽ ἄρα πόρτις
χαλκείη, χρυσοῦ δὲ τετυγμένος αὐτὸς ἔην Ζεύς.
ἀμφὶ δὲ δινήεντος ὑπὸ στεφάνην ταλάροιο
Ἑρμείης ἤσκητο· πέλας δέ οἱ ἐκτετάνυστο
Ἄργος ἀκοιμήτοισι κεκασμένος ὀφθαλμοῖσι.
τοῖο δὲ φοινήεντος ἀφ᾽ αἵματος ἐξανέτελλεν
ὄρνις ἀγαλλόμενος πτερύγων πολυανθέι χροιῇ,
ταρσὸν ἀναπλώσας ὡσείτε τις ὠκύαλος νηῦς·
χρυσείου ταλάροιο περίσκεπε χείλεα ταρσός. [3]
τοῖος ἔην τάλαρος περικαλλέος Εὐρωπείης.

αἱ δ᾽ ἐπεὶ οὖν λειμῶνας ἐς ἀνθεμόεντας ἵκανον, [4]
ἄλλη ἐπ᾽ ἀλλοίοισι τότ᾽ ἄνθεσι θυμὸν ἔτερπον.
τῶν ἡ μὲν νάρκισσον εὔπνοον, ἡ δ᾽ ὑάκινθον,
ἡ δ᾽ ἴον, ἡ δ᾽ ἕρπυλλον ἀπαίνυτο· πολλὰ δ᾽ ἔραζε
λειμώνων ἐαροτρεφέων θαλέθεσκε πέταλα.
αἱ δ᾽ αὖτε ξανθοῖο κρόκου θυόεσσαν ἔθειραν
δρέπτον ἐριδμαίνουσαι, ἀτὰρ μεσσίστη [5] ἄνασσα
ἀγλαΐην πυρσοῖο ῥόδου χείρεσσι λέγουσα,
οἷά περ ἐν Χαρίτεσσι διέπρεπεν Ἀφρογένεια.

οὐ μὲν δηρὸν ἔμελλεν ἐπ᾽ ἄνθεσι θυμὸν ἰαίνειν,
οὐδ᾽ ἄρα παρθενίην μίτρην ἄχραντον ἔρυσθαι.
ἦ γὰρ δὴ Κρονίδης ὥς μιν φράσαθ᾽, ὡς ἐόλητο

---

[1] mss also Ζ. ἐπ. ἠρ. χειρὶ θεείη   [2] Ἰναχίης τὴν Pierson:
mss εἰναλίης· τὴν or εἶναι ληϊστὴν   [3] ταρσὸς Wil: mss
-οῖς   [4] mss also ἐσήλυθον ἀνθεμόεντας   [5] μεσσίστη E,

43²

a great crowd and watched the sea-going heifer. Therein for the second piece was the Son of Cronus gently touching the same heifer of Inachus beside the seven-streamèd Nile, and so transfiguring the hornèd creature to a woman again; and the flowing Nile was of silver wrought, and the heifer of brass, and the great Zeus of gold. And beneath the rim of the rounded basket was Hermes fashioned, and beside him lay outstretched that Argus which surpassed all others in ever-waking eyes; and from the purple blood of him came a bird uprising in the pride of the flowery hues of his plumage, and unfolding his tail like the sails of a speeding ship till all the lip of the golden basket was covered with the same. Such was this basket of the fair beauteous Europa's.

Now when these damsels were got to the blossomy meads, they waxed merry one over this flower, another over that. This would have the odorous narcissus, that the corn-flag; here 'twas the violet, there the thyme: for right many were the flowerets of the lusty springtime budded and bloomed upon that ground. Then all the band fell a-plucking the spicy tresses of the yellow saffron, to see who could pluck the most; only their queen in the midst of them culled the glory and delight of the red red rose, and was pre-eminent among them even as the Child o' the Foam among the Graces.

Howbeit not for long was she to take her pleasure with the flowers, nor yet to keep her maiden girdle undefiled. For, mark you, no sooner did the Son of

cf. μέσατος, νέατος, τρίτατος : mss μέσσοισιν, μέσσῃσιν, μέσῃ ἔστη

θυμὸν ἀνωίστοισιν ὑποδμηθεὶς βελέεσσι
Κύπριδος, ἣ μούνη δύναται καὶ Ζῆνα δαμάσσαι.
δὴ γὰρ ἀλευόμενός τε χόλον ζηλήμονος Ἥρης
παρθενικῆς τ' ἐθέλων ἀταλὸν νόον ἐξαπατῆσαι
κρύψε θεὸν καὶ τρέψε δέμας καὶ γείνετο ταῦρος,
οὐχ οἷος σταθμοῖς ἐνιφέρβεται, οὐδὲ μὲν οἷος
ὦλκα διατμήγει σύρων εὐκαμπὲς ἄροτρον,
οὐδ' οἷος ποίμνης ἐπιβόσκεται, οὐδὲ μὲν οἷος
ὅστις ὑποδμηθεὶς ἐρύει πολύφορτον ἀπήνην.
τοῦ δή τοι τὸ μὲν ἄλλο δέμας ξανθόχροον ἔσκε,
κύκλος δ' ἀργύφεος μέσσῳ μάρμαιρε μετώπῳ,
ὄσσε δ' ὑπογλαύσσεσκε καὶ ἵμερον ἀστράπτεσκεν.
ἰσά τ' ἐπ' ἀλλήλοισι κέρα ἀνέτελλε καρήνου
ἄντυγος ἡμιτόμου κεραῆς¹ ἅτε κύκλα σελήνης.

ἤλυθε δ' ἐς λειμῶνα καὶ οὐκ ἐφόβησε φαανθεὶς
παρθενικάς, πάσῃσι δ' ἔρως γένετ' ἐγγὺς ἱκέσθαι
ψαῦσαι θ' ἱμερτοῖο βοός, τοῦ δ' ἄμβροτος ὀδμὴ
τηλόθι καὶ λειμῶνος ἐκαίνυτο λαρὸν ἀϋτμήν.
στῆ δὲ ποδῶν προπάροιθεν ἀμύμονος Εὐρωπείης,
καί οἱ λιχμάζεσκε δέρην, κατέθελγε δὲ κούρην.
ἡ δέ μιν ἀμφαφάασκε καὶ ἠρέμα χείρεσιν ἀφρὸν
πολλὸν ἀπὸ στομάτων ἀπομόργνυτο, καὶ κύσε
        ταῦρον.
αὐτὰρ ὁ μειλίχιον μυκήσατο· φαῖό κεν αὐλοῦ
Μυγδονίου γλυκὺν ἦχον ἀνηπύοντος ἀκούειν.
ὤκλασε δὲ πρὸ ποδοῖιν, ἐδέρκετο δ' Εὐρώπειαν
αὐχέν' ἐπιστρέψας καί οἱ πλατὺ δείκνυε νῶτον.
ἡ δὲ βαθυπλοκάμοισι μετέννεπε παρθενικῇσι·

¹ mss also ἄντα κεραίην ἡμιτόμου

Cronus espy her, than his heart was troubled and
brought low of a sudden shaft of the Cyprian, that is
the only vanquisher of Zeus. Willing at once to
escape the jealous Hera's wrath and beguile the
maiden's gentle heart, he put off the god and put
on the bull, not such as feedeth in the stall, nor yet
such as cleaveth the furrow with his train of the
bended plough, neither one that grazeth at the head
of the herd, nor again that draweth in harness the
laden wagon. Nay, but all his body was of a yellow
hue, save that a ring of gleaming white shined in
the midst of his forehead and the eyes beneath it
were grey and made lightnings of desire; and the
horns of his head rose equal one against the other
even as if one should cleave in two rounded cantles
the rim of the hornèd Moon.

So came he into that meadow without affraying
those maidens; and they were straightway taken
with a desire to come near and touch the lovely ox,
whose divine fragrance came so far and outdid even
the delightsome odour of that breathing meadow.
There went he then and stood afore the spotless may
Europa, and for to cast his spell upon her began to
lick her pretty neck. Whereat she fell to touching
and toying, and did wipe gently away the foam that
was thick upon his mouth, till at last there went a
kiss from a maid unto a bull. Then he lowed, and so
moving-softly you would deem it was the sweet cry
of the flute of Mygdony, and kneeling at Europa's
feet, turned about his head and beckoned her with a
look to his great wide back.

At that she up and spake among those pretty

"Mygdony": Phrygia, whence the flute was supposed to
have come with the worship of Dionysus.

435

'δεῦθ' ἑτάραι φίλιαι καὶ ὁμήλικες, ὄφρ' ἐπὶ τῷδε
ἑζόμεναι ταύρῳ τερπώμεθα· δὴ γὰρ ἁπάσας
νῶτον ὑποστορέσας ἀναδέξεται, οἷά τ' ἐνηὴς
πρηΰς τ' εἰσιδέειν καὶ μείλιχος, οὐδέ τι ταύροις
ἄλλοισι προσέοικε· νόος δέ οἱ ἠΰτε φωτὸς
αἴσιμος ἀμφιθέει, μούνης δ' ἐπιδεύεται αὐδῆς.'

ὣς φαμένη νώτοισιν ἐφίζανε μειδιόωσα,
αἱ δ' ἄλλαι μέλλεσκον. ἄφαρ δ' ἀνεπήλατο
        ταῦρος,
ἣν θέλεν ἁρπάξας· ὠκὺς δ' ἐπὶ πόντον ἵκανεν.
ἡ δὲ μεταστρεφθεῖσα φίλας καλέεσκεν ἑταίρας
χεῖρας ὀρεγνυμένη, ταὶ δ' οὐκ ἐδύναντο κιχάνειν.
ἀκτάων δ' ἐπιβὰς πρόσσω θέεν ἠΰτε δελφὶς
χηλαῖς ἀβρέκτοισιν ἐπ' εὐρέα κύματα βαίνων.

ἡ δὲ τότ' ἐρχομένοιο γαληνιάασκε θάλασσα,
κήτεα δ' ἀμφὶς ἄταλλε Διὸς προπάροιθε ποδοῖιν,
γηθόσυνος δ' ὑπὲρ οἶδμα κυβίστεε βυσσόθε
        δελφίς·
Νηρεΐδες δ' ἀνέδυσαν ὑπὲξ ἁλός, αἱ δ' ἄρα πᾶσαι
κητείοις νώτοισιν ἐφήμεναι ἐστιχόωντο.
καὶ δ' αὐτὸς βαρύδουπος ὑπείραλος[1] Ἐννοσίγαιος
κῦμα κατιθύνων ἁλίης ἡγεῖτο κελεύθου
αὐτοκασιγνήτῳ· τοὶ δ' ἀμφί μιν ἠγερέθοντο
Τρίτωνες, πόντοιο βαρύθροοι[2] αὐλητῆρες,
κόχλοισιν ταναοῖς γάμιον μέλος ἠπύοντες.
ἡ δ' ἄρ' ἐφεζομένη Ζηνὸς βοέοις ἐπὶ νώτοις
τῇ μὲν ἔχεν ταύρου δολιχὸν κέρας, ἐν χερὶ δ' ἄλλῃ
εἴρυε πορφυρέην κόλπου πτύχα,[3] ὄφρά κε μή μιν
δεύοι ἐφελκόμενον πολιῆς ἁλὸς ἄσπετον ὕδωρ.

---

[1] ὑπείραλος E, cf. ὑπείροχος and Il. 23, 227 ὑπερ ἁλα : mss
ὑπὲρ ἁλὸς or ὑπερ ἁλα   [2] mss also βαθύθροοι   αὐλ : mss
also ἐνναετῆρες   [3] mss also πορφυρέας and πτύχας

curly-pates saying "Come away, dear my fellows and my feres; let's ride for a merry sport upon this bull. For sure he will take us all upon his bowed back, so meek he looks and mild, so kind and so gentle, nothing resembling other bulls; moreover an understanding moveth over him meet as a man's, and all he lacks is speech." So saying, she sat her down smiling upon his back; and the rest would have sate them likewise, but suddenly the bull, possessed of his desire, leapt up and made hot-foot for the sea. Then did the rapt Europa turn her about and stretch forth her hands and call upon her dear companions; but nay, they might not come at her, and the sea-shore reached, 'twas still forward, forward till he was faring over the wide waves with hooves as unharmed of the water as the fins of any dolphin.

And lo! the sea waxed calm, the sea-beasts frolicked afore great Zeus, the dolphins made joyful ups and tumblings over the surge, and the Nereids rose from the brine and mounting the sea-beasts rode all a-row. And before them all that great rumbling sea-lord the Earth-Shaker played pilot of the briny pathway to that his brother, and the Tritons gathering about him took their long taper shells and sounded the marriage-music like some clarioners of the main. Meanwhile Europa, seated on the back of Zeus the Bull, held with one hand to his great horn and caught up with the other the long purple fold of her robe, lest trailing it should be wet in the untold waters of the hoar brine; and the robe

"unharmed of the water": the salt water was supposed to rot the hoofs of oxen

κολπώθη δ' ὤμοισι πέπλος βαθὺς Εὐρωπείης,
ἱστίον οἷά τε νηός, ἐλαφρίζεσκε δὲ κούρην.   1

ἡ δ' ὅτε δὴ γαίης ἀπὸ πατρίδος ἦεν ἄνευθεν,
φαίνετο δ' οὔτ' ἀκτή τις ἁλίρροθος οὔτ' ὄρος αἰπύ,
ἀλλ' ἀὴρ μὲν ἄνωθεν, ἔνερθε δὲ πόντος ἀπείρων,
ἀμφί ἑ παπτήνασα τόσην ἀνενείκατο φωνήν·
'πῇ με φέρεις θεόταυρε; τίς ἔπλεο; πῶς δὲ κέ-
          λευθα
ἀργαλέ' εἰλιπόδεσσι[1] διέρχεαι, οὐδὲ θάλασσαν
δειμαίνεις; νηυσὶν γὰρ ἐπίδρομός ἐστι θάλασσα
ὠκυάλοις, ταῦροι δ' ἁλίην τρομέουσιν ἀταρπόν.
ποῖόν τοι ποτὸν ἡδύ; τίς ἐξ ἁλὸς ἔσσετ' ἐδωδή;
ἦ ἄρα τις θεός ἐσσι· θεοῖς γ'[2] ἐπεοικότα ῥέξεις.   1
οὔθ' ἅλιοι δελφῖνες ἐπὶ χθονὸς οὔτε τι ταῦροι
ἐν πόντῳ στιχόωσι, σὺ δὲ χθόνα καὶ κατὰ πόντον
ἄτρομος[3] ἀΐσσεις, χηλαὶ δέ τοί εἰσιν ἐρετμά.
ἦ τάχα καὶ γλαυκῆς ὑπὲρ ἠέρος ὑψόσ' ἀερθεὶς
εἴκελος αἰψηροῖσι πετήσεαι οἰωνοῖσιν.
ὤμοι ἐγὼ μέγα δή τι δυσάμμορος, ἥ ῥά τε δῶμα
πατρὸς ἀποπρολιποῦσα καὶ ἑσπομένη βοΐ τῷδε
ξείνην ναυτιλίην ἐφέπω καὶ πλάζομαι οἴη.
ἀλλὰ σύ μοι μεδέων πολιῆς ἁλὸς Ἐννοσίγαιε
ἵλαος ἀντιάσειας, ὃν ἔλπομαι εἰσοράασθαι   1
τόνδε κατιθύνοντα πλόον προκέλευθον ἐμεῖο.
οὐκ ἀθεεὶ γὰρ ταῦτα διέρχομαι ὑγρὰ κέλευθα.'

ὡς φάτο· τὴν δ' ὧδε προσεφώνεεν ἠΰκερως[4] βοῦς·
'θάρσει παρθενική, μὴ δείδιθι πόντιον οἶδμα.
αὐτός τοι Ζεύς εἰμι, κεἰ[5] ἐγγύθεν εἴδομαι εἶναι
ταῦρος· ἐπεὶ δύναμαί γε φανήμεναι ὅττι θέλοιμι.

---

[1] thus Ahr : mss κέλευθον ἀργαλέην (or -λέοισι) πόδεσσι
[2] γ' E : mss δ'   [3] mss also ἄβροχος, cf. 114   [4] mss also
εὐρύκερως   [5] κεἰ Meineke : mss καὶ

438

went bosoming deep at the shoulder like the sail of
a ship, and made that fair burden light indeed.

When she was now far come from the land of her
fathers, and could see neither wave-beat shore nor
mountain-top, but only sky above and sea without
end below, she gazed about her and lift up her voice
saying: "Whither away with me, thou god-like
bull? And who art thou, and how come undaunted
where is so ill going for shambling oxen? Troth,
'tis for the speeding ship to course o' the sea, and
bulls do shun the paths of the brine. What water
is here thou canst drink? What food shalt thou get
thee of the sea? Nay, 'tis plain thou art a God;
only a God would do as thou doest. For bulls go no
more on the sea than the dolphins of the wave on the
land; but as for you, land and sea is all one for your
travelling, your hooves are oars to you. It may well
be you will soar above the the gray mists and fly like
a bird on the wing. Alas and well-a-day that I left
my home and followed this ox to go so strange a sea-
faring and so lonesome! O be kind good Lord of
the hoar sea—for methinks I see thee yonder
piloting me on this way—, great Earth-Shaker, be
kind and come hither to help me; for sure there's
a divinity in this my journey upon the ways of the
waters."

So far the maid, when the hornèd ox upspake and
said: "Be of good cheer, sweet virgin, and never thou
fear the billows. 'Tis Zeus himself that speaketh,
though to the sight he seem a bull; for I can put on
what semblance soever I will. And 'tis love of

σὸς δὲ πόθος μ' ἀνέηκε τόσην ἅλα μετρήσασθαι
ταύρῳ ἐειδόμενον· Κρήτη δέ σε δέξεται ἤδη,
ἥ μ' ἔθρεψε καὶ αὐτόν, ὅπῃ νυμφήϊα σεῖο
ἔσσεται· ἐξ ἐμέθεν δὲ κλυτοὺς φιτύσεαι υἷας,
οἳ σκηπτοῦχοι ἄνακτες ἐπὶ χθονίοισιν ἔσονται.᾽
    ὣς φάτο· καὶ τετέλεστο τά περ φάτο. φαίνετο
        μὲν δὴ
Κρήτη, Ζεὺς δὲ πάλιν σφετέρην ἀνελάζετο μορφήν,
λῦσε δέ οἱ μίτρην, καί οἱ λέχος ἔντυον Ὧραι.
ἡ δὲ πάρος κούρη Ζηνὸς γένετ' αὐτίκα νύμφη,
καὶ Κρονίδῃ τέκνα τίκτε καὶ αὐτίκα γίνετο μήτηρ.

thee hath brought me to make so far a sea-course
in a bull's likeness; and ere 'tis long thou shalt be
in Crete, that was my nurse when I was with her;
and there shall thy wedding be, whereof shall spring
famous children who shall all be kings among them
that are in the earth."

So spake he, and lo! what he spake was done;
for appear it did, the Cretan country, and Zeus
took on once more his own proper shape, and upon
a bed made him of the Seasons unloosed her
maiden girdle. And so it was that she that before
was a virgin became straightway the bride of Zeus,
and thereafter straightway too a mother of children
unto the Son of Cronus.

III.—THE LAMENT FOR BION

THIS *poem seems to have been suggested by Bion's own* Lament for Adonis; *in form it closely resembles the* Song of Thyrsis. *The writer was a pupil of Bion, and hailed from Southern Italy, but is otherwise unknown.*

III.—ΕΠΙΤΑΦΙΟΣ ΒΙΩΝΟΣ

Αἰλινά μοι στοναχεῖτε νάπαι καὶ Δώριον ὕδωρ,
καὶ ποταμοὶ κλαίοιτε τὸν ἱμερόεντα Βίωνα.
νῦν φυτά μοι μύρεσθε, καὶ ἄλσεα νῦν γοάοισθε,
ἄνθεα νῦν στυμνοῖσιν [1] ἀποπνείοιτε κορύμβοις,
νῦν ῥόδα φοινίσσεσθε τὰ πένθιμα, νῦν ἀνεμῶναι,
νῦν ὑάκινθε λάλει τὰ σὰ γράμματα καὶ πλέον αἰαῖ
βάμβανε [2] τοῖς πετάλοισι· καλὸς τέθνακε μελικτάς.

ἄρχετε Σικελικαὶ τῶ πένθεος ἄρχετε Μοῖσαι.
ἀδόνες αἱ πυκινοῖσιν ὀδυρόμεναι ποτὶ φύλλοις,
νάμασι τοῖς Σικελοῖς ἀγγείλατε τᾶς Ἀρεθοίσας,
ὅττι Βίων τέθνακεν ὁ βουκόλος, ὅττι σὺν αὐτῷ
καὶ τὸ μέλος τέθνακε καὶ ὤλετο Δωρὶς ἀοιδά.

ἄρχετε Σικελικαὶ τῶ πένθεος ἄρχετε Μοῖσαι.
Στρυμόνιοι μύρεσθε παρ' ὕδασιν αἴλινα κύκνοι,
καὶ γοεροῖς στομάτεσσι μελίσδετε πένθιμον ᾠδάν,
οἵαν ὑμετέροις ποτὶ χείλεσι γῆρας ἀείδει, [3]
εἴπατε δ' αὖ κούραις Οἰαγρίσιν, εἴπατε πάσαις
Βιστονίαις Νύμφαισιν 'ἀπώλετο Δώριος Ὀρφεύς.'

ἄρχετε Σικελικαὶ τῶ πένθεος ἄρχετε Μοῖσαι.

---

[1] στυμνοῖσιν E, cf. Bion i. 74: mss στυγν. [2] βάμβανε, cf.
Bion 6. 9: mss λάμβανε [3] γῆρας ἀείδει Wil: mss. γῆρυς
ἄειδε

III.—THE LAMENT FOR BION

CRY me waly upon him, you glades of the woods, and waly, sweet Dorian water; you rivers, weep I pray you for the lovely and delightful Bion. Lament you now, good orchards; gentle groves, make you your moan; be your breathing clusters, ye flowers, dishevelled for grief. Pray roses, now be your redness sorrow, and yours sorrow, windflowers; speak now thy writing, dear flower-de-luce, loud let thy blossoms babble ay; the beautiful musician is dead.

A song of woe, of woe, Sicilian Muses.

You nightingales that complain in the thick leafage, tell to Arethusa's fountain of Sicily that neatherd Bion is dead, and with him dead is music, and gone with him likewise the Dorian poesy.

A song of woe, of woe, Sicilian Muses.

Be it waly with you, Strymon swans, by the waterside, with voice of moaning uplift you such a song of sorrow as old age singeth from your throats, and say to the Oeagrian damsels and eke to all the Bistonian Nymphs "The Dorian Orpheus is dead."

A song of woe, of woe, Sicilian Muses.

"flower-de-luce": the petals of the iris were said to bear the letters AI, "alas." "Strymon": a river of Thrace, where Orpheus lived and died; swans were said to sing before their death. "Oeagrian damsels": daughters of Oeagrus king of Thrace and sisters of Orpheus. "Bistonian": Thracian.

κεῖνος ὁ ταῖς ἀγέλαισιν ἐράσμιος οὐκέτι μέλπει,   2
οὐκέτ' ἐρημαίαισιν ὑπὸ δρυσὶν ἥμενος ᾄδει,
ἀλλὰ παρὰ Πλουτῆι μέλος Ληθαῖον ἀείδει.
ὥρεα δ' ἐστὶν ἄφωνα, καὶ αἱ βόες αἱ ποτὶ ταύροις
πλαζόμεναι γοάοντι καὶ οὐκ ἐθέλοντι νέμεσθαι.

ἄρχετε Σικελικαὶ τῶ πένθεος ἄρχετε Μοῖσαι.
σεῖο Βίων ἔκλαυσε ταχὺν μόρον αὐτὸς Ἀπόλλων,
καὶ Σάτυροι μύροντο μελάγχλαινοί τε Πρίηποι·
καὶ Πᾶνες στοναχεῦντο[1] τὸ σὸν μέλος, αἵ τε καθ'
                                ὕλαν
Κρανίδες ὠδύραντο, καὶ ὕδατα δάκρυα γέντο.
Ἀχὼ δ' ἐν πέτραισιν ὀδύρεται, ὅττι σιωπῇ   3
κοὐκέτι μιμεῖται τὰ σὰ χείλεα. σῷ δ' ἐπ' ὀλέθρῳ
δένδρεα καρπὸν ἔριψε, τὰ δ' ἄνθεα πάντ' ἐμαράνθη.
μάλων οὐκ ἔρρευσε καλὸν γλάγος, οὐ μέλι σίμβλων,
κάτθανε δ' ἐν κηρῷ λυπεύμενον· οὐκέτι γὰρ δεῖ
τῶ μέλιτος τῶ σῶ τεθνακότος αὐτὸ τρυγᾶσθαι.

ἄρχετε Σικελικαὶ τῶ πένθεος ἄρχετε Μοῖσαι.
οὐ τόσον εἰναλίαισι παρ' ἀόσι μύρατο Σειρήν,[2]
οὐδὲ τόσον ποκ' ἄεισεν ἐνὶ σκοπέλοισιν Ἀηδών,
οὐδὲ τόσον θρήνησεν ἀν' ὥρεα μακρὰ Χελιδών,
Ἀλκυόνος δ' οὐ τόσσον ἐπ' ἄλγεσιν ἴαχε Κηΰξ,[3]   4
οὐδὲ τόσον γλαυκοῖς ἐνὶ κύμασι κηρύλος ᾆδεν,   4

---

[1] στοναχεῦντο : mss -εῦντι   [2] Σειρήν Buecheler : mss σε
(δέ, γέ) πριν or δελφίν   [3] Κηΰξ Aldus : mss κήρυξ

He that was lovely and pleasant unto the herds
carols now no more, sits now no more and sings
'neath the desert oaks; but singeth in the house
of Pluteus the song of Lethè, the song of oblivion.
And so the hills are dumb, and the cows that wander
with the bulls wail, and will none of their pasture.

A song of woe, of woe, Sicilian Muses.

Your sudden end, sweet Bion, was matter of weep-
ing even unto Apollo; the Satyrs did lament you,
and every Priapus made you his moan in sable garb.
Not a Pan but cried woe for your music, not a Nymph
o' the spring but made her complaint of it in the
wood; and all the waters became as tears. Echo,
too, she mourns among the rocks that she is silent
and can imitate your lips no more. For sorrow
that you are lost the trees have cast their fruit on
the ground, and all the flowers are withered away.
The flocks have given none of their good milk, and
the hives none of their honey; for the honey is
perished in the comb for grief, seeing the honey of
bees is no longer to be gathered now that honey of
yours is done away.

A song of woe, of woe, Sicilian Muses.

Never so woeful was the lament of the Siren upon
the beach, never so woeful the song of that Nightin-
gale among the rocks, or the dirge of that Swallow
amid the long hills, neither the wail of Ceÿx for the
woes of that Halcyon, nor yet the Ceryl's song among

"Pan, Priapus, Satyrs, Nymphs": the effigies of these
deities which stood in the pastures. "the Sirens":
these were represented as half bird, half woman, and
bewailed the dead.   lines 38–41: The references are to
birds who once had human shape; *see index.*

οὐ τόσον ἀῴοισιν [1] ἐν ἄγκεσι παῖδα τὸν Ἀοῦς   4
ἱπτάμενος περὶ σᾶμα κινύρατο Μέμνονος ὄρνις,
ὅσσον ἀποφθιμένοιο κατωδύραντο Βίωνος.

ἄρχετε Σικελικαὶ τῶ πένθεος ἄρχετε Μοῖσαι.
ἀδονίδες πᾶσαί τε χελιδόνες, ἅς ποκ' ἔτερπεν,
ἃς λαλέειν ἐδίδασκε, καθεζόμεναι ποτὶ πρέμνοις
ἀντίον ἀλλάλαισιν ἐκώκυον· αἱ δ' ὑπεφώνευν
'ὄρνιθες λυπεῖσθ' αἱ πενθάδες· ἀλλὰ καὶ ἡμεῖς.' [2]

ἄρχετε Σικελικαὶ τῶ πένθεος ἄρχετε Μοῖσαι.   50
τίς ποτὶ σᾷ σύριγγι μελίξεται ὦ τριπόθητε;
τίς δ' ἐπὶ σοῖς καλάμοις θήσει στόμα; τίς θρασὺς
        οὕτως;
εἰσέτι γὰρ πνείει τὰ σὰ χείλεα καὶ τὸ σὸν ἆσθμα,
ἀχὰ δ' ἐν δονάκεσσι τεᾶς ἔτι [3] βόσκετ' ἀοιδᾶς.
Πανὶ φέρω τὸ μέλισμα; τάχ' ἂν καὶ κεῖνος ἐρεῖσαι
τὸ στόμα δειμαίνοι, μὴ δεύτερα σεῖο φέρηται.

ἄρχετε Σικελικαὶ τῶ πένθεος ἄρχετε Μοῖσαι.
κλαίει καὶ Γαλάτεια τὸ σὸν μέλος, ἅν ποκ' ἔτερπες
ἑζομέναν μετὰ [4] σεῖο παρ' ἀϊόνεσσι θαλάσσας.
οὐ γὰρ ἴσον Κύκλωπι μελίσδεο· τὸν μὲν ἔφευγεν   6
ἁ καλὰ Γαλάτεια, σὲ δ' ἅδιον ἔβλεπεν ἅλμας.
καὶ νῦν λασαμένα τῶ κύματος ἐν ψαμάθοισιν
ἕζετ' ἐρημαίαισι, βόας δ' ἔτι σεῖο νομεύει.

ἄρχετε Σικελικαὶ τῶ πένθεος ἄρχετε Μοῖσαι.
πάντα τοι ὦ βούτα συγκάτθανε δῶρα τὰ Μοισᾶν,
παρθενικᾶν ἐρόεντα φιλήματα, χείλεα παίδων,

---

[1] ἀῴοισιν: mss also ἠώνοισιν and οἰών.   [2] λυπεῖσθ' αἱ Ahr:
mss λυπεῖσθαι, -θε, -θέ γε   mss also ἡμᾶς and ὑμεῖς   [3] ἄχα
δ' ἐν Ahr: mss ἀχεδνή, ἀχεδὼν, ἀχεδονεῖ   ἔτι β. Brunck:
mss ἐπιβ.   [4] μετὰ Hermann: mss παρὰ

the blue waves, nay, not so woeful the hovering bird of Memnon over the tomb of the Son of the Morning in the dells of the Morning, as when they mourned for Bion dead.

A song of woe, of woe, Sicilian Muses.

The nightingales and all the swallows, which once he delighted, which once he taught to speak, sat upon the branches and cried aloud in antiphons, and they that answered said "Lament, ye mourners, and so will we."

A song of woe, of woe, Sicilian Muses.

O thrice-belovèd man! who will make music upon thy pipe? Who so bold as to set lip to thy reeds? For thy lips and thy breath live yet, and in those straws the sound of thy song is quick. Shall I take and give the pipe to Pan? Nay, mayhap even he will fear to put lip to it lest he come off second to thee.

A song of woe, of woe, Sicilian Muses.

There's Galatea, too, weeps for your music, the music that was erst her delight sitting beside you upon the strand. For Cyclops' music was all another thing; she shunned him, the pretty Galatea, but she looked upon you more gladly than upon the sea. And lo! now the waves are forgotten while she sits upon the lone lone sands, but your cows she tends for you still.

A song of woe, of woe, Sicilian Muses.

All the gifts that come of the Muses have perished, dear Neatherd, with you, the dear delightful kisses

"bird of Memnon": The tomb of Memnon, son of the Dawn and Tithonus, was visited every year by birds called Memnonidae. "Galatea": Bion seems to have written a first-person pastoral resembling the *Serenade*, in which a neatherd lover of Galatea sang to her on the beach. If so, Fragment XII would seem to belong to it.

καὶ στυμνοὶ [1] περὶ σῶμα τεὸν κλαίουσιν Ἔρωτες.
χἀ Κύπρις ποθέει [2] σε πολὺ πλέον ἢ τὸ φίλημα,
τὸ πρώαν τὸν Ἄδωνιν ἀποθνάσκοντα φίλησεν.

τοῦτό τοι ὦ ποταμῶν λιγυρώτατε δεύτερον ἄλγος, 70
τοῦτο, Μέλη, νέον ἄλγος. ἀπώλετο πρᾶν τοι [3]
Ὅμηρος,
τῆνο τὸ Καλλιόπας γλυκερὸν στόμα, καί σε
λέγοντι
μύρασθαι [4] καλὸν υἷα πολυκλαύτοισι ῥεέθροις,
πᾶσαν δὲ πλῆσαι [5] φωνᾶς ἅλα· νῦν πάλιν ἄλλον
υἱέα δακρύεις, καινῷ δ' ἐπὶ πένθεϊ τάκῃ.
ἀμφότεροι παγαῖς πεφιλημένοι, ὃς μὲν ἔπινε
Παγασίδος κράνας, ὃ δ' ἔχεν πόμα τᾶς Ἀρεθοίσας.
χὠ μὲν Τυνδαρέοιο καλὰν ἄεισε θύγατρα
καὶ Θέτιδος μέγαν υἷα καὶ Ἀτρείδαν Μενέλαον·
τῆνος δ' οὐ πολέμους, οὐ δάκρυα, Πᾶνα δ' ἔμελπε, 80
καὶ βούτας ἐλίγαινε καὶ ἀείδων ἐνόμευε,
καὶ σύριγγας ἔτευχε καὶ ἁδέα πόρτιν ἄμελγε,
καὶ παίδων ἐδίδασκε φιλήματα, καὶ τὸν Ἔρωτα
ἔτρεφεν ἐν κόλποισι καὶ ἤρεθε τὰν Ἀφροδίταν.

ἄρχετε Σικελικαὶ τῶ πένθεος ἄρχετε Μοῖσαι.
πᾶσα Βίων θρηνεῖ σε κλυτὰ πόλις, ἄστεα πάντα.
Ἄσκρα μὲν γοάει σε πολὺ πλέον Ἡσιόδοιο·
Πίνδαρον οὐ ποθέοντι τόσον Βοιωτίδες ὗλαι·
οὐ τόσον Ἀλκαίω περιμύρατο Λέσβος ἐραννά· [6]
οὐδὲ τόσον ὃν ἀοιδὸν ὀδύρατο [7] Τήιον ἄστυ· 90
σὲ πλέον Ἀρχιλόχοιο ποθεῖ Πάρος· ἀντὶ δὲ
Σαπφῶς

[1] στυμνοὶ E, cf. Bion i. 74: mss στυγνοὶ or -ὸν   [2] χἀ Wil:
mss ἁ   ποθέει Herm: mss φιλέει   [3] τοι: mss also ποι and
μοι   [4] μύρασθαι Mein: mss -εσθαι   [5] Schaef: mss δ'
ἔπλησε, -σας   [6] ἐράννα Heringa: mss ἐρεννά, ἐρενέα, ἐρεμνά
[7] ὃν Wakefield: mss τὸν   ὀδύρατο Wakef: mss ἐμύρατο

of the maidens, the sweet lips of the lads; round
your corse the Loves weep all dishevelled, and
Cypris, she's fainer far of you than the kiss she gave
Adonis when he died the other day.

O tunefullest of rivers, this makes thee a second
grief, this, good Meles, comes thee a new woe. One
melodious mouthpiece of Calliopè is long dead, and
that is Homer; that lovely son of thine was mourned,
'tis said, of thy tearful flood, and all the sea was filled
with the voice of thy lamentation: and lo! now
thou weepest for another son, and a new sorrow
melteth thee away. Both were beloved of a water-
spring, for the one drank at Pegasus' fountain and
the other got him drink of Arethusa; and the one
sang of the lovely daughter of Tyndareüs, and of the
great son of Thetis, and of Atreid Menelaüs; but this
other's singing was neither of wars nor tears but of
Pan; as a herdsman he chanted, and kept his cattle
with a song; he both fashioned pipes and milked the
gentle kine; he taught the lore of kisses, he made
a fosterling of Love, he roused and stirred the passion
of Aphrodite.

A song of woe, of woe, Sicilian Muses.

O Bion! there's not a city, nay, not a humble
town but laments thee. Ascra makes far louder
moan than for her Hesiod, the woods of Boeotia long
not so for their Pindar; not so sore did lovely Lesbos
weep for Alcaeus, nor Teos town for the poet that
was hers; Paros yearns as she yearned not for Archi-

"the other day": The reference to Adonis' death is
doubtless to a recent Adonis-Festival. "Meles": the
river of Smyrna, birthplace of Bion and claiming to be the
birthplace of Homer. "the poet that was hers": Anacreon.

εἰσέτι[1] σεῦ τὸ μέλισμα κινύρεται ἁ Μιτυλάνα.
εἰ δὲ[2] Συρακοσίοισι Θεόκριτος· αὐτὰρ ἐγώ τοι
Αὐσονικᾶς ὀδύνας μέλπω μέλος, οὐ ξένος ᾠδᾶς
βουκολικᾶς, ἀλλ᾽ ἅντε διδάξαο σεῖο μαθητὰς
κλαρονόμος Μοίσας τᾶς Δωρίδος, ᾇ με[3] γεραίρων
ἄλλοις μὲν τεὸν ὄλβον, ἐμοὶ δ᾽ ἀπέλειπες ἀοιδάν.

ἄρχετε Σικελικαὶ τῶ πένθεος ἄρχετε Μοῖσαι.
αἰαῖ ταὶ μαλάχαι μέν, ἐπὰν κατὰ κᾶπον ὄλωνται,
ἠδὲ τὰ χλωρὰ σέλινα τό τ᾽ εὐθαλὲς οὐλον ἄνηθον,
ὕστερον αὖ ζώοντι καὶ εἰς ἔτος ἄλλο φύοντι·
ἄμμες δ᾽ οἱ μεγάλοι καὶ καρτεροί, οἱ[4] σοφοὶ ἄνδρες,
ὁππότε πρᾶτα θάνωμες, ἀνάκοοι ἐν χθονὶ κοίλᾳ
εὕδομες εὖ μάλα μακρὸν ἀτέρμονα νήγρετον ὕπνον.
καὶ σὺ μὲν ὦν[5] σιγᾷ πεπυκασμένος ἔσσεαι ἐν γᾷ,
ταῖς Νύμφαισι δ᾽ ἔδοξεν ἀεὶ τὸν βάτραχον ᾄδειν.
ταῖς[6] δ᾽ ἐγὼ οὐ φθονέοιμι· τὸ γὰρ μέλος οὐ καλὸν
    ᾄδει.

ἄρχετε Σικελικαὶ τῶ πένθεος ἄρχετε Μοῖσαι.
φάρμακον ἦλθε, Βίων, ποτὶ σὸν στόμα, φάρμακον
    ἦδες—
τοιούτοις χείλεσσι ποτέδραμε κοὐκ ἐγλυκάνθη;
τίς δὲ βροτὸς τοσσοῦτον ἀνάμερος ὡς[7] κεράσαι τοι
ἢ δοῦναι καλέοντι τὸ φάρμακον;—ἔκψυγεν ᾠδά.[8]

ἄρχετε Σικελικαὶ τῶ πένθεος ἄρχετε Μοῖσαι.
ἀλλὰ Δίκα κίχε πάντας. ἐγὼ δ᾽ ἐπὶ πένθεῖ τῷδε

---

[1] εἰσέτι = evermore   [2] εἰ δὲ Wil : mss ἐν δὲ, οὐδὲ   [3] ᾇ με
Briggs : mss ἅμμε, ἄμμε, ἄμμεγα   [4] καρτεροί, οἱ Briggs : mss
καρτεροὶ or καρτεροικοὶ   [5] ὦν Wakef : mss ἐν   [6] ταῖς Wil :

lochus, and Mitylenè bewails thy song evermore instead of Sappho's. To Syracuse thou art a Theocritus, and as for Ausonia's mourning, 'tis the song I sing thee now ; and 'tis no stranger to the pastoral poesy that sings it, neither, but an inheritor of that Dorian minstrelsy which came of thy teaching and was my portion when thou leftest others thy wealth but me thy song.

A song of woe, of woe, Sicilian Muses.

Ay me! when the mallows and the fresh green parsley and the springing crumpled dill perish in the garden, they live yet again and grow another year ; but we men that are so tall and strong and wise, soon as ever we be dead, unhearing there in a hole of the earth sleep we both sound and long a sleep that is without end or waking. And so it shall be that thou wilt lie in the earth beneath a covering of silence, albeit the little croaking frog o' the tree by ordinance of the Nymphs may sing for evermore. But they are welcome to his music for me ; it is but poor music he makes.

A song of woe, of woe, Sicilian Muses.

There came poison, sweet Bion, to thy mouth, and poison thou didst eat—O how could it approach such lips as those and not turn to sweetness? And what mortal man so barbarous and wild as to mix it for thee or give it thee at thy call?—and Song went cold and still.

A song of woe, of woe, Sicilian Muses.

Howbeit Justice overtaketh every man ; and as for me, this song shall be my weeping sad lamentation

mss τοῖς   7 ὡς Ahr : mss δs or ἢ   8 ἔκψυγεν ᾠδὰ E : mss
ἔκφυγεν (or ἢ φύγεν) ᾠδὰν

δακρυχέων τεὸν οἶτον ὀδύρομαι. εἰ δυνάμαν δέ,
ὡς Ὀρφεὺς καταβὰς ποτὶ Τάρταρον, ὥς ποκ’
        Ὀδυσσεύς,
ὡς πάρος Ἀλκείδας, κἠγὼ τάχ’ ἂν ἐς δόμον ἦνθον
Πλουτέος, ὥς κέ σ’ ἴδοιμι,[1] καὶ εἰ Πλουτῆι μελίσδῃ,[2]
ὡς ἂν ἀκουσαίμαν, τί μελίσδεαι. ἀλλ’ ἄγε[3] Κώρᾳ
Σικελικόν τι λίγαινε καὶ ἁδύ τι βουκολιάζευ.   120
καὶ κεῖνα Σικελά, καὶ ἐν[4] Αἰτναίαισιν ἔπαιζεν
ἀόσι, καὶ μέλος οἶδε τὸ Δώριον· οὐκ ἀγέραστος
ἐσσεῖθ’ ἁ μολπά. χὡς Ὀρφεῖ πρόσθεν ἔδωκεν
ἀδέα φορμίζοντι παλίσσυτον Εὐρυδίκειαν,
καὶ σὲ Βίων πέμψει τοῖς ὤρεσιν. εἰ δέ τι κἠγὼν
συρίσδων δυνάμαν, παρὰ Πλουτέι κ’ αὐτὸς ἄειδον.

---

[1] κέ σ’ Schaef: mss κεν   [2] Ahr: mss -σδης, -σδεις   [3] ἀλλ’
ἄγε Wil: mss ἀλλὰ πᾶσα, ἀλλ’ ἐπὶ, καὶ πᾶσα, καὶ παρὰ   [4] some
mss omit καὶ before κεῖνα   Σικελά, καὶ ἐν Teucher: mss
σικελικὰ ἐν (or καὶ ἐν), σικελικαῖσιν ἐν

for thy decease. Could I but have gone down into Tartarus as Orpheus went and Odysseus of yore and Alcides long ago, then would I also have come mayhap to the house of Pluteus, that I might see thee, and if so be thou singest to Pluteus, hear what that thou singest may be. But all the same, I pray thee, chant some song of Sicily, some sweet melodious country-song, unto the Maid; for she too is of Sicily, she too once sported on Etna's shores; she knows the Dorian music; so thy melodies shall not go without reward. Even as once she granted Orpheus his Eurydicè's return because he harped so sweetly, so likewise she shall give my Bion back unto the hills; and had but this my pipe the power of that his harp, I had played for this in the house of Pluteus myself.

"the Maid": Persephonè, who was carried off by Pluto—here called Pluteus—when she was playing in the fields of Sicily.

IV–VII

OF *the remaining poems the first three are quoted by* Stobaeus. *The last is found in the Anthology* (Anth. Plan., 4. 200), *and was wrongly ascribed to Moschus owing to its mention of Europa's bull.*

IV

Τὰν ἅλα τὰν γλαυκὰν ὅταν ὤνεμος ἀτρέμα βάλλῃ,
τὰν φρένα τὰν δειλὰν ἐρεθίζομαι, οὐδ' ἔτι μοι γᾶ[1]
ἐστὶ φίλα, ποθίει δὲ πολὺ πλέον ἁ μεγάλα μ' ἅλς.[2]
ἀλλ' ὅταν ἀχήσῃ πολιὸς βυθός, ἁ δὲ θάλασσα
κυρτὸν ἐπαφρίζῃ, τὰ δὲ κύματα μακρὰ μεμήνῃ,
ἐς χθόνα παπταίνω καὶ δένδρεα, τὰν δ' ἅλα φεύγω,
γᾶ δέ μοι ἀσπαστά, χἁ δάσκιος εὔαδεν ὕλα,
ἔνθα καὶ ἢν πνεύσῃ πολὺς ὤνεμος, ἁ πίτυς ᾄδει.
ἦ κακὸν ὁ γριπεὺς ζώει βίον, ᾧ δόμος ἁ ναῦς,
καὶ πόνος ἐστὶ θάλασσα, καὶ ἰχθύες ἁ πλάνος
    ἄγρα.
αὐτὰρ ἐμοὶ γλυκὺς ὕπνος ὑπὸ πλατάνῳ βαθυ-
    φύλλῳ,
καὶ παγᾶς φιλέοιμι τὸν ἐγγύθεν ἄχον ἀκούειν,
ἁ τέρπει ψοφέοισα τὸν ἀγρικόν,[3] οὐχὶ ταράσσει.

V

Ἤρατο[4] Πὰν Ἀχῶς τᾶς γείτονος, ἤρατο δ' Ἀχὼ
σκιρτατᾶ Σατύρω, Σάτυρος δ' ἐπεμήνατο Λύδᾳ.
ὡς Ἀχὼ τὸν Πᾶνα, τόσον Σάτυρος φλέγεν Ἀχώ,
καὶ Λύδα Σατυρίσκον· Ἔρως δ' ἐσμύχετ' ἀμοιβᾷ.

---

[1] μοι γᾶ Bosius : mss μοῖσα   [2] πλέον ἁ μεγάλα μ' ἅλς E :
mss πλέονα μεγάλαν ἅλα   [3] ἀγρικὸν Stephanus : mss ἀγροῖκον
[4] ἤρατο Wakef : mss ἦρα

IV.—[A COMPARISON]

WHEN the wind strikes gently upon a sea that is blue, this craven heart is roused within me, and my love of the land yields to the desire of the great waters. But when the deep waxes grey and loud, and the sea begins to swell and to foam and the waves run long and wild, then look I unto the shore and its trees and depart from the brine, then welcome is the land to me and pleasant the shady greenwood, where, be the wind never so high, the pine-tree sings her song. O 'tis ill to be a fisher with a ship for his house and the sea for his labour and the fishes for his slippery prey. Rather is it sleep beneath the leafy plane for me, and the sound hard by of a bubbling spring such as delights and not disturbs the rustic ear.

V.—[A LESSON TO LOVERS]

PAN loved his neighbour Echo; Echo loved a frisking Satyr; and Satyr, he was head over ears for Lydè. As Echo was Pan's flame, so was Satyr Echo's, and Lydè master Satyr's. 'Twas Love re-

ὅσσον γὰρ τήνων τις ἐμίσεε τὸν φιλέοντα,
τόσσον ὁμῶς φιλέων ἠχθαίρετο, πάσχε δ' ἃ ποίει.
ταῦτα λέγω πᾶσιν τὰ διδάγματα τοῖς ἀνεράστοις·
στέργετε τὼς φιλέοντας, ἵν' ἢν φιλέητε φιλῆσθε.

VI

'Αλφειὸς μετὰ Πίσαν ἐπὴν κατὰ πόντον ὁδεύῃ,
ἔρχεται εἰς 'Αρέθοισαν ἄγων κοτινηφόρον ὕδωρ,
ἕδνα φέρων καλὰ φύλλα καὶ ἄνθεα καὶ κόνιν
    ἱράν,
καὶ βαθὺς ἐμβαίνει τοῖς κύμασι, τὰν δὲ θάλασσαν
νέρθεν ὑποτροχάει, κοὐ μίγνυται ὕδασιν ὕδωρ,
ἁ δ' οὐκ οἶδε θάλασσα διερχομένω ποταμοῖο.
κῶρος λινοθέτας [1] κακομάχανος αἰνὰ διδάσκων
καὶ ποταμὸν διὰ φίλτρον Ἔρως ἐδίδαξε κολυμβῆν.

VII—ΕΙΣ ΕΡΩΤΑ ΑΡΟΤΡΙΩΝΤΑ

Λαμπάδα θεὶς καὶ τόξα βοηλάτιν εἵλετο ῥάβδον
    οὖλος Ἔρως, πήρην δ' εἶχε κατωμαδίην,
καὶ ζεύξας ταλαεργὸν ὑπὸ ζυγὸν αὐχένα ταύρων
    ἔσπειρεν Δηοῦς αὔλακα πυροφόρον.
εἶπε δ' ἄνω βλέψας αὐτῷ Διί· 'πλῆσον ἀρούρας,
    μή σε τὸν Εὐρώπης βοῦν ὑπ' ἄροτρα βάλω.'

---

[1] λινοθέτας E, cf. Theocr. 21. 10 : mss δεινοθέτας

ciprocal; for by just course, even as each of those
hearts did scorn its lover, so was it also scorned
being such a lover itself. To all such as be heart-
whole be this lesson read: If you would be loved
where you be loving, then love them that love you.

VI.—[A RIVER IN LOVE]

WHEN Alpheüs leaves Pisa behind him and travels
by the sea, he brings Arethusa the water that makes
the wild olives grow; and with a bride-gift coming,
of pretty leaves and pretty flowers and sacred dust,
he goeth deep into the waves and runneth his course
beneath the sea, and so runneth that the two waters
mingle not and the sea never knows of the river's
passing through. So is it that the spell of that
impish setter of nets, that sly and crafty teacher of
troubles, Love, hath e'en taught a river how to dive.

VII.—OF LOVE PLOUGHING

LOVE the Destroyer set down his torch and his
bow, and slinging a wallet on his back, took an ox-
goad in hand, yoked him a sturdy pair of steers, and
fell to ploughing and sowing Demeter's cornland;
and while he did so, he looked up unto great Zeus
saying "Be sure thou make my harvest fat; for if
thou fail me I'll have that bull of Europa's to my
plough."

"sacred dust": the dust of the race-course at Olympia
(Pisa).

MEGARA

MEGARA

THE *poem gives a picture of Heracles' wife and mother at home in his house at Tiryns while he is abroad about his Labóurs. The two women sit weeping. The wife bewails his mad murder of their children, and gently hints that the mother might give her more sympathy in her sorrow if she would not be for ever lamenting her own. To which the kind old Alcmena replies, " sufficient unto the day is the evil thereof" ; but though her own anxiety for the safety of the labouring Heracles, increased now by an evil dream, is food enough, God knows, for lamentation, she feels, as indeed Megara must know full well, for her sorrowing daughter too. The poem bears a resemblance to* [*Theocritus*] *XXV, and is thought by some to belong to the same author.*

ΜΕΓΑΡΑ

'Μῆτερ ἐμή, τίφθ' ὧδε φίλον κατὰ θυμὸν ἰάπτεις
ἐκπάγλως ἀχέουσα, τὸ πρὶν δέ τοι οὐκέτ' ἔρευθος
σῴζετ' ἐπὶ ῥεθέεσσι; τί μοι τόσον ἠνίησαι;
ἦρ' ὅτι ἄλγεα πάσχει ἀπείριτα φαίδιμος υἱὸς
ἀνδρὸς ὕπ' οὐτιδανοῖο, λέων ὡσείθ' ὑπὸ νεβροῦ;
ὤμοι ἐγώ, τί νυ δή με θεοὶ τόσον ἠτίμησαν
ἀθάνατοι; τί νύ μ' ὧδε κακῇ γονέες τέκον αἴσῃ;
δύσμορος, ἥτ' ἐπεὶ ἀνδρὸς ἀμύμονος ἐς λέχος ἦλθον,
τὸν μὲν ἐγὼ τίεσκον ἴσον φαέεσσιν ἐμοῖσιν
ἠδ' ἔτι νῦν σέβομαί τε καὶ αἰδέομαι κατὰ θυμόν·
τοῦ δ' οὔτις γένετ' ἄλλος ἀποτμότερος ζωόντων,
οὐδὲ τόσων σφετέρῃσιν ἐγεύσατο φροντίσι κηδέων.
σχέτλιος, ὃς τόξοισιν, ἅ οἱ πόρεν αὐτὸς Ἀπόλλων
ἠέ τινος Κηρῶν ἢ Ἐρινύος αἰνὰ βέλεμνα,
παῖδας ἑοὺς κατέπεφνε καὶ ἐκ φίλον εἵλετο[1] θυμὸν
μαινόμενος κατὰ οἶκον, ὃ δ' ἔμπλεος ἔσκε φόνοιο.
  τοὺς μὲν ἐγὼ δύστηνος ἐμοῖς ἴδον ὀφθαλμοῖσι
βαλλομένους ὑπὸ πατρί, τὸ δ' οὐδ' ὄναρ ἤλυθεν
    ἄλλῳ.
οὐδέ σφιν δυνάμην ἀδινὸν καλέουσιν ἀρῆξαι
μητέρ' ἑήν, ἐπεὶ ἐγγὺς ἀνίκητον κακὸν ἦεν.

<hr>

[1] εἵλετο : mss also ὄλεσε

MEGARA

Megara the wife of Heracles addresses his mother Alcmena.

"Mother dear, O why is thy heart cast down in this exceeding sorrow, and the rose o' thy cheek a-withering away?   What is it, sweet, hath made thee so sad? Is it because thy doughty son be given troubles innumerable by a man of nought, as a lion might be given by a fawn? O well-a-day that the Gods should have sent me this dishonour! and alas that I should have been begotten unto such an evil lot! Woe's me that I that was bedded with a man above reproach, I that esteemed him as the light of my eyes and do render him heart's worship and honour to this day, should have lived to see him of all the world most miserable and best acquaint with the taste of woe! O misery that the bow and arrows given him of the great Apollo should prove to be the dire shafts of a Death-Spirit or a Fury, so that he should run stark mad in his own home and slay his own children withal, should reave them of dear life and fill the house with murder and blood!

Aye, with my own miserable eyes I saw my children smitten of the hand of their father, and that hath no other so much as dreamt of.   And for all they cried and cried upon their mother I could not help them, so present and invincible was

467

ὡς δ' ὄρνις δύρηται ἐπὶ σφετέροισι νεοσσοῖς
ὀλλυμένοις, οὖστ' αἰνὸς ὄφις ἔτι νηπιάχοντας
θάμνοις ἐν πυκινοῖσι κατεσθίει· ἢ δὲ κατ' αὐτοὺς
πωτᾶται κλάζουσα μάλα λιγὺ πότνια[1] μήτηρ,
οὐδ' ἄρ' ἔχει τέκνοισιν ἐπαρκέσαι· ἢ γάρ οἱ αὐτῇ
ἆσσον ἴμεν μέγα τάρβος ἀμειλίκτοιο πελώρου·
ὡς ἐγὼ αἰνοτόκεια φίλον γόνον αἰάζουσα
μαινομένοισι πόδεσσι δόμον κάτα πολλὸν ἐφοίτων.
ὥς γ' ὄφελον μετὰ παισὶν ἅμα θνήσκουσα καὶ
    αὐτὴ
κεῖσθαι φαρμακόεντα δι' ἥπατος ἰὸν ἔχουσα,
Ἄρτεμι θηλυτέρῃσι μέγα κρείουσα γυναιξί.
τῷ χ' ἡμέας κλαύσαντε φίλησ' ἐνὶ χερσὶ τοκῆε[2]
πολλοῖς σὺν κτερέεσσι πυρῆς ἐπέβησαν ὁμοίης,
καί κεν ἕνα χρύσειον ἐς ὀστέα κρωσσὸν ἁπάντων
λέξαντες κατέθαψαν, ὅθι πρῶτον γενόμεσθα.
νῦν δ' οἱ μὲν Θήβην ἱπποτρόφον ἐνναίουσιν
Ἀονίου πεδίοιο βαθεῖαν βῶλον ἀροῦντες·
αὐτὰρ ἐγὼ Τίρυνθα κάτα κραναὴν πόλιν Ἥρης
πολλοῖσιν δύστηνος ἰάπτομαι ἄλγεσιν ἧτορ
αἰὲν ὁμῶς· δακρύων δὲ παρεστί μοι οὐδ' ἴ' ἐρωή.

ἀλλὰ πόσιν μὲν ὁρῶ παῦρον χρόνον ὀφθαλμοῖσιν
οἴκῳ ἐν ἡμετέρῳ· πολέων γάρ οἱ ἔργον ἑτοῖμον
μόχθων, τοὺς ἐπὶ γαῖαν ἀλώμενος ἠδὲ θάλασσαν
μοχθίζει πέτρης ὅγ' ἔχων νόον ἠὲ σιδήρου
καρτερὸν ἐν στήθεσσι· σὺ δ' ἠύτε λείβεαι[3] ὕδωρ,
νύκτας τε κλαίουσα καὶ ἐκ Διὸς ἥμαθ' ὁπόσσα.
ἄλλος μὰν οὐκ ἄν τις εὐφρήναι με παραστὰς
κηδεμόνων· οὐ γάρ σφε δόμων κάτα τεῖχος ἐέργει·

---

[1] πότνια = raving E, cf. Ποτνιαί, ποτνιάς, ποτνιάομαι   τοκῆε
Herm : mss τοκῆες   [3] mss also λείβεται

468

their evil hap. But even as a bird that waileth
upon her young ones' perishing when her babes
be devoured one by one of a dire serpent in the
thicket, and flies to and fro, the poor raving mother,
screaming above her children, and cannot go near
to aid them for her own great terror of that
remorseless monster; even so this unhappiest of
mothers that's before thee did speed back and forth
through all that house in a frenzy, crying woe upon
her pretty brood. O would to thee kind Artemis,
great Queen of us poor women, would I too had
fallen with a poisoned arrow in my heart and so
died also! Then had my parents taken and wept
over us together, and laid us with several rites on
one funeral pile, and so gathered all those ashes in
one golden urn and buried them in the land of our
birth. But alas! they dwell in the Theban country
of steeds and do till the deep loam of the Aonian
lowlands, while I be in the ancient Tirynthian hold
of Hera, and my heart cast down with manifold pain
ever and unceasingly, and never a moment's respite
from tears.

For as for my husband, 'tis but a little of the time
my eyes do look upon him in our home, seeing he
hath so many labours to do abroad by land and sea
with that brave heart of his so strong as stone
or steel; and as for you, you are poured out like
water, weeping the long of every day and night Zeus
giveth to the world: and none other of my kindred
can come and play me comforter; they be no next-
door neighbours, they, seeing they dwell every one

469

καὶ λίην πάντες γε πέρην πιτυώδεος Ἰσθμοῦ
ναίουσ᾽, οὐδέ μοί ἐστι πρὸς ὅντινά κε βλέψασα   5
οἷα γυνὴ πανάποτμος ἀναψύξαιμι φίλον κῆρ,
νόσφι γε δὴ Πύρρης συνομαίμονος· ἡ δὲ καὶ αὐτὴ
ἀμφὶ πόσει σφετέρῳ πλέον ἄχνυται Ἰφικλῆι,
σῷ υἱεῖ· πάντων γὰρ ὀϊζυρώτατα τέκνα
γείνασθαί σε θεῷ τε καὶ ἀνέρι θνητῷ ἔολπα.᾽

   ὣς ἄρ᾽ ἔφη· τὰ δέ οἱ θαλερώτερα δάκρυα μήλων [1]
κόλπον ἐς ἱμερόεντα κατὰ βλεφάρων ἐχέοντο,
μνησαμένη τέκνων τε καὶ ὧν μετέπειτα τοκήων.
ὣς δ᾽ αὕτως δακρύοισι παρήϊα λεύκ᾽ ἐδίαινεν
Ἀλκμήνη· βαρὺ δ᾽ ἧγε καὶ ἐκ θυμοῦ στενάχουσα   6
μύθοισιν πυκινοῖσι φίλην νυὸν ὧδε μετηύδα·

   ‘δαιμονίη παίδων, τί νύ τοι φρεσὶν ἔμπεσε τοῦτο
πευκαλίμαις; πῶς ἄμμ᾽ ἐθέλεις ὀροθυνέμεν ἄμφω
κήδε᾽ ἄλαστα λέγουσα; τὰ δ᾽ οὐ νῦν πρῶτα
      κέκλαυται.
ἦ οὐχ ἅλις, οἷς ἐχόμεσθα τὸ δεύτατον αἰὲν ἐπ᾽
      ἦμαρ [2]
γινομένοις; μάλα μέν γε φιλοθρηνής [3] κέ τις εἴη,
ὅστις ἀριθμήσειεν ἐφ᾽ ἡμετέροις ἀχέεσσι.
θάρσει· οὐ τοιῆσδ᾽ ἐκυρήσαμεν ἐκ θεοῦ αἴσης.

   καὶ δ᾽ αὐτὴν ὁρόω σε φίλον τέκος ἀτρύτοισιν
ἄλγεσι μοχθίζουσαν. ἐπιγνώμων δέ τοί εἰμι   7
ἀσχαλάαν, ὅτε δή γε καὶ εὐφροσύνης κόρος ἐστί·
καί σε μάλ᾽ ἐκπάγλως ὀλοφύρομαι [4] ἠδ᾽ ἐλεαίρω,
οὕνεκεν ἡμετέροιο λυγροῦ μετὰ δαίμονος ἔσχες,
ὅσθ᾽ ἡμῖν ἐφύπερθε κάρης βαρὺς αἰωρεῖται.

---

[1] cf. Theocr. 14. 38, *Il.* 6. 496   [2] ἐπ᾽ ἦμαρ : cf. Theocr.
Inscr. 8. 3   [3] mss also φιλοφρηνὴς   [4] mss also
ἐποδύρομαι

of them away beyond the piny Isthmus, and so
I have none to look to, such as a thrice-miserable
woman needs to revive her heart—save only my
sister Pyrrha, and she hath her own sorrow for her
husband Iphicles, and he your son; for methinks
never in all the world hath woman borne so ill-fated
children as a God and a man did beget upon you."

So far spake Megara, the great tears falling so big
as apples into her lovely bosom, first at the thought
of her children and thereafter at the thought of her
father and mother. And Alcmena, she in like man-
ner did bedew her pale wan cheeks with tears, and
now fetching a deep deep sigh, spake words of
wisdom unto her dear daughter :

"My poor girl," says she, "what is come over
thy prudent heart? How is it thou wilt be dis-
quieting us both with this talk of sorrows unforget-
table? Thou hast bewept them so many times
before; are not the misfortunes which possess us
enough each day as they come? Sure he that
should fall a-counting in the midst of miseries like
ours would be a very fond lover of lamentation.
Be of good cheer; Heaven hath not fashioned us of
such stuff as that.

And what is more, I need no telling, dear child,
of thy sadness; for I can see thee before me labour-
ing of unabating woes, and God wot I know what
'tis to be sore vexed when the very joys of life are
loathsome, and I am exceeding sad and sorry thou
shouldest have part in the baneful fortune that hangs
us so heavy overhead. For before the Maid I swear

"the misfortunes which possess us" : the Greek is 'Are
not the woes which possess us, coming every latest day,
enough?'

ἴστω γὰρ Κούρη τε καὶ εὔεανος Δημήτηρ,
ἅς κε μέγα βλαφθείς τις ἑκὼν ἐπίορκον ὀμόσσαι [1]
δυσμενέων,[2] μηθέν σε χερειότερον φρεσὶν ᾗσι
στέργειν [3] ἢ εἴπερ μοι ὑπὲκ νηδυιόφιν ἦλθες
καί μοι τηλυγέτη ἐνὶ δώμασι παρθένος ἦσθα.
οὐδ' αὐτήν γέ νυ πάμπαν ἔολπά σε τοῦτό γε λήθειν.
τῷ μή μ' ἐξείπῃς ποτ', ἐμὸν θάλος, ὥς σευ ἀκηδέω,
μηδ' εἴ κ' ἠϋκόμου Νιόβης πυκινώτερα κλαίω.
οὐδ' ὡς γὰρ νεμεσητὸν ὑπὲρ τέκνου γοάασθαι
μητέρι δυσπαθέοντος· ἐπεὶ δέκα μῆνας ἔκαμνον
πρὶν καί πέρ τ' [4] ἰδέειν μιν, ἐμῷ ὑπὸ ἥπατ' ἔχουσα,
καί με πυλάρταο σχεδὸν ἤγαγεν Ἀιδωνῆος·
ὧδέ ἑ δυστοκέουσα κακὰς ὠδῖνας ἀνέτλην.
νῦν δέ μοι οἴχεται οἷος ἐπ' ἀλλοτρίης νέον ἆθλον
ἐκτελέων· οὐδ' οἶδα δυσάμμορος, εἴτε μιν αὖτις
ἐνθάδε νοστήσανθ' ὑποδέξομαι, εἴτε καὶ οὐκί.

πρὸς δ' ἔτι μ' ἐπτοίησε διὰ γλυκὺν αἰνὸς ὄνειρος
ὕπνον· δειμαίνω δὲ παλίγκοτον ὄψιν ἰδοῦσα
ἐκπάγλως, μή μοί τι τέκνοις ἀποθύμιον ἔρδῃ.
εἴσατο γάρ μοι ἔχων μακέλην εὐεργέα χερσὶ
παῖς ἐμὸς ἀμφοτέρῃσι, βίῃ Ἡρακληείῃ·
τῇ μεγάλην ἐλάχαινε δεδεγμένος ὡς ἐπὶ μισθῷ
τάφρον τηλεθάοντος ἐπ' ἐσχατιῇ τινος ἀγροῦ,
γυμνὸς ἄτερ χλαίνης τε καὶ εὐμίτροιο χιτῶνος.
αὐτὰρ ἐπειδὴ παντὸς ἀφίκετο πρὸς τέλος ἔργου
καρτερὸν οἰνοφόροιο πονεύμενος ἕρκος ἀλωῆς,
ἤτοι ὁ λίστρον ἔμελλεν ἐπὶ προὔχοντος [5] ἐρείσας
ἀνδήρου καταδῦναι, ἃ καὶ πάρος εἵματα ἔστο·
ἐξαπίνης δ' ἀνελάμψεν ὑπὲρ καπέτοιο βαθείης

---

[1] ὀμόσσαι Brunck : mss -ση   [2] δυσμενέων participle
[3] στέργειν : syntax shifted owing to the intervention of

it, and before the robed Demeter—and any that
willingly and of ill intent forsweareth these will rue
it sore—I love thee no whit less than I had loved
thee wert thou come of my womb and wert thou the
dear only daughter of my house. And of this me-
thinks thou thyself cannot be ignorant altogether.
Wherefore never say thou, sweetheart, that I heed
thee not, albeit I should weep faster than the fair-
tressed Niobè herself. For even such laments as
hers are no shame to be made of a mother for the
ill hap of a child; why, I ailed for nine months big with
him or ever I so much as beheld him, and he brought
me nigh unto the Porter of the Gate o' Death, so ill-
bested was I in the birthpangs of him; and now he
is gone away unto a new labour, alone into a foreign
land, nor can I tell, more's the woe, whether he will
be given me again or no.

And what is more, there is come to disquiet my
sweet slumber a direful dream, and the adverse
vision makes me exceedingly afraid lest ever it
work something untoward upon my children. There
appeared unto me, a trusty mattock grasped in
both hands, my son Heracles the mighty; and
with that mattock, even as one hired to labour,
he was digging of a ditch along the edge of
a springing field, and was without either cloak or
belted jerkin. And when his labouring of the strong
fence of that place of vines was got all to its end,
then would he stick his spade upon the pile of the
earth he had digged and put on those clothes he
wore before; but lo! there outshined above the
deep trench a fire inextinguishable, and there rolled

ὀμόσσαι, cf. Theocr. 12. 4 ff.   ⁴ πρὶν καί πέρ τ' cf. Il. 15. 588,
Theocr. 2. 147   ⁵ mss also λίστρον ἐπὶ προύχοντος σπεῦδεν

πῦρ ἄμοτον, περὶ δ' αὐτὸν ἀθέσφατος εἰλεῖτο φλόξ.
αὐτὰρ ὅγ' αἰὲν ὄπισθε θοοῖς ἀνεχάζετο ποσσίν,
ἐκφυγέειν μεμαὼς ὀλοὸν μένος [1] Ἡφαίστοιο·
αἰεὶ δὲ προπάροιθεν ἑοῦ χροὸς ἠΰτε γέρρον
νώμασκεν μακέλην· περὶ δ' ὄμμασιν ἔνθα καὶ ἔνθα
πάπταινεν, μὴ δή μιν ἐπιφλέξει δήιον πῦρ.
τῷ μὲν ἀοσσῆσαι λελιημένος, ὥς μοι ἔικτο,
Ἰφικλέης μεγάθυμος ἐπ' οὐδεῖ κάππεσ' ὀλισθὼν
πρὶν ἐλθεῖν, οὐδ' ὀρθὸς ἀναστῆναι δύνατ' αὖτις,
ἀλλ' ἀστεμφὲς ἔκειτο, γέρων ὡσεί τ' ἀμενηνός,
ὅντε καὶ οὐκ ἐθέλοντα βιήσατο γῆρας ἀτερπὲς
καππεσέειν· κεῖται δ' ὅγ' ἐπὶ χθονὸς ἔμπεδον
   αὕτως,
εἰσόκε τις χειρός μιν ἀνειρύσσῃ παριόντων
αἰδεσθεὶς ὄπιδα προτέρην πολιοῖο γενείου.
ὣς ἐν γῇ λελίαστο σακεσπάλος Ἰφικλέης·
αὐτὰρ ἐγὼ κλαίεσκον ἀμηχανέοντας ὀρῶσα
παῖδας ἐμούς, μέχρι δή μοι ἀπέσσυτο νήδυμος
   ὕπνος
ὀφθαλμῶν, ἠὼς δὲ παραυτίκα φαινόλις ἦλθε. [2]
   τοῖα, φίλη, μοι ὄνειρα διὰ φρένας ἐπτοίησαν
παννυχίη· τὰ δὲ πάντα πρὸς Εὐρυσθῆα τρέποιτο
οἴκου ἀφ' ἡμετέροιο, γένοιτο δὲ μάντις ἐκείνῳ
θυμὸς ἐμός, μηδ' ἄλλο παρὲκ τελέσειέ τι δαίμων.'

---

[1] μένος : mss also βέλος   [2] φαινόλις ἦλθε : mss also
φαίνετο δῖα

about him a marvellous great flame. At this he went quickly backward, and so ran with intent to escape the baleful might of the God o' Fire, with his mattock ever held before his body like a buckler and his eyes turned now this way and now that, lest the consuming fire should set him alight. Then methought the noble Iphicles, willing to aid him, slipped or ever he came at him, and fell to the earth, nor could not rise up again; nay, but lay there helpless, like some poor weak old man who constrained of joyless age to fall, lieth on the ground and needs must lie, till a passenger, for the sake of the more honour of his hoary beard, take him by the hand and raise him up. So then lay targeteer Iphicles along; and as for me, I wept to behold the parlous plight of my children, till sleep the delectable was gone from my eyes, and lo! there comes me the lightsome dawn.

Such are the dreams, dear heart, have disquieted me all the night long; and I only pray they all may turn from any hurt of our house to make mischief unto Eurystheus; against him be the prophecy of my soul, and Fate ordain that, and that only, for the fulfilment of it."

THE DEAD ADONIS

THE DEAD ADONIS

THIS *piece of Anacreontean verse is shown both by style and metre to be of late date, and was probably incorporated in the Bucolic Collection only because of its connexion in subject with the* Lament for Adonis.

ΕΙΣ ΝΕΚΡΟΝ ΑΔΩΝΙΝ

Ἄδωνιν ἡ Κυθήρη
ὡς εἶδε νεκρὸν ἤδη
στυμνὰν[1] ἔχοντα χαίταν
ὠχράν τε τὰν παρειάν,
ἄγειν τὸν ὗν πρὸς αὐτὰν
ἔταξε τὼς Ἔρωτας.
οἳ δ᾿ εὐθέως ποτανοὶ
πᾶσαν δραμόντες ὕλαν
στυγνὸν τὸν ὗν ἀνεῦρον,
δῆσαν δὲ[2] καὶ πέδασαν.
χὠ μὲν βρόχῳ καθάψας
ἔσυρεν αἰχμάλωτον,
ὃ δ᾿ ἐξόπισθ᾿ ἐλαύνων
ἔτυπτε τοῖσι τόξοις.
ὁ θὴρ δ᾿ ἔβαινε δειλῶς,
φοβεῖτο γὰρ Κυθήρην.
τῷ δ᾿ εἶπεν Ἀφροδίτα
‘πάντων κάκιστε θηρῶν,
σὺ τόνδε μηρὸν ἴψω;
σύ μου τὸν ἄνδρ᾿ ἔτυψας;’
ὁ θὴρ δ᾿ ἔλεξεν ὧδε·
‘ὄμνυμί σοι Κυθήρη

---

[1] στυμνὰν E, cf. Bion i. 74 : mss στυγνὰν
[2] δὲ Wil : mss τε

THE DEAD ADONIS

WHEN the Cytherean saw Adonis
dead, his hair dishevelled and his
cheeks wan and pale, she bade the
Loves go fetch her the boar, and they
forthwith flew away and scoured the
woods till they found the sullen boar.
Then they shackled him both before
and behind, and one did put a noose
about the prisoner's neck and so drag
him, and another belaboured him with
his bow and so did drive, and the
craven beast went along in abject
dread of the Cytherean. Then up-
spake Aphrodite, saying, "Vilest of
all beasts, can it be thou that didst
despite to this fair thigh, and thou
that didst strike my husband?" To
which the beast "I swear to thee,

αὐτήν σε καὶ τὸν ἄνδρα
καὶ ταῦτά μου τὰ δεσμὰ
καὶ τώσδε τὼς κυναγώς·
τὸν ἄνδρα τὸν καλόν σευ
οὐκ ἤθελον πατάξαι
ἀλλ' ὡς ἄγαλμ' ἐσεῖδον,
καὶ μὴ φέρων τὸ καῦμα
γυμνὸν τὸν εἶχε μηρὸν
ἐμαινόμαν φιλᾶσαι.
καί μ' εὖ κατεκσίναζε·[1]
τούτους λαβοῦσα τέμνε,
τούτους κόλαζε, Κύπρι·
τί γὰρ φέρω περισσῶς
ἐρωτικοὺς ὀδόντας;
εἰ δ' οὐχί σοι τάδ' ἀρκεῖ,
καὶ ταῦτά μου τὰ χείλ'
τί γὰρ φιλεῖν ἐτόλμων
τὸν δ' ἠλέησε Κύπρις,
εἶπέν τε τοῖς Ἔρωσι
τὰ δεσμά οἱ 'πιλῦσαι.
ἐκ τῶδ' ἐπηκολούθει,
κὰς ὕλαν οὐκ ἔβαινε,
καὶ τῷ πυρὶ[2] προσελθὼν
ἔκαιε τοὺς ὀδόντας.[3]

---

[1] μ' εὖ: cf. Plat. *Theaet.* 169 B μάλ' εὖ (με) συγκεκφασιν and *Symp.* 194 A εὖ καὶ μάλ' ἂν φόβοιο: mss μευ   κατεκσίναζε Scaliger: mss κατεσίναζε   [2] τῷ πυρί Heinsius: mss τᾷ χερί   [3] ὀδόντας Faber: mss ἔρωτας

Cytherean," answered he, " by thyself and by thy husband, and by these my bonds and these thy huntsmen, never would I have smitten thy pretty husband but that I saw him there beautiful as a statue, and could not withstand the burning mad desire to give his naked thigh a kiss. And now I pray thee make good havoc of me ; pray take and cut off these tusks, pray take and punish them— for why should I possess teeth so passionate ? And if they suffice thee not, then take my chaps also—for why durst they kiss ? " Then had Cypris compassion and bade the Loves loose his bonds ; and he went not to the woods, but from that day forth followed her, and more, went to the fire and burnt those his tusks away.

THE PATTERN-POEMS

(Greek Anthology, XV, 21 ff.)

SIMIAS

I.—THE AXE

THIS *poem was probably written to be inscribed upon a
votive copy of the ancient axe with which tradition said
Epeius made the Wooden Horse and which was preserved
in a temple of Athena. The lines are to be read accord-
ing to the numbering. The metre is choriambic, and each
pair of equal lines contains one foot less than the pre-
ceding. The unusual arrangement of lines is probably
mystic. Simias of Rhodes flourished about* 300 B.C.
(*Anthology*, XV, 22.)

ΤΕΧΝΟΠΑΙΓΝΙΑ

ΣΙΜΙΟΥ

I.—ΠΕΛΕΚΥΣ

1 Ἀνδροθέα δῶρον ὁ Φωκεὺς κρατερᾶς μηδοσύνας ἦρα τίνων Ἀθάνᾳ

2 ὥπασ᾽ Ἐπειὸς πέλεκυν, τῷ ποτε πύργων θεοτεύκτων κατέρειψεν αἶπος

3 τᾶμος, ἐπεὶ τὰν ἱερὰν κηρὶ πυρίπνῳ πόλιν ᾐθάλωσεν

4 Δαρδανιδᾶν, χρυσοβαφεῖς δ᾽ ἐστυφέλιξ᾽ ἐκ θεμέθλων ἄνακτας,

5 οὐκ ἐνάριθμος γεγαὼς ἐν προμάχοις Ἀχαιῶν

6 ἀλλ᾽ ἀπὸ κρανᾶν ἰθαρᾶν νᾶμα κόμιξε δυσκλεῖς.[1]

7 νῦν ἐς Ὀμήρειον ἔβα κέλευθον

8 σὰν χάριν, ἀγρὰ πολύβουλε Παλλάς.

9 τρὶς μάκαρ ὃν σὺ θυμῷ

10 ἵλαος ἀμφιδέρχθης.

11 ὅδ᾽ ὄλβος

12 ἀεὶ πνεῖ.

13 Σιμμίας Βαίνων κλυτὸς ἴσα θεοῖς ὡς εὗρε Ῥόδου γεγαὼς ὁ πολύτροπα μαιόμενος[2] μέτρα μολπῆς.

---

[1] δυσκλεῖς = δυσκλεής E: mss δύσκλης, δυσκλεής, δυσηλεής   [2] μαιόμενος Wil : mss μόνος

This line, the handle of the Axe, is missing from some of the mss, and is in all probability an interpolation from the *Egg* l. 20.

THE PATTERN-POEMS

SIMIAS

I.—THE AXE

EPEIUS of Phocis has given unto the man-goddess Athena, in requital of her doughty counsel, the axe with which he once overthrew the upstanding height of God-builded walls, in the day when with a fire-breath'd Doom he made ashes of the holy city of the Dardanids and thrust gold-broidered lords from their high seats, for all he was not numbered of the vanguard of the Achaeans, but drew off an obscure runnel from a clear shining fount. Aye, for all that, he is gone up now upon the road Homer made, thanks be unto thee, Pallas the pure, Pallas the wise. Thrice fortunate he on whom thou hast looked with very favour. This way happiness doth ever blow.

489

II.—THE WINGS

THIS *poem seems to have been inscribed on the wings of a statue—perhaps a votive statue—representing Love as a bearded child. The metre is the same as that of the* Axe *with the difference that the lines are to be read in the usual order. The poem also differs from the* Axe *in making no reference, except by its shape, to the wings of Love. Moreover it contains no hint of dedication.* (*Anthology* XV, 24.)

II.—ΠΤΕΡΥΓΕΣ

Λεῦσσέ με τὸν Γᾶς τε βαθυστέρνου ἄνακτ' Ἀκμονίδαν τ' ἄλλυδις ἑδράσαντα
μηδὲ τρέσῃς, εἰ τόσος ὢν δάσκια βέβριθα λάχνα γένεια.
τᾶμος ἐγὼ γὰρ γενόμαν, ἁνίκ' ἔκραιν' Ἀνάγκα
πάντα δ' ἕκας εἶχε φράδεσσι λυγροῖς [1]
ἕρπετά, πάνθ' ὅσ' ἕρπε [2]
δι' αἴθρας

Χάους τε·
οὔτι γε Κύπριδος παῖς
ὠκυπέτας [3]   'Αρέιος [3]   καλεῦμαι·
10 οὔτε γὰρ ἔκρανα βίᾳ, πραϋνόῳ [4] δὲ πειθοῖ,
εἶκέ τέ μοι γαῖα θαλάσσας τε μυχοὶ χάλκεος οὐρανός τε·
τῶν δ' ἐγὼ ἐκνοσφισάμαν ὠγύγιον σκᾶπτρον, ἔκρινον [5] δὲ θεοῖς θέμιστας.

[1] ἕκᾶς εἶχε φράδεσσι λυγροῖς E, cf. Hesych. φραδέαι· βουλαῖς: mss ἐκπάσει καὶ φραδέει (εἶκε φράδεσσι) λυγραῖς   [2] ἕρπε E: mss ἕρπει   [3] 'Αρέιος E, for ᾶ cf. Il. 2, 676 and 'Αρραβία Theocr. 17. 86: mss δ' ἀέρμος, δ' ἀέρος   [4] Bgk: mss πραΰνω   [5] Salm: mss ἔκραυνον

II.—THE WINGS

BEHOLD the ruler of the deep-bosomed Earth, the turner upside-down of the Son of Acmon, and have no fear that so little a person should have so plentiful a crop of beard to his chin. For I was born when Necessity bare rule, and all creatures, moved they in Air or in Chaos, were kept through her dismal government far apart. Swift-flying son of Cypris and war-lord Ares—I am not that at all; for by no force came I into rule, but by gentle-willed persuasion, and yet all alike, Earth, deep Sea, and brazen Heaven, bowed to my behest, and I took to myself their olden sceptre and made me a judge among Gods

"Son of Acmon": Heaven.   "Chaos": *see index.*

493

```
          – ◡ –
        – ◡ – ◡ | – ◡ –
 5, 6 ◡ – ◡ – | ◡ – ◡ – | ◡ – –
      ◡ – ◡ – | ◡ ◡ ◡ – | > – ◡ – | ◡ – –
 9, 10 ◡ – ◡ – | ◡ – ⌣⌣ – | ◡ – | > – ◡ – | ◡ – –
      ◡ – ◡ – | ◡ – ◡ – | ◡ – | – ◡ ◡ | – ◡ ◡ | – ◡ – –
      ◡ – ◡ – | ◡ – ◡ – | – – | – – | – ◡ ◡ | – ◡ ◡ |
          – ◡ – –
15, 16  – – | – – | ◡ ◡ ◡ – | ◡ ◡ ◡ – | ◡ ◡ ◡ – | ◡ – ◡ – |
        ◡ – | ◡ – –
      – ◡ – ◡ | – ◡ – ◡ | – ◡ – > | – – | – – | – – |
        ◡ ◡ – | ◡ ◡ – | ◡ – ◡ –
19, 20  – – | ◡◡ – | ◡ ◡ – | ◡ ◡ – | ◡ ◡ – | ◡ ◡ – |
        ◡ ◡ ◡ – | ◡ ◡ ◡ – | – ◡ ◡ | – –
```

III.—THE EGG

THIS *piece would appear to have been actually inscribed upon an egg, and was probably composed merely as a* tour-de-force. *If so, it forms a link in the development of such pieces between the two preceding poems and Theocritus'* Pipe. *The lines, like those of the* Axe, *are to be read as they are numbered, and as there is no evidence here of dedication, the unusual order must have a different purpose ; the poem must be of the nature of a puzzle or riddle. The piece is marked out from the* Axe *and the* Wings *on the one side, and from the* Pipe *on the other, by the variety of its metrical scheme. The lines gradually increase from a trochaic monometer catalectic to a complicated decameter of spondees, anapaests, paeons, and dactyls.*

The " Dorian nightingale *" is the poet and the "* new weft *" the poem itself.* (*Anthology*, XV, 27.)

1 Κωτίλας

3 τῇ τόδ᾽ ἄτριον νέον [1]

5 πρόφρων δὲ θυμῷ δέξο· δὴ γὰρ ἀγνᾶς [2]

7 τὸ μὲν θεῶν ἐριβόας Ἑρμᾶς ἔκιξε [3] κᾶρυξ

9 ἄνωγε δ᾽ ἐκ μέτρου μονοβάμονος μέζω πάροιθ᾽ ἀέξειι

11 θοῶς δ᾽ ὕπερθεν ὠκυλέχριον νεῦμα ποδῶν σποράδα
    πίασκεν [5]

13 θοοῖσί [6] τ᾽ αἰολαῖς νεβροῖς κῶλ᾽ ἀλλάσσων ὀρσιπόδω
    ἐλάφων τέκεσσιν·

15 τηλεκραίπνοις [7] ὑπὲρ ἄκρων ἱέμεναι ποσὶ λόφων κα᾽
    ἀρθμίας ἴχνος τιθήνας,

17 καί τις ὠμόθυμος ἀμφίπαλτον αἶψ᾽ αὐδὰν θὴρ ἐ
    κόλπῳ δεξάμενος θαλαμᾶν πυκωτάτῳ [8]

19 κᾆτ᾽ ὦκα βοᾶς ἀκοὰν μεθέπων ὅγ᾽ ἄφαρ λάσιο
    νιφοβόλων ἀν᾽ ὀρέων ἔσσυται ἄγκος· [9]

20 ταῖς δὴ δαίμων κλυτὸς ἶσα θοοῖσι πόνον δονέων ποσὶ᾽
    πολύπλοκα μεθίει μέτρα μολπᾶς.

18 ῥίμφα πετρόκοιτον [11] ἐκλιπὼν ὄρουσ᾽ εὐνὰν ματρὸ
    πλαγκτὸν μαιόμενος βαλιᾶς ἑλεῖν τέκος·

16 βλαχᾷ δ᾽ οἰῶν πολυβότων ἀν᾽ ὀρέον νομὸν ἔβα
    τανυσφύρων τ᾽ ἀν᾽ ἄντρα [12] Νυμφᾶν,

14 ταὶ δ᾽ ἀμβρότῳ πόθῳ φίλας ματρὸς ῥώοντ᾽ αἶψ
    μεθ᾽ ἱμεροέντα μαζόν,

12 ἴχνει θενὼν τόνον [13] παναίολον, Πιερίδων μονόδουπο
    αὐδάν,

10 ἀριθμον εἰς ἄκραν δεκάδ᾽ ἰχνίων, κόσμον νέμοντ
    ῥυθμῶν. [14]

8 φῦλ᾽ ἐς βροτῶν ὑπὸ φίλας ἑλὼν πτεροῖσι [15] ματρός

6 λίγειά νιν κἄμ᾽ ἀμφὶ ματρὸς ὠδίς· [16]

4 Δωρίας ἀηδόνος·

2 ματέρος

For critical notes see p. 499.

III.—THE EGG

Lo here a new wett of a twittering mother, a Dorian nightingale ; receive it with a right good will, for pure was the mother whose shrilly throes did labour for it. The loud-voicèd herald of the Gods took it up from beneath its dear mother's wings, and cast it among the tribes of men and bade it increase its number onward more and more—that number keeping the while due order of rhythms— from a one-footed measure even unto a full ten measures : and quickly he made fat from above the swiftly-slanting slope of its vagrant feet, striking, as he went on, a motley strain indeed but a right concordant cry of the Pierians, and making exchange of limbs with the nimble fawns the swift children of the foot-stirring stag.—Now these fawns through immortal desire of their dear dam do rush apace after the belovèd teat, all passing with far-hasting feet over the hilltops in the track of that friendly nurse, and with a bleat they go by the mountain pastures of the thousand feeding sheep and the caves of the slender-ankled Nymphs, till all at once some cruel-hearted beast, receiving their echoing cry in the dense fold of his den, leaps speedily forth of the bed of his rocky lair with intent to catch one of the wandering progeny of that dappled mother, and then swiftly following the sound of their cry straightway darteth through the shaggy dell of the snow-clad hills.—Of feet as swift as theirs urged that renownèd God the labour, as he sped the manifold measures of the song.

SIMIAS III

[1] thus Bergk-Wil : mss (with incorporated glosses) τῇ τόδ᾽ ὠδν νέον ἀγνᾶς ἀηδόνος· πανδιωνίδας δωρίας· νασιώτας ἀτριον- ρόδου (or τί τόδ᾽ ὠδν νέον ἀηδόνος Δωρίας ἀγρίου) [2] δὴ γὰρ ἀγνᾶς Salmasius : mss δεῖ γὰρ ἀγνᾶ, δὴ ἀγνᾶ [3] ἔκιξε : mss also ἥκιζε [4] mss also ὄνῳ δ᾽ μέζω E : mss μέγαν ἀέξειν : mss also ὤυξε [5] ὠκυλέχριον E : mss ὠκὺ λέχ. φέρων π̃ασκεν, cf. Pind. P. 4. 150 : mss also πίφαυσκεν [6] θοοῖσι E : mss θοαῖσι [7] τηλεκρ. E : mss παλαικραιπνοῖς [8] θαλαμᾶν Haeberlin : mss -ων πυκνοτάτῳ : mss πουκότατον, πουκότητα [9] κᾶτ᾽ Wil : mss καὶ τάδ᾽ λάσιον Salm : mss -ων ἔσσυται ἄγκος Salm : mss ἔσσυτ᾽ ἀνάγκαις [10] κλυτὸς Bgk : mss -αῖς Ἴσα θοοῖσι πόνον δονέων ποσὶ Jacobs-E : mss ἴσα θεοῖς ποσὶ δονέων or θε. π. πονέων [11] πετρόκ. Salm : mss πτερόκ. or περίκ. [12] βλαχᾷ E : mss βλαχαὶ, λαχαὶ ὀρέων = ὀρεῖον E : mss ὀρέων τ᾽ ἀν᾽ ἄντρα Salm : mss τ᾽ ἄντρα, ἄντρα [13] θενὼν τόνον E : mss θένον τὸν, θενὼ τὰν [14] mss also ἄκρον thus Bgk : mss κόσμιος νέμοντο ῥυθμῷ, κόσμον νέμοντα ῥυθμὸν [15] πτεροῖσι Scaliger : mss πέτροις, πέτροισι [16] κάμ᾽ ἀμφί Salm : mss καμφι ὠδίς : mss also ὠδὶς ἀγνᾶς

THEOCRITUS

THE SHEPHERD'S PIPE

THE *lines of this puzzle-poem are arranged in pairs,
each pair being a syllable shorter than the preceding, and
the dactylic metre descending from a hexameter to a
catalectic dimeter. The solution of it is a shepherd's
pipe dedicated to Pan by Theocritus. The piece is so
full of puns as to preclude accurate translation. The
epithet Merops, as applied to Echo, is explained as
sentence-curtailing, because she gives only the last
syllables (?), but there is also a play on Merops
"Thessalian." The strongest reason*[1] *for doubting the
self-contained ascription of this remarkable* tour-de-force
*to Theocritus is that the shepherd's pipe of Theocritus'
time would seem to have been rectangular, the tubes being
of equal apparent length, and the difference of tone
secured by wax fillings. But to the riddle-maker and his*

---

[1] Advanced by Mr. A. S. F. Gow in *Journ. Philol.* 33. 128 ;
see also *Class. Rev.* 1934. 121.

public a poem was primarily something heard, not some-
thing seen, and the variation in the heard length of the
lines would correspond naturally enough to the variation
in note of the tubes of the pipe. Moreover, every
musical person must have known that, effectively, the tubes
were unequal. The doubling of the lines is to be
explained as a mere evolutionary survival. The applica-
tion of puzzles or riddles to this form of composition was
new, but in giving himself the patronymic Simichidas the
author is probably acknowledging his debt to his pre-
decessor, Simichus being a pet-name form of Simias, as
Amyntichus for Amyntas in VII. If so, the Pipe *is*
anterior to the Harvest Home, *and we have here the*
origin of the poet's nickname. (Anthology, XV, 21.)

Οὐδενὸς εὐνάτειρα μακροπτολέμοιο δὲ μάτηρ
μαίας ἀντιπέτροιο θοὸν τέκεν ἰθυντῆρα,
οὐχὶ κεράσταν, ὅν ποτε θρέψατο ταυροπάτωρ,
ἀλλ' οὗ πειλιπὲς αἶθε πάρος φρένα τέρμα σάκους,
οὔνομ' ὅλον δίζων, ὃς τᾶς Μέροπος πόθον
κούρας γηρυγόνας ἔχε τᾶς ἀνεμώκεος.
ὃς Μοίσᾳ λιγὺ πᾶξεν ἰοστεφάνῳ
ἕλκος ἄγαλμα πόθοιο πυρισμαράγου,[1]
ὃς σβέσεν ἀνορέαν ἰσανδέα
παπποφόνου Τυρίας τ' ἐξήλασεν·[2]   10
ᾧ τόδε τυφλοφόρων ἐρατὸν
πῆμα Πάρις θέτο Σιμιχίδας·
ψυχὰν ᾇ[3] βροτοβάμων
στήτας οἶστρε Σαέττας
κλωποπάτωρ ἀπάτωρ
λαρνακόγυιε χαρεὶς[4]
ἁδὺ μελίσδοις
ἕλλοπι κούρᾳ,
Καλλιόπᾳ
νηλεύστῳ.   20

---

[1] mss also πυρισφαράγου   [2] so Haeb : mss ἀφείλετο or gap
[3] ᾇ Hecker : mss ἀεὶ or ὡ   [4] χαρεὶς Heck : mss χαίρεις

THEOCRITUS.—THE SHEPHERD'S PIPE

Odysseus   Tele-
THE bedfere of nobody and mother of the war-
machus   herdsman of (goats) the goat
abiding brought forth a nimble director of
that suckled one (Zeus) for whom a stone was substituted   Cerastas,
the nurse of the vice-stone, not the
long-horned=Comatas, long-haired   bees, cf. 7. 80 and Verg. G. 4. 550
hornèd one who was once fed by the son of a bull,
Pitys (Pine)=P+itys; itys=shield-rim; ine (old
but him whose heart was fired of old by the P-less
spelling)=eyes, i.e. bosses   lit. whole; pan=all   goat-
ine of bucklers,   dish   by name and double
legged
by nature, him that loved the wind-swift voice-born
Echo   lit. voice-dividing (of Man)   Syrinx also=fistula
maiden of mortal speech, him that fashioned a sore
that shrilled with the violet-crowned Muse into a
for Syrinx
monument of the fiery furnace of his love, him that
the Persian at Marathon
extinguished the manhood which was of equal sound
Perseus   Europa (Europe) was daughter
with a grandsire-slayer and drove it out of a maid of
of a Phoenician   Theo-critus=judge between
Tyre, him, in short, to whom is set up by this Paris
Gods[1] nickname of Theocritus   woe=possession, ref. to the
that is son of Simichus this delectable piece of un-
sore above   i.e. moleskin wallet, lit. wearers of the blind;
peaceful goods dear to the wearers of the blindman's
blind=wallet   lit. man-treading; Prometheus made
skin, with which heartily well pleased, thou clay-
Man of clay   beloved   Omphalè (cf. Ovid, Fast. 2. 305)   son of
treading gadfly of the Lydian quean, at once thief-
Hermes, and, in a sense, son of Odysseus   lit. box-legged
begotten and none-begotten, whose pegs be legs,
box=hoof
whose legs be pegs, play sweetly I pray thee unto
Echo cannot speak of herself
a maiden who is mute indeed and yet is another
=of beautiful voice
Calliopè that is heard but not seen.

[1] Strictly the compound should mean 'judged by God.'

DOSIADAS

THE FIRST ALTAR

THIS *puzzle is written in the Iambic metre and composed of two pairs of complete lines, five pairs of half-lines, and two pairs of three-quarter lines, arranged in the form of an altar. Of the writer nothing is known; he was obviously acquainted with the* Pipe *and also with Lycophron's* Alexandra. *The poem is mentioned by Lucian (Lexiph. 25), but metrical considerations point to its being of considerably later date than the* Pipe. *Moreover, the idea of making an altar of verses presupposes a change in the conception of what a poem is. It was now a thing of ink and paper; and Dosiadas seems to have interpreted the* Pipe *in the light of the pipes of his own time, as representing the outward appearance of an actual pipe.* (Anthology, XV, 26.)

ΔΩΣΙΑΔΑ ΔΩΡΙΕΩΣ

ΒΩΜΟΣ

Εἰμάρσενός με στήτας
πόσις, μέροψ δίσαβος,
τεῦξ᾽, οὐ σποδεύνας ἶνις Ἐμπούσας μόρος
Τεύκροιο βούτα καὶ κυνὸς τεκνώματος,
χρυσᾶς δ᾽[1] ἀΐτας, ἆμος ἐψάνδρα
τὸν γυιόχαλκον οὖρον ἔρραισεν,
ὃν ἀπάτωρ δίσευνος
μόγησε ματρόριπτος·
ἐμὸν δὲ τεῦγμ᾽ ἀθρήσας
Θεοκρίτοιο κτάντας
τριεσπέροιο καύστας
θώυξεν αἶν᾽ ἰύξας[2]
χάλεψε γάρ νιν ἰῷ
σύργαστρος ἐκδυγήρας[3]
τὸν δ᾽ αἰλινεῦντ᾽[4] ἐν ἀμφικλύστῳ
Πανός τε ματρὸς εὐνέτας φὼρ
δίζωος ἶνίς τ᾽ ἀνδροβρῶτος Ἰλοραιστᾶν[5]
ἦρ᾽ ἀρδίων ἐς Τευκρίδ᾽ ἄγαγον τρίπορθον.

---

[1] χρυσᾶς E: mss χρυσᾶς, -οῖς, -οῦς   δ᾽: added by
Valckenaer   [2] αἶν᾽ ἰύξας Salm: mss ἀνιύξας   [3] ἐκδυγήρας
Salm: mss ἐκδὺς γῆρας   [4] αἰλινεῦντ᾽ Hecker: mss ἀεὶ
λινεῦντ᾽ or ἐλλινεῦντ᾽   [5] mss ἰνοραίσταν, ἰλοραίστας, ἰλιο-
ραίστας

DOSIADAS

THE FIRST ALTAR

<small>Jason   Medea put on man's clothes</small>

I AM the work of the husband of a mannish-
<small>to fly into Media   rejuvenated in Medea's caldron   this also = Thessalian</small>

mantled quean, of a twice-young mortal, not
<small>i.e. Thetis, who could   Thetis put Achilles in   active</small>
<small>change her form like E.   the fire to immortalise him   and passive</small>

Empusa's cinder-bedded scion, who was the killing
<small>he was killed by Paris   and killer of Hector son of Hecuba, who</small>

of a Teucrian neatherd and of the childing of a
<small>   i.e. Jason, who built this altar to</small>
<small>became a dog   Chrysè (= Golden) on the way to Colchis</small>

bitch, but the leman of a golden woman; and he
<small>   Medea</small>

made me when the husband-boiler smote down
<small>Talos the brazen man</small>
<small>protected Crete   also = guardian and other things   Hephaestus</small>

the brazen-leggèd breeze wrought of the twice-
<small>wedded Aphrodite and Aglaia, and was a virgin-</small>
<small>birth of Hera who cast him from Olympus</small>

wed mother-hurtled virgin-born; and when the
<small>   Philoctetes   Paris, see the Pipe lighter of the pyre   Heracles</small>

slaughterman of Theocritus and burner of the three-
<small>was begotten on three nights   the Altar</small>

nighted gazed upon this wrought piece, a full
<small>   a</small>

dolorous shriek he shright, for a belly-creeping
<small>serpent   poison = arrow</small>

shedder of age did him despite with enshafted venom;
<small>   isle of Lemnos</small>

but when he was alackadaying in the wave-ywashen,
<small>   Odysseus carried off the</small>
<small> Penelopè   Palladium and came alive from Hades</small>

Pan's mother's thievish twy-lived bedfellow came
<small>Diomed, son of Tydeus who ate Melanippus' head</small>

with the scion of a cannibal, and carried him into
<small>by Heracles, the Amazons, the Greeks   also = land of Troy</small>

the thrice-sacked daughter of Teucer for the
<small>the arrows of Heracles brought by Philoctetes</small>
<small>caused (Troy's fall and) the destruction of the</small>
<small>   tomb (and corpse) of Ilus</small>

sake of Ilus-shivering arrow-heads.

VESTINUS

THE SECOND ALTAR

THE Besantinus *of the manuscripts is very probably a
corruption of* Bestinus, *that is L. Julius Vestinus, who is
described in an inscription as " High-priest of Alexandria
and all Egypt, Curator of the Museum, Keeper of the
Libraries both Greek and Roman at Rome, Supervisor of
the Education of Hadrian, and Secretary to the same
Emperor." The dedication to Hadrian is contained in
the acrostic, which runs, " O Olympian, mayst thou
sacrifice in*[1] *many years." The* Altar *is composed of
three Anacreontean lines, three trochaic tetrameters, three
phalaecians, eleven iambic dimeters, three anapaestic
dimeters, and three choriambic tetrameters. The poem is
not a puzzle, except in so far as the acrostic furnishes
this element ; for, unlike its predecessors, it refers to itself
in definite terms. The author has confined his imitation
of Dosiadas to the shape of the poem and the use of out-
of-the-way words and expressions. (Anthology,* XV, 25.)

[1] Or perhaps " for," *i.e.* " in honour of."

ΒΗΣΤΙΝΟΥ[1]

ΒΩΜΟΣ

Ο λὸς οὔ με λιβρὸς ἱρῶν
Λ ιβάδεσσιν οἷα κάλχης[2]
Υ ποφοινίῃσι τέγγει,
Μ αύλιες δ᾽ ὕπερθε πέτρῃ Ναξίῃ[3] θοούμεναι
Π αμάτων φείδοντο Πανός, οὐ στροβίλῳ[4] λιγνύϊ
Ι ξὸς εὐώδης μελαίνει τρεχνέων με Νυσίων·
Ε ς γὰρ βωμὸν ὅρῃ με μήτε γλούρου[5]
Π λίνθοις μήτ᾽ Ἀλύβης παγέντα[6] βώλοις,
Ο ὐδ᾽ ὃν Κυνθογενὴς ἔτευξε φύτλη
Λ αβόντε μηκάδων κέρα,
Λ ισσαῖσιν ἀμφὶ δειράσιν
Ο σσαι νέμονται Κυνθίαις,
Ι σόρροπος πέλοιτό μοι·
Σ ὺν οὐρανοῦ γὰρ ἐκγόνοις
Ε ἰνάς μ᾽ ἔτευξε γηγενής,
Τ άων ἀείζωον τέχνην
Ε νευσε πάλμυς ἀφθίτων.
Σ ὺ δ᾽, ὦ πιὼν κρήνηθεν ἣν
Ι νις κόλαψε Γοργόνος,
Θ ύοις τ᾽ ἐπισπένδοις τ᾽ ἐμοὶ
Υ μηττιάδων πολὺ λαροτέρην
Σ πονδὴν ἄδην· ἴθι δὴ θαρσέων
Ε ς ἐμὴν τεῦξιν, καθαρὸς γὰρ ἐγὼ
Ι ὸν ἱέντων τεράων, οἷα κέκευθ᾽ ἐκεῖνος,
Α μφὶ Νέαις Θρηϊκίαις ὃν σχεδόθεν Μυρίνης
Σ οί, Τριπάτωρ, πορφυρέου φὼρ ἀνέθηκε κριοῦ.

[1] Βηστίνου Haeb : mss Βησαντίνου   [2] κάλχης Brunck-E :
mss κάχλην   [3] mss πέτρης ναξίας   [4] στροβίλῳ Salm : mss
-ων   [5] mss ὀρῆς   μ. γλούρου Bgk : mss μ. ταγχούρου,
μηταχούρου   [6] λαβόντε Wil : mss -τα

VESTINUS

THE SECOND ALTAR

THE murky flux of sacrifice bedews me not with ruddy trickles like the flux of a purple-fish, the whittles whetted upon Naxian stone spare over my head the possessions of Pan, and the fragrant ooze of Nysian boughs blackens me not with his twirling reek; for in me behold an altar knit neither of bricks aureate nor of nuggets Alybaean, nor yet that altar which the generation of two that was born upon Cynthus did build with the horns of such as bleat and browse over the smooth Cynthian ridges, be not that made my equal in the weighing. for I was builded with aid of certain offspring of Heaven by the Nine that were born of Earth, and the liege-lord of the deathless decreed their work should be eterne.   And now, good drinker of the spring that was strucken of the scion of the Gorgon, I pray that thou mayst do sacrifice upon me and pour plentiful libation of far goodlier gust than the daughters of Hymettus ; up and come boldly unto this wrought piece, for 'tis pure from venom-venting prodigies such as were hid in that other, which the thief who stole a purple ram set up unto the daughter of three sires in Thracian Neae over against Myrīnè.

"possessions of Pan": sheep and oxen.   "fragrant ooze of Nysian boughs": frankincense.   "nuggets Alybaean" explained by *Iliad*, 2. 857.   "offspring of Heaven": the Graces.   "the Nine": the Muses.   "daughter of three sires": an etymological variation of Tritogeneia.   The last few lines refer to the *Altar* of Dosiadas, Myrīnè being another name for Lesbos.

INDEX

INDEX

INDEX

INDEX

Atreus : XVIII. 6, XVII. 118; Mosch., III. 79; son of Pelops and father of Agamemnon and Menelaus.

Augeas : XXV. 7, etc.; son of the Sun, and king of the Epeians of Elis.

Ausonia : Mosch., III. 94; S. Italy (Magna Graecia).

Autonoë : XXVI. 1, etc.; daughter of Cadmus mythical king of Thebes.

Bacchus : XXVI. 13, *Inscr.*, XVIII. 3.

Battus : IV. 41, 56.

Bebrycians : XXII. 29, etc.; a people of Bithynia.

Bellerophon : XV. 92; son of a king of Corinth; riding the winged horse Pegasus, he killed the Chimaera.

Bembina : XXV. 202; a town of the Peloponnese near Nemea.

Berenicë : XV. 107, 110, XVII. 34, etc.; wife of Ptolemy I.

Bias : III. 44; *see* Melampus.

Biblus : XIV. 15; a town of Phoenicia.

Bion : Mosch., III. 2, etc.

Bistonian : Mosch., III. 18; Thracian.

Blemyans : VII. 114; a people of Ethiopia, who lived at the source of the Nile.

Boeotia : Mosch., III. 88; a district of central Greece.

Bombўca : X. 26, 36.

Brasilas : VII. 11.

Bucaeus : XI. etc.

Buprasium : XXV. 11; a city of Elis.

Burina : VII. 6; the fountain of Cos.

Byblis : VII. 115; a fountain of Miletus.

Cadmus : XXVI. 36; mythical king of Thebes.

Caïcus : *Inscr.*, XIV. 3.

Calliopë : Mosch., III. 72; *Pipe*, 19; one of the Muses.

Calydon : XVII. 54; a town of Aetolia in Central Greece.

Calymna : I. 57; an island of the Aegean near Cos.

Camirus : *Inscr.*, XXII. 4; a Dorian City of Rhodes.

Caria : XVII. 89; a district of S.W. Asia Minor.

Carnea : V. 83; the Dorian festival of Apollo.

Castalia : VII. 148; a fountain of Mt. Parnassus, sacred to the Muses.

Castor : XXII. 22, etc., XXIV. 129, 132; son of Zeus and Leda, the wife of Tyndareüs king of Sparta; the twin-brother of Polydeuces and brother of Helen.

Caucasus : VII. 77.

Ceos : XVI. 44; an island of the W. Aegean, birthplace of the great Lyric and Elegiac poet Simonides (556–467 B.C.)

Cerberus : XXIX. 38; the watch-dog of the lower world.

Ceÿx : Mosch., III. 40, *see* Halcyon.

Chalcon : VII. 6, *where see note.*

Chaos : *Wings*, 7; according to Orphic notions, the Void which, with the Aether or Air, existed before the universe and was the child of Chronus or Time and Anankè or Necessity.

Charites (the Graces) : XVI. 6, etc., 109, *where see note,* XXVIII. 7; Bion, I. 91; Mosch., II. 71.

Chios : VII. 47; XXII. 218; an island of the E. Aegean, one of the cities which boasted to be the birthplace of Homer.

Chiron : VII. 150; the Centaur; he lived in a a cave on Mt. Pelion in Thessaly, where he taught Peleus and other heroes.

Chròmis : I. 24.

Chrysa : Dos., 5, *where see note.*

Chrysogonè : *Inscr.*, XIII. 2.

Cianians : XIII. 30; a mythical people of the Propontis.

Cilicia : XVII. 88; a district of S.E. Asia Minor.

Cinaetha : V. 102; the name of a sheep.

Cinyras : Bion, I. 91; king of Cyprus and father of Adonis.

Circè : II. 15, IX. 36; a mythical sorceress who turned Odysseus' companions into pigs.

Cissaetha : I. 151; the name of a goat.

INDEX

519

INDEX

king of Tiryns, **taskmaster** of Heracles.

Eurȳtus : XXIV. 108; a famous archer, king of Oechalia in Thessaly.

Eusthĕnes : *Inscr.*, XI. 1.

Eutȳchis : XV. 67.

Evening Star (Hesperus) : Bion, IX. 1.

Fate : I. 93, 140, II. 160, XXIV. 70; Bion, I. 94, VII. 3, 6, 15, XI. 4.

Foam, Child of the : Bion, IX. 1; Mosch., II. 71; Aphrodite; according to one story she was born of the sea-foam.

Fury (Erĭnys) : *Meg.*, 14; the Furies were avenging deities who pursued wrong-doers.

Galatĕa : VI. 6, XI. 8, etc.; Bion, II. 3, XII. 3; Mosch., III. 58, 61; a sea-nymph, daughter of Nereus.

Ganymed : XII. 35; a beautiful youth carried off by eagles to be the cupbearer of Zeus.

Glaucè : IV. 31; a poetess contemporary with Theocritus.

—— *Inscr.*, XXIII. 2.

Golgi : XV. 100; a town of Cyprus, a seat of the worship of Aphrodite.

Gorgo : XV. 1, etc.

Gorgon : Vest., 19; a woman-like monster with serpents for hair; every one that looked upon her became stone; when she was slain by Perseus the winged horse Pegasus sprang from her blood.

Greek : Bion, II. 12.

Hades : I. 63, 103, 130, II. 33, 160, IV. 27, XVI. 30, 52, *Inscr.*, VI. 3; Bion, I. 94, VIII. 3; Mosch., I. 14; *Meg.*, 86.

Haemus : VII. 76; a mountain of Thrace.

Halcȳon (Alcyonè) : Mosch., III. 40, *cf. also* Theocr. VII. 59 *and note;* daughter of Aeolus and wife of Ceȳx king of Trachis; he perished at sea, and his body was found by his wife upon the shore; she threw herself into the sea and was changed into a kingfisher or halcyon.

Hăleis : V. 123; a river of the district of Sybaris in S. Italy.

—— VII. 1; a river or river-valley of Cos.

Harpalȳcus : XXIV. 116; a teacher of Heracles, called elsewhere Autolycus.

Hēbè : XVII. 32; Goddess of Youth, wife of Heracles in heaven.

Hebrus : VII. 112; a river of Thrace.

Hecatè : II. 12, 14.

Hector : XV. 139; son of Priam and chief hero of the Trojan side.

Hecuba : XV. 139; wife of Priam king of Troy.

Heilisson : XXV. 9; a river of Arcadia and Elis.

Helen : XV. 110, XVIII. 6, etc., XXII. 216, XXVII. 1, 2; Bion, II. 10; daughter by Zeus of Leda the wife of Tyndareüs, king of Sparta. After she became the wife of Menelaüs, she was carried off by Paris, and this gave rise to the Trojan War.

Helicè : I. 125; Callisto, daughter of Lycaon king of Arcadia; she was beloved by Zeus, and having been changed by the jealous Hera into a bear, was placed by him among the stars as the constellation of the Great Bear (Helicè).

—— XXV. 165, 180; the chief city of Achaea.

Helicon : XXV. 209, *Inscr.*, I. 2; a mountain of Boeotia sacred to the Muses.

Hellespont : XIII. 29.

Hēphaestus : II. 134; Mosch., II. 38; *Meg.*, 106.

Hera : IV. 22, XV. 64, XVII. 133, XXIV. 13; Mosch., II. 77; *Meg.*, 38.

Heracles (Hercules) : II. 121, IV. 8, VII. 150, XIII. 37, 70, 73, XVII. 20, 26, 27, XXIV. 1, etc., XXV. 71, etc.; *Meg.*, 95.

Hermes : I. 77, XXIV. 115, XXV. 4; Bion, V. 8; Mosch., II. 56; *Egg*, 7.

INDEX

Hesiod, Mosch. III., 87; the early Epic poet; he was regarded as second to Homer.

Hesperus : Bion, IX. 1.

Hiero : XVI. 80, etc.; king of Syracuse, 270–216 B.C.

Himera : V. 124; a river of the district of Sybaris in S. Italy.

Himeras : VII. 75; a river near the town of Himera in N. Sicily.

Hippocoön : VI. 41, X. 16

Hippomenes : III. 40, *where see note.*

Hipponax : *Inscr.*, XIX. 1; the Iambic poet of Ephesus; he was famous for his lampoons, and flourished about 540 B.C. at Clazomenae in Asia Minor.

Homer : XVI. 20; Mosch., III. 71; *Axe,* 7.

Hômôlê : VII. 103; a mountain of Thessaly, a seat of the worship of Pan.

Hyĕtis : VII. 115; a spring near Miletus in Asia Minor.

Hylas : XIII. 7, etc.; a youth beloved by Heracles.

Hymen : XVIII. 58; Bion, I. 87, 90,

Hymettus : Vest., 21; a mountain of Attica famous for its marble and its honey.

Iasion : *see* Jasion.

Icaria : IX. 26; an island of the E. Aegean.

Ida : I. 105, XVII. 9; Bion, II. 10; a mountain of the Troad.

Idalium : XV. 100; a town of Cyprus, a seat of the worship of Aphrodite.

Idas : XXII. 140, etc.; son of Aphareus mythical king of Messenia.

Ilium : XXII. 217; Troy.

Ilus : XVI. 75; Dos., 17; grandfather of Priam and king of Troy.

Inachus : Mosch., II. 44, 51; son of Oceanus and first king of Argos; he was the father of Io.

Inhospitables : Bion, VIII. 4, *where see note.*

Ino : XXVI. 1, 22; daughter of Cadmus mythical king of Thebes.

Io : Mosch., II. 44; an Argive princess beloved by Zeus; owing to Hera's jealousy he turned her into a cow, in which shape, pursued by a gadfly sent by Hera, she wandered over land and sea till she reached Egypt, where Zeus restored her to human form and she became by him mother of Epaphus king of Egypt.

Iolcus : XIII. 19; the city of Thessaly whence Jason set out in quest of the Golden Fleece.

Ionia : XVI. 57, XXVIII. 21; the Greek cities of the mid-Aegean coast of Asia Minor.

Iphicles : XXIV. 2 etc.; *Meg.,* 53, 111, 118; brother of Heracles; *see* Alcmena.

Iris : XVII. 134; messenger of the Gods.

Isthmus : *Meg.*, 49; the neck of land joining the Peloponnese to central Greece.

Jasion (Iasion) : III. 50; a son of Zeus and Electra; he was beloved by Demeter.

Jason : XIII. 16, 67, XXII. 31; son of Aeson the rightful king of Iolcus, was sent by the usurper Pelias, who hoped thus to be rid of him, to fetch the Golden Fleece from Colchis.

Justice : Mosch., III. 114.

Lăbas : XIV. 24.

Lacedaemon : *see* Sparta.

Lacinium : IV. 33; a promontory near Croton in S. Italy, a seat of the worship of Hera.

Lâcon : V. 2, etc.

Laërtes : XVI. 56; father of Odysseus.

Lagid (son of Lagus) : XVII. 14; Ptolemy I, Soter, king of Egypt, 323–287 B.C.

Lampriadas : IV. 21.

Lampūrus (White-tail) : VIII. 65; the name of a dog.

Laocoösa : XXII. 206; wife of Aphareus.

Lapiths : XV. 141; a Thessalian tribe who waged a famous war against the Centaurs.

INDEX

INDEX

INDEX

524

INDEX

INDEX

INDEX

ADDITIONAL NOTE ON THEOCRITUS I. 29 ff.

(1) Some scholars, following Suidas' explanation, take ἑλι-χρύσῳ as the ivy-flower. This meaning may have been invented to explain the passage ; it is not recorded in the Scholia. But it cannot be denied that κεκονιμένος (or κεκονισμένος, as some mss give it) "dusted" suits the groups of dots which represent the ivy-flower on many ancient cups. (2) In these days when what were thought unlikely emendations, e.g. at 2. 82, 15. 7, 145, have found support in papyri, it is perhaps only natural that I should wish to record, against the advice of most of the friends I have consulted, that I have thought of ἐνὶ χρυσῷ κεκοπισμένος (ενι from ελι below, cf. πενία ~ πέλεν ά 21. 16–17), "carved," or perhaps "stamped," i.e. *repoussé*, "in gold"—intended as an ignorant exaggeration in describing what appears to have been a wooden cup with painted decorations (cf. ἀργυροκοπιστήρ, ἐναργυρίζομαι, and ἔγχρυσος which presupposes the phrase ἐν χρυσῷ). In either of these cases ἁ δὲ ἑλιξ must mean "the ivy-tendril." It should be noted that however we take the passage, in accordance with Greek custom the first δέ and not the second must mark the contrast with περὶ μὲν χείλη. For this reason I now (1937) favour Meineke's κατ' ὤτων (cf. ἀμφῶες above), a proposal of which I have been reminded by Professor Campbell.

J. M. E.

Printed in Great Britain by
Fletcher & Sons Ltd, Norwich

THE LOEB CLASSICAL LIBRARY

VOLUMES ALREADY PUBLISHED

Latin Authors

AMMIANUS MARCELLINUS. Translated by J. C. Rolfe. 3 Vols.

APULEIUS: THE GOLDEN ASS (METAMORPHOSES). W. Adlington (1566). Revised by S. Gaselee.

ST. AUGUSTINE: CITY OF GOD. 7 Vols. Vol. I. G. E. McCracken. Vols. II and VII. W. M. Green. Vol. III. D. Wiesen. Vol. IV. P. Levine. Vol. V. E. M. Sanford and W. M. Green. Vol. VI. W. C. Greene.

ST. AUGUSTINE, CONFESSIONS OF. W. Watts (1631). 2 Vols.

ST. AUGUSTINE, SELECT LETTERS. J. H. Baxter.

AUSONIUS. H. G. Evelyn White. 2 Vols.

BEDE. J. E. King. 2 Vols.

BOETHIUS: TRACTS and DE CONSOLATIONE PHILOSOPHIAE. Rev. H. F. Stewart and E. K. Rand. Revised by S. J. Tester.

CAESAR: ALEXANDRIAN, AFRICAN and SPANISH WARS. A. G. Way.

CAESAR: CIVIL WARS. A. G. Peskett.

CAESAR: GALLIC WAR. H. J. Edwards.

CATO: DE RE RUSTICA. VARRO: DE RE RUSTICA. H. B. Ash and W. D. Hooper.

CATULLUS. F. W. Cornish. TIBULLUS. J. B. Postgate. PERVIGILIUM VENERIS. J. W. Mackail.

CELSUS: DE MEDICINA. W. G. Spencer. 3 Vols.

CICERO: BRUTUS and ORATOR. G. L. Hendrickson and H. M. Hubbell.

[CICERO]: AD HERENNIUM. H. Caplan.

CICERO: DE ORATORE, etc. 2 Vols. Vol. I. DE ORATORE, Books I and II. E. W. Sutton and H. Rackham. Vol. II. DE ORATORE, Book III. DE FATO; PARADOXA STOICORUM; DE PARTITIONE ORATORIA. H. Rackham.

CICERO: DE FINIBUS. H. Rackham.

CICERO: DE INVENTIONE, etc. H. M. Hubbell.

CICERO: DE NATURA DEORUM and ACADEMICA. H. Rackham.

CICERO: DE OFFICIIS. Walter Miller.

CICERO: DE REPUBLICA and DE LEGIBUS. Clinton W. Keyes.

1

Cicero: De Senectute, De Amicitia, De Divinatione. W. A. Falconer.

Cicero: In Catilinam, Pro Flacco, Pro Murena, Pro Sulla. New version by C. Macdonald.

Cicero: Letters to Atticus. E. O. Winstedt. 3 Vols.

Cicero: Letters to His Friends. W. Glynn Williams, M. Cary, M. Henderson. 4 Vols.

Cicero: Philippics. W. C. A. Ker.

Cicero: Pro Archia, Post Reditum, De Domo, De Haruspicum Responsis, Pro Plancio. N. H. Watts.

Cicero: Pro Caecina, Pro Lege Manilia, Pro Cluentio, Pro Rabirio. H. Grose Hodge.

Cicero: Pro Caelio, De Provinciis Consularibus, Pro Balbo. R. Gardner.

Cicero: Pro Milone, In Pisonem, Pro Scauro, Pro Fonteio, Pro Rabirio Postumo, Pro Marcello, Pro Ligario, Pro Rege Deiotaro. N. H. Watts.

Cicero: Pro Quinctio, Pro Roscio Amerino, Pro Roscio Comoedo, Contra Rullum. J. H. Freese.

Cicero: Pro Sestio, In Vatinium. R. Gardner.

Cicero: Tusculan Disputations. J. E. King.

Cicero: Verrine Orations. L. H. G. Greenwood. 2 Vols.

Claudian. M. Platnauer. 2 Vols.

Columella: De Re Rustica. De Arboribus. H. B. Ash, E. S. Forster and E. Heffner. 3 Vols.

Curtius, Q.: History of Alexander. J. C. Rolfe. 2 Vols.

Florus. E. S. Forster. Cornelius Nepos. J. C. Rolfe.

Frontinus: Stratagems and Aqueducts. C. E. Bennett and M. B. McElwain.

Fronto: Correspondence. C. R. Haines. 2 Vols.

Gellius. J. C. Rolfe. 3 Vols.

Horace: Odes and Epodes. C. E. Bennett.

Horace: Satires, Epistles, Ars Poetica. H. R. Fairclough.

Jerome: Selected Letters. F. A. Wright.

Juvenal and Persius. G. G. Ramsay.

Livy. B. O. Foster, F. G. Moore, Evan T. Sage, and A. C. Schlesinger and R. M. Geer (General Index). 14 Vols.

Lucan. J. D. Duff.

Lucretius. W. H. D. Rouse. Revised by M. F. Smith.

Martial. W. C. A. Ker. 2 Vols.

Minor Latin poets: from Publilius Syrus to Rutilius Namatianus, including Grattius, Calpurnius Siculus, Nemesianus, Avianus and others, with " Aetna " and the " Phoenix." J. Wight Duff and Arnold M. Duff.

Ovid: The Art of Love and Other Poems. J. H. Mozley.

Ovid: Fasti. Sir James G. Frazer.

2

Ovid: Heroides and Amores. Grant Showerman.
Ovid: Metamorphoses. F. J. Miller. 2 Vols.
Ovid: Tristia and Ex Ponto. A. L. Wheeler.
Persius. Cf. Juvenal.
Petronius. M. Heseltine. Seneca: Apocolocyntosis. W. H. D. Rouse.
Phaedrus and Babrius (Greek). B. E. Perry.
Plautus. Paul Nixon. 5 Vols.
Pliny: Letters, Panegyricus. Betty Radice. 2 Vols.
Pliny: Natural History. 10 Vols. Vols. I–V and IX. H. Rackham. VI.–VIII. W. H. S. Jones. X. D. E. Eichholz.
Propertius. H. E. Butler.
Prudentius. H. J. Thomson. 2 Vols.
Quintilian. H. E. Butler. 4 Vols.
Remains of Old Latin. E. H. Warmington. 4 Vols. Vol. I. (Ennius and Caecilius) Vol. II. (Livius, Naevius Pacuvius, Accius) Vol. III. (Lucilius and Laws of XII Tables) Vol. IV. (Archaic Inscriptions)
Sallust. J. C. Rolfe.
Scriptores Historiae Augustae. D. Magie. 3 Vols.
Seneca, The Elder: Controversiae, Suasoriae. M. Winterbottom. 2 Vols.
Seneca: Apocolocyntosis. Cf. Petronius.
Seneca: Epistulae Morales. R. M. Gummere. 3 Vols.
Seneca: Moral Essays. J. W. Basore. 3 Vols.
Seneca: Tragedies. F. J. Miller. 2 Vols.
Seneca: Naturales Quaestiones. T. H. Corcoran. 2 Vols.
Sidonius: Poems and Letters. W. B. Anderson. 2 Vols.
Silius Italicus. J. D. Duff. 2 Vols.
Statius. J. H. Mozley. 2 Vols.
Suetonius. J. C. Rolfe. 2 Vols.
Tacitus: Dialogus. Sir Wm. Peterson. Agricola and Germania. Maurice Hutton. Revised by M. Winterbottom, R. M. Ogilvie, E. H. Warmington.
Tacitus: Histories and Annals. C. H. Moore and J. Jackson. 4 Vols.
Terence. John Sargeaunt. 2 Vols.
Tertullian: Apologia and De Spectaculis. T. R. Glover. Minucius Felix. G. H. Rendall.
Valerius Flaccus. J. H. Mozley.
Varro: De Lingua Latina. R. G. Kent. 2 Vols.
Velleius Paterculus and Res Gestae Divi Augusti. F. W. Shipley.
Virgil. H. R. Fairclough. 2 Vols.
Vitruvius: De Architectura. F. Granger. 2 Vols.

Greek Authors

ACHILLES TATIUS. S. Gaselee.

AELIAN: ON THE NATURE OF ANIMALS. A. F. Scholfield. 3 Vols.

AENEAS TACTICUS. ASCLEPIODOTUS and ONASANDER. The Illinois Greek Club.

AESCHINES. C. D. Adams.

AESCHYLUS. H. Weir Smyth. 2 Vols.

ALCIPHRON, AELIAN, PHILOSTRATUS: LETTERS. A. R. Benner and F. H. Fobes.

ANDOCIDES, ANTIPHON. Cf. MINOR ATTIC ORATORS.

APOLLODORUS. Sir James G. Frazer. 2 Vols.

APOLLONIUS RHODIUS. R. C. Seaton.

THE APOSTOLIC FATHERS. Kirsopp Lake. 2 Vols.

APPIAN: ROMAN HISTORY. Horace White. 4 Vols.

ARATUS. Cf. CALLIMACHUS.

ARISTIDES: ORATIONS. C. A. Behr. Vol. I.

ARISTOPHANES. Benjamin Bickley Rogers. 3 Vols. Verse trans.

ARISTOTLE: ART OF RHETORIC. J. H. Freese.

ARISTOTLE: ATHENIAN CONSTITUTION, EUDEMIAN ETHICS, VICES AND VIRTUES. H. Rackham.

ARISTOTLE: GENERATION OF ANIMALS. A. L. Peck.

ARISTOTLE: HISTORIA ANIMALIUM. A. L. Peck. Vols. I.–II.

ARISTOTLE: METAPHYSICS. H. Tredennick. 2 Vols.

ARISTOTLE: METEOROLOGICA. H. D. P. Lee.

ARISTOTLE: MINOR WORKS. W. S. Hett. On Colours, On Things Heard, On Physiognomies, On Plants, On Marvellous Things Heard, Mechanical Problems, On Indivisible Lines, On Situations and Names of Winds, On Melissus, Xenophanes, and Gorgias.

ARISTOTLE: NICOMACHEAN ETHICS. H. Rackham.

ARISTOTLE: OECONOMICA and MAGNA MORALIA. G. C. Armstrong (with METAPHYSICS, Vol. II).

ARISTOTLE: ON THE HEAVENS. W. K. C. Guthrie.

ARISTOTLE: ON THE SOUL, PARVA NATURALIA, ON BREATH. W. S. Hett.

ARISTOTLE: CATEGORIES, ON INTERPRETATION, PRIOR ANALYTICS. H. P. Cooke and H. Tredennick.

ARISTOTLE: POSTERIOR ANALYTICS, TOPICS. H. Tredennick and E. S. Forster.

ARISTOTLE: ON SOPHISTICAL REFUTATIONS.
On Coming to be and Passing Away, On the Cosmos. E. S. Forster and D. J. Furley.

ARISTOTLE: PARTS OF ANIMALS. A. L. Peck; MOTION AND PROGRESSION OF ANIMALS. E. S. Forster.

ARISTOTLE: PHYSICS. Rev. P. Wicksteed and F. M. Cornford. 2 Vols.
ARISTOTLE: POETICS and LONGINUS. W. Hamilton Fyfe DEMETRIUS ON STYLE. W. Rhys Roberts.
ARISTOTLE: POLITICS. H. Rackham.
ARISTOTLE: PROBLEMS. W. S. Hett. 2 Vols.
ARISTOTLE: RHETORICA AD ALEXANDRUM (with PROBLEMS. Vol. II). H. Rackham.
ARRIAN: HISTORY OF ALEXANDER and INDICA. New Vol. I by P. A. Brunt. Vol. II by E. Iliffe Robson.
ATHENAEUS: DEIPNOSOPHISTAE. C. B. Gulick. 7 Vols.
BABRIUS and PHAEDRUS (Latin). B. E. Perry.
ST. BASIL: LETTERS. R. J. Deferrari. 4 Vols.
CALLIMACHUS: FRAGMENTS. C. A. Trypanis. MUSAEUS: HERO AND LEANDER. T. Gelzer and C. Whitman.
CALLIMACHUS: HYMNS and EPIGRAMS. LYCOPHRON. A. W. Mair. ARATUS. G. R. Mair.
CLEMENT OF ALEXANDRIA. Rev. G. W. Butterworth.
COLLUTHUS. Cf. OPPIAN.
DAPHNIS AND CHLOE. Thornley's Translation revised by J. M. Edmonds. PARTHENIUS. S. Gaselee.
DEMOSTHENES I: OLYNTHIACS, PHILIPPICS and MINOR ORATIONS I–XVII and XX. J. H. Vince.
DEMOSTHENES II: DE CORONA and DE FALSA LEGATIONE. C. A. Vince and J. H. Vince.
DEMOSTHENES III: MEIDIAS, ANDROTION, ARISTOCRATES, TIMOCRATES and ARISTOGEITON I and II. J. H. Vince.
DEMOSTHENES IV–VI: PRIVATE ORATIONS and IN NEAERAM. A. T. Murray.
DEMOSTHENES VII: FUNERAL SPEECH, EROTIC ESSAY, EXORDIA and LETTERS. N. W. and N. J. DeWitt.
DIO CASSIUS: ROMAN HISTORY. E. Cary. 9 Vols.
DIO CHRYSOSTOM. J. W. Cohoon and H. Lamar Crosby. 5 Vols.
DIODORUS SICULUS. 12 Vols. Vols. I–VI. C. H. Oldfather. Vol. VII. C. L. Sherman. Vol. VIII. C. B. Welles. Vols. IX and X. R. M. Geer. Vol. XI. F. Walton. Vol. XII. F. Walton. General Index. R. M. Geer.
DIOGENES LAERTIUS. R. D. Hicks. 2 Vols. New Introduction by H. S. Long.
DIONYSIUS OF HALICARNASSUS: ROMAN ANTIQUITIES. Spelman's translation revised by E. Cary. 7 Vols.
DIONYSIUS OF HALICARNASSUS: CRITICAL ESSAYS. S. Usher. 2 Vols.
EPICTETUS. W. A. Oldfather. 2 Vols.
EURIPIDES. A. S. Way. 4 Vols. Verse trans.
EUSEBIUS: ECCLESIASTICAL HISTORY. Kirsopp Lake and J. E. L. Oulton. 2 Vols.

GALEN: ON THE NATURAL FACULTIES. A. J. Brock.

THE GREEK ANTHOLOGY. W. R. Paton. 5 Vols.

GREEK ELEGY AND IAMBUS with the ANACREONTEA. J. M. Edmonds. 2 Vols.

THE GREEK BUCOLIC POETS (THEOCRITUS, BION, MOSCHUS). J. M. Edmonds.

GREEK MATHEMATICAL WORKS. Ivor Thomas. 2 Vols.

HERODES. Cf. THEOPHRASTUS: CHARACTERS.

HERODIAN. C. R. Whittaker. 2 Vols.

HERODOTUS. A. D. Godley. 4 Vols.

HESIOD and THE HOMERIC HYMNS. H. G. Evelyn White.

HIPPOCRATES and the FRAGMENTS OF HERACLEITUS. W. H. S. Jones and E. T. Withington. 4 Vols.

HOMER: ILIAD. A. T. Murray. 2 Vols.

HOMER: ODYSSEY. A. T. Murray. 2 Vols.

ISAEUS. E. W. Forster.

ISOCRATES. George Norlin and LaRue Van Hook. 3 Vols.

[ST. JOHN DAMASCENE]: BARLAAM AND IOASAPH. Rev. G. R. Woodward, Harold Mattingly and D. M. Lang.

JOSEPHUS. 9 Vols. Vols. I–IV. H. Thackeray. Vol. V. H. Thackeray and R. Marcus. Vols. VI–VII. R. Marcus. Vol. VIII. R. Marcus and Allen Wikgren. Vol. IX. L. H. Feldman.

JULIAN. Wilmer Cave Wright. 3 Vols.

LIBANIUS. A. F. Norman. Vols. I–II.

LUCIAN. 8 Vols. Vols. I–V. A. M. Harmon. Vol. VI. K. Kilburn. Vols. VII–VIII. M. D. Macleod.

LYCOPHRON. Cf. CALLIMACHUS.

LYRA GRAECA. J. M. Edmonds. 3 Vols.

LYSIAS. W. R. M. Lamb.

MANETHO. W. G. Waddell. PTOLEMY: TETRABIBLOS. F. E. Robbins.

MARCUS AURELIUS. C. R. Haines.

MENANDER. F. G. Allison.

MINOR ATTIC ORATORS (ANTIPHON, ANDOCIDES, LYCURGUS, DEMADES, DINARCHUS, HYPERIDES). K. J. Maidment and J. O. Burtt. 2 Vols.

MUSAEUS: HERO AND LEANDER. Cf. CALLIMACHUS.

NONNOS: DIONYSIACA. W. H. D. Rouse. 3 Vols.

OPPIAN, COLLUTHUS, TRYPHIODORUS. A. W. Mair.

PAPYRI. NON-LITERARY SELECTIONS. A. S. Hunt and C. C. Edgar. 2 Vols. LITERARY SELECTIONS (Poetry). D. L. Page.

PARTHENIUS. Cf. DAPHNIS AND CHLOE.

PAUSANIAS: DESCRIPTION OF GREECE. W. H. S. Jones. 4 Vols. and Companion Vol. arranged by R. E. Wycherley.

Philo. 10 Vols. Vols. I–V. F. H. Colson and Rev. G. H. Whitaker. Vols. VI–IX. F. H. Colson. Vol. X. F. H. Colson and the Rev. J. W. Earp.

Philo: two supplementary Vols. (*Translation only.*) Ralph Marcus.

Philostratus: The Life of Apollonius of Tyana. F. C. Conybeare. 2 Vols.

Philostratus: Imagines. Callistratus: Descriptions. A. Fairbanks.

Philostratus and Eunapius: Lives of the Sophists. Wilmer Cave Wright.

Pindar. Sir J. E. Sandys.

Plato: Charmides, Alcibiades, Hipparchus, The Lovers, Theages, Minos and Epinomis. W. R. M. Lamb.

Plato: Cratylus, Parmenides, Greater Hippias, Lesser Hippias. H. N. Fowler.

Plato: Euthyphro, Apology, Crito, Phaedo, Phaedrus. H. N. Fowler.

Plato: Laches, Protagoras, Meno, Euthydemus. W. R. M. Lamb.

Plato: Laws. Rev. R. G. Bury. 2 Vols.

Plato: Lysis, Symposium, Gorgias. W. R. M. Lamb.

Plato: Republic. Paul Shorey. 2 Vols.

Plato: Statesman, Philebus. H. N. Fowler. Ion. W. R. M. Lamb.

Plato: Theaetetus and Sophist. H. N. Fowler.

Plato: Timaeus, Critias, Clitopho, Menexenus, Epistulae. Rev. R. G. Bury.

Plotinus. A. H. Armstrong. Vols. I–III.

Plutarch: Moralia. 17 Vols. Vols I–V. F. C. Babbitt. Vol. VI. W. C. Helmbold. Vols. VII and XIV. P. H. De Lacy and B. Einarson. Vol. VIII. P. A. Clement and H. B. Hoffleit. Vol. IX. E. L. Minar, Jr., F. H. Sandbach, W. C. Helmbold. Vol. X. H. N. Fowler. Vol. XI. L. Pearson and F. H. Sandbach. Vol. XII. H. Cherniss and W. C. Helmbold. Vol. XIII 1–2. H. Cherniss. Vol. XV. F. H. Sandbach.

Plutarch: The Parallel Lives. B. Perrin. 11 Vols.

Polybius. W. R. Paton. 6 Vols.

Procopius: History of the Wars. H. B. Dewing. 7 Vols.

Ptolemy: Tetrabiblos. Cf. Manetho.

Quintus Smyrnaeus. A. S. Way. Verse trans.

Sextus Empiricus. Rev. R. G. Bury. 4 Vols.

Sophocles. F. Storr. 2 Vols. Verse trans.

Strabo: Geography. Horace L. Jones. 8 Vols.

Theophrastus: Characters. J. M. Edmonds. Herodes, etc. A. D. Knox.

7

Theophrastus: De Causis Plantarum. B. Einarson and
G. K. K. Link. Vol. I.
Theophrastus: Enquiry into Plants. Sir Arthur Hort,
Bart. 2 Vols.
Thucydides. C. F. Smith. 4 Vols.
Tryphiodorus. Cf. Oppian.
Xenophon: Cyropaedia. Walter Miller. 2 Vols.
Xenophon: Hellenica. C. L. Brownson. 2 Vols.
Xenophon: Anabasis. C. L. Brownson.
Xenophon: Memorabilia and Oeconomicus. E. C. Marchant.
Symposium and Apology. O. J. Todd.
Xenophon: Scripta Minora. E. C. Marchant and G. W.
Bowersock.

IN PREPARATION

Latin Authors

Manilius. G. P. Goold.

DESCRIPTIVE PROSPECTUS ON APPLICATION

CAMBRIDGE, MASS.   **HARVARD UNIVERSITY PRESS**
LONDON   **WILLIAM HEINEMANN LTD**